Studies in the Legal History of the South

EDITED BY PAUL FINKELMAN, TIMOTHY S. HUEBNER, AND KERMIT L. HALL

This series explores the ways in which law has affected the development of the southern United States and in turn the ways the history of the South has affected the development of American law. Volumes in the series focus on a specific aspect of the law, such as slave law or civil rights legislation, or on a broader topic of historical significance to the development of the legal system in the region, such as issues of constitutional history and of law and society, comparative analyses with other legal systems, and biographical studies of influential southern jurists and lawyers.

Jury Discrimination

CHRISTOPHER WALDREP

Jury Discrimination

The Supreme Court,

Public Opinion, and

a Grassroots Fight for

Racial Equality in Mississippi

The University of Georgia Press

Athens and London

© 2010 by the University of Georgia Press
Athens, Georgia 30602
www.ugapress.org
All rights reserved
Set in Minion by Graphic Composition, Inc.

Printed digitally in the United States of America

Library of Congress Cataloging-in-Publication Data
Waldrep, Christopher, 1951–
    Jury discrimination : the Supreme Court, public opinion,
and a grassroots fight for racial equality in Mississippi /
Christopher Waldrep.
        p. cm. — (Studies in the legal history of the South)
    Includes bibliographical references and index.
    ISBN-13: 978-0-8203-3002-0 (hardcover : alk. paper)
    ISBN-10: 0-8203-3002-7 (hardcover : alk. paper)
1. Jury selection—Mississippi—History.
2. Discrimination in justice administration—Mississippi—History.
3. Race discrimination—Mississippi—History.
4. African Americans—Civil rights—Mississippi—History.
5. Mississippi—Race relations. I. Title.
    KFM7142.W35 2010
    347.762'07520973—dc22   2009047689

British Library Cataloging-in-Publication Data available

Contents

Acknowledgments

AT THE OUTSET OF THIS PROJECT, Robert Palmer offered useful suggestions. James Martel met with me to discuss Emerson. My graduate assistant, Melissa Barthelemy, read over the entire manuscript and provided me with fourteen pages of commentary. Two other graduate students, Mike Caires and Tina Speidel, journeyed with me to the National Archives to examine records of the Secret Service. Les Benedict read the entire manuscript, offering many valuable comments and suggestions. Pam Brandwein shared her thoughts on Joseph Bradley and the Supreme Court via a running e-mail dialogue that forced me to rethink my initial ideas. Jarbel Rodriguez and Charles Donahue Jr. offered detailed critiques of the first chapter. Eva Sheppard Wolf led the San Francisco State University history colloquium in a helpful critique of a portion of this manuscript. My first thoughts about John G. Cashman appeared in a special issue of *Nineteenth Century American History*, edited by Bill Carrigan. His encouragement and commentary clarified my thinking about that Mississippi conservative. My initial ideas about Joseph Bradley can be found in *Journal of Supreme Court History* (34 [2009]: 149–63), thanks to the encouragement of Mel Urofsky. I also presented my findings about Bradley at the American Society for Legal History meeting, where Linda Przybyszewski and Tim Huebner offered useful comments. Mike Fitzgerald took time out from his vacation not only to read over the entire manuscript but also to spend two hours going over it in the Martinez Starbucks (my first visit). Maureen O'Rourke of the New Jersey Historical Society provided essential assistance as I explored the Joseph P. Bradley Papers. For the University Press of Georgia, Nancy Grayson offered encouragement, John Joerschke asked good questions, and Barbara Wojhoski provided superb copyediting. My family, Pamela, Janelle, and Andrea, as always, provided the foundational support that made it possible for me to write this book.

Introduction

THE CROSS-EXAMINATION BEGAN WITH the basics. "Your name is P. C. Dowan?" the white lawyer asked. That was not quite right, and Pinkard C. Dowans pointed out that his name ended with an *s*. Pride in his name had brought Dowans to court in the first place. In 1909, when he testified, Dowans had been a grand lecturer of the Colored Knights of the Pythians for four years. Traveling from one Mississippi black fraternal organization to the next, Dowans helped formulate and spread the values that tied black fraternalists together. Dowans not only preached moral values, but he also made the contacts that allowed blacks across Mississippi to form social networks, organize collective identities, and pool resources to counter white efforts to disparage, oppress, and marginalize them.[1]

Dowans was in court because he had been denounced as "unmanly, unchristian, and ungentlemanly . . . unfit to be a member of the Pythian and Calanthian Order" by the *Calanthian Journal*, a newspaper published by a fraternal organization called the Court of Calanthe. Fraternal organizations paid Dowans's speaking fees based on their assessment of his moral character. The *Calanthian Journal* article appeared on November 28, 1908. Thereafter, Dowans's speaking invitations dried up, cutting off his income. Dowans sued its sponsor, the Court of Calanthe.

When questioned by his own lawyer, Dowans had described himself as a fifty-year resident of Vicksburg and a former schoolteacher. He was, in short, a person worthy of respect with a reputation worth money.

Edward N. Scudder represented the Court of Calanthe. Born in 1861, Scudder had not fought in the Civil War, but at the time he confronted Dowans, he was serving in the Sons of Confederate Veterans (SCV) as an assistant judge advocate general. Later he became a division commander and a member of the SCV's executive council. The trial transcript of Dowans's case described him as "Col. Scudder." According to his daughter, he served as captain (not colonel) in the Issaquena Guards, an all-white militia group most certainly formed to intimidate blacks. At the time of Dowans's trial, Scudder lived north of Vicksburg, in Issaquena County, an area he had once represented in the state senate. He had served only one term, but in that time he made a signal contribution to Mississippi culture. In 1894, he had joined the senate committee organized to design a new state flag for Mississippi. This was four years after whites ousted blacks entirely from jury lists and almost entirely from voting rolls. Scudder celebrated this accomplishment by designing a flag with three broad stripes intended to recall the Confederate Stars and Bars flag. To make his commitment to triumphant white supremacy even clearer, Scudder placed the Confederate battle flag in the new state flag's upper left corner. In 1924, Scudder's daughter, Fayssoux, wrote that her father had told her "that it was a simple matter for him to design the flag because he wanted to perpetuate in a legal and lasting way that dear battle flag under which so many of [Mississippi's] people had so gloriously fought."[2] Now, in 1909, the designer of Mississippi's pro-Confederate state flag confronted the man who may well have been the first black juror in the state after Reconstruction.

Scudder approached his target gingerly. "You have been a school teacher in this County?" he asked.

"Yes sir and served in this court here a long time in juries and bailiff in this court." Dowans must have held this information back to catch Scudder off guard. Now he revealed that court officials had so trusted him that they made him a bailiff and allowed him to sit on juries. Scudder's next question suggested that he could not imagine that any black man could serve on a jury after whites had regained power and passed laws to keep blacks from voting.

"Those were the old black and tan days when they used to have and elect Republican Sheriffs?"

White Southerners derided the period after the Civil War as "the old black and tan days," a brief and, from their point of view, entirely unsuccessful experiment with biracialism when black people and white, or "tan," people voted and sat together in the legislature and on juries. For a white man in 1909, the black and tan days were of historical interest only, a distant memory from a thoroughly discredited time. In those days, as bailiff, Dowans had sometimes selected the bystanders who served on juries. But now Dowans answered that he had been on juries much more recently than during Reconstruction.

"Last year," he said, "I served right here."

Scudder found that hard to believe. He tried to break down Dowans's claim by asking for details: "In which court?"

"This court right here."

Scudder pressed harder. "What case did you get to try?"

Dowans had no trouble answering that question. "Of Mr. Wright; Wright brothers."

Dowans was not lying. On April 22, 1907, Warren County's circuit court organized eight panels of thirty potential jurors, one for each week of its term. The circuit clerk wrote each man's name in his big minute book, not identifying any by race. The second name in the first panel was "P. C. Downs." Not all the men called for jury duty actually served. Later in the same term, a black man whom the clerk identified as "Jeff. Prentes" came to court as a potential juror, but there is no evidence that he stayed long or received pay for his jury service. He never sat on a jury. Later, on the same day that Dowans came to court as a potential juror, the court heard the case of *Merchants and Planters Packet Company v. Wright Brothers*, a suit for debt. The jury heard the evidence and arguments and deliberated, but could not reach a verdict. The next day they tried again but still could not agree. The clerk identified the jurors only as "J. E. Whitaker and eleven others," but Dowans had to be one of the eleven others as he claimed because on April 26 the court paid him for five days' jury service and two miles of travel. He received $12.60. The official record validated Dowans's claim.[3]

Defeated, Scudder moved on to other topics, but Dowans won his case. The jury, though entirely white, found in his favor.[4]

Dowans's lawsuit was an obscure litigation over a forgotten man's pride and reputation in a small town deep in the Mississippi Delta. Nonetheless, Dowans's testimony seems to document the impossible. White Southerners kept blacks off juries because they understood that jury service represented rights both political and civil. Dowans and Scudder dueled over jury service as a form of democratic participation in the operations of government, akin to voting. Justice Anthony Kennedy has recently recognized the long-standing link between voting and jury service. Both had long offered a path toward democratic participation in government, he said. "Jury service," he wrote, "is an exercise of responsible citizenship by all members of the community, including those who otherwise might not have the opportunity to contribute to our civic life." Kennedy then went on to say that both Congress and the Supreme Court had recognized this in the nineteenth century.[5] Scholars look at voting more often than jury service, but it is worth noting that white Southerners guarded their juries more strictly than their voting booths. In every southern state, a handful of blacks managed to vote, but whites tried very hard to keep every last black person off their juries. The import is clear: a few votes did not really matter, but the power to investigate and define crime and determine guilt did.

The impulse to discriminate has been nearly universal throughout American history. Jury discrimination, in fact, has been so common that it is hard to dispute James Oldham, who dismisses the idea of a jury of peers as always "a fairy tale."[6] True, but it would also be accurate to call it an ideal even if it is one not always realized, like all constitutional principles. For defendants from despised groups, trapped in the midst of pervasive prejudice, the power of that ideal determined their chances at something like a fair trial. In some places, at some moments, some judges tried to live up to the ideal. For example, in 1870, a Wyoming territorial judge placed women on a grand jury because, he said, women had been "the victim of the vices, crimes and immoralities of man" tolerated by government for too long. Government should allow women on juries so they could protect themselves, he said.[7] The ideal gave hope to the oppressed. At her 1873 trial for illegal voting, Susan B. Anthony argued that disfranchised women could not get a fair trial from a jury made up entirely of enfranchised male jurors. Such men were not her peers, she said and charged that the state put them on her jury as a device to oppress her, depriving her of jurors who might understand her plight.[8]

Though no book-length examination of how the juries came to be all-white exists, few historians would doubt that the American habit of restricting jury service to white men has played an important role in shaping the nation's racial history.[9] In 1955, defense attorney John Whitten told the jury trying the murderers of Emmett Till, "[I am sure that] every last Anglo-Saxon one of you men on this jury has the courage to set these men free." They did.[10] From the Civil War to the period of the civil rights struggle, numerous trials sustained segregation, lynching, and discrimination. In examining such instances, scholars routinely observe that all-white juries decided the cases without asking how those juries got to be so white. Perhaps the answer seems obvious: they were the result of entrenched local prejudice that the nation could not overcome.[11] The answer, however, is obvious only if we assume that the Supreme Court played no independent role in preserving white dominance. Many historians assume precisely that: in his great book on Reconstruction, Eric Foner observes that in deciding Reconstruction cases the Supreme Court responded "to the shifting currents of Northern public opinion."[12]

It is the argument here that the great difficulty early twentieth-century Mississippi blacks faced as they agitated for trial by jury and juries of their peers can be accounted for by the U.S. Supreme Court's actions after the Civil War. The justices debated the possibility of deferring to public opinion and, if so, to which kind of public opinion. This opinion would be white, of course—that they did not debate—but even defined as white, opinion took more than one form. One kind was indeed a shifting current, fleeting, transient, poisoned by racial prejudice, but there were more deeply imagined and more permanent values that also came from the public, what historians call "memory." Memory is popular historical consciousness, the lessons ordinary people derive from their past, narratives that legitimize or challenge current practices.[13] The U.S. Supreme Court broached the problem of its power over state jury-selection procedures after centuries of debate over who should be allowed onto juries. This history established a powerful mythology, national in scope: defendants should be tried by a jury of their peers. After the Civil War, when freed people became citizens, this sentiment conflicted with other, white, interests. White people had an economic interest in keeping black laborers under strict and sometimes violent control in ways that could not withstand serious scrutiny by fairly selected juries. Despite its considerable abstract popular appeal, the sentiment had been so contested during the Civil War era that the Court had considerable latitude when making its rules. In choosing interest over sentiment, the Court sided with the supposed wisdom of crowds over memory.[14]

Yet that memory persisted. At the bottom of the Mississippi Delta, a peculiar confluence of cultural, political, social, and constitutional forces converged with small-town politics to produce two lawyers, one black and one white, both determined together to crack Mississippi's all-white jury system. They, and everyone else in their world, worked according to rules set by the Supreme Court. Had the Supreme Court set different evidentiary rules, making it easier to prove discrimination, there might have been tens of thousands of black jurors throughout the nation at the time when whites tried to make and enforce segregation laws. Instead, only a very few served and only for a few months. That a white native of Mississippi could partner with a black civil rights leader to break through Mississippi law and prejudice to get blacks admitted to juries at all suggests that legal reasoning plausibly founded on constitutional principle could trump even the most stubbornly prejudiced public opinion. Anyone who thinks that the Supreme Court could not possibly overcome racial practices in the South should consider Willis Mollison and Dabney Marshall's success in Mississippi. Why this success was so hard to achieve and so rare and how it could happen at all are the subjects of this book.

CHAPTER ONE

Making the Fairy Tale

THOMAS DABNEY MARSHALL WAS BORN *on his father's plan-*
tation November 20, 1860, two weeks after Abraham Lincoln's election to the
presidency. The Marshalls did not vote for Lincoln—his name was not on the
ballot in Mississippi. There is no surviving record of their vote, but the Mar-
shalls adamantly opposed secession, and most voters in and around Vicksburg
voted Whig and then Constitutional Unionist. Dabney Marshall's parents al-
most certainly supported John Bell, the Constitutional Unionist candidate.
Dabney's uncle went to Mississippi's secession convention, on every roll call
stubbornly voting not to secede despite heckling and jeers from his fellow del-
egates and the crowd watching the proceedings. It is tempting to conclude that
Marshall's family history of unionism explains—at least in part—his later
commitment to blacks' civil rights and his willingness to call on federal au-
thorities to protect them.[1]

At the University of Mississippi, Marshall's professor L. Q. C. Lamar chal-
lenged his commitment to national rights. Lamar, the bête noire of Marshall's
uncle at the secession convention, had been a leading congressional opponent
of the 1875 Civil Rights Act, which he denounced as an invasion of state sov-
ereignty. Even as a child, Marshall seemed precocious, perhaps brilliant, and
Lamar could not shake his commitment to national patriotism. Dabney grad-
uated in 1882 with honors and returned to Vicksburg filled with literary eru-
dition and scholarly knowledge and speaking French. At Vicksburg's Fourth of
July celebrations, he made speeches celebrating northern soldiers' valor along
with the Southerners'.

Despite Marshall's remarkable commitment to the Union, it is more likely
that history—what James Oldham has called "the fairy tale," the popular no-
tion that defendants have a right to be tried by a jury of their peers—hardened

this southern-born white man's ambition to litigate on behalf of black rights.
The term "fairy tale" suggests a delusion or a myth in the minds of poorly in-
formed citizens, something no experienced lawyer would take seriously, but it
was too real for white Mississippians to entirely ignore. The myth had power
for being so old. In medieval English legal treatises, but also in ballads, folk-
tales, and doggerel—the kind of texts written and consumed by ordinary
folk—citizens came to expect a jury of their peers as a "right." Against state
laws, adverse court decisions, and intractable racial prejudice, Dabney Mar-
shall went into battle armed with nothing more than a fairy tale.

Fortunately, it was a powerful tale; unfortunately for Marshall, it also
was one shot through with troubling complications. The state of Mississippi
might well cite it to show that the provinces—the states—had long controlled
who could sit on juries. In the heroic story of jurors' independence, it was the
Crown and the Parliament against whom local jurors fought, not neighbor-
hood prejudice. They proudly brought that independence into court to stand
against the central authority. For Dabney Marshall, however, that same inde-
pendence was not so helpful. He needed to fight against his neighbors' preju-
dices with national rights enforced by national power.

Before the Declaration of Independence and the U.S. Constitution, people
in the Atlantic world had already discovered through a long and complex
process stretching over centuries that trial by jury was a meaningful right
only when juries had a measure of independence from centralized governmental power. Jurors could represent the king or their neighbors, but there
was a natural tension between the two, between the national and the local.
To represent their neighbors, jurors had to at least seem to reflect the diversity of their communities. This truth took root in historical memory, mythology, and stories about the past, narratives that gave Americans tools
against which they could measure the Constitution and other formal texts
produced by the government.

One common story credits the origins of trial by jury to an aggressive
and centralizing monarchy. In 1086, when the king of England decided to
inventory his possessions, he dispatched subordinates into the countryside
to summon men from throughout the kingdom to represent their communities, rendering verdicts about the value of property in their locales.
The resulting Domesday Book recorded the findings of this elaborate in-
quest. Although the king's inquiry reached into the smallest settlements,

called hundreds and vills, seeking representative men, it hardly transformed Saxon juries into a democratic institution. Such inquiries seemed more a "relentless government prying" than a "bastion of liberty," legal scholar John Baker has observed.[2] In such inquests, it might have appeared to make sense to swear in almost anyone as a juror so as not to miss valuable information. But it was not really sensible because not everyone could be trusted. The simplest solution was to disqualify some classes of people, and at least by 1215 Romano-canonical procedure excluded slaves, children, the insane, the infamous, paupers, and infidels as witnesses. According to the theory, such persons might lie with abandon, while a respectable, propertied juror had something to lose by rendering a mischievous verdict. In practice, though, overburdened judges eager to get on with their work sometimes ignored the rules. Surviving texts do not often document English judges' refusing to allow a witness's testimony, whereas some do show judges proceeding to sentence even when the winning side's witnesses came from despised groups.[3]

Henry II (r. 1154–89) more regularly relied on local men for information and judgment. Twelve lawful men from each hundred and four from each vill should report serious crimes to royal officers, he said. The idea that twelve men should hear controversies quickly spread through the kingdom, with some claiming to see biblical sanction for the holy number. Juries listened to the complaints and rumors about alleged crimes that circulated through their vills and hundreds. Those failing to report crimes faced punishment themselves, a reality that discouraged any feeling of authority or influence, but juries could stop a prosecution in its tracks by announcing they did not believe an accuser.[4]

Juries became still more important after 1215, when the church forbade clerical participation in ordeals. Ordeals required prisoners to perform a painful task, testing their claims of innocence against fire or water on the theory that God would rescue the innocent from torture. Priests determined the outcome by examining prisoners' wounds. With priests no longer available to judge ordeals, juries became still more important; *vox populi* substituted for *vox dei*.[5] In the same year, King John (r. 1199–1216) signed the Magna Carta, which recognized trial by jury:

> 38 In future no official shall place a man on trial upon his own unsupported statement, without producing credible witnesses to the truth of it.

> 39 No free man shall be seized or imprisoned, or stripped of his rights or possessions, or outlawed or exiled, or deprived of his standing in any other way, nor will we proceed with force against him, or send others to do so, except by the lawful judgment of his equals or by the law of the land.[6]

Scholars once exaggerated the Magna Carta's force, but it at least contributed to the mythology that a prisoner had a right to "the lawful judgment of his equals." Because the nobles imposed the Magna Carta on their reluctant king, it once seemed to show that juries really were a palladium of liberty, resistant to centralizing authorities. But historians long ago found that the jury system developed very gradually and not in a clap of heroic thunder, so the idea of juries' independence has not been credible for some time. Nonetheless, the Magna Carta became part of jury folklore, perhaps the linchpin of the fairy tale.

Some of the earliest English juries were "mixed," which most often meant geographically diverse. As early as 1101, royal writs required that juries include men from different shires to render a verdict. But a "mixed" jury could also be one that was religiously diverse. In 1190, King Richard (r. 1189–99) required that mixed juries decide cases between Christians and Jews. Juries could also be "mixed" in the sense that judges seated foreigners. A jury of six burgesses and six outsiders decided a 1233 Colchester quarrel. In 1303, Edward I (r. 1272–1307) granted foreign merchants a charter (the Carta Mercatoria) guaranteeing various privileges, including juries with at least some non-English members. Authorities allowed foreigners and even Jews on their juries because they believed people must be judged according to their own laws or customs, rules native to their home community. In 1308, a half-English and half-Welsh jury decided a land dispute in Shropshire. The same logic that allowed Welshmen on juries also permitted Jews on some juries. When members of an alien group came to court, the law took into account the customs and practices of the particular foreign community.[7] This idea became statutory law in 1353, when Parliament enacted the Statute of the Staple, which, in addition to designating certain ports where particular goods could be exported or imported, allowed aliens to serve as jurors. Such charters and laws adopted local procedures that judges had devised with no advice from Parliament or the king. Nationalizing these local practices substituted formalized, national principle for community justice.[8]

Despite concessions to local court practices, Parliament scrambled—unsuccessfully—to control jury membership, trying to keep poorer people and members of despised groups out. In 1285, the Statute of Westminster limited jury service to those holding freehold estates of an annual value of twenty shillings. This amount increased in 1293. Judges saw such laws as an inconvenience that could be safely ignored, so unfree tenants continued to appear on juries, a fact documented by a 1285 statute complaining that such unfree men, the land poor or the landless, still slipped onto juries. These people made their presence obvious, proving they did not share the values of elite power holders by drinking, swearing, and stealing while in court. Judges disliked this situation, but by the 1340s the Black Death further challenged efforts to limit jury service to men of quality by reducing the number of people available for service.[9]

Over time the ordinary inconvenience of finding and seating members of the wealthier classes as jurors took on national significance. Kings published and circulated books designed to woo better people onto juries. While in exile, Henry VI had one of his minions draft a manuscript titled *In Praise of the Laws of England*. Sir John Fortescue (ca. 1395–ca. 1477) had considerable familiarity with juries, having served as a justice of the peace thirty-five times in seventeen counties and boroughs. He imagined a dialogue between a prince (Henry VI's son Edward) and the Chancellor, "a certain aged knight," dedicated to preserving the teachings of Augustine, Aristotle, and other ancient writers. Fortescue's "aged knight" tells Edward that jurors should own property and be of the vicinage, familiar with the dispute and the parties. Such "witnesses," he wrote, "are neighbours, able to live of [sic] their own, sound in repute and fair-minded, not brought into court by either party, but chosen by a respectable and impartial officer, and compelled to come before the judge." Nothing, he said, can be concealed from such jurors. For Fortescue, such objective men, fairly chosen, embodied every element of the law, as it ought to be. Jurors, he said, represented the king but could not be influenced by him. Strong kings sought justice, meaning that they used the law politically, not mischievously manipulating outcomes, but demonstrating to their subjects their adherence to the law's sacred principles crafted from customs and nature. Bound by oath to follow the law, kings won their legitimacy by carrying out the principled will of the people. For three hundred years, English lawyers cited Fortescue's argument for justice against tyranny as an authority on the English constitution; he may not have invented the idea of the fairly chosen, objective jury, but he did more than almost anyone else to perpetuate the idea.[10]

Fortescue's book, with its picture of the independent-minded, property-owning juror, circulated for centuries after its initial publication. By complaining that the "poor and simpler sort" and "men of weake judgement and verie meane estate" often served as jurors, various royal proclamations and statutes continued to confirm that people without property found seats on juries.[11] The jury lists that survive from this era tend to be battered documents with deletions and interlineations. Officers had to scramble to replace summoned men who did not appear.[12] In some places, at some times, it could seem that the wealthy served less often than the down-and-out—some complained that corrupt sheriffs excused those who could pay, relegating jury service to the poor and ignorant. Such complaints were exaggerated. By and large, jurors had at least moderate wealth.[13]

Authorities mixed different kinds of people into their jury pools not just because people without property sometimes slipped by. Special problems required that courts look to the trades for jurors. Likewise, cases involving the forest required jurors with the appropriate knowledge. Courts also needed jurors to decide the guilt or innocence of lawyers charged with misconduct. Masters of ships and travelers served on juries deciding nautical matters.[14] Women sometimes served on even the earliest English juries, although only in very specialized circumstances. During his reign, Edward the Confessor (r. 1042–66) had held that women could be in a state of *legalitas*, or "law-worthy," meaning they had the trust of their neighbors. They could be witnesses but not jurors, at least not routinely. In a practice dating back to Roman times, however, women could sit on juries when a female prisoner tried to "plead her belly," seeking to escape punishment for being pregnant. Women appeared as jurors more regularly from the reign of Elizabeth I (r. 1558–1603) to that of James I (r. 1603–25). Matrons determined questions of inheritance, determining whether widows feigned pregnancy to exclude another heir. Matrons also investigated women seeking an annulment on grounds of their husband's impotency. The women checked to see if the wife had remained a virgin. They also sat on the juries of witchcraft trials to inspect the bodies of accused females. Women were not as stringently barred from juries as some others, and their chance of being seated on a jury was better than that of Quakers and reputed Quakers.[15]

It is not clear that women or poorer people summoned onto juries saw their service as a bastion of liberty against despotism. It did not help that the men who called them into service were the lowest-ranking court officials, notorious for haphazard fumbling. Those summoned often dreaded being called for jury duty and sometimes fled when they had the chance; judges sometimes made jurors virtual prisoners of the court, denying them food while they deliberated in order to speed verdicts. It became a crime to smuggle meals to sequestered juries.[16] In the sixteenth century and later, English kings tried to force convictions by disciplining recalcitrant jurors through the Star Chamber and other judicial inquiries.[17] Kings increasingly initiated prosecutions and more closely managed trials, winning a higher conviction rate. Judges began insisting that juries decide cases based on evidence presented in court by prosecutors, not from their own knowledge. A new round of property requirements tried to limit jury service.[18]

These efforts once again ran afoul of widely held beliefs that jurors should be independent of royal authority. When Henry VII (r. 1485–1509) tried to eliminate grand juries from trials involving noncapital offenses, judges and lawyers would not go along. The new property requirements did not really work, for would-be jurors often refused to attend the panel at the criminal courts, called assizes, forcing judges to rely on tales or talesmen, persons summoned to act as jurors from among the bystanders in court. Dissidents loudly protested that juries should have a right to decide law as well as find facts.[19] In 1601, when Christopher Blunt went on trial for joining a conspiracy against the queen, the judge ruled that the new laws setting high property requirements applied only to cases "between Party and Party" and not to criminal cases prosecuted by the state. The common law, after all, only asked that jurors have some property, the judge noted. Further, he continued, there were places in England where no resident owned any property. It would be unjust to exclude people in those areas from jury service. "After so long a practice to the contrary," the judge said, it would be "inconvenient" to change procedures now. Including jurors without freeholds seems not to have hurt the government's case against Blunt. The jury pronounced him guilty, and the authorities beheaded him.[20]

Blunt's execution demonstrated that even with nonelite jurors, the government often achieved its purposes. Nonetheless, some groups hoped to gain ground by using the increasingly widespread belief that jurors represented liberty against national power. The seventeenth-century political movement known as the Levellers invoked as ancient custom the rule that juries acted independently of royal authority, representing their neighborhoods and not the government. In 1649, a Leveller tract titled *Agreement of the People* insisted that persons charged with felonies should be tried by "twelve sworn men of the neighborhood; to be chosen in some free way by the people . . . and not picked and imposed, as hitherto in many places they have been." John Lilburne believed so strongly that juries should represent their communities that he opposed any appeal of convictions in local courts, except to Parliament. Levellers like Lilburne mythologized the jury as an institution that actually preceded the judiciary.[21]

In 1662, as the Levellers continued to try to turn jurors' supposed autonomy to their own advantage, Parliament set in motion a fresh challenge to that independence when it passed the Quaker Act and two years later the Conventicles Act, forbidding nonconformist religious meetings. London officials arrested Quaker preachers and locked Friends' meeting places, stationing troops to ensure that Quakers did not break the locks. This measure only forced Quaker preachers onto the streets. On August 14, 1670, Quakers William Penn and William Mead preached to a large crowd on London's Gracechurch Street. Constables stood at the ready with warrants signed by Mayor Sir Samuel Starling. Prosecutors charged that Penn and Mead disturbed the peace and produced witnesses to support their allegations. When Edward Bushel refused to kiss the Bible when sworn as a juror, Penn realized he had at least one nonconformist on his jury. Seeing an opening, he argued that the jury should consider whether his indictment was legal. Penn may have hoped to provoke the judge into losing his temper in front of the jury. If so, he succeeded. "You are an impertinent fellow," the judge snapped. When Penn continued to argue law to the jury, citing cases to make his point, the judge exclaimed, "You are a troublesome fellow" before ordering Penn removed to the bail dock. As officers escorted him away, Penn continued his performance: "Must I therefore be taken away because I plead for the fundamental laws of England?" he called out as the officers hustled him away. Mead then took up the argument, telling jurors that English law limited the meaning of riot to three or more people meeting together to beat a man or forcibly trespass on another man's land. The court angrily interrupted, "I thank you, Sir, that you will tell what the Law is."[22]

Penn exhorted the jurors to consult their conscience. Edward Bushel, along with three others, did so and refused to find Penn guilty. When the jury returned their verdict, finding that Penn had merely spoken to a crowd and not raised a tumult, the mayor denounced Bushel as "a silly fellow . . . an impudent canting fellow." As court officers argued with the jury, Penn reiterated his point: the "Verdict should be free, the Bench ought to wait upon them, but not forestall them." The judge first tartly insisted, "I will have a Verdict," and then threatened Bushel: "I will set a mark upon you, and whilst I have any thing to do in the City, I will have an eye upon you." This was not strong enough for the mayor, who interjected, "Have you no more wit than to be led by such a pitiful fellow?" and then helpfully explained that such impudence really needed an extralegal response: "I will cut his nose," Starling announced. To this Penn retorted, "It is intolerable that my Jury should be thus menaced." Penn continued with a short speech praising juries for following the fundamental law of England. This was too much for the mayor, who answered in words that Penn rendered in italics in his account: "*Stop his mouth: Jailor, bring fetters, and stake him to the ground.*" The jurors stood their ground—heroically, Penn thought—and the court retaliated by fining every juror. Yet they still would not yield.[23]

In a series of tracts, Penn applauded the jurors, saying, "Nothing could have been more wisely conceived by our ancestors" than constructing the jury as a popular institution standing "against the will of Arbitrary Power," neighborhood prejudice triumphant over the central power. A prisoner, Penn continued, should have as his jury "men who know his character." Penn called juries "proper Judges of Law and Fact." Starling accused Penn of treason, called the Quakers "a turbulent and inhumane sort of People," and blasted Penn's book as a "Blasphemous Treatise." He accused Penn of reviling all law.[24]

Meanwhile, Bushel sat in jail for refusing to pay his fine. He asked for a writ of habeas corpus, claiming his fine had no basis in law. Chief Justice Sir John Vaughan of the Court of Common Pleas added to the growing literature celebrating jurors' independence when he ruled in favor of Bushel, finding that jurors could not be fined or imprisoned for their verdicts.[25]

Penn's tracts went into the culture, becoming part of the collective memory of independent jurors standing up to the government. The government itself sometimes promoted exactly the same trope. It needed to. After efforts to punish jurors for rendering verdicts, it is no wonder that judges sometimes could not find enough jurors. In 1680, Sir John Hawles sought to persuade people reluctant to serve on juries that they should willingly do so. Though more imaginative than most judges, Hawles had exactly the same purpose as the numerous magistrates who published their charges to grand juries: he wanted to persuade his readers that jury service preserved the nation. To accomplish this, he published a dialogue with a would-be juror. This man explained that he had been summoned for jury duty but hoped to avoid actually serving, complaining, "There is something of Trouble and Loss of Time in it." Hawles replied by emphasizing the importance of jury service and invoked the ancient constitution. Juries have existed, he said, since the beginning of the nation, "as soon as the People were reduced to any Form of *Civil* Government." The custom of deciding quarrels through a sworn jury had survived all of England's conquests, revolutions, invasions by foreigners, and internal struggles. According to Hawles, the Anglo-Saxon king Alfred the Great (r. 871–99) had judges killed for daring to encroach on the privileges of juries. Paraphrasing Vaughan, Hawles assured the juror that he need not fear punishment for any verdict he might render in court.[26]

Hawles did not urge resistance to authority, but some jurors thought the history he recounted entitled them to frustrate those in power. On the eve of the Glorious Revolution, an English jury made itself the subject of folklore and mythology when it resisted royal authority. In 1688, James II (r. 1685–89) required that the clergy read his declaration for liberty of conscience twice in every church and that all bishops circulate it through their dioceses. The archbishop of Canterbury, with six other bishops, petitioned James II, noting that the king could not constitutionally force them to read his declaration. The king then summoned the seven bishops to appear before the King in Council. The bishops came but refused to give recognizance guaranteeing their appearance before the Court of King's Bench. To this impertinence, the king responded by jailing the bishops in the Tower of London, where they publicized their plight, and the government indicted them for sedition. The trial of the seven bishops squeezed jurors into the space between growing opposition to James II and the king's determination to defend his authority against dissent. When the jury acquitted the bishops, it both repudiated James II's Catholicism and asserted continued jural independence.[27]

In scores of less famous and more ordinary cases, juries continued to enforce local customs in court, as was evident in cases of self-defense. The common law required that a killer claiming self-defense prove that he had exhausted every avenue of escape before turning on his tormentor. Thus the law contradicted the feeling in hundreds and vills that a person violently attacked had a right to strike back and not run away. Juries sometimes fictionalized facts to fit the legal requirement when they wanted to enforce the community's view that a violent attack justified a violent response, even if the attacked person still had an opportunity to escape. In Sussex County, grand jurors carefully weighed the evidence, applying common sense and prudence as well as the law. Jurors stubbornly refused to indict without solid evidence; they made sheriffs hustle to find witnesses, and they dismissed suspicions based on nothing more than circumstances, opportunity, or malice. Accusations made too quickly raised their hackles, but so too did accusations made too slowly. Grand jurors sometimes bent the law to extend mercy to people accused of serious crimes. "Foolish pity," one officer scoffed, but there was nothing to do about it.[28]

Seditious libel cases presented jurors with an important battleground over governmental authority. Courts tried to instruct jurors on the law, telling them whether published writings were libelous, in an effort to leave jurors with little to do. Champions of a free press asked why juries had to convict printers for publishing tracts that people outside government found unobjectionable, and jurors sometimes brought those questions to their deliberations.[29] Jurors willing to defy their instructions and acquit printers and writers obnoxious to those in authority won the praise of balladeers. "Your pens are free," one anonymous writer proclaimed in 1729. "Your *Thoughts* and the *Press* are at full Liberty."

> Let no *Pamphleteers*
> Be *concern'd* for their *Ears*,
> For ev'ry Man now shall be try'd by his *Peers*.
> *Twelve good honest* Men shall decide each Cause,
> And be Judges of *Fact*, though not Judges of *Laws*.[30]

Juries balanced judges' "Interests, Ambitions, Pleasures, other Passions and Frailties," an anonymously published *Guide to English Juries: Setting Forth Their Antiquity, Power and Duty* explained in 1725. Judges menaced the people with "Miseries, Law-oppression, Oppression under color of law." Judges were easily corrupted, the *Guide* averred, while jurors had no fear of losing their offices. "Opportunity makes many a whore," the *Guide* observed.[31]

Juries were small crowds, ordinary folk controlling crime not only through formal court functions but outside the law as well. Very likely almost every person living in England believed that he or she could participate in the apprehending of criminals if the need arose. This was true through the legal process but also outside the law. "The private individual," one scholar has written, "was the most important law-enforcing officer in the community."[32] Mobs of Londoners captured most suspected criminals in that city. Victims of street crime looked to passersby, not constables, to locate stolen goods and capture the thief. Sometimes the line between official and popular punishment blurred as when jeering crowds gathered at trials and public punishments. Before 1737, Old Bailey trials took place in an open area called the

Sessions House Yard, which onlookers entered from an alley. Since authorities wanted to humiliate convicted persons, punishment required popular participation to be fully effective. Thus officials encouraged such participation at the pillory. When officials sanctioned crowds' abuse of prisoners, they permitted punishments outside the formal rule of law. Magistrates sometimes found mobbing a useful method of social control. Exactly when crowds enjoyed their greatest power and popular acceptance remains uncertain, but Londoners turned to mobbing less often as the eighteenth century progressed, coming to rely on professional law enforcers.[33]

Grand rhetoric about the great responsibility that every juror held in his hands inspired fresh restrictions on who could serve on juries. Jurors should be men of fortune, the *Complete Juryman* explained, because a juror's wealth stood as his pledge for good behavior. These new challenges fared no better than earlier efforts. Although the *Complete Juryman* hoped jurors would be men of fortune, it nonetheless admitted that juries represented their communities: British law required that at least two jurors come from the vicinity or hundred of the dispute, the *Complete Juryman* explained. Property qualifications limited access to jury service in theory, the *Complete Juryman* conceded, but helpfully confessed that judges rarely enforced property qualifications. If the parties did not object, then property really did not matter, whatever the statute said. Officials moving cases through the Old Bailey structured their proceedings to discourage jury challenges. Juries heard cases in batches; one jury heard twenty-one cases and only deliberated three times. The Old Bailey clerk ritually informed accused persons that they should "look to their challenges." They almost never did. "In some cases it may not be necessary for a juror to have so great an Estate, Real or Personal, as these Statutes respectively require," the author of the *Complete Juryman* observed. Judges could find ways around property qualifications, even when the parties raised challenges. The common law did not require a freehold for jury service; the juror merely needed to have the use of a freehold, not be its owner. Constables, tithingmen, and headboroughs met yearly to prepare lists of jurors. Court officers placed their jury lists on the church door to allow would-be jurors to challenge themselves, pleading their lack of qualification as a way of avoiding jury duty.[34]

England's myth that ordinary people could find ways onto juries, challenging the central authority with local ideas of justice, did American lawyers no good unless it crossed the Atlantic Ocean with the colonists. It did. Early colonial authorities, like those in England, felt compelled to include even despised portions of the population. Massachusetts officials organized a jury of six Indians and six colonists to try an Indian.[35] Despite that example, colonials, in fact, did not always adopt the jury as a bulwark against tyranny. Colonies with strong leaders often eschewed juries, while those with weaker magistrates relied on juries. Criminal defendants in seventeenth-century Plymouth rarely saw a jury; Massachusetts regarded its General Court as an alternative to a jury trial; Rhode Islanders guarded their right to trial by jury, but New Haven Colony abolished trial by jury. In Virginia colonists scattered themselves along rivers and streams, making the assembly of a jury impracticable and overly expensive. Such inconveniences could not long suppress old values. As new generations of colonists increasingly claimed the liberty of movement, they came to believe more strongly that communities should rely on jurors to represent their interests against laws issued from central authorities.[36] Especially in civil cases, colonists expected jurors to protect rights both natural and civil by expressing the community consensus. In the most serious criminal cases, authorities hesitated to take a settler's life without securing community approval. This desire for community participation reached progressively less-serious crimes as time passed. By the last decades of the seventeenth century, New England was "mad" for juries.[37]

The most famous instance involved John Peter Zenger in a trial that achieved mythological status as an instance of a representative jury resisting imperial authority. Zenger lived in the colony of New York, where tensions between the legislature and the New York Supreme Court ran high. Governors had long fought to extract quitrents from colonial gentry and had consistently advocated the use of juryless equity courts to enforce their demands for money. Landlords very commonly refused to pay the quitrents, and royal officials sought a method to force them to yield.[38] The legislature tried to create a supreme court, but the governor followed Crown policy and created a court based on ordinances issued by the governor.

In 1732, William Cosby arrived in New York to become governor. He immediately feuded with Rip Van Dam, the most senior member of the council and acting governor of New York for the thirteen months preceding Cosby's arrival. Cosby named James DeLancey chief justice in 1733, the same year Zenger began publishing the *New York Weekly Journal*. New York politicians financed Zenger's paper and used it to attack and ridicule Cosby. For his part, Cosby intended to use DeLancey against his political enemies. DeLancey twice tried to get grand jurors to indict Zenger, but the jurors refused both times, and the *Weekly Journal* continued to churn out anti-Cosby propaganda. Even after he failed with two grand juries to win an indictment of Zenger, Cosby ordered him arrested anyway. To better ensure the result he wanted at trial, DeLancey excluded Zenger's lawyers from any further practice before his court. In their place, DeLancey appointed John Chambers to represent Zenger, probably anticipating that Chambers would make only a perfunctory effort to defend the printer.[39]

Chambers surprised DeLancey by demanding a "struck jury," which would allow him more latitude in challenging potential jurors. Feeling he could not deny the request, the judge granted it. The sheriff chose forty-eight names, of which each side could strike as many as twelve. From the remaining twenty-four names, the sheriff selected twelve. On the evening of July 29, the sheriff presented his forty-eight names, which Chambers quickly recognized as Cosby's friends and cronies rather than men randomly drawn from the freeholders' list. Chambers probably shocked DeLancey when he objected, but it was through his vigorous efforts that Zenger got a fairly picked jury, one that represented a more genuine cross section of the public than Cosby and DeLancey had intended.[40]

After the fight over the jury, the trial began, and at this moment the political faction financing Zenger's defense dismissed Chambers and replaced him with Andrew Hamilton. Hamilton faced a task that seemed impossible. Eighteenth-century English law deemed any publication seditious if it defamed the authority of the government. The political nature of the crime made it difficult for defense lawyers to delineate precise boundaries around what could be prosecuted and what could not. Anything designed to bring the government into contempt could be seen as seditious libel. At trial, the prosecutor pointed out that Zenger did not deny that he had printed materials ridiculing Cosby. Hamilton famously asked jurors to reject British libel and slander law to find in favor of freedom of the press. That the jury did so probably owed as much to Chambers's work as to Hamilton's rhetoric.[41]

In 1747, New York grand jurors continued such independent thinking when they refused to indict rioters, making a political statement against British authorities. Virginia grand jurors also acted politically when they indicted aristocrats for petty offenses. British colonial officers, including William Kempe, New York attorney general, fought back by complaining that such troublesome jurors lacked the competence necessary to decide questions of law.[42] Demanding more-competent jurors circumvented their independence since judges used such rhetoric to justify picking more-cooperative men with ties to the government. But over time, grand juries nonetheless became a means to protest English imperial policies. British efforts to eliminate trial by jury in its Stamp Act and subsequent Townshend Acts hardened a developing colonial tendency to see juries as a bulwark against tyranny and oppression. John Adams wrote that jury service invested the common, ordinary people, what he called society's democracy, in executing the laws. Juries introduced "a mixture of popular power" into the system, he said. By turning to vice-admiralty courts, as Parliament did in 1765 and 1767, single judges, acting with no jury at all, seemed scandalously empowered to arbitrarily subvert the English constitution.[43]

Juries heroically battling arbitrary power emerged as an increasingly potent symbol during the imperial crisis, one that encouraged the notion that a constitution should be fundamentally superior to legislative acts. The idea of fundamental law had a long history in England, but John Locke and other English Whigs thought it enforceable only through revolution. Nothing in this history logically led Americans to believe they could invoke constitutional principle in court; instead the Americans learned to seize sovereignty through their juries.[44] In 1768, Bostonians thwarted efforts by British officers to prosecute their rioting opponents by placing members of their mob on the Suffolk County grand jury. Adams defended John Hancock, accused of smuggling, by accusing British officers, "the Barons of modern Times," of proceeding against his client "not by jury, not by the Law of the Land." Adams charged that Parliament protected British subjects' right to a jury trial in England "and by the next Clause deprive[d] all Americans of the Privilege." Denying trial by jury degraded Americans, Adams argued, and repealed the Magna Carta. Adams and other Whig lawyers fought for trials before representative juries.[45]

In 1774, the First Continental Congress did not forget trial by jury when it issued its Declaration and Resolves outlining American rights. Article V stated "that the respective colonies are entitled to the common law of England, and more especially to the great and inestimable privilege of being tried by their peers of the vicinage, according to the course of that law." Article VII claimed "immunities and privileges granted and confirmed to them by royal charters, or secured by their several codes of provincial laws." This ill-defined phrase had great potential. The Continental Congressmen obviously had in mind the rule of law, as articulated in their colonial charters and provincial codes, which promised the colonists the same "liberties, franchises, and immunities" as Englishmen enjoyed. These words sometimes implied a limit on governmental authority but at other times suggested a requirement imposed on local government. Communities could not discriminate against immigrating nonresidents.[46]

By the time the Americans came to draft the fundamental laws of their new nation, the fairy tale that defendants had a right to trials by juries of their peers seemed well established in popular folklore and mythology. For Pinkard Dowans and other black Americans who might want to avail themselves of such a right, though, the history of trial by jury had structured the right to a jury of peers in a troubling way. Jury service was a right, but one profoundly decentralized, a right against, rather than enforced by, national power. A colonial jury had saved Zenger; colonial juries had vexed the British in Boston. When the colonies became states, trial by jury became a right protected and enforced by the states. For black Americans like Pinkard Dowans, however, state control of jury selection became an almost insurmountable obstacle to a fair trial.

The conflict between state power and natural rights enforceable by the national authority became evident at the moment of independence. In 1776, the Continental Congress organized two committees. In one, Thomas Jefferson drafted the Declaration of Independence, which included a complaint that King George denied his colonial subjects access to trial by jury. Jefferson invoked natural law, holding it to be a self-evident truth that the Creator had endowed people with certain inalienable rights, and he proceeded to charge the king with assenting to pretended legislation "depriving [the American colonists] in many cases, of the benefits of Trial by Jury." Another committee, led by John Dickinson, drafted the Articles of Confederation. Dickinson lacked Jefferson's enthusiasm for natural law. With regard to states' rights, Dickinson had to tread carefully, and the Articles of Confederation acknowledged state sovereignty. But Dickinson did state that American citizens had a right to their "privileges and immunities," implying a national right that could trump states' rights, at least theoretically. In Article IV, Dickinson wrote, "The better to secure and perpetuate mutual friendship and intercourse among the people of the different States in the Union, the free inhabitants of each of these States, paupers, vagabonds, and fugitives from justice excepted, shall be entitled to all the privileges and immunities of free citizens in the several States." But the articles created no federal courts and suggested intervention in state trials or selection of jurors might not be possible. Dickinson urged "privileges and immunities" but offered no way of protecting those rights.[47]

The first challenges to state power came in the first decade after independence. Throughout the 1780s, it became clear to many that Dickinson had been too deferential to the states. Although James Madison recorded no particular dissatisfaction with their administration of justice, the states' lawmaking troubled him. In 1783, he complained of "the variance of their policy & interests in the article of commerce." When he summarized his disquiet in 1787, Madison noted the failure of the states to contribute tax revenues to the central government, their tendency to encroach on federal authority, their trespasses on the rights of one another, and the mutability of state laws. The states daily, Madison wrote, repealed or superseded laws without giving them a fair trial. Madison had become disenchanted with majority rule at the local and state level. "Whenever an apparent interest of common passion unites a majority," he wrote, nothing restrains it from invading the rights of the minority. He meant legislative majorities, not juries, but his comment reveals no concern with protecting the rights of ordinary people to sit in judgment of their fellows as members of trial juries.[48]

Although delegates to the 1787 Constitutional Convention later claimed that they gave ample consideration to trial by jury, Max Farrand's *Records of the Federal Convention* suggests otherwise.[49] When the Committee of Detail presented a draft document on August 6, it included a provision that trials of criminal defendants be in the state where the offense was committed and be before a jury. In September, as the delegates finished their business, Hugh Williamson of North Carolina urged expanding the right to jury trials by extending the privilege to civil cases. Nathaniel Gorham of Massachusetts, an influential nationalist, spoke for the majority when he rebuffed this overture by saying that civil matters should be handled by state legislatives, and not constitutionally. "The Representatives of the people may be safely trusted in this matter," he contended. Elbridge Gerry, also of Massachusetts, intervened to say that juries guarded against corrupt judges, the argument commonly made in English pamphlet literature. George Mason, a Virginian rapidly losing confidence in the convention's work, commented that he understood Gorham's point but still favored "a general principle laid down on this." This brief discussion inspired Mason to add that he thought a bill of rights covering this and other points should be added to the document. It could be drafted very easily, he observed. On September 15, Charles Pinkney and Elbridge Gerry tried again, suggesting that Article III be revised to preserve trial by jury in civil as well as criminal cases. Gorham again objected, repeating his concern that the convention must not intrude on practices in different states. The "trial itself is *usual* in different cases in different States." Rufus King of Massachusetts and Charles Cotesworth Pinkney agreed with Gorham, and after short, sharp rejoinders from three sides, the proposal died. The Constitution guaranteed criminal defendants' access to a jury trial but did not extend the same right to civil litigants.[50]

It is a measure of just how thoroughly ordinary Americans had internalized their right to trial by jury that the delegates had to defend their neglect of this issue. Ironically, they now found themselves making long and complex speeches on a topic scarcely covered at the convention. James Wilson took the lead. In a speech delivered on October 6, 1787, Wilson began by explaining that the federal constitution "was not local but general." The framers wrote it mindful not only that they were creating fundamental law for an entire continent but that they had to respect "the views and establishments" of thirteen independent sovereignties. The various states had different rules regarding civil juries. Some states did not allow juries in categories of civil cases where other states did. The delegates could not create a general rule that covered so many conflicting rules. "The convention found the task too difficult for them," Wilson said. He continued his argument at the Pennsylvania ratifying convention. In criminal cases, he explained, the government had to be restricted from abusing its powers by giving defendants access to a jury trial. Defenders of the new Constitution asked voters to trust the men they elected to Congress not to trample the right of trial by jury. Even if the framers failed to inscribe such a right in the Constitution's text, they said, members of Congress could be relied on not to impinge on the right to a jury. Edmund Randolph conceded to the Virginia Convention that he would have liked to have a guarantee of the right to a jury in civil cases explicitly placed in the Constitution. Nonetheless, he said, he would stake his property that Congress would institute trial by jury in a way that accommodated the conveniences of the inhabitants in every state.[51]

Arguments made by Charles Pinkney, Elbridge Gerry, and George Mason for the right to a jury trial in civil cases foreshadowed Anti-Federalist opposition to the proposed Constitution. Few Anti-Federalist writers neglected to warn that the new Constitution failed to protect trial by jury in civil cases. In heartily rejecting Wilson's explanations, they spoke as one. Some charged that the Constitution created an overly powerful Supreme Court that would overturn jury verdicts by reviewing both facts and the law. The Pennsylvania writer "Centinel," probably Samuel Bryan working with his father,

Judge George Bryan, said that the Constitution "threatened" trial by jury and in another article flatly said that the Constitution "abolished" trial by jury. Centinel added that the chief justice of the United States would be both judge and jury, becoming an all-powerful arbiter of law and equity.[52] The Anti-Federalist calling himself "Brutus" thought allowing appeals in criminal trials "a new and unusual thing." According to Brutus, it meant subjecting criminal defendants to double jeopardy, since Brutus worried that persons acquitted might be tried again if a federal appeals court reversed the acquittal.[53] Numerous Anti-Federalists worried that the Constitution endangered trials by a jury of the vicinage, an institution they particularly cherished, fearing that taking trials out of the vicinage would force litigants to travel great distances to have their day in court.[54] But Anti-Federalists also argued that trials of the vicinage opened jury service to poorer and less privileged members of society. Anti-Federalists worried that holding trials far from the scene of the crime or dispute necessarily relied on written evidence in the form of depositions. Since only elite members of society could read, this process denied the poor a chance to serve on juries. Evidence had to come from the mouths of live witnesses for the poorest of the poor, the illiterate, to understand it.[55] Although many Anti-Federalists appeared concerned that the Constitution threatened the right of trial by jury for litigants, some Anti-Federalists wanted juries to truly represent their communities. They did not, of course, expect the landless or their women or their slaves to serve on juries. So even the most determined champion of public jury service had only an enfeebled concept of popular participation, by modern standards. Nonetheless, Richard Henry Lee called the "full and equal representation of the people" on juries essential to a free and good government. "Every order of men in the community" had to have access to jury service, Lee asserted.

Anti-Federalists relied on history to make their pro-jury arguments. In Maryland, Luther Martin reminded his state's general assembly that trial by jury had a long history as a barrier against arbitrary power.[56] Centinel quoted Blackstone, as did the "Federal farmer" who asserted that "every political and legal writer" recognized the importance of juries. Brutus called juries "the boast of our forefathers."[57] A Maryland Anti-Federalist calling himself "a Farmer" wrote that the right to a jury trial had been preserved and handed down from generation to generation for two thousand years, celebrated by the most enlightened statesmen of every age.[58] Cincinnatus reminded his readers of the Zenger trial.[59] Given such a long and celebrated history, some Anti-Federalists wondered why their own generation would "trifle . . . away" such a heritage.[60]

Proponents of the Constitution in New York published a series of newspaper columns to rebut the Anti-Federalist clamor. In an essay numbered 83, Federalist Alexander Hamilton smoothly reassured New Yorkers that both the Constitution's proponents and its opponents agreed on the value of trial by jury. Hamilton wrote that one group, the Anti-Federalists, saw the jury trial as a valuable safeguard of liberty, while the other saw it politically, as the very palladium of free government. As a Federalist, Hamilton recognized jurors' political value but doubted they were "competent to investigate questions involving complicated legal issues." The answer, of course, was to restrict jurors to questions of fact, leaving law to the judges, a solution Thomas Jefferson favored. Hamilton, though, did not believe such a separation feasible. In most cases, he explained, law becomes too entangled with questions of fact for a separation of the two.[61]

In 1789, James Madison went to the first session of the first Congress prepared to rewrite the Constitution to add protections for trial by jury. Though Madison was initially hostile to the Anti-Federalists' demands for a bill of rights, North Carolina's refusal to ratify the Constitution without amendments the previous fall had converted him, and he now offered amendments to make the Constitution "acceptable to the whole people of the United States." A majority had ratified the document, but Madison wanted to win over the last holdouts, "to extinguish from the bosom of every member of the community, any apprehensions" that the new government threatened the liberty won with blood from the British. On June 8, 1789, Madison stood in the House with his proposed amendments. He urged Congress to guarantee "due process of law," which implied trial by jury. More explicitly, he wanted to guarantee that "in all criminal prosecutions, the accused shall enjoy the right to a speedy and public trial." The Anti-Federalists saw the Bill of Rights as a check on the national government's powers, but Madison, for his part, hoped to add a protection against state assaults on due process. He proposed changing Article I, Section 10, so that it included language that foreshadowed the Fourteenth Amendment: "No State shall violate the equal rights of conscience, or the freedom of the press, or the trial by jury in criminal cases."[62] Congress would not agree to this proposal, and no limitation of the states' authority over trials made it into the Bill of Rights. The Bill of Rights that Congress proposed and the states ratified, however, required a grand jury for persons held to answer for a capital or "infamous" crime (Fifth Amendment) and guaranteed the right to a speedy and public trial by an impartial jury (Sixth Amendment) and the right to trial by jury in suits at common law (Seventh Amendment). These protections served as limitations on federal and not state courts, where most trials occurred.

Despite these constitutional endorsements of trial by jury, in 1800 Samuel Chase continued Hamilton's theory that juries should be limited to facts, scolding a lawyer who tried to argue law to the jury in *United States v. Callender*: "It is not competent to the jury to decide" law.[63] Both Hamilton and Chase feared an invasion of the jury box by the less-well-off or the down-and-out. But neither man could misunderstand the meaning of jury service: it offered ordinary people a path into the inner workings of government.

Given the democratic connotations associated with jury service, it is not surprising that after the Revolutionary War many states required the random selection of jurors. One writer contrasted the English system, where jurors were "returned by the sheriff" with the more equitable American procedure, where they were "draughted by lot, from each town."[64] Women, children, African Americans, and men without property would not be called, but revolutionary ideology demanded that every white male freeholder have an equal opportunity to represent his community on a jury. In 1784, Massachusetts required town constables to assemble freeholders and other inhabitants qualified to vote "to elect and choose by ballot, so many good and lawful men of their town . . . to serve on the Grand jury." Selectmen chose potential petit jurors, putting their names in a box for random selection.[65] In Maine the selectmen made lists of persons of good moral character and "then lay the whole of their doings before the town for a revision, who [might] confirm the same, or make such alterations therein as they [might] deem proper." Thereafter the court randomly drew the names from a box.[66] Rhode Island lawmakers told their town councils in 1798 to make lists of "all persons liable by law, and whom they [should] judge to be qualified as Jurors, and put the names of such persons on separate pieces of paper into a box." Officials picked grand and petit jurors in blind drawings.[67]

North Carolina went to the greatest lengths of all to ensure selection of grand and petit jurors who were truly representative of the white male population. That state ordered court clerks to select potential jurors from freeholders listed on the county tax returns. North Carolinians, however, worried that some freeholders might not be on the tax rolls, prompting a resolution: "If said tax returns shall not contain the names of all the inhabitants of their said county, who in their opinion are well qualified to act as such jurors, they shall cause the names of all such persons to be inserted on their said jury list." But legislators thought that even such a measure might not ensure that every last freeholder made it onto the list and so went on to require judges "to examine carefully the jury lists ... and diligently inquire if any persons qualified to be jurors as above mentioned [were] omitted." The names produced by this process went into a box. To guarantee a random selection, the law required that the drawing be performed by a child under ten years of age, who would presumably be unable to read the names of the persons in the box.[68]

Random selection of jurors explains the persistent complaints about the low quality of jurors. Newspapers periodically reported that jurors drank or read newspapers while on duty. In 1843, the *New York Herald* announced that it had had enough with weak-minded jurors' sympathy for criminal defendants. "The great mass of the intelligent and reputable portion" of the population knew that juries perpetrated great evils, the *Herald* grumbled before adding that if northern jurors did not shape up, the North would soon have no choice but to adopt the vigilante and lynching techniques so common in the South.[69]

Legislators tried to accommodate relentless popular complaints about juror incompetence by specifying that jurors be "good and lawful," "discrete," "reputable," and "judicious" "gentlemen" of "good moral character." One recent student of Illinois juries estimates that Illinois law used such language to eliminate all but 10 percent of the population from jury service. Custom sometimes prompted jury commissioners to prefer the wealthier and more influential over the less-well-off, but they often chose poorer people, a fact documented by the common criticism charging that unworthy persons too often sat on juries. James Wilson answered that the "untutored" would make mistakes when they served on juries, but their mistakes could be corrected and would never grow into a dangerous system. Ordinary people summoned to jury service, Wilson argued, cannot develop the esprit de corps often found among elites and professionals; that lack of professionalism guards property, character, freedom, and life against arbitrary power.[70]

The law allowed lawyers to further restrict access to actual jury service. State law based on common law principles rather than the U.S. Constitution controlled jury selection procedures for almost every criminal trial in the United States before the Civil War, and those laws recognized that defendants had two competing expectations. First, defendants could demand that juries be chosen fairly, meaning sheriffs had to proceed neutrally and randomly, not seating friends or enemies of one side or the other. This stipulation suggests that very plain folk should serve on juries, including the town drunk or neighborhood loafers. Attorneys, though, could insist that only competent persons serve on their juries. Defense lawyers, then, could attack juries as irregularly summoned and impaneled, or they could try to eliminate individual jurors as incompetent. In legal parlance, this meant that lawyers attacked jurors in two ways: by challenging either the array or the polls. Challenges to the array alleged partiality or some procedural error by the sheriff or his deputies in their method for picking jurors. In the first half of the nineteenth century, defense lawyers enjoyed numerous grounds for attacking the array. Some must have seemed a bit outlandish even at the time. Henry St. George Tucker, in lectures delivered to the Winchester (Virginia) Law School, said that foreigners could challenge an array that included only U.S. citizens, though they had no right to demand their own countrymen. Tucker acknowledged that he had never actually seen a jury that included foreigners. Some responsible authorities tried to rein in defense counsel. Joseph Chitty emphasized the very limited number of legitimate challenges to the array. A defense lawyer needed to show the sheriff's actual affinity to either of the parties through a pecuniary interest in the case or "if an action of battery [were] depending between the sheriff and the defendant."[71]

In an 1833 North Carolina case, Judge Thomas Ruffin agreed that even small procedural mistakes, such as swearing Joes Jones as Joel Jones, constituted a reversible error. A grand jury can only consist of those actually summoned, he maintained. But Ruffin meant to put a stop to the many challenges to grand jurors on such trivial errors. Had defense counsel objected "in due season," the objection would have been unanswerable. "In strictness," Ruffin stated, objections had to be raised at the proper time, before the grand jury was sworn. "Thus it was at common law," Ruffin said, adding that nothing in North Carolina law provided any other alternative.[72] Despite such concerns, judges very often sternly enforced rules against anomalies in jury selection procedures. In 1834, New York lawyer David Graham observed that the practice in his state had once been so strict, "the jurymen [so] rigidly scanned," that lawyers could even set aside almost any indictment by finding trivial errors made by the sheriff when assembling the jury.[73]

Challenges to the polls took exception to individuals as unsuitable for jury service. Antebellum lawyers commonly cited Sir Edward Coke's four categories of challenges to the polls. Some of these were irrelevant in the American context, such as *propter honoris respectum,* which excused lords of Parliament. The important one was *propter affectum,* suspicion of bias or partiality. Good defense lawyers energetically sought statements indicating bias when examining potential jurors. Appeals courts threw out convictions when defense lawyers produced evidence that a juror had made remarks revealing prejudice. Also, persons rendered infamous could not serve, nor could slaves.[74]

Trial by jury took a firm foothold not only in the Constitution but in the consciousness of ordinary people, becoming an "emerging isthmus," in James Wilson's words, amid the instability of arbitrary power. It is interesting to compare the place juries held in the Constitution with that occupied by slavery. Article IV used confusing and elliptical language to guarantee slave owners the right to reclaim "Person[s] held to Service or Labour in one State, under the Laws thereof." By contrast, Article III forthrightly promised that "The Trial of all Crimes . . . shall be by Jury." The Sixth Amendment guaranteed "an impartial jury" in "all criminal prosecutions." The framers seemed less embarrassed to guarantee trial by jury than slave labor. Some scholars now disagree, but Don Fehrenbacher has observed that slavery held only a muddled and provisional place in the Constitution. Trial by jury stood as a mightier fortress.[75]

Yet even as trial by jury as a democratic institution secured its place in American constitutionalism, a rival model began to challenge it: the ideal of the upright, competent, fully qualified juror. Victims of crime, defendants, and the neighborhoods where crime occurred all had good reason to want capable jurors who were invested in society deciding the guilt or innocence of accused persons. This expectation opened one more door for race to enter. White people held power, and white people perceived competence as white. At the end of the eighteenth century, few dared even imagine challenging such local convictions with some nationally held ideal of inclusiveness. Nonetheless, the model of the genuinely representative jury existed, sitting on the shelf of the nation's historical imagination, ready for use when the public opinion necessary to enforce constitutional rules shifted in a new direction. But there were other shelves and other ideals as well. Nothing was determined in advance of history.

CHAPTER TWO

The Discovery That Race
Politicizes Due Process

DABNEY MARSHALL WAS ONE MEMBER *of a three-man alliance determined to win justice for Mississippi blacks. Willis Mollison was the second. While Marshall enjoyed all the privileges of wealth and whiteness, Mollison had all the disadvantages of being born black in Mississippi. Nonetheless, he found his opportunities where he could, studying law under a Republican carpetbagger, the former Mississippi Supreme Court justice Elza Jeffords, and finagling a job as clerk of the Issaquena County circuit chancery court. He apparently performed his duties to the satisfaction of whites as well as African Americans, since he won election to the job in 1883 and reelection in 1887. Admitted to the bar in 1887, he first practiced law in his hometown of Mayerville before moving to Vicksburg, where he ran a bank, operated a newspaper, and continued his law practice.[1]*

Mollison attributed the worst of white racism to politics, firmly believing that Mississippi's notoriously demagogic governor, James K. Vardaman, had egged on the most evil and violent white racists to gain office. His evidence came from his own experience: Before Vardaman became governor in 1903, white lawyers and judges freely shared their offices and libraries with black colleagues, a practice that ended with Vardaman's election. Vardaman hated Booker T. Washington's variety of self-help since it implied that with education blacks could be made worthy citizens. This rankled Mollison, driving him to prove Washington right. To show black accomplishment and success, Mollison published a book titled The Leading Afro-Americans of Vicksburg, Miss., Their Enterprises, Churches, Schools, Lodges and Societies. *He gave speeches arguing that blacks could be educated, could be successful, could be deserving of white respect.[2]*

Shortly after Vardaman took office, the Mississippi legislature passed a new segregation law, one that required streetcar companies to separate black from white passengers. The law took effect June 1, 1904, and the Vicksburg Street Railway readied its cars for the big day by building screens for seatbacks to make separate compartments. Whites anticipated that blacks would boycott the segregated cars. Sure enough, when the first segregated cars rolled on June 1, blacks refused to ride and continued to do so for three months, but in September Mollison urged black Vicksburgers to call off the boycott.[3] Boycotting the streetcars did not fit with his strategy of presenting his race as respectable and earnest. Better to protest in a way that promoted the talents and abilities of the best men whom the black race had to offer, Mollison believed.

To Mollison, pursuing the right of blacks to serve on juries seemed a better way to fight for civil rights than a trolley boycott. It was not only a lawful and entirely dignified way to challenge segregation; it also offered an opportunity to confront whites with talented, responsible, and educated blacks obviously qualified for such civic service. Moreover, although Mollison fought against white opponents organized to violent and frightening proportions, he nonetheless imagined that he did so with the highest law of the nation on his side. So, like Marshall, Mollison relied on "the fairy tale" of democratic jury service when making his arguments.

Just as Dabney Marshall had to grapple with a history riddled with contradictions, so too did Mollison. As a black man, Mollison also knew well African Americans' long effort just to be heard before a jury, let alone to serve as jurors. More than Marshall, Mollison knew the history of the black struggle for access to law before the Civil War. The rights Mollison demanded had not been won before the Civil War, but they had been articulated, argued, and advanced. Before the Civil War, efforts to secure the right to trial by jury for black Americans ran into opposition based more in politics than in constitutionalism. White slave owners and their allies claimed that the Constitution itself was primarily a political document, a sectional compromise. The antebellum compromises that white Americans made with the nation's most sacred principles—including the foundational idea that defendants should be tried by a jury of their peers—presaged compromises made in the Jim Crow era.

After the Revolutionary War and the Constitutional Convention, slavery and racism challenged the principles that had seemed so well established not just in the Constitution's text but in the public imagination. Proponents of slavery argued for a kind of popular constitutionalism, the notion that the Constitution represented political compromise between the sections of the country more than an articulation of profound principle. The Fugitive Slave Law, they said, necessarily abrogated trial by jury for a political purpose, but did so for a worthy cause, preserving the Union. Abolitionists fought back, collecting a portfolio of natural-law arguments against slavery and in favor of trial by jury for all Americans, including blacks. Ralph Waldo Emerson insisted that true law came from nature and not from politics. The Supreme Court played only a slight role in this quarrel, but the arguments assembled, the doctrines tested, and, most importantly, the evidence of public support for race-based exceptions to the principle of trial by jury would prove important to its deliberations later. Even Emerson came to understand that politics, influenced by race, could eat into the vitals of the higher-law doctrine he so treasured. The antebellum compromises that white Americans made with the nation's most sacred principles, including trial by jury, made it harder for postbellum jurists to remain true to that foundational tenet.

In the beginning, the importance of guarding principle from the wanton influences of public opinion seemed clearer than it would later. Of the men most often thought of as the framers of the Constitution, at least one, James Madison, warned against "the inconveniences of democracy" and sought to build a structure that would fortify constitutional rights against the strongest political challenges, the conflagrations Madison could see coming. The fires he feared were political, waves of emotionalism sweeping the population away from consensus, reckless and feckless factions more concerned with immediate advantage than the good of the whole. Madison doubted that either religion or individual conscience could sufficiently restrain a majority determined to oppress a minority.[4] Black Americans could see the racial implications in political threats to constitutional principle. In 1800, James Forten, a black businessman and Revolutionary War veteran in Philadelphia, wrote that "principles of natural law" rendered blacks' "thralldom"—slavery—unjust. Forten saw no sanctuary for human liberty in politics. His was a truth self-evident in the founding documents, "one of the most prominent features in the Declaration of Independence, and in that glorious fabrick of collected wisdom, our noble Constitution."[5] Around 1801, an anonymous writer, calling himself A Friend to the Constitution, mythologized Madison and the other framers as acting in "that day of genuine patriotism," a time before faction or party, even before politics, "to

establish wise and correct principles" to be protected by judges acting outside popular passions.[6]

That trial by jury was such a wise and correct principle, few Americans
could doubt. This fact was quickly recognized by the authors of legal treatises, who warned that any state trying to evade it ran the risk of rendering its legal proceedings a nullity.[7] Nonetheless, Madison's fears that such
rights would be challenged proved well founded. In the time between the
American Revolution and the Civil War, Americans quarreled over their
commitment to abstract doctrine over majority rule, the idea that ordinary
people should have a veto over even the most important constitutional pre-
cepts. Following the evolving balance of power between politics and the
principle of trial by jury tracks the most important controversies Americans faced before the Civil War. As neither side could entirely prevail over
the other, drama characterized their fights for dominance.

From the beginning, state politics intervened in the right to trial by jury.
Not many months after *A Friend to the Constitution* praised the framers for
setting principles outside politics, the Pennsylvania legislature enlarged the
powers of magistrates, eliminating trial by jury in some instances. Critics
charged that the legislators acted politically against both the Constitution's
"sacred principles" and the common law. In 1803, one anonymous writer
complained that a Pennsylvania faction sought to "change and undermine
this ancient and rightful mode of trial." The right to trial by jury, this author
declared, came from "ancient, immemorial usage," codified in the common
law of England, which had survived ruthless despots, corruption, and anar-
chists. A Philadelphia newspaper concluded that the bill contradicted "our
ancient habits." In the end, Governor Thomas McKean invoked those principled arguments when he vetoed the bill.[8]

More often legislative enactments about juries were not vetoed. The
founding generation trusted state legislatures to set the rules for who could
sit on American juries, federal and state, and used Section 29 of the Judiciary
Act of 1789 to instruct federal judges that they must follow state law when
choosing jurors. To make sure they conformed with this requirement, federal judges in New York and New England employed as jurors men selected
by state officers.[9] This practice seemed right because the states had defended
the common law against British attempts to overturn it in the Revolution,
some said. Not only did Congress lack the states' experience standing up for
common-law rights, but some thought it imitated British tyranny when it

passed the Alien and Sedition Acts in 1798. This poison even spread into the judiciary. Federalist judges steered grand and trial juries to indict and convict Jeffersonians. Thomas Jefferson decried the "germ of rottedness" soiling trial by jury and asked his state, not Congress, to fix the problem by requiring that jurors be elected by popular vote. Jefferson considered his state's courts less political—more dedicated to neutral common-law principles— than the Federalist-dominated federal courts. State courts generally did the bidding of their legislatures, but state judges weighed legislative enactments against the common law with its time-tested principles.[10]

The common law could not long be confined to the state courts. Federal judges and the lawyers appearing before them sometimes reshaped the neutral principles that Jefferson and others favored into powerful polemics that achieved greater fame than state pronouncements. In *Calder v. Bull* (1798), Supreme Court justice Samuel Chase wrote that "vital principles" constrained legislative power. Twenty-one years later, while arguing *Dartmouth College v. Woodward* (1819), Daniel Webster insisted that constitutions articulate "those fundamental and unalterable principles of justice, which must lie at the foundation of every free and just system of laws."[11] State courts found the great advocate's language useful when reversing their legislatures and echoed Webster that those bodies did not have a free hand to act on every popular whim. North Carolina's Thomas Ruffin declared in 1833 that "law of the land" meant something more than "merely" any act by any legislature.[12]

Nonetheless, it seems likely that when Congress reiterated its concession to the states in 1840, affirming that state rules controlled federal jury selection, it expected state politics more than ancient principle to set jury selection rules. By 1840, many state legislatures had beaten back abolitionists' assertions of common-law rights for blacks. In the New York senate, abolitionists mounted a campaign challenging the federal Fugitive Slave Law with a state law that guaranteed accused fugitives a jury trial. A similar proposition in Ohio stirred a hysterical response from the *Ohio Statesman*. "Breakers Ahead," the paper shrieked, adding that agitation for trial by jury increased the "Insolence of the Blacks!" "Shall we extend the rights and privileges of the blacks, and hold out inducements for them to settle among us?" the *Statesman* wailed.[13] Such expressions stood as the main line of defense against abolitionist demands.

Slave owners said that the Constitution itself included language allowing them to challenge trial by jury. Article IV guaranteed Southerners' right to retrieve runaway slaves: "No person held to Service or Labour in one State, under the Laws thereof, escaping into another, shall in Consequence of any Law or Regulation therein, be discharged from such Service or Labour, but shall be delivered up on Claim on the Party to whom such Service or Labour may be due."[14] Responding to a case involving three Virginia men charged with kidnapping into slavery a free black Pennsylvania citizen, Congress tried, and failed, to enact a fugitive slave law in 1791. Pennsylvania had wanted to extradite the three suspects and Virginia resisted. U.S. attorney general Edmund Randolph stepped in to criticize both Virginia and Pennsylvania, but he sided with Virginia less than with Pennsylvania. He pointed out that before facing extradition the three Virginians had enjoyed the benefits of a jury: Pennsylvania had asked to extradite only after a grand jury considered the evidence. This was no "wanton or unauthorized" accusation, he observed.[15]

At the end of 1792, Congress returned to the issue. The Senate first considered a bill that would have required northern state officers to track down and arrest persons whom white Southerners accused of being their slaves. This failed either because Northerners did not want their tax dollars used to hunt slaves, or because they did not care about due process for free blacks living in the North. Instead, the Senate authorized slave owners and their agents to enter the North and arrest blacks outside the law, effectively denying alleged fugitive slaves access to trial by jury. The law required that they present proof of ownership to a magistrate or judge, who then issued a certificate legalizing the seizure, but the original arrest would be done by ordinary citizens, acting outside legal institutions. Nothing in the federal law allowed a jury to review the arrest or weigh the evidence against the accused slave. Black people living in the North lost their right to trial by jury because their congressmen failed to rally to their protection while southern congressional delegations united against them.[16]

The *Annals of Congress* leaves only a parsimonious record of debates, but it seems likely that Congress enacted the 1793 law because it assumed that enforcing the fugitive slave clause would promote sectional harmony.[17] Only afterward did lawyers work out a constitutional justification for Congress's political encroachment on such a fundamental element of due process of law as trial by jury. In 1819, Pennsylvania's chief justice William Tilghman thought it "well known" that Southerners would not have consented to the Union without constitutional protection for their slave property. The citizens of Pennsylvania freely entered into an agreement that made it their duty to return fugitive slaves to their owners, he wrote, adding that Congress had decided this must be done in a summary manner, "without the delay of a formal trial."[18] One of the most important nineteenth-century American jurists, Joseph Story, agreed with Tilghman, writing that the Union could not have been formed without protection for slavery built into the Constitution.[19] Under this theory, trial by jury could be set aside to accommodate white Southerners' demands. Principle yielded to politics.

Every state prevented participation on juries by black people. Northern whites thought it would be "derogatory" to sit with a black man and more so to consult with him to reach a verdict, according to an English traveler.[20] Eighteen state legislatures wrote jury laws that overtly discriminated, either by specifying that jurors had to be white men or that they had to be freeholders or householders, requirements that excluded many whites but virtually all blacks. (See appendix 1.)

In contrast to past practice, lawmakers now linked jury service to voting. Twelve states made suffrage a precondition for jury service. This did not necessarily guarantee racial exclusion. Maine, Massachusetts, Minnesota, Vermont, and Wisconsin (and Michigan after 1850) did not put a racial limitation on voting in their state constitutions. The other states passed jury laws with no overt racial discrimination, but by linking jury service to voting, constitutionally limited to white males, lawmakers made certain that no black person could serve as a juror. California, Connecticut, Delaware, Iowa, Michigan (before 1850), Ohio, and Texas all limited voting to white male citizens in their constitutions and then restricted jury service to voters. Most states using this stratagem wrote language into their laws suggesting that they did not want all their white voters participating on juries. Delaware insisted its jurors be not only voters but also "sober and judicious persons"; Iowa wanted not just voters but those with "good moral character, sound judgment, and in full possession of the senses of hearing and seeing." California insisted its voters have possession of their "natural faculties" before becoming jurors. (See appendix 2.)

Five New England states did not use either constitutional voting restrictions or overt statutory discriminations to eliminate black jury service. Nonetheless, in the first decades of the nineteenth century, Maine, Massachusetts, New Hampshire, Rhode Island, and Vermont all wrote laws that permitted or perhaps encouraged informal discrimination.[21] In Maine, municipal officers prepared lists of "such persons only as are of good moral character qualified to vote for representatives of each town." These states all tried to change jury service from an onerous obligation to a mark of public citizenship. Even men lucky enough to get on the lists prepared by the municipal officers could not count on jury service, as they had to win the approval of their neighbors, assembled in town meetings. The municipal officers put their lists "before the town for their approval," and a majority of the voters assembled could "strike names but [could] not insert any others."[22] In Massachusetts, the selectmen of each town chose "inhabitants they [thought] well qualified to serve as jurors . . . persons of good moral character, or sound judgment." New Hampshire had a similar system, as did Rhode Island and Vermont. (See appendix 3.)

In every state, jury commissioners or even lower-ranking public officials, deputy clerks and deputy sheriffs, exercised considerable discretion in picking jurors. Of course, not only the New England states relied on low-ranking officers to pick the right jurors. Alexis de Tocqueville thought such deputies in every state exercised "very arbitrary" powers to select jurors.[23] This could have the effect of putting nonelites on juries. Maryland depended so much on county officials to round up jurors that lawmakers found they had to plead with sheriffs to summon better-quality jurors. Sheriffs, the lawmakers complained, "frequently return[ed] jurors very inadequate to the discharge of the important duties assigned to them."[24]

However far down the white social hierarchy sheriffs went for jurors, though, they did not select blacks, and even whites opposed to slavery hardly noticed. Before 1830, abolitionists rarely linked the right to a trial by jury with emancipation, not because they did not see trial by jury as an immutable principle, but because they hoped to end slavery without involving the question of rights for the freed people. Reformers, including James G. Birney and Theodore Weld, wanted to send emancipated American slaves to Africa and thus avoid the issue of the former slaves' rights. Even so, due process for black Americans was not entirely forgotten. The 1793 federal Fugitive Slave Law so obviously outraged common-law due process standards that some northern states challenged it by throwing legal protections around persons accused of being slaves. Pennsylvania's 1826 law required state judges to demand from slave owners, and their agents, better proof than the federal law required. But Pennsylvania did not guarantee that its citizens would get a jury trial when Southerners claimed they were fugitive slaves.[25]

Colonization with its concession that constitutional rights need not be accorded to slavery's victims never appealed to many blacks; African

Americans themselves argued for the same inherent and lawful rights that white Americans enjoyed.[26] By the 1830s, some whites had begun to move closer to the black position. The fiery William Lloyd Garrison emerged to lead a different kind of abolitionist movement than Birney and Weld, rejecting rights based on citizenship rooted in the nation state. He instead placed the individual over the collective and disdained all conventional organizations. In itself this was not a philosophy likely to persuade Birney and Weld, but his demands for immediate emancipation over colonization did. [27] In 1834, Birney resigned from the colonizers and joined Garrison's American Anti-Slavery Society, turning his lengthy letter of resignation, which he published as a pamphlet, into a devastating critique of his former allies. All great revolutions in sentiment, he said, must rest on some foundational principle. With the swift and sure moves of a surgeon, Birney charged that conditioning emancipation on expulsion essentially acknowledged slavery as "lawful, right, just, before God and man, *in certain cases, in existing circumstances.*" Everywhere colonization societies seemed atrophied by the 1830s, no doubt for many reasons, but Birney's rights-based argument struck a chord.[28]

Whether they advocated colonization or immediate emancipation, abolitionists other than Garrison found that higher law nerved their cause even in the face of overwhelming scorn from their opponents. There is no law, no authority, and no precedent "except in harmony with *His Will,*" New York abolitionist William Goodell (1792–1878) wrote. Although abolitionists faced overwhelming opposition and derision from Americans in all walks of life, Goodell nonetheless put considerable faith in popular will; he simply thought that politics had to be a path toward higher law, the certainty of God-ordained principles. Justice could not be found only in the common law, Goodell conceded. Eminent English jurists such as Blackstone "yielded to the claims of equity, and the rising voice of human nature." People are the divinely appointed architects of their own destinies, Goodell thought. God taught people justice, "the alphabet of that sublime truth," and people must find the immutable and eternal laws of God. Rather than trying to reconstruct the original intent of the framers, many of whom owned slaves, he argued for a strict construction of the Constitution's text and its promise to establish justice and guarantee justice and liberty for all. He vigorously denied that any constitutional principle had been compromised or limited or balanced or "crippled, forestalled, fettered, thumb-screwed, and gagged." The framers of the Constitution disagreed over how much power to give the

central government, and the ratification process produced widespread political agitation. But God had guided the people to decisively ratify the Constitution's guarantees of natural-law rights to liberty and justice.[29]

Garrison countered such textual analysis by insisting that the original
intent of the Constitution's framers had been to preserve slavery. His fol-
lower Frederick Douglass, after reading Madison's notes on the conventions, agreed that the founding fathers accommodated slavery, a position he
maintained as late as 1849 and 1850, when he debated the black abolitionist
Samuel Ringgold Ward. Ward urged the audience to set aside the framers'
sentiments and focus on the Constitution's text. Any legal document must
be understood on the basis of what it said, not the supposed intentions of
its authors, Ward told the assembled crowd. Douglass responded by pointing to the three-fifths clause as proof that the Constitution's text actually did
support slavery.[30]

Thereafter, Douglass broke with Garrison and began publicly using the
words of the Constitution against slavery, while for a time privately continuing to believe that Washington, Jefferson, and Henry were "strangers to any
just idea of liberty," apparently forgetting that of the three, only Washington
attended the Constitutional Convention, and even he contributed little to
the deliberations. Douglass made a political calculation that he could better turn white Americans against slavery if they thought their Constitution
favored liberty than by criticizing the founding generation. Within a few
years, Douglass's textual approach could hardly be distinguished from that
of Goodell and Ward. There may be a proslavery Constitution "floating in
the brains of Pro-Slavery Doughfaces in the North," he observed, but that
was not the true Constitution of 1789. People favoring an original-intent
reading of the Constitution, Douglass said, looked for "subtle and occult"
meanings hidden beneath the plain words. The people did not adopt "un-
dercurrent meanings" when they ratified the Constitution. They adopted
its plain meaning with its "obvious intentions." As for the old argument
that the framers owned slaves, Douglass now pointed out that the generation that wrote and ratified the Constitution overwhelmingly favored
gradual emancipation.[31]

Douglass was no lawyer, but abolitionist attorneys followed his approach
and adopted Goodell's natural-law argument. In 1845, the New York lawyer Alvan Stewart (1790–1849) represented Mary Tebout, held as an apprentice, and William, held as a slave for life, before New Jersey's supreme
court. Stewart relied on New Jersey's new constitution, which guaranteed

"all men ... certain natural and inalienable rights" including liberty. He cited the U.S. Constitution as well, "an Anti-slavery document, in its general spirit and tendencies." Stewart argued that while the Constitution guaranteed natural rights, slaveholding presidents, members of Congress, and Supreme Court justices had created an "invisible Constitution of slaveholding construction" that thwarted "the good honest anti-slavery Constitution which should have gone into operation on the fourth of March, 1789." The New Jersey Supreme Court rejected Stewart's natural-law arguments, ruling that New Jersey positive law had always recognized slavery.[32]

During the 1830s, abolitionists increasingly focused their attention on the right to trial by jury until it became the central feature in their argument. This happened in New York, when abolitionist lawyers sought to free a slave named Jack from his putative owner, Mary Martin. Martin claimed Jack under federal law, the 1793 Fugitive Slave Act; Jack turned to the state courts for a writ of personal replevin, or *de homine replegiando*. This writ was similar to the writ of habeas corpus, but while habeas corpus only got the prisoner before a judge, the writ of personal replevin promised to put the prisoner in front of a jury. Abolitionists wanted to get alleged fugitives from slavery before northern juries, hoping that the juries would nullify the law and decide against slavery even if the slave owner proved his or her case. In July 1834, the Supreme Court of Judicature of New York ruled against Jack, finding that the states could not interfere with slave owners' rights. The fugitive slave clause of the Constitution, Judge Samuel Nelson wrote, is "peremptory and unqualified" and gives Congress, not the states, the power to determine the terms by which slave owners reclaim their escaped slaves. Nelson's opinion not only sent Jack back to slavery but instructed New York not to use trial by jury as a device to thwart the federal Fugitive Slave Law.[33]

In New York, the traditional American doctrine holding that governmental powers should be separated from each other did not prevent decisions by the state supreme court from being appealed to the Court for the Correction of Errors, consisting of the president of the senate, the senators, the chancellor, and the justices of the supreme court. New York law provided that the justices should "have no voice" when the Court for the Correction of Errors reviewed one of their decisions.[34] In *Jack, a Negro Man, v. Mary Martin*, the Court for the Correction of Errors returned two opinions, both ruling against Jack as an individual, though one favored the principle of trial by jury for fugitives. New York state senator Isaac W. Bishop's

opinion denounced "zealous efforts for a premature and immediate abolition of slavery" and thought it "singular" that abolitionist lawyers had discovered a right to trial by jury for fugitives unknown to our forefathers or
their descendants. Bishop could not understand how a law "so benign in
its practical effects" as the Fugitive Slave Law could be unconstitutional.[35]

Chancellor Reuben Hyde Walworth also ruled against Jack, affirming
the state supreme court, but would not agree that Congress had the power
under the Constitution to allow a state magistrate to strip a citizen of his
freedom without trial by jury. Suppose, Walworth asked, the person claimed
as a slave insisted he was a free, native-born citizen of the state where he
was found. Could such a person be shipped into slavery based on nothing
more than a cursory examination by a judge? Walworth said no. Congress
had only enumerated powers, he argued, and that was not one of them. All
powers not specifically delegated to Congress by the Constitution remain
with the states. Walworth ruled against Jack, as an individual, for failing to
rebut Mary Martin's evidence that he really was a slave. But in cases where
that question remained open, Walworth believed the state of New York
should require trial by jury to make sure the person going into slavery really
was a slave.[36]

Walworth's opinion became a key document in the antislavery canon of
constitutional arguments, but it was only one piece in an expanding body
of work. In 1838, the abolitionist William Yates published a compendium of
speeches, court decisions, and other documents that included Walworth's
ruling denying the power of Congress to strike down trial by jury.[37] In 1842,
John Quincy Adams added his voice to the canon, warning that slavery
threatened Americans' "self-evident truths," which included trial by jury.[38]
The Cincinnati lawyer Salmon Chase used the case of John Van Zandt,
accused of helping eight slaves escape to freedom above Cincinnati, as a
vehicle to launch a broad attack against the constitutionality of the 1793
Fugitive Slave Act on the grounds that it violated the Seventh Amendment's
guarantee of trial by jury: "Congress has no power to authorize the seizure and trial of any person without a jury." Abolitionists added Chase's
Van Zandt brief to their growing collection of trial-by-jury arguments
against slavery.[39]

Other authors followed. Lysander Spooner (1808–87), a lawyer and writer
from Massachusetts, had a long history of writing protest pamphlets, criticizing plans to drain the Maumee River, congressional bans on private mail
deliveries, and a state law requiring would-be lawyers to read law for three

years before practicing. But he devoted himself most enthusiastically to abolition. His pamphlet *Unconstitutionality of Slavery* went through five editions and became the Liberty Party's ready reference before he published *An
Essay on the Trial by Jury* in 1852. This detailed and well-researched book
argued that juries represented the whole population, and no male segment of society could be denied access to jury service without violating the
common law. Spooner took the side of those lawyers, like Story, who had
argued that the common law could trump state power to determine qualifications for jury service. The common law, Spooner wrote, required that
juries be chosen entirely at random from the entire adult male population.
Since neither the states nor the federal government did this, Spooner—
unafraid of rhetorical excess in the service of consistency—said that there
had never been a legal jury in the entire history of the United States.[40]

The American Anti-Slavery Society armed itself with the publications of
Yates, Spooner, and others, but it fully understood that the constitutional
principles it favored could not be advanced outside the political process.
The well-known lawyer and abolitionist Henry B. Stanton (1805–87), husband of Elizabeth Cady Stanton, argued that slavery only existed by political action—legislative enactments that violated the common law. Stanton sometimes marveled at the progress he had seen, and his optimism
convinced him that through the political process the free states could exter-
minate slavery. He urged abolitionists to demand a jury trial for every fugitive slave in the nation, confident that once given this "inestimable right,"
fugitives would be safe, remarking, "for, where can you find twelve impartial men among us" who will return black people to slavery. Stanton and
other abolitionists urged their followers to petition state legislators for the
right to trial by jury for alleged fugitive slaves, and petitions began appearing in state capitals by the late 1830s.[41]

The petitioners' best chance for success was in Massachusetts, where
James C. Alvord (1808–39), of the Massachusetts House of Representatives'
Judiciary Committee, wrote his legislature's response to abolitionist petitioning. Alvord began cautiously, saying that the fugitive slave clause imposed a duty on Massachusetts that violated the common law, but which
"she [could] not shrink from performing, to the full" since the Constitution was a contract "into which she [had] voluntarily entered." Alvord then
warned abolitionists that no state could dictate to the federal government
how to enforce rights awarded by the Constitution. Anticipating Justice Joseph Story's opinion in *Prigg v. Pennsylvania*, Alvord wrote that Congress

could not make the states assist slave owners in retrieving fugitives, a federal right they had only through the U.S. Constitution. Nor could the states force a jury into a federal proceeding. Alvord then proceeded to challenge the constitutionality of the Fugitive Slave Law, in part because it violated constitutional guarantees to trial by jury. To opponents' argument that constitutional protections for trial by jury could not apply to slaves, Alvord answered that freemen accused of being slaves had every right to a state trial before a jury. Persons violating the rights of freemen, Alvord cautioned, acted at their own peril. A person falsely accused of being a slave could not only demand a jury to win his freedom but could then sue for damages, before another jury.[42]

Alvord's report, written in a neutral, factual style, citing numerous precedents, and initially published not as an abolitionist tract but in *American Jurist*, provided lawyerly ammunition for abolitionists in other states. In 1839 and 1840, New Yorkers considered bills allowing alleged fugitive slaves to have a trial by jury. In New York, legislators debated an "Act to extend the right of trial by jury" with proponents proclaiming that "every presumption" must favor liberty, while opponents said that the proposed law would violate the U.S. Constitution.[43] In 1837, the abolitionists' petition campaign launched the drive for trial by jury in that state, and within three years the white majority saw blacks and their abolitionist allies as a menacing horde, threatening to "settle" among them.[44]

This politicking on behalf of constitutionalism ran into opposition based on the crudest of racial appeals. When the Philadelphia lawyer James C. Biddle proposed allowing jury trials for alleged fugitives in Pennsylvania, Jacksonian Democrat Charles Jared Ingersoll erupted in outrage: "Trial by jury for fugitive slaves! For blacks by whites! What a solecism, an absurdity. From the Magna Charta down, trial by jury has been a trial by peers, by equals." Since trial by jury implied a jury of one's peers, no white man could sit on a jury trying a case involving a black person without making the white man a "peer" of the black person, Ingersoll said. Biddle's proposal went down in defeat.[45] Those writing on behalf of slave owners denounced the proponents of trial by jury for alleged fugitive slaves as guilty of "fanaticism or folly." That was the position taken by the General Assembly of South Carolina in 1841. In 1840, New York abolitionists finally passed a law extending trial by jury to persons arrested as fugitive slaves, "An Act to extend the right of trial by jury." The law provided that "upon the return of any writ of habeas corpus issued to bring up the body of an alleged fugitive from service or labor to which he is held under the laws of any other state, who shall have escaped into this state, the claim to the service of such fugitive, his identity, and the fact of his having escaped from another state of the United States into this state, shall be determined by a jury."[46] The South Carolinians furiously denounced this "obnoxious" law for confining "the adjudication of these questions to juries" and precluding "the consideration of them by the judiciary."[47]

To defeat such racism, abolitionists appealed to natural law, an approach that had the advantage of invoking Madison and the framers' concern for rights against populist "conflagrations." Although white Southerners could find natural law appealing, some also recognized in its logic worrisome implications, as became clear at Virginia's 1829 constitutional convention. Virginia's population had extended westward into areas unable to easily sustain a slave-based economic system, creating new interest groups unhappy with the old structures. To claim a fairer share of state power, the westerners began arguing that they had a natural-law right to equal representation and to vote without property restrictions; the constitutional convention gathered to consider their complaints. Western delegates had at least one advantage over their opponents: they could point out that other states had already accommodated slave-poor whites. Even South Carolina—hardly the most democratic of southern states—had eliminated property requirements for voting and reapportioned representation in its state legislature. Virginia's westerners came to the convention armed with petitions from their constituents demanding removal of all property restrictions on voting and citing the founding principles to support their appeal. And at least one aging member of the founding generation showed up to say that the westerners had a point. "That all men are by nature equally free" is foundational to government, Chief Justice John Marshall reminded them.[48]

It soon became clear that some men in the older parts of the state intended not only to defend their privileges but were willing to jettison what the westerners and John Marshall saw as the nation's founding principles to do so. Defenders of property restrictions on voting repudiated the old Revolutionary ideals and denied that abstract truths could be found in nature. Political maxims, Philip N. Nicholas conceded, had some value, but he was unwilling to decide policy on the basis of abstract truths. Judge Abel P. Upshur of the General Court of Virginia bluntly told the convention that, in truth, *there are no original principles of Government at all.* Principles come from government and do not precede it, Upshur said. Nicholas and

Upshur carried the day. Virginia's new constitution retained property qualifications for voting.[49]

Virginia academics sometimes found natural-law arguments more per-
suasive than did their state's great planters. At the University of Virginia,
Professor Henry St. George Tucker lectured his students that natural law
formed the foundation for all systems of human law. People feel natural
law in their consciences, and remorse, Tucker told his students, "is a drop
of God's wrath falling upon the soul." Tucker expressed alarm at lynching,
which he saw as evil because it denied trial by jury. In the Seventh Amendment, he said, can be found the echoes of the Magna Carta and centuries of
human struggle for liberty wrung from the Crown. But Tucker would not
go as far as the abolitionists on this point. He agreed that there was an innate sense of right found in all humankind, but said it had to be improved
by judicious attention and cultivation. Tucker warned his students that "our
own short-sighted and imperfect estimate of consequences" meant that no
particular case could be decided by the law of nature. People should not
turn their backs on the "treasures of experience" left by previous generations, recorded in law. Like Hobbes, Tucker also believed that having entered society, "it is our duty to submit" to its rules, including those allowing slavery. And although Tucker believed in natural law, he thought nature
yielded few principles: self-preservation, the relationship of parent to child,
the right of property, and the inherently social condition of humankind.
Tucker also differentiated between perfect and imperfect rights found in
nature. Rights clearly stated, fixed, and determined, Tucker said, must be
respected as perfect. The right to own property, therefore, was perfect. A
poor man, though, had only an imperfect right to the public's charity. Relief was a vague and indeterminate thing; the master's right to command
the service of his servant was perfect, Tucker lectured. Unlike Nicholas and
Upshur, Tucker would not deny natural law—he called it the cornerstone of
all law—but he believed he could make it useful for slavery.[50]

However sensible the abolitionists' constitutional argument seemed to
later generations, it never held or even dominated the field of constitutional rights before the Civil War. The abolitionists' constitutional argument
against slavery had trouble winning widespread support because it seemed
undemocratic; it challenged—some might say insulted—majority opinion.
More-democratic ideas about politics took hold in the public imagination
at almost the precise moment that critics of slavery radically reinterpreted
their opposition to slavery, taking a more dogmatic, rights-based approach.
Andrew Jackson's movement emphasized democracy over inborn or his-

torical rights. Jackson lost his bid for the presidency in 1824, though he received more votes than his opponent. John Quincy Adams had been made president by means of a corrupt bargain among politicians, Jackson alleged, and his administration lacked legitimacy for not truly representing the people. Opposition to Adams grew throughout his term. In urban areas, nascent labor unions promoted democratic ideals, as in 1828 Philadelphia, when the Working Men's Party began marching under the banner of equal rights. In rural Kentucky, farmers resented central banking, and their opposition to it led to scandals over the legitimacy of law, which helped spark a grassroots democratic revolt. By 1828, Jackson and his followers rode a wave of popular demands for democracy into power. Jackson served two terms as president, becoming an icon for an era, espousing a set of beliefs that dominated American politics until the Civil War. The democratic impulse he represented transformed American politics, prompting white Americans everywhere to demand greater popular participation in government: judges should be elected; courts should represent popular will. The leading historian of Jacksonian-era mobbing acknowledges that Jackson himself disliked rioting but argues that his rhetoric nonetheless encouraged riotous popular sovereignty.[51]

Jacksonian reform led Americans to question how they might democratize trial by jury, something that many whites paradoxically thought required increased racial restrictions. New York's 1821 constitutional convention severely restricted black voting. Samuel Young of Saratoga vowed to oppose black voting so as to discharge the duty that he owed "the people." "Public sentiment" would not allow black voting, he insisted, and as proof cited the fact that no black man had ever been selected for jury duty. "If he were, no jury would sit with him."[52] New York, though, did not inaugurate the wave of Jacksonian constitutions; instead a long dry spell followed that state's convention. Between 1830 and 1838, six southern states and Pennsylvania wrote new constitutions that democratized officeholding and voting for white males. A second, and larger, wave of constitution writing first appeared in Rhode Island, where Democrats not only favored black voting but tried to write constitutional protections for trial by jury for blacks into their state's organic law. Rhode Island's experience shows that Jacksonian reform did not require hostility to abolitionist demands for trial by jury for black Northerners.

Initially, Rhode Island had barely felt the tremors from Andrew Jackson's seismic transference of sovereignty to the people. Rhode Island's state government still operated under its colonial charter, issued by Charles II in

1663, which limited voting to the "freemen of the said Company" without defining the term. Unrestrained by the state's constitution, the Rhode Island General Assembly so limited suffrage that 60 percent of the population had no vote or say in their government at a time when Andrew Jackson had inspired the nation to agitate for popular sovereignty. As in Virginia, through the first decades of the nineteenth century new ways of making money emerged, allowing industrious citizens to accumulate wealth and pay taxes without owning land. These taxpayers had no vote under Rhode Island's archaic charter system of government. Representation was so malapportioned that fifty-one members of the legislature represented half the population, while twenty-one members represented the other half. Rhode Island's ruling elite saw no advantage in opening voting or jury service to a broader segment of the population, and the legislature rejected repeated efforts to call a state constitutional convention.[53]

In 1834, Thomas Dorr declared that political reform could be accomplished only by writing a new Rhode Island constitution based on natural law. Participation in government, he said, was a natural right "which cannot be abridged, nor suspended any further than the greatest good of the greatest number imperatives requires." Thus, to critics charging that his claims of natural rights did not include women, Dorr answered that women had once voted in New Jersey. That experiment had been suspended, Dorr said, "upon a just consideration of the best good of society, including that of the sex itself." Women themselves had assented to "this arrangement of their natural protectors." Dorr focused almost the entirety of his speech on voting, turning to the judiciary only at the end. When he did, he called for an independent judiciary, warning that allowing politics into the law would allow politicians to dispense with "that palladium of liberty," trial by jury.[54]

After the Rhode Island legislature considered and rejected a proposal allowing "every male inhabitant of [the] State" over twenty-one years of age and a resident of the state for two years to vote for delegates to a constitutional convention, Dorr's insurgents drafted a new state constitution and organized an ex officio election to ratify their work.[55] The Dorr rebels called their constitution the People's Constitution and filled its text with claims to natural law that echoed the Declaration of Independence. "All men are created free and equal and are endowed by their Creator with certain natural, inherent, and inalienable rights." The People's Constitution guaranteed the right of trial by jury, as did every other state bill of rights, but it also guaranteed trial by jury for alleged fugitive slaves:

14. Any person in this State who may be claimed to be held to labor or service, under the laws of any other State, territory, or district, shall be entitled
to a jury trial, to ascertain the validity of such claim.[56]

For a time, two state governments vied for control of Rhode Island, but in
June 1842, the charter government declared martial law and snuffed out its
rival. A state court tried Dorr for treason. Dorr protested that the government denied him a fair trial by packing the jury with his political opponents, even moving his trial from Providence to the more hostile Newport
to better ensure a conviction. Arguing that the court denied him an impartial jury, a fundamental right, Dorr won over some of the judges sitting
on his case, but he nonetheless faced a jury entirely made up of men opposed to him politically. Dorr's lawyers reviewed the history of trial by jury
and cited English authorities to demonstrate that trial by jury emerged as
a fundamental law recognized under the common law and secured by the
U.S. Constitution. One of Dorr's lawyers, George Turner, attacked a Rhode
Island law passed in 1842 that allowed the government to indict defendants
in one county and try them in another of its choosing. The chief justice interrupted to note that the only question was whether the general assembly
could alter the common law on the question of trial by jury. Turner answered that the chief justice's question depended on another: whether trial
by jury rested on fundamental law. "Ordinary legislation" cannot abrogate
fundamental principles of law, Turner argued. The state court thought it
could and convicted Dorr, sentencing him to prison.[57] In federal court, one
of Dorr's lieutenants, Martin Luther, sued several state soldiers for illegally
breaking into his home and ill-treating his family. The U.S. Supreme Court
ruled that the question of who held sovereignty in Rhode Island was a political question for elected legislators to decide, not a matter for the courts.
The practical effect of the decision left the charter government in power and
ended a revolutionary effort at majority rule.[58]

After Dorr's effort in Rhode Island, nine states wrote new state constitutions between 1848 and 1851, and the delegates to these conventions included some white men sympathetic to blacks, but even they could hardly
imagine placing blacks on juries. At the Ohio convention, William Sawyer, an ardent Democratic politician and former speaker of the Ohio House
of Representatives, insisted that the foundational principles articulated in
the Declaration of Independence gave blacks the right to serve on juries—
if they were present. In Sawyer's mind, the fact that all Ohioans had

constitutional rights meant that black people had to be moved out of the state to avoid giving them rights or funding their education. Sawyer had little concern about keeping blacks enslaved and, in fact, praised slavery. Saying blacks "were very little removed from the condition of dumb beasts," Sawyer could not contain his indignation that anyone would petition on their behalf and insisted that the convention spurn their petitions. In theory blacks could be jurors, he said—but not in Ohio. Every man, Sawyer believed, should stay "in his own place and in his own order."[59]

Ohio was one of four states that debated how to eliminate blacks entirely from within their borders. In Indiana several delegates took Sawyer's position, saying that to keep blacks from having "political rights," "we ought not to have them amongst us." One delegate warned that three-quarters of the state's white population would flee the state if the convention made it possible for blacks to vote. When a delegate asked if there was anyone in the hall willing to allow blacks to vote, several voices chorused, "No one—no one."[60] On September 19, 1849, California delegates instructed their legislature to find ways to prevent black immigration into the Golden State. These efforts to racially "purify" states failed and sometimes prompted principled opposition. Edward Gilbert, founder and editor of the newspaper *Alta California* representing San Francisco at the California constitutional convention, warned his fellow delegates that such a restriction would violate the U.S. Constitution's clause guaranteeing privileges and immunities. Nonetheless, some white politicians stubbornly persisted in efforts to make their states entirely white. The leader of efforts to keep blacks out of California argued that the privileges and immunities clause did not apply to blacks because they could not be citizens. Antiblack delegates also made a political argument, pointing out that their constituents overwhelmingly favored forbidding black entry into the state. The restriction passed, but in October, when the California convention revisited the issue, more delegates warned against contradicting the U.S. Constitution, and the convention reversed itself.[61] Not long after California's convention adjourned, Maryland's convention appointed a committee to gather statistics on the free black population to build a case for outlawing free blacks.[62] The next year, Virginia debated expelling free blacks.[63] In the minds of most Jacksonian-era whites, blacks had no place on juries. The question was whether they had the right to be in the states at all.

Some Jacksonians thought real democracy required elimination of the whole grand jury system. Three state conventions, in Ohio, Michigan, and Indiana, debated abolishing or limiting grand juries on the grounds of the expense and their practice of meeting in secret. Grand jurors' secrecy seemed undemocratic and elitist, and most delegates valued cutting taxes almost as much as the extension of suffrage. In Indiana a delegate estimated that grand juries cost $20,000 a year, while in Michigan another delegate countered a similar argument by saying that the grand jury system cost only $3,871 a year, or one cent per person in the state. Those in favor of abolishing or limiting grand juries admitted that they proposed using popular power to overturn rights rooted in the common law, challenging centuries of history. But they insisted that grand juries had been invented to curb kingly power, a problem Americans no longer faced. Opponents of the grand jury system faltered on one important question: Did grand juries really represent a majority of the public? Defenders of the grand jury system invoked constitutional principle, but politically they had better luck when they questioned whether those seeking to eliminate or limit grand juries really represented the people. Newspapers had not agitated against grand juries. There had been no public meetings clamoring for grand jury reform, and no petitions had been written demanding an end to the system. In these constitutional conventions, a true clash between constitutional principle and the public had not really occurred.[64]

Few abolitionist voices could be heard at the state conventions, and delegates spent little time debating trial by jury for fugitive slaves. In Ohio, Sawyer rejoiced over the new fugitive slave law and predicted that it would help eliminate blacks from the North entirely. As in other states, the Illinois convention considered a provision guaranteeing the right of trial by jury as "inviolate." Unlike in other states, one of the Illinois delegates documented just how closely abolitionists associated the rights of blacks with trial by jury. Hurlbut Swan interrupted debate over trial by jury to propose an amendment:

> The Legislature shall pass no law, nor shall any law be in force after the adoption of this constitution, that shall prohibit the citizens of this state from feeding the hungry, or clothing the naked, nor restrain them from exercising the common principles of philanthropy or dictates of humanity. Nor shall any law remain in force that recognizes the principle that a person of color is presumed to be a slave until he has proved himself to be free; or that prescribes whipping as a punishment for offences. But the legislature shall provide by law for the support of schools for the education of colored children, and shall adopt other measures as they may deem expedient for the benefit and improvement of colored persons in this state.[65]

On the surface, Swan's language had nothing to do with trial by jury, but in fact it had everything to do with it. Swan was a Connecticut native who had moved to Illinois in 1845, a Whig until he became a Free Soiler and later a Republican. Swan regarded the Illinois constitution's protection of trial by jury as prime real estate for philanthropic demonstrations on behalf of black people. No doubt he realized that his proposal had no chance of success, and it went down in defeat by a lopsided vote of 97 to 28.[66]

Andrew Jackson greatly emboldened those forces dedicated to the popular appeal over hidebound constitutional principle. Jackson's majoritarian ideals triumphantly dealt his opponents a stunning blow, but even as this happened, intellectual cavalry from the most unlikely fort imaginable rallied in reply. Unitarianism had a long history in the United States, but its appeal expanded just as Jackson and his supporters gathered strength, especially in Boston, where doubts about original sin became widespread. To the religiously faithful, Jacksonian Democracy seemed irreligious since it put majority will ahead of moral principle. Reform societies organized to combat the threat. One of these groups, the Transcendentalists, sought higher law through individual reflection. The German philosopher Immanuel Kant (1724–1804) had posited that human-made categories of cognition organized perceptions in ways that had little to do with reality, which, ultimately, remained unknowable. These rules of seeing transcended everything else. American Transcendentalists may not have carefully read Kant, but they adopted elements of his skepticism. They questioned the Bible, which got them into trouble, but never doubted natural law. Rejecting the doubts about religion and individual conscience that animated Madison's thinking in *Federalist* No. 10, Ralph Waldo Emerson and fellow Transcendentalists sought truths they could know only intuitively. Like Madison, though, Emerson doubted that rights should be entrusted to politics. Political quarreling did not produce truth, he said. Principle mattered more than material force. The soul of true reform relied not on "outward and vulgar means," certainly not on a majority vote, "numbers." Knowing that truth could all too easily be outvoted, Emerson favored not "numbers" but the "sentiment of man," a moral clarity most apparent when approached privately.[67]

No nineteenth-century politician or author influenced American thought more than Emerson, students of his writing claim. Some have said that his emphasis on individualism defined the American character. In the antebellum United States, leading legal scholars reflected Emerson's thinking as they began advocating a more scientific approach to the law, with themselves as the scientists. Legal science identified law as resting on transcendent principles found through thoughtful research rather than politics. Rufus Choate (1799–1859) of Massachusetts personified the new lawyer, disdainful of "unreasoning liberty" and hostile to suggestions that the law might be "the transient and arbitrary creation of the majority will."[68] Emerson's reputation flourished throughout the 1850s, but as it did, the core of Transcendentalism changed, becoming more focused on opposition to slavery by political means.[69]

Abolitionists and their opponents faced off in their own high-noon melodrama when they confronted questions of natural law and political power during congressional debates over what became the 1850 Compromise. War with Mexico had greatly expanded the territory of the United States, adding a great swath of western lands. A new generation of Southerners expected to do what their fathers had done: take a few slaves, move west, and build vast plantations with cheap land and enslaved labor. Northerners understood that if slavery developed in the West, there would be no chance to pursue the kind of free market economy they knew and valued. As the two regions faced off, tensions and talk of civil war swept the nation. President Zachary Taylor exacerbated the potential for a bloody disaster by proposing that California skip the territorial stage and immediately become a state. With no chance for Southerners to move their slaves to the West Coast, this meant that California would certainly join the Union as a free state. Southerners exploded in outrage. Contemptuous of Taylor's naïveté, Senator Henry Clay of Kentucky stepped forward to resolve the problem, offering a complex series of measures designed to effect a compromise that would hold the Union together.[70]

Abolitionists' efforts to undermine slavery by winning trial-by-jury rights for accused fugitive slaves bedeviled Clay and other compromisers but drew sustenance from Emerson's higher-law doctrines. Despite the increasing influence of Emerson's thinking in American culture, the political process demonstrated its limits, as congressmen moved to preserve the Union through harder and sterner protections for slave owners' rights based on political compromise. On January 29, Clay rose to announce that he held in his hand a series of resolutions proposing "an amicable arrangement of all questions in controversy between the free and the slave States, growing out of the subject of slavery."[71] His resolutions included the following:

7th. *Resolved*, That more effectual provisions ought to be made by law, according to the requirement of the Constitution, for the restitution and

delivery of persons bound to service or labor in any State who may escape
into any other State or Territory of the Union.[72]

Clay's effort to craft a new fugitive slave law had its roots in the 1842 Supreme Court decision *Prigg v. Pennsylvania*. In that decision, the Court
had ruled that the northern states could not pass laws interfering with enforcement of the federal Fugitive Slave Act. Chief Justice Roger B. Taney's
concurring opinion mischaracterized the majority decision as forbidding
northern states from assisting in the capture and rendition of escaped
slaves. Some Northerners used Taney's concurrence to justify their refusal
to allow the use of state facilities in fugitive slave cases. Southerners responded with demands for a new fugitive slave law to offset the effects of
Prigg v. Pennsylvania, and by making it easier for slave owners to recap-
ture their escaped slaves, Clay's proposal met their demands.[73] This meant
making certain that no state could offer trial by jury to persons accused of
escaping slavery.

When Clay unveiled this resolution, the Senate was already deep in debate over a new fugitive slave bill that James Murray Mason of Virginia had
proposed. Mason had introduced his bill on January 4, disingenuously declaring that since he merely wanted to enforce a provision of the Constitution, he took "it for granted . . . that it [would] meet with no resistance
whatever." Mason crafted his proposed law to make certain that persons
in the North accused of being southern slaves would never get a trial by
jury. Mason urged that federal judges, but also such minor officers as clerks,
postmasters, and collectors of customs, be empowered to issue warrants authorizing white Southerners to take black persons south. The *Philadelphia
North American and United States Gazette* complained that postmasters and
clerks should not be deciding questions of liberty and slavery, "especially
without the aid of juries to assist them in deciding the merits of claims often
obscure and intricate."[74]

The day before Clay offered his eight resolutions, Senator William Henry
Seward of New York proposed his own fugitive slave law, one that guaranteed trial by jury for all persons accused of being fugitive slaves. Southerners charged that Seward violated principles of fairness and patriotism to
insult the "truly national" bill that Mason had proposed. By the time Clay
stood with his eight resolutions in hand, the Senate had already bitterly divided along sectional lines, at least in part over trial by jury.[75] Clay's political
assault on a constitutional principle forced Emerson to rethink his commit-

ment to private reflection and higher law. "The last year has forced us all into politics," he said a year later.[76]

When Clay introduced his resolutions, he had already forged an alliance with the leading political figure in the Northeast, Daniel Webster. The two consulted on January 21, 1850. They had never been particularly close and had often maintained a formal distance from each other, but now they shared a passionate determination to save the Union at all costs. Webster was ardently nationalistic. He had changed his party affiliations as the decades rolled by, but he began life as a Federalist and never abandoned his commitment to strong national government. His goal was to "cultivate a truly national spirit."[77] When South Carolina had tried in 1832 to nullify the tariff laws that Congress had passed, threatening to leave the Union, Webster pioneered the idea of a perpetual Union. Webster opposed slavery as "unjust" and "evil," but he always put the Union first and he believed that attacking the peculiar institution with force of arms would only "rivet the chains of slavery more strongly." His best hope was that southern whites' Christianity would temper their treatment of slavery's victims. By 1850, Webster had drifted away from his constituents, many of whom had come to see slavery as an evil too monstrous to be tolerated for the sake of preserving the Union.[78]

Nonetheless, on March 7, Webster stood ready to go even further for the Union, abandoning trial by jury as a constitutional principle. Initially unimpressed by southern demonstrations, by March Webster had become alarmed at the prospect of disunion. At times it seemed that the entire nation pleaded with him to save the Union; one Democrat even predicted he could make himself greater than George Washington by steering a course that took the country away from civil war. If he did so, it would be with a speech. Oratory was Webster's great talent; he spoke with a voice many found unforgettable, "one carried the sound of it to the grave."[79] His March the Seventh Speech, as it came to be known, proved Webster's most significant contribution to American letters. In it he did not mention trial by jury directly, but he challenged the natural-law foundations that underlay abolitionists' demands for due process. Nothing in the Bible, he said, could be read as an injunction against slavery. Although in his younger days he had blasted affronts to trial by jury as unconstitutional, "monstrous" affronts to "fundamental principles of liberty," he now endorsed a political interpretation of the Constitution, asserting it did nothing more than reconcile the North with the South by imposing a duty on the North to return runaway slaves to the South. Webster identified the Constitution so much with political compromising that he could no longer see assertions of rights as anything but a threat to the Union. "Is the great Constitution," he asked, "to be thawed and melted away by secession, as the snows on the mountains?"[80]

Webster's oration for the Union sent patriotic hearts fluttering, but two senators soon zeroed in on his willingness to abandon trial by jury. John Parker Hale of New Hampshire, the first antislavery candidate elected to the Senate, warned that without the protections of trial by jury nothing prevented southern slave owners from coming North to "seize [one's] wife or . . . child" as slaves. This was too much for Senator Andrew Pickens Butler of South Carolina. "Blacks," he spat back. With this single word, he meant to give the lie to Hale's purple prose about "the wife of your bosom of the children of your love . . . wrenched from your protection." Butler had a completely racialized view of slavery: Only black people were slaves and black people should be slaves; trial by jury merely offered northern jurors a chance to nullify southern slavery. White people were not slaves and needed no trial by jury to prove themselves. To this Hale had an answer. Persons with only a single, remote African ancestor were "black" no matter how white they appeared and would not get a jury under Clay's plan, endorsed by Webster. "I have seen some that are holden as slaves, that it would be very difficult to tell by their complexions what their parentage was." Any free person, Hale continued, black or white, must have trial by jury to ensure his or her freedom.[81]

Those in Congress seeking to deny trial by jury for fugitives received further support on May 8. In reporting Clay's resolutions favorably, the Senate's Select Committee of Thirteen took the opportunity to denounce northern resistance to white Southerners' efforts to reclaim their slaves as "deplorable" and repeated Webster's argument that the Constitution required no trial by jury when slave owners sought to retrieve their slaves. The "forms and ceremonies of a final trial" never take place in the state where the arrest is made, the committee reported. "When the trial does take place, it is in the State or country from which the party has fled." The committee took note of the numerous petitions demanding trial by jury in fugitive slave cases and then condemned them for using a cherished institution to make a mockery of justice, "so far as the owner of the fugitive [was] concerned." Requiring trial by jury, the committee continued, would amount to a refusal to enforce the Constitution, that is, the fugitive slave clause. The committee urged Congress to smooth the recovery of all fugitives, thereby removing all causes for complaint—by white Southerners. The committee expressed no desire to satisfy northern petitioners demanding trial by jury for alleged fugitives.[82]

Webster only implied his willingness to abandon trial by jury in his great speech; on May 15 he said so directly in a letter explaining his speech to a group of his constituents in Newburyport. This "Newburyport letter" caused a minor sensation, further outraging those abolitionists convinced that some rights—including trial by jury—really did come from natural law and should not be frittered away through political compromise and bargaining. Webster began by noting that in the last twenty years some Northerners had tried to shift the question of trial by jury for alleged slaves from a political matter to "a question of religion and humanity." Retrieving any kind of fugitive from justice, Webster said, never involved trial by jury. Fugitives from justice faced a judge and, on production of an indictment or an affidavit, the judge ordered the prisoner returned to the jurisdiction seeking to prosecute him. The procedure was exactly the same for persons accused of being escaped slaves as it was for persons accused of crimes. "In both cases," Webster wrote, "the proceeding is to be preliminary and summary." In both cases, it is the state from which the prisoner fled that must hold the trial. To those skeptical that slaves could get jury trials in the slave states, Webster insisted that slaves had fair access to courts in the southern states. "There is not a slave State in the Union, in which independent judicial tribunals are not always open to receive and decide upon petitions or applications for freedom." Moreover, Webster concluded that he had never heard an allegation that southern courts did not render fair and upright decisions in such cases. Webster reported that he had searched the original records of the debate over the 1793 law and could find no hint that anyone thought trial by jury should be required for persons accused of being fugitive slaves. Webster derided "the cry of universal freedom." Most pointedly, Webster complained that northern states' "ill-considered" personal liberty laws made trial by jury impossible for alleged fugitive slaves. The thrust of the North's dissent was aimed at denying southern slave catchers access to the state facilities necessary to have a trial, jails, courts, and judges, which had the effect of shutting blacks out of court as well.[83]

Webster also reviewed the Bill of Rights and found that none of its provisions applied to persons accused of being escaped slaves. The Constitution requires that all criminal prosecutions shall be by a trial by jury, but reclaiming a fugitive slave was not a criminal prosecution nor was it a "suit at common law," requiring a trial by jury under the Seventh Amendment, he added. On this point, Webster disagreed with Massachusetts congressman and abolitionist Horace Mann. Webster quoted Mann as saying that a man may not lose his horse without a trial, but he may lose his freedom. Webster countered by saying that under Mann's theory a neighbor could not reclaim a horse that wandered off his property without a trial by jury to ascertain his right to do so.[84] Webster's analogy threatened to become a widespread and effective answer to abolitionists' demand for juries in fugitive slave cases. The *Boston Courier* liked it so much that it offered its own variant. Abolitionists, the *Courier* said, believed that if a man lost his hat he could not pick it up without a trial by jury.[85]

Despite his letter and despite the support he received from friends like the *Boston Courier*, Webster soon had second thoughts about the position he had taken against trial by jury. On June 3 (the same day the *Courier* published its hat version of his analogy), he backtracked. On that day, Webster announced in Congress that he had prepared a fugitive slave bill the previous February after consulting eminent lawyers and "a high judicial authority." He had been holding it back, he said, waiting for "a proper time." When he laid this bill before the Senate, it had a provision for those fugitives who denied that they had been slaves. In such cases, the commissioner or judge should "forthwith" summon a jury to determine the facts. Although Webster insisted this had been his preference all along, it contradicted his earlier statements, and it seems extremely unlikely that he had written any such a bill in February. This was a new position.[86]

The congressman whom Webster had singled out for criticism, Horace Mann, ignored Webster's tricky maneuvering and penned a ten-thousand-word reply to the Newburyport letter for the *Boston Daily Atlas*. On June 14 and 21, William Lloyd Garrison cleared space for it on the pages of the *Liberator*, omitting a large amount of interesting foreign and domestic intelligence to do so, he said. Mann acknowledged that he was taking on an American giant, a formidable intellect with thirty-seven years of experience in politics. Webster had been first elected to Congress in 1813; Mann had been elected just two years before, in 1848, taking the seat made vacant by John Quincy Adams's death. Known now principally as a founder of public education, Mann had served in the Massachusetts state legislature in the 1830s before withdrawing from politics for twelve years, ignoring the political process so completely that he remained neutral even in presidential elections.[87] Mann served in Congress only briefly, from 1848 to 1852, but during that time he became increasingly militant in his criticism of slavery and the South. Since he believed slavery was "the salt of all political cooking," he could hardly avoid it once he returned to politics. Slavery, he came to believe, challenged the fundamental principles of American republicanism.[88]

The quarrel between Webster and Mann once again laid bare the two different readings of the Constitution that divided American society. Webster predicated his defense of Clay's compromise on an understanding of the Constitution, not as an articulation of fundamental values, but as a political compromise between the North and the South. The North had a duty to the South, which it performed by returning fugitive slaves to their masters. Webster regretted that "a new degree of feeling" in the North had infected what had always been a political question with religious principles, which, he warned, produced fanaticism that excited the public unnecessarily.[89] In his reply to Webster, Mann made repeated references to the "power above us," cited the New Testament, and urged his readers to "look to the perfect law of God." Natural law needed human law for its enforcement and that was the role played by the Constitution. It articulated and defended natural-law principles. For Mann the Constitution was far more than a political compromise.[90]

Mann began his response to Webster by taking on the lost-horse analogy. "I said," Mann wrote, "a man may not *lose* his horse, or his property in a horse, without a right to the trial by jury." In other words, no one can *take* another person's property without facing a jury trial. Webster had malevolently reversed the facts, Mann charged, saying that no one could find a lost horse without going to trial.[91]

Mann devoted the bulk of his letter to a close analysis of the Constitution designed to prove that it did indeed guarantee trial by jury. Webster had observed that in the original, unamended Constitution, Article III protected trial by jury in criminal prosecutions, but noted, "There is no other clause or sentence in the Constitution having the least bearing on the subject." Mann countered this assertion by pointing out that when Congress met in 1789, before the Bill of Rights became part of the Constitution, it passed a law establishing the federal court system and provided for trial by jury in civil suits. Congress must have derived this power to require jury trials in civil cases from the Constitution, Mann said. Moreover, in the states' ratifying conventions, the delegates gave speeches assuming that the new Constitution authorized trial by jury. Every student of the Constitution, Mann insisted, understood that the only reason the Constitution did not expressly mandate trial by jury in civil cases was "the difficulty of running the dividing line between the many cases that should be so tried, and the few that should not." Mann also noticed that the joint resolutions proposing the Bill of Rights to the states called the new amendments "further declaratory and restrictive clauses." He took this to mean that when the Seventh Amendment promised to protect trial by jury in civil cases, it merely "preserved" an existing right. It instituted no rights de novo. The spirit of the Constitution, Mann argued, "yearns toward liberty and the rights of man. Trial by jury is essential to those rights." As evidence of this, Mann pointed to the first laws enacted by colonial legislatures, which protected trial by jury. He also quoted the Declaration of Independence, which attacked King George for "depriving [Americans], in many cases, of the benefits of trial by jury." Such commentators as Blackstone and Story described trial by jury as a "fundamental right."[92]

Mann challenged Webster's reading of the Seventh Amendment. Webster had said, "Nothing is more false" than any claim that the Seventh Amendment accords persons accused of being fugitive slaves a right to trial by jury. Part of the problem involved the meaning of the word "suit." The Seventh Amendment guaranteed trial by jury in "Suits at common law," and Webster averred that reclaiming an escaped slave did not amount to a "suit." Mann disagreed and cited *Cohens v. Virginia* (1821) as his authority. In that case, the Court had asked, "What is a suit?" and then answered, "It [is] the prosecution of some *claim*, demand or request." The Constitution said slaves had to be delivered "on *claim*" of the owner. In another case, *Parsons v. Bedford* (1830), the Supreme Court defined "suit at common law" as any proceeding to determine a legal right, a meaning broad enough to include alleged fugitive slaves, Mann maintained.[93]

Like Webster, lawyers on the proslavery side insisted that they more truly defended the U.S. Constitution than did abolitionists like Mann. In 1851, Thomas Irwin, a federal district court judge in Pennsylvania, told his grand jury that the parties to the Constitution "were sovereign states" and as such had "surrendered for the welfare of the whole, portions of that sovereignty." Retrieving runaway slaves without trial by jury was a piece of that surrendered sovereignty. This bargain had to be respected, Irwin insisted: "No State can therefore without a breach of this compact make its territories . . . an asylum for fugitive slaves." Like Webster, Irwin warned that "the fallacy of the 'higher law'" threatened "the peace and safety of the community."[94]

Lawyers representing slave owners commonly made the same argument as Irwin. The ties of the Union are fragile, they said. To continue the Union, Northerners must honor their commitments under the fugitive slave clause, with no holding back, "no hesitancy to comply."[95]

The chief justice of the U.S. Supreme Court, Roger B. Taney, would have no part of any such fallacies or threats, but in an 1852 case involving not slavery but murder on the high seas, he sounded more like Mann than Webster. After a circuit court had convicted Thomas Reid and Edward Clemens of murder, two jurors offered affidavits saying that they had consulted a newspaper account of the evidence when deliberating. That was enough to overturn the conviction, Taney decided. The right of trial by jury was no state-created right, legitimate only for having a long history in state courts, Taney said, but rather existed *before* the formation of states, even before the first colonists set foot in America. Colonists coming to North America "undoubtedly brought with them" trial by jury, that "most cherished and familiar" common-law principle, Taney observed. Taney came perilously close to recognizing trial by jury as a national right when he noted that when trial by jury had seemed insufficiently protected by the new constitution, "it was the people of these thirteen States" who "ingrafted on it provisions which secures the trial by jury." Taney emphasized trial by jury as a state right, but only because the states followed the English common law. Not the people acting through their states, but rather "the people of these thirteen states" adopted the common law. That description sounded more like a national community than a collection of states. Taney's ruling shows just how pervasive Mann's ideas about trial by jury as a fundamental right set outside politics really were—when race was not involved.[96]

After 1850, stories of escaping black men, women, and children began to appear more frequently in the press. The most sensational case involving the question of escaped slaves' right to a jury trial involved Anthony Burns, arrested as a fugitive slave in 1854. Boston abolitionists rallied around Burns and turned his arrest and rendition into a national issue. For a time, Burns became the most famous slave in America. His lawyer, Richard Henry Dana, demanded a jury. He did so by asking for a writ of personal replevin. By filing a writ of personal replevin, Dana hoped to appeal beyond the narrow confines of technical law to the broader consciousness of ordinary citizens likely to be summoned onto a Boston jury. When Dana went to the U.S. district court, the judge told him his writ was unknown in federal law. Another lawyer actually did get the writ from a state judge, but the U.S.

marshal holding Burns refused to honor it. Appealing for the right to a jury trial did not free Burns or save him from returning to slavery. Burns had a legal hearing before a commissioner, with no jury present. Charles Mayo Ellis represented Burns at the hearing, where he condemned the Fugitive Slave Law as a product of political negotiation, a violation of due process. "This trial is political," Ellis told the federal commissioner hearing the case. "Only in your narrow power of satisfying your mind on the narrowest of points," he continued, can be found "the semblance of justice."[97] The transcript of Ellis's speech paints a terrifying picture of the mockery of due process that blacks accused of being slaves faced: "I wish to look the men in the eye who dare to come here with pistols in their pockets, to ask us to meet with our opposing counsel armed, hemmed in with armed men, entering court with muskets at our breasts, trying a case under the muzzles of their guns."[98]

Congress had enacted the Fugitive Slave Law not on its legal merits but as part of a political deal. Law, Ellis orated, should be insulated from politics. "Matters not of legal character" have determined the rules of proceeding. Rather, "a system of grants and concessions" enacted "with a view to the political relations not of the parties but of the country" had stripped blacks of their rights to a jury trial. As proof that the Fugitive Slave Law represented bad law, a product of political compromise rather than the purer kind of internally consistent law that Ellis favored, he pointed out that the Fugitive Slave Law forbade trial by jury. Neither Dana nor Ellis prevailed, and Burns went back to slavery though abolitionists eventually purchased his freedom. He died in 1862.[99]

The federal commissioner who decided the Burns case, Edward Greely Loring, had blood ties to Boston's influential Curtis family, which, in turn, had connections with Daniel Webster. Representing slave owners seeking to retrieve their escaped slaves in Massachusetts, Benjamin Curtis carried Webster's ideas into Boston's courts, arguing against common-law conceptions of rights and claiming that the states' slave laws had to be respected. Curtis got a seat on the Supreme Court through Webster's recommendation.[100]

Once on the Court, Associate Justice Curtis abandoned Webster's relativism and consciously worked to invigorate due process as a natural-law right rather than a mere political privilege. In an opinion based more on imagination than research, *Murray's Lessee v. Hoboken Land and Improvement Co.* (1856), Curtis found that the framers of the Fifth Amendment "undoubtedly" meant to constitutionalize the Magna Carta's "law of the land" formulation when they wrote due process protections into the Fifth

Amendment. The framers had available the whole phrase as it had appeared in the Magna Carta: "by the judgment of his peers and the law of the land." Had they adopted that language in its entirety, Curtis speculated, the framers would have duplicated the jury protections found in the Sixth and Seventh Amendments and in Article III. But if they left out "judgment of his peers" to avoid the duplication, they ran the risk of degrading Americans' rights to a trial by jury. So, Curtis wrote, they substituted "due process of law" for the whole phrase, suggesting the term protected jury trials and had ancient origins long before the advent of American politics. Thus, Curtis placed due process above politics, enduring doctrine that restrained the legislature. Congress could not, under Curtis's formulation, intrude on due process by its "mere will." Curtis continued this line of reasoning in his *Dred Scott v. Sandford* dissent.[101]

Dred Scott v. Sandford stands as the Supreme Court at its worst, making a brazen attempt to use judicial power to solve a political problem. Born in Virginia, Dred Scott had come to St. Louis as a slave with his owner, Peter Blow. John Emerson then purchased Scott and traveled to various army posts, taking his slave with him, even to forts in Illinois and Wisconsin, free-soil states. Scott and his wife went to court, arguing that since they had been taken to jurisdictions that did not recognize slavery, they should be set free. They had precedent on their side, but in 1852 the Missouri Supreme Court ruled against Scott. By this time, Emerson had died and his widow had turned her affairs over to her brother, a New Yorker, giving the federal courts jurisdiction under the Constitution's diversity of citizenship clause. In 1857, Chief Justice Roger B. Taney eschewed judicial restraint and recklessly wrote that no black person could ever be a citizen and that the Missouri Compromise, which forbade slavery in some parts of the West while allowing it in others, was unconstitutional.[102]

Curtis advanced his due process ideas for a unanimous Court in *Murray's Lessee v. Hoboken Land and Improvement Co.*, but in *Dred Scott v. Sandford* he could only speak in dissent. To Taney's assertion that blacks had never been part of the political process, Curtis answered that blacks had been voting in five states that ratified the Constitution. "It would be strange," Curtis wrote, if the Constitution "deprived of their citizenship any part of the people of the United States who were among those by whom it was established." Curtis argued for freedom as a natural right, a "universal abstract truth" articulated in the Declaration of Independence. Republican politicians took heart from Curtis's dissent.[103] One Republican blasted

Taney and his fellow justices for making "an unhallowed interference . . . with the great political question of the day." Another critic called the opinion "a sheer usurpation of the powers of Congress."[104]

Curtis's switch documented the bifurcated view that antebellum Americans had of their Constitution and its role in politics. Curtis's struggles with these contradictions were not so different from those of Ralph Waldo Emerson. Emerson insisted he believed in democracy, but he understood society as hierarchical, divided between the great and the nongreat; in short, his belief in democracy competed with the natural aristocracy he experienced empirically. He expected great men to think for themselves, finding within themselves the natural laws that governed society. A man's rank, Emerson wrote, "depends on some symmetry in his structure." Those at the top of the intellectual hierarchy had minds structured to allow them to comprehend that parallel symmetry in the larger society. Emerson has become such an important icon in American life that rival groups and succeeding generations have battled over what he really represented.[105] Few can doubt, though, that Emerson shared Madison's pessimism about "the inconveniences of democracy" and the threat that numbers posed to rights. Emerson's recognition that politicians like Webster had forced the champions of liberty through natural law into politics marked a decisive turn in American life. Trial by jury had always been an element in the larger political game, but liberty's friends found it useful to hide that truth, to imagine trial by jury as coming from natural law and constitutional principle. Imagination holds power, but racism and slavery persuaded a majority of white men that trial by jury had to be set aside for the essentially political purpose of appeasing the white South.

By the time the first artillery fired, beginning the Civil War between North and South, the right to trial by jury had been thoroughly politicized. Whether white people would grant black people the privilege of trial by jury had become a political question, to be debated by politicians and their constituents. The mythology of a trial by a jury of the defendant's peers had been unmasked. It really was a fairy tale. At the same time, abolitionists had collected a body of legal arguments and constitutional doctrines supporting their contention that black people had a right to trial by jury, a right that stood outside political dispute. It may have been hanging by a thread, but natural law remained a force in American thought.

CHAPTER THREE

How Revolutionary Was the Civil War?

AFTER GRADUATING FROM COLLEGE *and setting up his law practice, Dabney Marshall found he had to balance his core beliefs against the demands of society, public opinion. At first, Marshall simply refused to compromise. Though he lived in Vicksburg, a place notorious for its brothels and drinking, Marshall sided with abstract law against the more popular pleasures of the flesh. He joined the prohibitionists, a beleaguered minority in Vicksburg but one with an important patron — John Cashman, editor of the* Vicksburg Evening Post, *and a law-and-order opponent of alcohol, free silver, and lynching. Cashman published articles by Marshall and praised his skills as a lawyer. In their writings, both Cashman and Marshall applauded the basic decency of Mississippi whites. Both wanted to be majoritarians, but their faith in the public really amounted to a hope that most white Mississippians shared their confidence in the rule of law. The weakness in this proposition ultimately became apparent to both men.*[1]

Favoring prohibition necessarily meant endorsing increased national power. Both Cashman and Marshall could do this and not just to control the evils of liquor. In 1886, Cashman endorsed a proposal to require federal judges to investigate reports of persons killed or injured for expressing their opinions. Cashman was even unconcerned that this notion came from Senator George F. Hoar (1826–1904), a Massachusetts Republican long notorious for his criticism of white southern racism and violence. For most white Southerners, the entire Hoar family seemed distasteful as the embodiment of northern anti-slavery extremism. In 1844, Hoar's father, Samuel Hoar, had even gone to South Carolina to rescue African American sailors whom local authorities had locked up to prevent slave rebellions. One southern newspaper dismissed the younger Hoar's bill as "nothing more or less than another of Mr. Hoar's oft-repeated thrusts at the South." Cashman took a different view. To the Vicksburg editor, Hoar's bill seemed "excellent and much-needed," and he argued, "It is the duty of the Nation to protect its citizens, and as some of the States fail in this respect, Senator Hoar's bill should become a law."[2] This willingness to call on federal power foreshadowed Marshall's later campaign to put blacks on Mississippi juries—something that Mississippi courts would never do without prodding by the national government. Everything depended on the federal government's willingness to assert itself. Before the Civil War, the national government rarely if ever prodded a state. After the war, the question facing Congress was the extent to which that policy had changed. Some in Congress—most notably James M. Ashley—insisted that a revolution in the public's thinking had occurred and the national government had vast new powers. Ordinary Mississippians like Cashman and Marshall could interpret these new powers as allowing federal supervision of the nation's drinking or how the states picked their jurors. It mattered a great deal how much power Congress decided the national government had in 1866 and that depended on public opinion and its power to control Congress or be led by Congress.

Despite his public protestations to the contrary, Marshall developed a skepticism about public opinion that stemmed in part from his interest in poetry, literature, and drama. To many nineteenth-century Americans, artists seemed suspiciously unmanly. This thinking Oscar Wilde did not contradict when he toured the United States in 1882, reaching Vicksburg on June 14, just as Marshall considered his own interests in literature and drama. Wilde's effeminate dress and behavior challenged conventions; more than that, they changed the popular image of artist. Being an artist meant not just making art; it meant performance, adapting a distinctive manner and dress. How Marshall dressed after Wilde's visit is not recorded, but, like Wilde, Marshall loved flowers and he wrote poetry that resembled Wilde's. After Wilde's theatrical productions hit the London stage, Marshall followed suit in Vicksburg, drafting a script filled with high-toned literary allusions.[3]

Marshall did not really become a Mississippi Oscar Wilde. For one thing, Wilde put faith in himself ahead of his trust in God, something Marshall would never do, lacking the self-confidence, or arrogance, to go that far. When he first encountered Wilde, Marshall still proclaimed his faith in popular opinion and progress far more than the Englishman did—or than he himself would later. The public, he thought, had an "instinctive feeling of humanity which is never deluded." The proof of this, Marshall thought, could be seen in the public's eagerness to read any book promising to uplift humanity. Such public feelings,

Marshall believed, contributed to past progress and promised further improvement in the future. Marshall felt Christianity made all men equal, and on this
point he had more in common with Oscar Wilde than with his fellow Mississippi Christians—somehow they had missed this doctrine when reading the
Bible. Marshall further asserted that the working classes had to be placed on
an equal footing with the capitalist classes before mankind could achieve its
goal of universal Christianity. At times Marshall sounded a critique of Mississippi society that seemed almost Marxian. "The capitalist's purse is the laborer's life," he said. For a capitalist, the laborer is nothing more than a "salable,
buyable property" with a liberty "merely fictive." The worker has a free body,
but his will is enslaved. Marshall's Marxism was a peculiar kind of Christian Marxism, steadied by the hand of God: "God works slowly," he explained.
Marshall apparently believed that what the public would tolerate limited the
work of God. "A universal sense," he said, set limits on "what can be done at a
given time and what it were vain to try." Trying to sound like a tough-minded
realist, Marshall urged reformers to remember they lived in an actual world,
not an ideal one. He also urged patience. Marshall's youthful confidence in
human progress convinced him that "the possible of to-morrow" will be better
than the "possible of to-day."[4]

Marshall's greatest struggle with public opinion came when he shot a man
to death. In 1895, Marshall, then serving in the Mississippi House of Representatives, campaigned for a seat in the state senate. When his political enemies—
the silver Democrats—spread ugly rumors about his sexuality, Marshall found
himself in an impossible position. The South's honor system required that he
confront his accuser, a man named Rufus Tilford Dinkins. Marshall could reject Vicksburg's alcoholism, he could insist on his art, but he could not so easily
reject the honor code. When he embraced prohibition, he found allies; when
he turned to art, he had a role model. He would find no similar comforts if he
did not confront the man who accused him of homosexuality. He ran the risk
not only of losing his law practice and his political career—prizes he valued
greatly—but of being cast out of society entirely, even by his own family. To his
parents, Marshall decried "that public opinion which bade me kill." He wrote
that he "deeply and powerfully suffered" before deciding to confront Dinkins.
But as a product of the South's honor culture, Marshall knew some insults and
wrongs could only be washed away with blood. In 1895, he understood that
on some matters he had no choice but to follow public opinion, no matter
what commitments he might have to law and constitutionalism. This was the
truth that Marshall learned in 1895: there were some public principles that the

individual spurned at his peril. In 1866, Congress struggled with a similar di-
lemma, mapping out new protections for civil rights in a culture still—in great
measure—hostile to the whole idea of nationally protected rights.

After the Civil War, members of Congress fiercely disagreed with one another, in agitated and angry words; it was the same political theater senators and representatives had always employed when debating slavery, but
now they considered more fundamental questions: whether to restructure
the basic tenets of the Union by taking important powers from the states.
In 1866, Congress wrote what would become the Fourteenth Amendment
amid a long debate over civil rights that at the outset saw members haltingly
inserting themselves into the states' police powers and concluded when
Congress boldly ordered the U.S. Army to reconstitute government in the
South. In the middle of this transition, Congress placed protections of citizens' "privileges and immunities" in the care of the federal government.
Many congressmen, perhaps most, saw those three words as the key to the
whole amendment, and for a moment some could glimpse their revolutionary potential. They intended to expand national power and to use the federal judiciary to enforce citizens' rights. An examination of congressional
speeches shows that about half of the Republicans voting for civil rights legislation did so based on their perceptions of public opinion. The other half
acted as old party men, much better at spreading the word through old cli-
chés and rhetoric than at following changes in their constituents' thinking
about race.[5] These men felt more comfortable not deciphering public opinion but rather repeating old homilies they claimed represented the original
principles established at the founding of the nation. It was this latter group
that dominated congressional thinking. Every statement of rights that Congress wrote came from existing texts from the Revolutionary era. Public
opinion had not obviously changed so much that Congress could amend
the Constitution in ways that violated or even expanded on the founders'
language. The old texts were a safe harbor, but they did conceal real change.
Some in Congress expected—in many ways for the first time—that federal
courts would protect citizens' rights.

Members of Congress came to their debates in Washington after having
tested their ideas in party conventions and election campaigns. In 1862, the
future chief justice of the U.S. Supreme Court, Morrison Waite, challenged
Ohio Congressman James M. Ashley for his seat. Both candidates favored
defeating the South and winning the war, and in fact they quarreled over

which one did the most to encourage enlistments. Both wanted to end slavery.[6] Unlike Ashley, though, Waite believed that the Constitution allowed Congress only limited powers against slavery. Waite obviously hoped and probably believed that most people in northwest Ohio agreed with him, but he clung to his conservatism under difficult circumstances. For voters it was obvious that events had already rapidly marched beyond old ideas about federal power over slavery. Congress had already passed a confiscation law authorizing the president to emancipate slaves employed in the rebellion. In Missouri Union general John C. Frémont—some thought rashly—freed those slaves owned by persons taking up arms against the United States. What Waite could do in the face of such dramatic events was to invoke the name of his party's leader, President Lincoln. Both the law and Frémont's declaration discomforted Lincoln, just as they did Waite. Waite presented himself to the voters as Lincoln's ally, but in fact Waite did not really understand Lincoln's position. Waite opposed extending congressional power over race relations on constitutional grounds; Lincoln had more practical matters on his mind: he needed to keep the border states, especially Kentucky, in the Union, something best accomplished by not directly confronting slavery in those states. Except in cases of fugitive slaves crossing state lines, policing black people had always been the job of the states, not the federal government, and both Congress and Frémont threatened that structure of power. Though known now as the Great Emancipator, in the summer of 1861 Lincoln designed everything he did in public to show that he had decided to stick with the traditional deference to the states' sovereignty. He did little or nothing to enforce the Confiscation Act. He had fired Frémont. On November 7, 1861, the Union army captured South Carolina's Sea Islands and found itself with eleven thousand ecstatic slaves on its hands. The following May, Major General Thomas Hunter, fearing a Confederate counterattack, had freed the Sea Island slaves and armed them for self-defense. Lincoln cancelled Hunter's order.[7]

Waite's opponent, Congressman Ashley, "a large, good-natured, popular style of man" according to fellow Ohioan Rutherford Hayes, came from the ranks of those Republicans impatient with Lincoln, eager to shift power from the states to the national government.[8] He looked to the public more than the Constitution for support, though he could certainly cite the Constitution and Supreme Court decisions when necessary. Into the summer of 1862, Ashley favored a second confiscation act, authorizing the national government to seize civilian property without the impediment of trial by jury. The First Confiscation Act, passed in 1861, had authorized seizing the property of rebels only when it was actually used in aid of the rebellion. The second law went much further, freeing the slaves of any Confederate refusing to surrender within sixty days of its enactment. Slaves escaping to the Union army would be freed. The law even authorized Lincoln to use blacks to put down the rebellion. The Confiscation Acts subordinated property rights to more-abstract constitutional values of liberty and union. Ashley's congressional allies quoted Supreme Court precedents to argue that under the Constitution the federal government was "not so weak as some gentlemen believe[d]" and possessed "slumbering powers."[9] Against constitutional principle, Ashley's opponents sallied public opinion. The people will stand the legislation, one congressman said, "they will be made to stand it" as events turned against the rebellious Southerners' barbarism.[10] For their part, Democrats united to condemn the proposed bill as an outrage. To the Republicans, they said, "You have no power to interfere with slavery in the States."[11] The Constitution, they insisted, allowed Congress to declare war and provide the means for waging war, nothing more. Democrats recognized that the proposed new Confiscation Act expanded congressional power, "a terrible innovation," based, they contended, on "vague and erroneous ideas which prevail[ed]."[12] Some Republicans, including Lincoln, disliked it as well for the same reason. It seemed, they thought, to increase national power too much, but although some Republicans held that view, most did not, and Congress passed the measure into law on July 16, 1862.[13]

During much of this time, Lincoln preferred a plan more consistent with antebellum understandings of national power. If the slaves were to be emancipated, the job should be done by the states, not the national government, albeit encouraged with federal money for compensation. On Saturday morning, July 12, 1862, Lincoln invited the border-state congressmen to the White House. Reading from a prepared text, he made an elaborate appeal for gradual emancipation with compensation, asking that state governments carry it out. Garrett Davis of Kentucky, along with nineteen others, rebuffed Lincoln two days later, complaining that compensating slave owners in the border states would cost nearly five million dollars, greatly swelling the national debt. They also raised constitutional concerns that revealed how they saw the founding charter—as a political compromise that protected slavery. Any federal attack on slavery, even indirectly, they said, threatened to blow apart fundamental constitutional understandings—the political compromise that had created the Union and the Constitution in

1787 and had held it together ever since. The people of the seceded states, these border-state men argued, had left the Union only because they feared that the North threatened their interests, their property, rights protected by the Constitution. If Lincoln pressed ahead with a plan to emancipate border-state slaves, he would confirm Southerners' worst fears and unify them against the Union. Lincoln warned that if the border states rejected his proposal, he would accept "the indispensible necessity" of military emancipation and arm the slaves against their former masters. The congressmen spurned Lincoln.[14]

It was at this point that Lincoln began moving toward emancipation. Lincoln had a politician's respect for the voters, but he had an equal respect for divine will. The Civil War, he said, was a "People's contest." When masses of people rise up, nothing can prevail against them. At the same time, there were deeper values to be considered. To continue as the "hope to the world," America had to represent something more than individual avarice and politics. There had to be a common purpose, a communal will that rose above mere politics. Convinced that no society wholly dedicated to the individual could long survive, Lincoln searched for what he could find in the will of the people that harmonized with that of God. "While man exists," Lincoln said, "it is his duty to improve not only his own condition, but to assist in ameliorating mankind."[15]

On July 13, while taking a carriage ride, Lincoln confided to two cabinet officers that he had decided to free the slaves by a proclamation. Publicly, he gave no hint of this. Waite, Ashley, and nearly everyone else at this time still associated Lincoln with only the most painfully tepid commitment to liberty—gradual, compensated emancipation, carried out by the states. Two days after Lincoln's carriage ride, the New York Times reported that the country supported gradual emancipation "with unexampled unanimity." Given what he had decided to do, this was hardly good news for the president. Orville Hickman Browning of Illinois, not privy to the secret, came to the White House and found Lincoln working alone in his library, looking strangely troubled and sad. Lincoln probably did not feel free to share his decision with Browning, knowing that his friend opposed freeing the slaves. Browning even urged Lincoln to veto the Confiscation Act. If he would only do that, Browning pleaded, the border states would applaud his act and contribute one hundred thousand additional soldiers to the war effort. Browning did not know that Lincoln had already decided against his advice and against the public opinion reported in the press as unanimous.

Lincoln startled Browning with his fatalism. "I must die sometime," Lincoln told the puzzled Browning, who noted that the president spoke with "a cadence of deep sadness in his voice."[16]

By the end of August, Waite and Ashley had begun their political campaigns in earnest. Both agreed that slavery could be abolished militarily. Waite's campaign speeches reveal that although he opposed slavery because it held the United States back, thwarting its ambition to be first among the nations of the earth, he also believed that the Constitution did not permit Congress to interfere with slavery, a state institution. However much he might personally loathe slavery, as a legislator there would be nothing he could do about it. Congress could pass laws punishing individuals, but it could not punish a whole class of people by confiscating their property. The Constitution, Waite told Ohio voters, would not permit Congress to interfere with slavery in the states. This rule remained the same in peace and in war. The laws of war, however, did strengthen the president's hand, Waite said, and laid out his argument that emancipation was a legitimate war measure. Without a doubt, Waite explained, slavery strengthened the rebels. In fact, since it freed white men from labor details for combat duty, slavery was the South's only advantage over the North. Therefore, the necessity of war allowed the president, as commander in chief, to abolish slavery and put the national government in charge of race relations—temporarily; one day the war would end, and responsibility for those matters would return to the states. Waite trusted the states not to revive slavery, but he feared Congress might permanently expand its powers. Waite's position that the president had wartime powers the Congress could never have meant that there could be no permanent federal power over race relations.[17]

Ashley, though, believed Congress had ample power to conquer the rebels, confiscate their property, and emancipate their slaves. He quoted portions of the Constitution authorizing Congress to declare war, raise armies, make rules for the army, call forth the militia, and make all laws necessary and proper to execute its powers. The express letter of the Constitution, Ashley said, clothed the Congress with power to end slavery.[18] In the midst of the fall campaign season, Lincoln released his Emancipation Proclamation, based entirely on his powers as commander in chief of the army. In the end, Ashley defeated Waite, and he returned to Congress confident—he said—that the people supported his emancipationist vision. If Ashley really believed that, he would have done well to consider evidence that Waite articulated widespread northern concerns about expanded national power.

Two years after Waite went down in defeat, another Ohio politician, Columbus Delano, won election to the House from another district running on a platform nearly identical to Waite's.[19]

Doubts about national power turned up close to the center of power in wartime Washington. Secretary of the Treasury Salmon Chase had a much stronger record of hostility to slavery than either Waite or Delano or even Lincoln. Lincoln never put his body between a lynch mob and an abolitionist editor; Chase had. As a lawyer, Lincoln only rarely involved himself in the fugitive slave controversy, defending just three harborers of fugitive slaves. Once he represented a Kentucky slave owner seeking to retrieve his escaped slave in Illinois; Chase, on the other hand, made a name for himself representing slaves.[20] As secretary of the treasury, Chase enlarged the government's power in ways that seemed permanent, realizing Alexander Hamilton's program of centralizing control of the nation's money through a national bank. The national bank had run afoul of Andrew Jackson's hard-money principles and concerns for states' rights, but the Civil War won Chase over to centralized banking. With the North's overwhelming industrial superiority, failing to find enough money may have been the only way that the North could lose the war. Losing the war would mean continuing slavery. Having grown up in Jacksonian America, Chase had absorbed Old Hickory's economic principles, and Chase had to set aside his doubts when he "earnestly" called on Congress to turn on the printing presses and unleash the paper money Jackson so hated. In 1863, Chase wrote David Dudley Field that he was "much gratified" by reports that the court of appeals would unanimously support the Legal Tender Law.[21] A few months later, he wrote Edward Mansfield to say that "seizing" the currency did "great good in more ways than one." Government-printed money, Chase asserted, made financial transactions more reliable and had "obtained for the Government a great resource, almost without cost." But even as he argued for paper money, he could not entirely hide his misgivings. Too much paper money was irresponsible, he wrote Mansfield and other friends. He criticized Lincoln for failing to lead with "energy & economy." Leadership meant paying for the war with higher taxes and real money, gold and silver, using paper money as little as possible.[22] At times the contradictions in Chase's thinking fairly leap off the pages of his letters. Chase criticized Lincoln for not moving fast enough to guarantee literate blacks the right to vote ("I don't like the way reconstruction is managed," he griped in 1864),[23] but at the same time, he argued against overly centralized government. He seemed to imagine

that white Southerners would allow black voting without extensive supervision by a strong central government.

In 1863, as Chase harnessed the nation's currency to the war effort,
General Lorenzo Thomas carried the news of the Emancipation Proclamation to the troops arrayed around Vicksburg, telling them not only that
blacks would be freed from slavery but that they would be armed and made
soldiers in the army. That seemed even more revolutionary than printing
money, but as the Civil War concluded, Congress had to decide whether to
make permanent such a national intrusion into racial matters. Continuing
the states' authority to try persons charged with crimes with little or no federal supervision promised a grim future for the emancipated people, leaving them to the mercies of their former masters. Emancipation had dramatically changed social and economic relations, but unless it also shifted
responsibility for policing crime away from the states, its full revolutionary
potential would not be realized.

Congress seemed to move in that direction when it established the Freedmen's Bureau in March 1865. To many members of Congress, this step portended a particularly dangerous form of paternalism. On those grounds,
Massachusetts senator Charles Sprague cast his vote for the bill under protest. It would be far better to ensure the freed slaves their "rights and privileges of freedom" rather than subject them to slow death by paternalism, he
said. He voted for the bill only because his colleagues would not give blacks
full citizenship rights. Without their rights, blacks would be exterminated
by their former masters without some kind of protection, and the Freedmen's Bureau was better than nothing. Congress appropriated no money;
the legislation merely formalized and expanded what the army had already
been doing, distributing clothing, food, and advice to destitute freedmen.
The army officers assigned to the bureau quickly found themselves adju-
dicating disputes between white employers and their laborers. They acted
administratively, without juries. Even so, Freedmen's Bureau courts offered
the freed slaves access to the first institutionalized justice that was not designed to oppress them. Freed people flocked to these courts for the redress
of their grievances. Some whites thought the experience of slavery had so
demoralized blacks as to render them incapable of understanding the value
of formal law. The former slaves disproved that contention by aggressively
demanding justice from the Freedmen's Bureau, demonstrating an awareness of what the law should do for them. They brought a wide variety of
grievances involving contract disputes, domestic relations, and labor rights.
They expected to be part of the law and not outside it.[24]

After Congress authorized formation of the Freedmen's Bureau, events carrying the war to its conclusion seemed to accelerate. Dispatches reporting that the capital of the Confederacy had fallen to Union forces reached Washington on the morning of April 3. Some thought the victory sweeter for having been won by black troops: "The certainty that Richmond has been taken, and taken by negro troops, is creating the wildest excitement," a Vermont newspaper reported. Washingtonians abandoned their homes and businesses to celebrate in the streets. Courts shut down, with one judge commenting that no one could be convicted of a misdemeanor on such a day of celebration. Bostonians spontaneously started singing "The Star Spangled Banner." New Yorkers ransacked their city for American flags to fly everywhere.[25] Good news came so fast that one editor happily lamented that he could not keep up.[26]

Even as they celebrated victory, some northern journalists urged the national government to curb its expanded wartime powers, cautioning against imposing harsh penalties on the defeated Southerners. If the national government insisted on further concessions from the southern states, white Southerners might flee to the mountains and wage a guerrilla war, the *Milwaukee Daily Sentinel* warned on April 6. The *Sentinel* assured its readers that the masses of white Southerners remained loyal to the Union and would not continue fighting unless it became a "strong necessity" to do so.[27] On April 10, northern newspapers reported the exciting news that Robert E. Lee had surrendered his army at Appomattox. The *Boston Daily Advertiser* summarized the news in a single word: "Peace."[28] From the White House, Lincoln delivered a speech, acknowledging, "We loyal people differ among ourselves as to the mode, manner and measure of a reconstruction."[29] As if to confirm Lincoln's observation, northern newspapers quarreled over how and on what terms to readmit the southern states to Congress. Senator Charles Sumner argued that by seceding, the southern states had reduced themselves to territorial status, an idea many Republicans, including Salmon Chase, had talked about as early as 1861. The *New York Herald* reported that most people rejected Sumner's view. The "popular" consensus was that the states had never really been out of the Union and should be quickly readmitted to representation in Congress. Many white Northerners assured themselves that Lincoln would take a just and forgiving approach toward white Southerners. Then, on April 14, Lincoln died, assassinated by John Wilkes Booth.[30]

In the months after Lincoln's death, as Congress remained out of session, members of his party carried to their constituents a constitutional argument for equal rights across racial lines. In Massachusetts George S. Bout-well told a Fourth of July audience that emancipation meant that the nation could finally realize the cardinal truths in the Declaration of Independence. The government, Boutwell said, had attempted to compromise the prin-ciples of freedom with the principles of slavery, an experiment defeated in the Civil War. In that summer of triumph, Boutwell felt confident that the people stood ready to reestablish the government on the doctrine that "all men are created equal." Boutwell had no doubt that blacks should vote and that the "judgment of the country" demanded black suffrage. Boutwell ac-knowledged that even some free states did not yet allow black voting, "but all these [were] errors, misfortunes, and wrongs," not real obstacles to the popular will. Nor did Boutwell think southern white public opinion should be allowed to stand in the way—after all, white Southerners were almost all enemies of the country. Boutwell acknowledged that in normal times illit-erate men should not be allowed to vote, but now such caveats missed the point. Blacks needed to vote because they supported the government; white Southerners should not be allowed to vote because they did not. Boutwell favored giving the black man the vote, he said, "because his power at the ballot-box is now essential to us." Boutwell did not take these positions to place himself in advance of public opinion. As he said himself at the end of 1865, "I am always disposed to listen to the will of the people."[31]

President Andrew Johnson and other conservatives saw no need for any kind of revolutionary transfer of power away from the states. Born in North Carolina before moving to eastern Tennessee as a teenager, Johnson be-came a Democrat; served as a state legislator, congressman, and governor; and as U.S. senator, always championing the common man against privi-leged elites. From the outset of the Civil War, most residents of Tennes-see's mountainous eastern region sided with the Union, and Johnson did as well. Named military governor of occupied Tennessee in 1862, Johnson energetically worked against both slavery and lingering Confederate influ-ence, attracting favorable notice from the Republicans. In 1864, when Lin-coln and the Republicans hoped to broaden their appeal by reaching out to Democratic supporters of the Union, Johnson seemed the logical choice for vice president.[32]

Johnson was a good choice only in theory, not in practice. His selection as vice president proved a dreadful miscalculation with consequences that lasted more than a century. Lincoln and the Republicans overlooked John-son's continued loyalty to Democratic Party ideology, with its persistent commitment to states' rights. Now, as president, the Tennessean told confidants that whites had always treated southern blacks humanely, could be trusted to do so in the future, and the freed people needed no further federal assistance. The Freedmen's Bureau, he said, was "a great nuisance" that should be removed as soon as possible. Policing, he insisted, should revert to the states as soon as practicable.[33]

Just months after the Confederate armies surrendered, white Southerners demonstrated that they expected to use state police powers to regulate freed people's labor and their conduct. Mississippi did this first. On November 22, 1865, the Mississippi legislature passed into law "An Act to Regulate the Relation of Master and Apprentice as Relates to Freedmen, Free Negroes, and Mulattoes." This law instructed sheriffs and justices of the peace to arrest not just orphaned children but all African Americans under the age of eighteen whose parents could not support them. It instructed state officers to place these children in the custody of suitable "masters," giving their former owners preference. It further authorized masters and mistresses to inflict "moderate corporeal chastisement" and made it a crime to "entice away" "apprentices" from their "masters."[34] Other laws created county courts authorized to administer physical punishment for small crimes, punished vagrancy, and limited hunting in a way designed to disarm black people. These laws did not allow blacks to even testify against whites (except as plaintiffs) and certainly did not envision black jurors.[35]

Seemingly oblivious to the implications of their actions, many Northerners wanted to reestablish civilian responsibility for policing at the first opportunity. Even officers assigned to the Freedmen's Bureau worried that northern public opinion would not long support continued military occupation of the South. The day after Mississippi enacted its first race law, Samuel Thomas, a Freedmen's Bureau officer in Mississippi, reassured his superiors that the army could soon draw down its presence in the Magnolia State, as the legislature proposed to regulate "the whole matter" through a system of laws legalizing civilian policing of black people. Thomas thought this a most positive development since it apparently indicated that white Southerners understood they now had to discipline the black population through law rather than rely on the informal methods favored by slave owners. The Freedmen's Bureau officer said that Mississippi police had already taken charge of crime control, at his request. Thomas assured his superiors that he kept his men on a short leash. He did not allow them to make arrests, and he instructed them to assist white Mississippians in settling the freed people under a labor system that would guarantee their employers a good day's work for fair pay.[36]

Northern press reaction surprised Thomas. Some editors thought the Mississippi statutes resembled an attempt to revive slavery through law. The *Chicago Tribune* led the attack. "Not to put too fine a point on it," the *Tribune* said, but "we tell the white men of Mississippi that the men of the North will convert the State of Mississippi into a frogpond before they will allow any such law to disgrace one foot of soil in which the bones of our soldiers sleep and over which the flag of freedom waves." The *Tribune* coined the term "Black Code" for the Mississippi statutes, which in fact were never codified. The *Tribune* used the term "code" to recall the slave codes.[37]

Mississippi's Black Codes, and the reaction of such northern newspapers as the *Chicago Tribune*, encouraged those Republicans most determined to expand federal authority. In December 1865, before Congress opened, the Republicans caucused to map out their strategy. The problem they faced was clear. If the southern states came back into the Union, they would constitute a sizable bloc in Congress. Under slavery they had been allowed to count three-fifths of their slaves for purposes of representation, which gave white Southerners disproportionate congressional power. After emancipation they stood ready to count five-fifths of their former slaves, further swelling their power in Congress, while still not allowing black voting. Ex-Confederates would gain an advantage from their defeat. All over Washington, groups of Republicans met to plot their response. When the Ohio Republican delegation gathered on December 1, 1865, Rutherford Hayes advocated what he called "the Ohio idea." He wanted to amend the Constitution so that representation would be based on voters instead of population. From the beginning, then, important House Republicans wanted to amend the Constitution.[38]

The "Ohio idea" could be read two ways, both reflecting timidity rather than strength. It could be seen as an effort to leverage better behavior from white Southerners, expecting them to allow black voting to increase their representation in Congress. But the Ohio idea could also be seen more cynically, as recognizing that white Southerners would very likely never register blacks to vote for any reason. By this understanding the Ohio idea was a device to permanently limit southern representation in Congress. Seen either way, the Ohio idea was a timid use of federal power. The Ohioans hesitated to mobilize national power to force black voting. When the Ohio Republicans presented their idea to the larger Republican caucus, Congressman

Thaddeus Stevens of Pennsylvania erupted in outrage. Hayes wrote that Stevens angrily threatened to walk out of the caucus if the idea was not dropped. "He is radical throughout," Hayes wrote.[39]

Stevens took a bolder stance than that advocated by Hayes and the Ohioans. On December 18, 1865, he told the House that the Civil War had changed American power arrangements more than the Ohio delegation realized. "Nobody," he began, "pretends" that the southern states "can be permitted to claim their old rights" under their old constitutions and frames of government. He saw no reason to pussyfoot around with the defeated states, trying to coax them into treating all their citizens equally. It was time for direct action.[40] Stevens explained that the southern states had "killed" themselves when they seceded; they were "dead" "as to all national and political action" and would come back to life only when Congress would "breathe into them the breath of life anew." Until then, the seceded states were "only dead carcasses lying within the Union." Dead states reverted to territorial status, to be governed by Congress under the Constitution's Article IV, Section 2. Under the Constitution, Congress had "absolute" power over territories, Stevens said. Like Hayes, he wanted to amend the Constitution, but his proposal differed greatly from the Ohio idea: "All national and State laws shall be equally applicable to every citizen, and no discrimination shall be made on account of race or color."[41]

While House Republicans debated how to amend the Constitution, Senate Republicans wondered why the great document should be amended at all. In the Senate, Charles Sumner wanted to do the same thing as Stevens, but through law rather than by constitutional amendment. Sumner laid out his philosophy two days after Stevens spoke, saying that Congress needed to carry out and maintain the Emancipation Proclamation, ending slavery. The president's pledge to end slavery, Sumner told his colleagues, had not been simply a wartime measure. It had no limitations in space or time. The federal government could not trust the states to carry out its pledge to end slavery. "The performance of that pledge cannot be intrusted to another." It certainly could not be left to the old slave masters, "embittered against their slaves." Slavery could only be ended by the national government.

Sumner's second point urged an even further expansion of federal power. If the federal government merely ended slavery as a formal institution, he insisted, the job would be only half done. The U.S. government had to make sure that all Americans, black and white, stood equally before the law. Sumner wanted "the absolute obliteration of all legal discriminations founded on color, whether in the court-room or at the ballot box." Like Stevens, Sumner claimed to be certain that the balance of power between the states and the federal government had shifted decisively in favor of the central authority. "As to the power of Congress over this question," Sumner said, "I cannot doubt it." There was no need to amend the Constitution because it already gave Congress sufficient power to do what needed to be done, Sumner believed.[42]

To some members of Congress, the revolutionary transfer of power away from the states that Stevens and Sumner proposed seemed plausible because emancipation had already worked a revolution on the public mind, and as lawmakers they were bound to write the new public will into law. This meant, of course, that only a dramatic change in public opinion justified the kind of revolutionary constitutional transformation that Stevens and Sumner proposed. If the public mind had not shifted so dramatically, then the foundation for Reconstruction would be compromised. Representative Henry P. H. Bromwell of Illinois, a proponent of civil rights, observed that *only* popular consent can truly make the law. "This is a truth of constitutions, as of statutes, charters, and contracts. According to our legal principles we recognize no other foundation for any law whatever." Bromwell did not feel bound by the original Constitution, a document that fell short of its goals. It was now time to more completely achieve what the framers had originally intended but failed to carry out.[43] James Ashley said an antislavery revolution had swept the country, a force too powerful to be stopped by the president or Congress.[44] Criticized for so long for being too far ahead of popular opinion, Ohio senator Ben Wade now chortled that the public was turning abolitionist so fast, he might not be able to keep up.[45]

Some on the conservative side feared that Wade and the Radicals might be right, but this, they theorized, was a sign of momentary "group dementia."[46] The Philadelphia diarist and commentator Sidney George Fisher (1809–71) wrote that emancipation had brought a mania for universal suffrage, and he shared Davis's worries that the Civil War had unleashed an exaggerated "popular passion for liberty & equality." Once that "madness" had passed, he predicted, the evils of Negro equality would become apparent. Fisher feared the inevitable reversal might come too late to permit a retreat from philanthropic concessions made at a weak moment. The Republicans' passion for civil rights also seemed "insane" to Samuel Smith Nicholas (1798–1869), the eccentric Kentucky-based legal commentator and former judge.[47] Election results at this time suggest that many Americans rejected the kind of thinking that Fisher and Nicholas espoused, but a segment of the public actually did diagnose the Republican ascendancy in Congress as a kind of temporary insanity. Fisher wrote books, newspaper columns, and articles. His diary suggests that editors saw him as sensible and level headed, which means they saw in his writing ideas that resonated with their own thinking and that of their readers. He was the kind of writer whose texts sometimes seemed to represent something larger than himself: public opinion.[48]

Insane or not, many members of Congress thought they understood their constituents' will based on their correspondence and local elections. But those sources of information lacked precision and often contradicted each other. White Northerners did not necessarily agree with Stevens and Sumner that the newfound distaste for slavery required or even permitted greater congressional oversight of state policing. Even Massachusetts senator Charles Sumner initially urged Congress to pass a law requiring only that federal—not state—judges in the South include freed slaves on their juries. He proposed a quota system, requiring, for example, that blacks make up half the membership of federal grand juries in places where African Americans formed a significant portion of the population.[49] In December 1865, most members of Congress considered even that approach, limited to federal courts, too far in advance of public opinion, and Sumner's proposal never received serious consideration.

Representatives kept up with their constituents' thinking by corresponding with the leading men in their districts. Senators stayed in touch with the legislatures in their home states, the very bodies that elected them to office in the first place. Some members of state legislatures freely offered advice, sometimes with pointed reminders about who had put the senator in his seat. "I assisted your first advent into public life," one Ohio legislator wrote John Sherman before adding, "I hope to continue our mutual good will."[50] But even the most assiduous congressman could only maintain contact with a small number of his constituents. It did not help when correspondents authoritatively asserted that "every prominent Union man" or "the sensible men of our party" in their part of the county held a particular view when another correspondent claimed all his friends believed the opposite.[51] Nevada senator William Stewart observed, "Everyone is liable to estimate the sentiments of the whole country by the views of a few friends or a small portion of his constituents, modified by his own peculiar ideas and wishes."[52] In the House, Ohio Republican Ralph Buckland, a former

Union army general, agreed, observing that while many members had offered their opinions, "unfortunately, scarcely any two of these distinguished gentlemen . . . agree on any one point."[53] Even those with the most peculiar ideas struggled to follow public opinion. Kentucky's Garrett Davis at first seemed nonplussed by the ease with which his opponents justified their views on changes in voters' thinking, but by June he saw the people as "all divided in their judgment" with no "considerable portion" favoring Republican constitutional initiatives.[54] Davis charged that the Republicans actually prevented Congress from truly representing popular thinking, calling them "wrong-doers" for "mutilating" Congress and passing revolutionary measures with less than a majority. The courts, he predicted, would right things, since they more truly represented the whole of white public opinion. He thought that while the public—more properly, the segment of the public that the Republicans represented—might temporarily accept equal rights or might be confused, one day soon the public mind would come clear again. "Ere long," he said, the [white] people "will rise up with earthquake force and fling you from power and place."[55]

Congressional confusion about public opinion became especially clear when the House considered whether to extend the vote to blacks living in the District of Columbia. No one doubted the constitutional power of Congress to determine suffrage in the district. In contrast to its relationship with the states, Congress directly ruled the District of Columbia. Democrats could only call on public opinion. Benjamin Boyer, a Pennsylvania Democrat, insisted that popular sentiment supported his position against black voting. Congress had the constitutional authority to allow black voting in the District of Columbia, he acknowledged, but it lacked the moral right to pass a bill so contrary to public opinion.[56]

Boyer, of course, defined white people as "the public." Every member of Congress carved out particular sections of the total population to serve as "the public." Hezekiah Bundy, an Ohio Republican, said that the Civil War had united public opinion, "the popular heart," behind the idea that only loyal people should govern. According to Bundy, not a single patriotic heart uttered even one sentiment in dissent. The whole country had rendered a "well-defined and clearly pronounced judgment" in favor of the national government protecting the rights of citizens in every state. Bundy meant Northerners only, of course, but not even all Northerners. During the Civil War, dissent and discord had riddled the North, so Bundy's statements are plausible only if his popular and patriotic hearts are limited to the Republican Party.[57] Republicans like George Lawrence of Pennsylvania could criticize Democrats' "indecent haste" to seat rebel leaders in Congress, because they did not yet accept white Southerners as legitimate members of the body politic.[58]

To test just how Congress understood its power after the Civil War requires looking at not only members' confusion over public opinion but also their use of the Constitution itself. For some Republicans and many Democrats as well, constitutional law seemed a surer guide than something so uncertain, and unknowable, as public opinion. Many Republicans agreed with George Boutwell that the founding documents contained the potential to revolutionize the protection of rights. In 1866, Republicans quickly identified powerful promise in Article IV, with its heretofore toothless guarantee of citizens' privileges and immunities. For Democrats the Constitution had historically defended states' powers and had created a white man's government, which must be defended, even in the face of a congressional majority and public opinion.

The first step, of course, was to state frankly that constitutional principle mattered more than public opinion. Roughly one-third of House Republicans took that step (see appendix 4, table A4.3). William D. Kelley of Pennsylvania claimed to have "consulted no popular impulse" but rather to have "seated [himself] at the feet of the fathers of our country."[59] Standing with the founding fathers gave Republicans like Kelley the confidence necessary to challenge Democrats' claims that this was "a white man's Government," an argument with a long history of electoral success. Democrats spoke demagogically, speaking to the crowd, while Republicans invoked first principles. In 1778, they pointed out, Congress had considered and rejected a proposal to limit privileges and immunities to white persons.[60] The foundation of the government rested on the rights of man, regardless of color, Senator Daniel Clark of New Hampshire asserted.[61]

Democrats tried to match the Republicans' constitutionalism with their own variety. They made it their mission to guard the Constitution from "invasion" by the Republicans. Years later the *Atlantic Monthly* published an obituary for state sovereignty, a "discredited" notion. In 1866, though, some members of Congress still defended state sovereignty and considered the rights of the states beyond their reach. They sometimes offered a historical argument: the people of the individual states had won freedom from England, created the United States, and guarded individual liberties.[62] New Jersey Democrat Andrew Jackson Rogers thought the founders made the states exempt from congressional assaults on their sovereignty; false assertions of privileges and immunities that pretended to guard civil rights, he charged, recklessly expanded federal power. Better to leave such matters to the judiciary, guarding the founders' intent, not to politicians acting on some temporary popular whim. "That matter," he said, "was left entirely to the courts."[63] For Kentucky's Garrett Davis, such questions went beyond abstract arguments over sovereignty to an organic law of race. He insisted that no black person had ever been a citizen, an argument he also based on the framers' original intent, or at least his version of it. At the time the framers wrote the Constitution, no blacks had been citizens; therefore, "we the people" meant white people only. He claimed that Congress lacked the power to make black people citizens, although he acknowledged that the Constitution's Article I, Section 8 gave Congress power "To establish a uniform Rule of Naturalization." The constitutional power to naturalize people applied only to foreigners, Davis insisted. Under gentle questioning by Reverdy Johnson, a fellow defender of states' rights, Davis went even further, adding that even immigrants from Africa could not be naturalized as American citizens. This assertion surprised Johnson. "Why not?" he asked.

"This is a Government and a political organization by white people. It is a principle of that Government and that organization before and below the Constitution, that nobody but white people are or can be parties to it."[64] Davis then demanded to know what part of the Constitution authorized the federal government to legislate on behalf of black people.

Davis's aggressively stated assertions nonplussed Johnson: "I do not know that there is any particular clause that says the child of a native born negro is to be a citizen, but it would be an extraordinary thing if under the judiciary clause it were not in the power of Congress to authorize a native-born negro . . . to sue."

Davis persisted. He did not think blacks should have access to the federal courts because of their color. Immigrants from Africa, naturalized as citizens, could not have access to the federal courts, regardless of the federal government's power to naturalize foreigners. The Constitution, he said, leaves "the whole subject of free negroes and slave negroes" to the states. The federal government can do nothing for African American people. It sets up a white man's government, he reiterated.[65]

Republicans, of course, could dismiss Davis's arguments. He could call on few votes to support his seemingly outlandish opinions. Determined to transfer power to protect rights from the states to the federal government, Republicans had only to decide how to characterize the rights they wanted protected, confident that they had the votes to pass whatever program they could rally around. But they began their debates sharply divided. In the Senate, three leading Republicans spelled out in some detail just what these new federal powers might be: Henry Wilson of Massachusetts, John Sherman of Ohio, and Lyman Trumbull of Illinois. In the House, Ohio's John Bingham played the most important role of all, pressing for a privileges and immunities clause in the new Fourteenth Amendment. This guaranteed that Congress would leave the question of just what power the nation now had over the states uncertain, ambiguous, and subject to judicial interpretation.

On December 13, 1865, Wilson spelled out his understanding of these new powers when he introduced a bill aimed at voiding the Black Codes. Wilson's bill did not list specific rights to be protected but used sweeping general language to assert national power over state law:

> Be it enacted &c. That all laws, statutes, acts, ordinances, rules and regulations, of any description whatsoever . . . whereby or wherein any inequality of civil rights and immunities among the inhabitants of said States is recognized . . . in consequence of any distinctions or differences of color, race, or descent . . . are hereby declared null and void.[66]

Senator John Sherman of Ohio, a far more moderate and conservative influence in Congress than either Stevens or Sumner, immediately identified Wilson's "civil rights and immunities" as language that paralleled the Constitution's guarantee of privileges and immunities. Article IV, Section 2, he said, merely guaranteed that citizens of one state "had the right to go anywhere within the United States and exercise the immunity of a citizen of the United States." The privileges and immunities clause had its origins in the Articles of Confederation, which had explained the meaning of the term more fully than the Constitution: "The free inhabitants of each State—paupers, vagabonds, and fugitives from justice excepted—shall be entitled to all the privileges and immunities of free citizens in the several States; and the people of each State shall have free ingress and egress to and from any other State." Sherman argued that before the Civil War the southern states routinely flouted the Constitution's guarantee of privileges and immunities and pointed to "the celebrated case of Mr. Hoar."[67] In 1822, South Carolina had enacted a law that required the arrest of every African American person found on a ship in a South Carolina port. The law did not allow for trial by jury, simply saying, "Persons of color shall be liable to be seized and confined in jail until said vessel shall clear out and depart from this State."[68] Under this law, black citizens of Massachusetts and other states went to jail, plainly denied their privileges and immunities. South Carolina persisted in its policy of jailing the black citizens of other states even after a federal judge declared the law unconstitutional. Determined to challenge the South Carolina law, Massachusetts dispatched a lawyer, Samuel Hoar, to the Palmetto State in 1844 with instructions to gather facts and litigate on behalf of imprisoned Massachusetts citizens. In South Carolina, the legislature denounced Hoar as a seditious person, and citizens threatened him with mob violence. Hoar fled the state. Congress was so toothless that it could not even protect the most elemental citizenship right, the privilege of travel from one state to the next, immune from harassment.[69]

The problem, Sherman said, was not that Hoar had lacked the constitutional right to travel into South Carolina. Sherman said that the privileges and immunities clause in Article IV did not empower Congress to enforce it. This was what Salmon Chase had said before the war as part of an argument that the same rule applied to the fugitive slave clause: Congress had no constitutional authority to enforce the right. Article IV, Sherman said, guaranteed freedom of travel only in theory. "There never was any doubt about the construction of this clause," Sherman contended, adding, "the trouble was in enforcing" it. In essence, "this constitutional provision was in effect a dead letter." The Thirteenth Amendment fixed this problem. Its second section, providing that Congress "shall have power to enforce this article by appropriate legislation," solved "the very difficulty" posed by the Constitution's failure to authorize Congress to protect privileges and immunities. Sherman urged the Senate to pass a law giving Congress power to protect privileges and immunities based on the Thirteenth Amendment.[70]

Sherman thought Hoar's experience demonstrated that privileges and immunities had to mean more than merely the freedom to travel. A traveler entering a state might well want to do something while he was there. Did that traveler have a constitutional right to free speech? Could he demand a fair trial by a jury of his peers, based on the U.S. Constitution? Hoar, for example, had wanted to use the courts in South Carolina. Sherman complained that Wilson had failed to produce a concrete list of "civil rights and immunities." So, on December 21, Wilson produced his own list. Civil rights and immunities included a citizen's right:

to go where he pleases;

to work for whom he pleases;

to sue and be sued;

to lease and buy and sell his own property, real and personal;

to go into the schools and educate himself and his children;

to the rights and guarantees of the good old common law;

that his cabin is protected by the just and equal laws of his country.[71]

Since Wilson said he wanted to protect the freedmen's "natural rights," he apparently considered the rights he listed to be "natural." Wilson did not mention trial by jury, but "the rights and guarantees of the good old common law" must have included it, especially since that was the one right Samuel Hoar had most needed in South Carolina and Sherman focused so much of his argument on Hoar's travails.

It is unlikely that Sherman or anyone else thought incompetent people should be allowed on juries, but there is evidence that Sherman did not consider freed people inherently incompetent. He did not engage in the racist rhetoric favored by Democratic opponents of privileges and immunities, and he insisted that the U.S. government was "bound by every consideration of honor . . . to protect the freedmen from the rebels." Sherman remembered that during the war blacks had "aided [the Union] in this conflict," arguing, "Therefore we are bound by every consideration of honor, of faith, of pubic morals, to protect and maintain all essential incidents of freedom to them."[72]

More than either Wilson or Sherman, Senator Lyman Trumbull of Illinois emerged to lead efforts to outlaw state discriminations against freed blacks through law rather than through a constitutional amendment. He wanted to protect "civil rights or immunities," but Trumbull also spelled out the specific rights he wanted protected:

the . . . right to make and enforce contracts

  To sue

  Be parties and give evidence

  To inherit, purchase, lease, sell, hold and convey real and person property

  To full and equal benefit of all laws and proceedings for security of person and property

  And shall be subject to like punishment, pains, and penalties, and to none other, any law, statute, ordinance, regulation, or custom to the contrary notwithstanding.[73]

Trumbull offered two bills guaranteeing privileges and immunities. In addition to his civil rights bill, he also proposed converting the Freedmen's Bureau into a police agency. Freedmen's Bureau agents would extend military jurisdiction over all cases "wherein . . . any State of local law, ordinance, police or other regulation, custom or prejudice" threatened "civil rights or immunities." Freedmen's Bureau officers could "take jurisdiction of, and hear and determine . . . all cases affecting negroes, mulattoes, freedmen, refugees, or other persons" subject to state discrimination. Trumbull proposed a radical shift of power from state to federal tribunals. His bill gave federal officers oversight power over state agents. The Freedmen's Bureau bill also substituted federal proceedings for state trials. To Trumbull's aid came Maryland senator John Creswell, with positive proof that the states could not be trusted to fairly try blacks. In some parts of Maryland, Creswell said, rebels murdered returning black veterans. To make sure no white man ever went to jail for killing a black person, Creswell explained, rebel sheriffs not only made certain that the juries were all white but also packed them with rebels.[74] Trumbull's opponents tried to turn the fair-trial argument against him, charging reverse discrimination, that the Freedmen's Bureau bill would take away trial by jury for white people.[75] The Senate nonetheless passed Trumbull's Freedmen's Bureau bill on January 25, by a vote of 37 to 10. Though he expected Johnson to sign the bill, Trumbull had more than enough votes to override a presidential veto.[76]

With the Freedmen's Bureau bill passed, Trumbull moved on his second priority, the civil rights bill, and on February 2, the Senate passed that bill as well, albeit by a slightly less comfortable margin, 33 to 12.[77] President Andrew Johnson then vetoed the Freedmen's Bureau bill, and Trumbull mounted his defense of the bill, expecting a quick override. In the Senate, though, his opponents forced him to concede that the military trials of civilians envisioned in the bill would, in some cases, deprive white Southerners of the right to trial by jury. At this point, Johnson was still ostensibly allied with congressional Republicans, and his veto portended a division among those working to reconstruct the South. Sherman rushed to make a conciliatory speech. As one of his constituents put it, he threw himself into the breach to prevent an irreparable split in the Republican Party, a split the Democrats would be sure to exploit.[78]

Sherman's correspondence reveals the problems faced by members of Congress trying to read public opinion through the mail. R. P. L. Baber warned Sherman that the entire Ohio legislature feared that neither John-

son's friends in the Republican Party nor his opponents could triumph without destroying the party. Baber said that while Ohio Republicans favored
protecting freed blacks' civil rights, the use of military tribunals to police
the South gave them pause. "Our people, while a unit that these rights must
be protect[ed] by constitutional laws, don't relish the trying of men without a jury in time of peace."[79] Some Ohioans had no sympathy for black
rights whatsoever. A Cincinnati doctor gave his professional opinion that
proponents of civil rights suffered from "nigger on the brain," an intractable mental disease with no known cure.[80] Another Ohioan reported that
he had canvassed every leading Republican in Columbus and found near-
unanimous support for the president.[81]

While most of the letters Sherman received from his constituents urged
reconciliation with the president and disdained the so-called "Radical" proponents of civil rights, a handful of correspondents offered unsettling warnings about a possible massacre of loyal men in the South. Others simply offered abstract praise for equal rights. In Lucas County, John Pease hailed
Sumner and Stevens as patriots, insisting that rights had to be protected.[82]
Another writer praised Sherman for pouring oil on waters troubled by the
president's alarming veto message but also insisted that Congress must
act to protect human rights, regardless of color.[83] A man signing his name
A. Stone Jr. wrote more authoritatively, after touring the South. Stone's trav-
els convinced him that black suffrage could not be forced on the South
without losing the support of white Republicans. But Stone's conversations
with white Southerners also convinced him that if the government with-
drew the Freedmen's Bureau from the South, no Union man would be safe.[84]

On February 20, the Senate failed to override Johnson's veto, falling three
votes short.[85] The confusion and tension that accompanied the Senate's failure to override can be best measured by looking to the House side of the
Capitol. The House was on edge anyway because Thaddeus Stevens had introduced a resolution declaring that Congress would admit no senator or
representative from the eleven seceded states until Congress declared those
states entitled to representation. News from the Senate about the veto vote
escalated tensions. Defenders of states' rights leapt to protest Stevens's proposal, prompting tumult and cries of "Order!" and "No!" To prevent a vote
on the proposed resolution, Democrats repeatedly moved that the House
adjourn and demanded a roll-call vote each time, which they repeatedly
lost. Democrats made further procedural motions, demanding more roll-
call votes. Common courtesy went by the board as more shouts rang out

across the hall. No doubt the worst of the racial epithets went unrecorded, but in the midst of one dilatory roll-call vote, a reporter caught Pennsylvania Democrat Philip Johnson denouncing the issue as "one of the biggest 'nigger' questions that could be brought up." When Democrats tried to offer a compromise, angry Republicans shouted them down. Finally, during yet another roll-call vote, Daniel W. Voorhees, an Indiana Democrat only days from being ousted from the House in a controversy over his election, interrupted to announce that the Senate had sustained the president. Republicans responded with more cries of "Order!" "Order!"[86] The president's veto had thrown the House into confusion, exposing the anger and hostility that lay just below the surface of ordinary courtesy.

In the House, even Republicans friendly to Trumbull's intentions had doubts about the constitutionality of a law allowing federal officers to take over state police functions. Ohioan John A. Bingham took the lead in raising such objections. He had made his position clear from the beginning: he wanted to amend the Constitution in a way that would protect citizens' privileges and immunities.[87] In March, Bingham spoke against Trumbull's civil rights bill. Bingham believed that "civil rights and immunities" or "privileges and immunities" implied more rights than those listed by Trumbull. Bingham did not need to concoct a list of protected rights; he took his list from the Bill of Rights. Guaranteeing privileges and immunities against state action meant applying the Bill of Rights to the states. "I know," he said, "that the enforcement of the bill of rights is the want of the Republic." Nonetheless, the Constitution made enforcing the rights listed in the Bill of Rights a state, not a federal, responsibility. It was a power reserved to the states, he asserted. Bingham then discussed the meaning of civil rights. "By all authority," he said, " the term 'civil rights' as used in this bill does include and embrace every right that pertains to the citizen as such." Since all the states discriminated, Bingham asked how the federal government could enforce a federal law against state discrimination. "What do you propose to do?" he asked. "Jail the governor?" Bingham's answer to the dilemma was clear: amend the Constitution.[88]

Morrison Waite's conservative ally in Congress, Columbus Delano, warned that Bingham's plans dangerously threatened the states' powers to limit jury service to competent persons. On March 8, he asked the Judiciary Committee chairman if his long list of protected rights might not include jury service. James Wilson of Iowa assured Delano that it did not. Delano complimented Wilson's legal acumen, but said, "I must confess that it does seem to me that this bill necessarily confers the right of being jurors." The bill provides for "full and equal benefit of all laws," Delano pointed out, asking how the full and equal benefit of the laws can be conferred without also conferring the right to jury service. Wilson protested that he had added that language to the bill himself, to limit rather than extend its provisions. The language read: "full and equal benefit of all laws and proceedings for the security of person and property, as is now enjoyed by the white citizens." Wilson saw this as limiting because "white citizen" did not include women or minors and said he had added the language to make certain that this part of the population would not benefit from the bill. When Wilson asked Delano if any rights at all resulted from national citizenship, Delano revealed the depth of his commitment to states' rights. Citizens of states are entitled to many rights, he answered, adding that he expected the states to guarantee, sustain, and enforce those rights. Congress could protect rights, too, "when there is power given by the Constitution of the United States to enforce those rights."[89]

Unlike Delano, Bingham really wanted to accomplish the goals of Trumbull's civil rights bill, albeit by constitutional amendment. He had worked out the language:

> That Congress shall have power to make all laws which shall be necessary and proper to secure to the citizens of each State all privileges and immunities of citizens of the several States, and to all persons in the several States equal protection in the rights of life, liberty and property.[90]

Bingham emphasized that his proposed amendment gave Americans no new rights; the Bill of Rights already listed all the rights he wanted to protect. The task was simply to shift responsibility for the protection of those rights from the states to the national government. Everybody in the world knows, Bingham orated, that the eleven states of the Confederacy disregarded the Bill of Rights and did not protect their citizens' rights, "the enforcement of which are absolutely essential to American nationality."[91] Bingham ridiculed his opponents for not daring to challenge the Bill of Rights. "What do gentlemen say to these provisions?" Bingham asked, and mimicked their response: "Oh, we favor that [the Bill of Rights]," but added that it should not be enforced, except by the states. "Why are gentlemen opposed to the enforcement of the bill of rights, as proposed?" Bingham demanded and then answered his own question with withering sarcasm: "Because they aver it would interfere with the reserved rights of the States!" States have no rights to deprive citizens of their rights, Bingham declared, and they never did.[92]

Iowa Republican Hiram Price touched a nerve when he sought to explain the meaning of privileges and immunities in Bingham's proposed amendment. Price started with a fairly minimalist definition. A traveler had a right to expect states to extend him the same protections that it offered native citizens. This was the very least that Article IV could mean, but then Price began delineating the implications of a federal right to state protections. If a Northerner went to South Carolina or Georgia, Price said, he should "have the same protection of laws there that he would have had had he lived there for ten years." He would, for example, have the right to freedom of speech, including (before the war) the right to criticize slavery. Price then continued, relating that he had recently heard of Illinoisans murdered while traveling in Mississippi. If Congress had the right to protect citizens' privileges and immunities, then it might well intervene in such a case of ordinary murder. This was too much for Edwin R. V. Wright, a virulently racist New Jersey Democrat. He raised a point of order, claiming that Price had strayed from his topic. "We are not trying murder cases," Wright said. In fact, Wright missed the point. Under Bingham's amendment, the federal government might well try murder cases or supervise more closely state trials of murder cases. Price insisted that his remarks were relevant, and after an exchange of insults with Wright, the Speaker agreed.[93]

A few days after the House quarreled over Bingham's proposed amendment guaranteeing privileges and immunities, it decided to eliminate that phrase from Trumbull's civil rights bill. On March 13, the House voted to delete privileges and immunities and then passed the bill, with only a list of rights and no general language available for interpretation by future congresses or judges.[94]

On March 15, the Senate concurred in the House version of Trumbull's civil rights bill. The president vetoed the bill, but this time the House and the Senate quickly overrode the veto on April 6 and April 9, respectively. Johnson's veto of the Freedmen's Bureau bill had attracted some support even from Republicans, in part because it threatened to deprive white Southerners of trial by jury, subjecting them to military trials. The civil rights bill did not have that baggage; it simply protected the rights of black Southerners, who had proven to be the most loyal to the Union—and to the Republican Party as well. One Ohio legislator wrote that this veto "hits harder" than the Freedmen's Bureau bill veto "and has fewer friends by far."[95] Another

Ohio Republican applauded the civil rights bill as equivalent to some of the North's most decisive battlefield victories in the war.[96] Some Republicans saw the president as abandoning principles of rights that had won electoral victories for their party in 1864.[97] With such grassroots support, Republicans voted almost unanimously for the bill, even representatives from places once notorious for their racism. Though born in Maryland, Congressman Henry P. H. Bromwell called Charleston, Illinois, home in 1866. In 1858, Lincoln had debated Stephen A. Douglas in Charleston, making the most racist statements of his campaign for the Senate that year. During the Civil War, copperhead supporters of the Confederacy had rioted in Charleston. After Bromwell cast his vote for civil rights, his political opponents tried to take advantage, circulating a handbill making a racist appeal (see fig. 3.1). Despite such tactics, which greatly exaggerated the reach of the Civil Rights Act, shorn as it was of the privileges and immunities clause, Bromwell's opponents failed to defeat him and he was reelected to the Fortieth Congress.[98]

As Congress debated proposed constitutional amendments and civil rights bills, the Joint Committee on Reconstruction worked privately to craft the actual language of an amendment. Robert Dale Owen was not a member of the committee, but the committee took his recommendations seriously, including his suggestion that the words "privileges and immunities" not appear in any constitutional amendment. In 1863, Secretary of War Edwin M. Stanton had appointed Owen, with Samuel Gridley Howe and James McKaye, to the American Freedmen's Inquiry Commission. Though the son of a utopian reformer, Owen had throughout his life very often reflected majority opinion. He advocated expansionism and Manifest Destiny when it was popular to do so and drafted that part of Indiana's constitution excluding blacks from the state when racism swept the Hoosiers. When the war came, he joined many Northerners to vigorously champion the Union. As a member of the Freedmen's Inquiry Commission, he gathered evidence that both confirmed the more positive prevailing racial stereotypes and promoted an expanded role for the U.S. government in race relations. Historians commonly describe the commission's report, largely written by Owen, as the blueprint for "Radical Reconstruction." In his report, Owen fended off criticism of emancipation, defended the character of black people — "Scarcely any beggars are found among them" — and called for "justice," a term he studiously refused to define.[99] As he waited through January, February, and March, Owen claimed later that he thought the Joint Committee

EXAMINE THE CIVIL RIGHTS BILL.
Examine the Veto!

The Bill makes the negro the equal of the white man; before the law no State can now discriminate between them.

It destroys State law, and fines and imprisons a judge who decides in accordance thereto.

It makes the negro a citizen, whether he is fit or unfit for a discharge of his high duties; the intelligent foreigner must wait five years

Perfect equality betwixt the races in all civil rights, is created by it. No State can make laws to protect the purity of blood, or forbid marriage between white and negro.

The negro can under its provisions, force himself into our company on cars, in lecture rooms, in hotels, and in all public assemblages.

The negro under its provisions, can hold office—all offices within the gift of the Government—whether the people will or no; nor can any State exclude the negro from office!

The Bill creates a swarm of officers to eat out our substance! Who pays these officials!—the white man! For whose benefit?—the negro's!

The negro can now take his seat in the jury box, and you cannot challenge him as a negro, (but your State court cannot try him without his consent, for any crime or misdemeanor, theft, burglary, arson, rape, murder, &c.)

The Bill makes the United States Courts and all their ministers, migratory bodies, at the will of the President, not to punish crimes done, alone, but to anticipate their commission.

In all cases, the negro has a final appeal to the Supreme Court of the United States.

BROMWELL VOTED FOR THE BILL.

FIGURE 3.1. Opponents of the 1866 Civil Rights Act exaggerated its reach, claiming, as this handbill shows, that it would desegregate juries.

Source: Bromwell Papers, Library of Congress, Washington, D.C.

had been inactive. Frustrated, Owen went to Washington, where he met Thaddeus Stevens and proposed a five-step plan. Owen's version of what would become the Fourteenth Amendment contained no reference to privileges or immunities:

> No discrimination shall be made by any State, nor by the United States, as to the civil rights of persons, because of race, color, or previous condition of servitude.[100]

Owen's version closely resembled what Stevens had urged in December, and Stevens pronounced himself happy with Owen's text. By the time Owen made his proposal, the committee, unbeknown to Owen, had already debated similar language for a new constitutional amendment. In January the committee considered a draft amendment guaranteeing to all American citizens "the same political rights and privileges." In February Bingham pressed for a version that more fully replicated the language of Article IV, Section 2:

> The Congress shall have power to make all laws which shall be necessary and proper to secure to the citizens of each state all the privileges and im-

munities of citizens of the several states; and to all persons in the several
States equal protection in the rights of life, liberty, and property.[101]

Bingham's version repeated language taken directly from the Constitution.
The only change came in the form of an explicit authorization for Congress to defend citizens' rights. Bingham proposed a transfer of police
power from the states to the federal government through the privileges and
immunities clause. His draft passed by the narrowest of margins, 7 to 6.[102]
The joint committee did not record its debates, but the atmosphere must
have been positively poisonous. On February 26, Andrew Jackson Rogers,
a member of the committee, attacked its deliberations on the floor of the
House as akin to edicts issued by Emperor Tiberius and Louis XIV. "This is
wicked, pestilent, and odious despotism," the New Jersey Democrat told the
House. The committee, he raged, planned treason against the Constitution.
He obviously had Bingham's transfer of power in mind.[103]

On February 26, the committee presented Bingham's version to the
House.[104]

Unlike Owen, Bingham had not couched this draft as a limitation on the
states; he wanted to expressly expand the powers of Congress. The House
debated Bingham's language at length, but on February 28 decided to post-
pone consideration by a vote of 110 to 37. The Reconstruction Committee
resumed consideration knowing that the House was not ready to pass such
an express grant of power to Congress.[105]

Stevens presented Owen's draft to the committee on April 21. The committee voted for it 10 to 2, with Rogers and Henry Grider, a Kentucky congressman, casting the only "No" votes. But although he voted yes, Bingham
could not have been satisfied. He saw privileges and immunities as a device
for applying the Bill of Rights to the states, his goal. After voting in favor
of Owen's Section 1, Bingham proposed a new section, one that guaranteed
privileges and immunities, due process, and equal protection. This language
passed as well, with Rogers and Grider again casting the only negative votes.
When the committee met just four days later, on April 25, Senator George H.
Williams, an Oregon Republican, urged striking out Bingham's new section and the committee agreed to that as well, 7 to 5. A few days later, on
April 28, Bingham proposed eliminating Owen's Section 1 and replacing
it with his deleted section, including privileges and immunities. This also
passed, 10 to 3.[106]

On April 30, the Joint Committee on Reconstruction reported Bingham's proposed constitutional amendment:

> No State shall make or enforce any law which shall abridge the privileges or immunities of citizens of the United States; nor shall any State deprive any person of life, liberty, or property without due process of law, nor deny any person within its jurisdiction the equal protections of the laws.[107]

Democrats charged that such general language might lead to a backdoor expansion of federal power on behalf of black rights. (For a summary of Democrats' views on the amendment, see appendix 4, table A4.1.) They particularly worried that Republicans might be surreptitiously slipping black voting rights into the bill. Some historians now argue that Congress mattered more as a protector of rights than the Supreme Court, but Democrats counted on the Supreme Court to vindicate their position and limit privileges and immunities. Perhaps they did so because they believed judicial supremacy logically followed the Constitution's design. The justices themselves have sometimes made that argument. But not all leading American leaders saw such logic in the Constitution's design; Jefferson, Jackson, and Lincoln had all argued that every department of government had equal interpretive authority. Congress, though, rarely challenged judicial supremacy. To do so would imply legislative supremacy, undercutting judicial review, a fundamental principle in the American system. Legislative supremacy was not impossible; the British constitutional system featured a supreme Parliament, its laws unreviewable except by itself. Congress manifestly understood that Americans so completely accepted judicial review that they would never tolerate legislative supremacy. Judicial review represented a fundamental commitment, a thing about which we no longer disagree, to paraphrase the constitutional theorist Keith Whittington. Whittington finds a political basis underlying judicial supremacy, a history of its development, but not for judicial review.[108] The enduring presence of judicial review in the American system apparently explains why Democrats so readily deferred to the judiciary.

This was true even though the fruits of judicial supremacy frightened some Democrats. Andrew J. Rogers, the same man who had accused Bingham of treason, told the House that in *Corfield v. Coryell*, Supreme Court justice Bushrod Washington had found that voting was a privilege or immunity.[109] Illinois Democrat Anthony Thornton said he did not personally believe civil rights included voting, "but with the loose and liberal mode of construction adopted in this age" judges might decide that it did.[110]

Once the Supreme Court implanted an expansive interpretation of privileges and immunities in the Constitution, conservatives worried, there was no telling what some future Congress might do. Unionist congressman Charles E. Phelps of Maryland objected that Congress might one day define the privileges and immunities of citizens so as to include voting, serving on juries, and holding office. Phelps understood "civil rights" as meaning only suing and testifying in courts and being amenable to the same punishments as other citizens. "Privileges and immunities," Phelps warned, are a much broader and more comprehensive term, and may, by definition, include suffrage, jury duty, and eligibility to office. Phelps vigorously opposed black voting. Slavery caused the Civil War, he said, meaning that the war was wholly and exclusively about ending slavery, and nothing more. The proposed constitutional amendment, he argued, might covertly introduce black voting in a way "so artfully framed as almost to escape observation and avoid odium."[111]

New Jersey Democrat Andrew Rogers made the same points as Phelps, warning that privileges and immunities would place blacks on juries, but he did so in language even more apocalyptic.

> If a negro is refused the right to be a juror, that will take away from his privileges and immunities as a citizen of the United States, and the Federal Government will step in and interfere, and the result will be a contest between the powers of the Federal Government and the powers of the States. It will result in a revolution worse than that through which we have just passed. It will rock the earth like the throes of an earthquake until its tragedy will summon the inhabitants of the world to witness its dreadful shock.[112]

Rogers formulated an impressive list of privileges and immunities. According to him, the list would have to include the right to vote, the right to marry, the right to contract, the right to serve on a jury, and, indeed, the right to be president of the United States. And Rogers meant his list to be illustrative only. Adding privileges and immunities to the Constitution, he warned, would prevent any state from "refusing to allow anything to anybody."[113]

Republicans defended privileges and immunities, saying the term had a much more limited meaning than that alleged by the Democrats. (For

Republicans' arguments, see appendix 4, tables A4.2 and A4.3.) Iowa Republican James Wilson said that privileges and immunities covered only great fundamental rights and relied on the great English jurist Blackstone for their meaning. There were just three: personal security, personal liberty, and the right of personal property.[114] Congress should have the authority to enforce such natural rights, he asserted. Minnesotan William Windom agreed, saying that voting was a political right, not one covered by the bill. For good measure, Windom added that privileges and immunities would not award former slaves "social privileges" either.[115]

Five days after Phelps spoke, the House nonetheless passed the proposed amendment.[116] Michigan senator Jacob Howard managed the debate in the Senate. Like Bingham, Howard forthrightly identified the purpose of the privileges and immunities language. The term includes "the personal rights guarantied and secured by the first eight amendments of the Constitution," Howard explained.[117] On June 8, the Senate passed the proposed amendment as did the House on June 13. The secretary of state certified it as the Fourteenth Amendment on July 28, 1868. The Constitution had been amended in a tumultuous political process that had failed to resolve issues on which society was deeply divided. A majority in Congress wanted the federal government to protect citizens' privileges and immunities. Leading proponents of the new amendments, specifically Bingham and Howard, expected that it would give the federal government power to protect rights listed in the Bill of Rights from state discrimination. These rights included trial by jury. Some Democrats feared it would do all that and even more. Some of them took comfort from this, feeling confident that public opinion would decisively shift away from such a drastic expansion of civil rights and the justices would have no choice but to follow suit.

In drafting the Fourteenth Amendment, Bingham and his fellow Republicans consciously constructed organic law from the founding documents. (For these arguments, see appendix 4, table A4.3.) They relied on the abolitionists' definition of citizenship, but every claim regarding rights came either from the 1787 Constitution or the Declaration of Independence.

In assembling the Fourteenth Amendment from existing documents, Bingham wanted to give Congress "the power to pass all laws necessary and proper to secure to all persons . . . their equal personal rights." He clearly did not feel confident that public opinion had changed enough to permit construction of wholly new rights. Better to rely on what everyone presumably, theoretically, already agreed on. He then added, "I desire to see the

Federal judiciary clothed with the power to take cognizance of the question, and assert those rights by solemn judgment, inflicting upon the offenders such penalties as will compel a decent respect for this guarantee to all the citizens of every State." Bingham expected the Supreme Court and all federal courts to enforce citizens' old rights in new ways.[118]

In the 1866 midterm elections, which extended into 1867, the Republicans retained their two-thirds domination of Congress, though in most off-year elections the party in power loses seats.[119] A close look at the results nonetheless suggests the seeds of future shifts in public opinion against what Congress had done. The best place to look for the public's mood is the House of Representatives, since at that time ordinary citizens could not vote directly for their U.S. senators. Those House Democrats who voted against the Fourteenth Amendment but made no speeches or comments about civil rights during the entire session generally retired (see appendix 4, table A4.4). Republicans replaced them about half the time.

Those Democrats voting against the Fourteenth Amendment who made speeches or remarks during the debates often made very racist appeals or offered constitutional arguments based on states' rights (see appendix 4, table A4.1). Of twenty five such men, nine chose not to stand for reelection, and three of those seats were then won by Republicans. Of all the House Democrats running for reelection in 1866, only two stood for reelection and went down in defeat. One was John Hogan, and he had originally won his seat only by a plurality in a three-way race. He actually gained votes in 1866, though not enough to win a two-way race. Kentucky held its congressional races the following May, and Burwell C. Ritter went down in a decisive defeat. But though elected as a Democrat, he had run as a Constitutional Unionist, and a Democrat defeated him. Of all the House Democrats taking decisive positions in Congress against black rights and for states' rights, voters rejected only two. A few Democrats actually benefited from their outspoken opposition to civil rights. The most spectacular example of this came from western Kentucky's First Congressional District. Lawrence Trimble—who expressed his regrets that slavery had not been made permanent constitutionally in 1860—went from 62 percent in 1864 to 85 percent in 1866. This no doubt reflects the pro-southern nature of his district, originally settled by South Carolinians. Western Kentuckians had so sympathized with the rebellion that they tried to secede from Kentucky and join the Confederacy. That effort failed, but through 1866 a low-grade guerrilla war persisted. Such pockets of resistance to civil rights for freed people persisted across the country, even in 1866, a year of Republican triumph. For anyone relying on public opinion as a foundation for civil rights, trouble lay ahead.[120]

By February 1867, Congress had again passed a bill calling for military policing of the southern states. This was a different and better-written version of Trumbull's beefed-up Freedmen's Bureau bill, which had failed in the Senate when Republicans could not find enough votes to override Johnson's veto. The 1867 bill divided the South into military districts and authorized military commanders to arrest and try civilians. It did so only temporarily and called for the states to write their own constitutions, so it had strict limits on federal power. It was, one congressman said, "a mere police bill," though the final version actually did much more than that. While the earlier Freedmen's Bureau bill had the reputation of denying American citizens trial by jury, this bill authorized black voting in elections to create new state constitutions. It seemed more democratic, though, in fact, it also authorized military trials without juries of civilians arrested by the army. In contrast to the uncertainty that had plagued Republicans the previous year, this time they acted with confidence, feeling vindicated by the 1866 elections. They found it much easier to denounce Andrew Johnson, and after a year of violence—one member flatly said the Civil Rights Act had failed—Republicans felt the burden of having abandoned southern Republicans, both black and white, to vigilantes. "The American people demand that we shall do something and quickly," Connecticut Republican Augustus Brandegee said.[121] Henry J. Raymond, an opponent of the bill, acknowledged that there was "no sentiment more deeply rooted in the public mind" than the need to protect Southerners loyal to the Union.[122] The turn in public opinion seemed especially poignant when James R. Doolittle of Wisconsin, a marginal Republican, gave a remarkable speech that bordered on the self-pitying. His own state legislature had denounced him for not supporting civil rights and demanded that he resign. He refused, but the rebuke from his home state wounded him deeply. He delivered a rambling autobiographical lecture pleading his cause to the Senate, but he had obviously lost the support of his constituents by siding with the Democrats. Since he could no longer claim to speak for Wisconsin, he now professed to represent the whole United States, including white Southerners. Later he claimed to have sacrificed his political hopes to his love for and fidelity to the Constitution. "That is a good thing for a boy to do," chortled Timothy Howe, the other senator from Wisconsin, who had been long convinced that the Constitution supported his opposition to slavery.[123] Johnson vetoed the 1867 bill, just as he had vetoed the 1866 Freedmen's Bureau bill, but this time both houses easily overrode the veto the same day they received the president's veto message.[124]

Yet even in this moment of Republican triumph, there were signs that the public had not embraced, perhaps not fully understood, the revolutionary possibilities inherent in the Fourteenth Amendment. Henry J. Raymond of New York correctly warned that there was no unanimity of sentiment supporting military occupation of the South. In New Jersey, the lawyer Joseph P. Bradley thought the Fourteenth Amendment might well have drastically enlarged the powers of Congress to police civil rights. Later, though, he described himself as uncertain, "rather in the condition of *seeking the truth*, than that of dogmatically laying down opinions."[125] Nonetheless, Congress forged ahead, and the South became five military districts, with a general in command of each, ready to appoint new sheriffs and county officials across the South. These new officers would seat black men on southern state juries for the first time in American history.

CHAPTER FOUR

Privileges and Immunities in the Supreme Court

ON AUGUST 9, 1895, DABNEY MARSHALL *put himself outside the law when, accompanied by two cousins, he shot and killed Rufus Tilford Dinkins at the train depot in Brandon, Mississippi.*[1] *Through the newspapers, Dinkins had circulated a rumor that Marshall had committed acts so unspeakable they could not be printed. What the newspapers would not say, though most readers must have realized, was that Dinkins was accusing Marshall of homosexual acts. Marshall believed he had no choice but to confront and shoot the man saying such things about him. Although Marshall followed the South's code of honor and enjoyed a measure of public support for doing so, he nonetheless went to jail and faced the death penalty at trial. For his enemies, though, this was not enough. They wanted to orchestrate those "circumstances of overwhelming humiliation" so characteristic of a shaming ritual.*[2] *Newspaper etiquette did not permit open discussion of homosexuality; it could only be implied or suggested. Marshall's enemies had to find another way to blacken his name. Though Marshall had been in the news because of his writing, his erudition, and his promising political career before the shooting, no journalist had ever before described his physical appearance. Now the silver press reported that he weighed less than ninety pounds, was "very fragile," and had a most unfortunate nickname in a hyper-masculinized culture: "the Little Shrimp." Marshall wore thick glasses but even with correction saw so poorly that he had to ask Dinkins to identify himself before shooting him.*[3] *Dinkins, by contrast, seemed a pillar of masculinity, athletic, married twice, father of children, and able to make an engine or build a house.*[4]

Marshall's obvious guilt and effeminate appearance did not necessarily mean that the majority of white Mississippians would agree that he had dishonored himself by shooting Dinkins. Even in jail awaiting trial, with some newspapers snickering at his appearance and comparing him to Oscar Wilde, the "Little Shrimp" still had cards he could play. His political connections led the best lawyers in the state to his side, including Anselm Joseph McLaurin, who had just been nominated by the Democrats for governor and would, therefore, soon have the power to pardon his client. Congressman Thomas Catchings volunteered to defend Marshall, as did Solomon S. Calhoon, already reputed to be one of Mississippi's best lawyers and destined to serve on the Mississippi Supreme Court.[5] The whole state waited for a spectacular trial. The Jackson Clarion-Ledger predicted—perhaps hoped, since it despised Marshall and wanted his name dragged through the mud for as much as possible—that the trial would be "long and exciting."[6]

There was no trial. Marshall's dream team negotiated a plea agreement that sent Marshall and his cousins to prison but saved them from the death penalty. Rumors immediately circulated that McLaurin would quickly pardon Marshall once he became governor and that Marshall had pleaded guilty to keep Dinkins's slander from being made public. McLaurin denied both charges, issuing a statement pledging not to pardon his client and insisting, perhaps implausibly, that even in a trial what Dinkins had said would never be admitted into evidence and become public.[7]

After Marshall went to prison, the Clarion-Ledger *washed its hands of him, implying with evident satisfaction that it did not expect to hear from the troublesome Marshall ever again: "After today the* Clarion-Ledger *closes its columns to the Brandon tragedy."[8] Misplaced optimism. Marshall would be back, his talents channeled in a direction that lay outside formal politics. When he returned from prison, Marshall would base his attack on the system that had sent him to prison for obeying the dictates of his culture on constitutional principles. The only flaw in Marshall's plan was that he had to operate under rules crafted by the U.S. Supreme Court. He could use the Constitution against Mississippi's prejudiced legal system only to the extent that the Supreme Court's rulings made such a challenge possible.*

The Supreme Court both interprets and constructs constitutional meanings. Interpretation is a legal process in which the judge finds meaning embedded in some legal text, the Constitution, or a statute. Sometimes, however, the text does not have the answer to the particular question that the judge must answer, and he turns to the more creative process of constitutional construction. When constructing constitutional law, the judge cannot honestly claim to have discovered some preexisting, hidden meaning but instead writes law without guidance from the text.[9] In the case of the Fourteenth Amendment, Congress made construction necessary when it finessed the public's divisions and uncertainties about what the Civil War meant. Many Americans shared Democrats' fears of despotism and centralized power, while others favored Republican efforts to expand national power. Both sides knew that the real outcome of the Civil War—the battle over its meaning for citizens' rights—hung in the balance, to be decided by the Supreme Court.

Before the Supreme Court had time to act, though, U.S. Army generals, acting under the Reconstruction Act, ordered southern state judges to admit blacks onto their juries (see table 4.1). On April 27, 1867, Charles Griffin, a Republican-sympathizing general in charge of the military district that included Texas, opened juries to black participation. Subsequently, on May 30, Major General Daniel Sickles, commanding the Second Military District (North and South Carolina), ordered state court judges to draw their jurors from all taxpayers. On August 19, Major General John Pope opened juries in Georgia, Alabama, and Florida, the Third Military District, to black participation, "without discrimination."[10] Whites reacted with shock and indignation. In Texas they angrily demanded to know Griffin's authority. No law authorized federal interference in state trials, they said. They thought it unfair that Griffin could force blacks onto Texas juries, while authorities in northern states continued to keep their juries entirely white. Most of those who argued against black jury service, however, complained that blacks were too ignorant, "even of the commonest circumstances of daily life," to effectively decide cases. One Texas newspaper offered to paint a picture: a distinguished federal judge on the bench, the leading members of the Texas bar on each side, a corporation as litigant, "and in the jury-box, to complete the picture, twelve plantation hands, not one of whom can read or spell his own name." Such a "ludicrous" scene, most whites believed, demonstrated the impossibility of meaningful black jury service. Governor James W. Throckmorton complained to the president, but he also advised state judges to follow Griffin's order. Such severe criticism forced Griffin to explain himself to his superiors. His order was necessary, he said, to protect the lives and property of loyal Texans. Besides, he added, nothing in his order interfered with state requirements that jurors be voters and freeholders, requirements that shut almost every black Texan out of jury service. By the end of 1867, General Winfield S. Hancock had taken command of Texas, and he

TABLE 4.1 Commanding generals' orders regarding jury service in
congressional reconstruction

Military district	States	Commanding general	Date of order	
First	Virginia	John M. Schofield		
Second	North and South Carolina	Daniel Sickles	May 30, 1867	All citizens assessed for taxes and who shall have paid taxes for the current year are qualified to serve as jurors.
Third	Georgia, Alabama, Florida	John Pope	August 19, 1867	Grand and petit jurors, and all other jurors . . . will hereafter be taken exclusively from the lists of voters without discrimination.
Fourth	Mississippi, Arkansas	E. O. C. Ord	September 6, 1867	As freed people bear their share of taxation, no denial to them of the benefit of those laws will be tolerated.
Fifth	Texas, Louisiana	Charles Griffin	April 27, 1867	[P]ersons disqualified by law are drawn to serve as jurors in the civil courts of Texas, directed that hereafter no person shall be eligible to serve as a juryman until he shall have taken the test oath.
Fifth		Joseph A. Mower	September 28, 1867	All persons duly registered in Texas, and no others, will be eligible as jurors.
Fifth		Winfield S. Hancock	December 5, 1867	[T]he trial by jury [shall] be henceforth regulated and controlled by the Constitution and civil laws without regard to any military orders heretofore issued from these headquarters.

Source: Major General D. E. Sickles, General Orders no. 32, May 30, 1867, Order Volume 594; Brevet Major
General Pope, General Orders no. 53, August 19, 1867, Order Volume 598; Brevet Major General Ord, General
Orders no. 25, September 6, 1867, Order Volume 601C; Brevet Major General Joseph A. Mower, Special Orders
no. 151, Order Volume 606; General Winfield Hancock, Special Orders no. 203, December 5, 1867, Order Volume 606, all in RG 94, National Archives, Washington, D.C.; E. McPherson, *Political History of the United States*,
316–25.

backed away from Griffin's order, saying that civil authorities ought not be "embarrassed" by military interference with jury selection.[11]

General Edward O. C. Ord took charge of the district that included Mississippi on March 26, 1867. His superiors had directed him to police the state, protecting "all persons in their rights of persons and property . . . and to punish, or cause to be punished, all disturbers of the public peace and criminals."[12] To Ord the economic foundations that underlay whites' racism made the obstacles to his task especially formidable. The problem lay with poor and laboring white men newly forced to compete for jobs with freed blacks willing to underbid the whites. White laborers would not tolerate the presence of black labor if they could help it, Ord explained to his superiors. Laboring whites violently and bloodily disregarded the laws to save themselves from black economic competition and moreover elected justices and judges to office who would "defer to their feelings and who [would] not punish outrages upon freedmen." Although uncertain at first whether he could legally interrupt the civil law, Ord soon moved aggressively to dismiss sheriffs, mayors, justices of the peace, and other civil officers, replacing them with his appointees. In Vicksburg he made a Union army veteran sheriff and appointed the first black justice of the peace in the state's history. The practical effects of these actions for ordinary Southerners could be seen most clearly in the changing composition of juries. In Vicksburg, Mississippi, no blacks sat as jurors for five years after the city fell to Union forces. In 1869, two years after Congress passed its Reconstruction Act, the first African American grand jurors took their oaths. A year later, blacks made up nearly half of Vicksburg's grand jurors.[13] For the first time in their lives, or the lives of their parents and grandparents, black victims of crime could find institutional sympathy in Mississippi. They may well have thought that things had taken a permanent turn for the better, but the Supreme Court had not yet ruled. Everything accomplished in Mississippi lacked permanence, as it came from a congressional act built on the shifting sands of public opinion.

Ord believed that the distasteful business of policing American civilians should be terminated as quickly as possible. "I am of the opinion that sooner or later the administration of the laws for the government and good of freedmen will have to be left to the legitimate authority of the States."[14] Congress had passed a Reconstruction Act, but how long the public would support military occupation of the South was uncertain. What mattered was how the Supreme Court would rule on crucial questions of national power against state sovereignty.

At this moment, intellectual control of the Supreme Court teetered between Justices Samuel Miller of Iowa and Joseph Bradley of New Jersey, who dueled over what powers the Supreme Court would allow the federal government to exercise over the states. The Court initially approached the problem obliquely, through two celebrated cases that dealt with paper money and the slaughtering of animals for meat in New Orleans. Miller emphasized the importance of public opinion in a way that raised doubts about centralized power; Bradley considered a more principled approach that favored national protection of individual rights. Both men considered where to limit congressional power over rights.

Their contest began amid a fight over legal tender, the traditional battleground for disputes over national power. The Civil War and Reconstruction had shown many Americans the validity of Alexander Hamilton's insight that the path to national power meant getting control of the money. Salmon Chase wanted to mobilize all the nation's resources toward winning the war, even if doing so meant compromising his hard-money philosophy. By February 1862, he had reluctantly concluded that the government had to issue legal tender, paper money. When he lobbied Congress, Chase pointed out that the troops had not been paid in months. The hard-money men in Congress fought Chase's financial treason in debates that raged for weeks, but on February 25, 1862, the president signed into law the first legal tender act, authorizing $150 million in greenbacks. Another legal tender act came a year later.[15]

By putting the federal government in charge of the nation's money, Salmon Chase had enlarged national power just as Hamilton had envisioned seventy-one years earlier. And more, Chase's law had a policing component, making counterfeiting and certain kinds of embezzlement federal crimes. In 1863, Congress appropriated twenty-five thousand dollars to suppress counterfeiting, a figure it increased to one hundred thousand dollars a year later. In 1865, the Treasury Department established the Secret Service, acting administratively without formal congressional authorization. This action promised to permanently involve the federal government in the kind of ordinary police work that once had been the exclusive preserve of the states in a way no temporary military surge into the South could ever accomplish. The Treasury Department organized the Secret Service with offices in most major cities. Agents interviewed witnesses, kept files (with photographs, a controversial step) of likely suspects, developed confidential informants, and gathered clues, the kind of ordinary policing previously performed only by local cops. In the summer of 1871, Attorney General Amos Akerman asked the head of the Secret Service to dispatch agents into the South to investigate the Ku Klux Klan. When Mississippians murdered a U.S. deputy marshal in 1873, Secret Service agents gathered evidence and interviewed witnesses. Attached to the Justice Department as "special agents," members of the Secret Service investigated civil rights violations, infiltrating the Ku Klux Klan to gather information. The Legal Tender Law thus brought federal police into the states and localities.[16]

Democrats condemned Chase's actions not only as an unconstitutional assault on the states' powers but also as an offense that used political muscle to expand national power in violation of deeply held moral values. President Andrew Jackson had established hard money, gold and silver, as the only true "constitutional" currency, they said, meaning that he left politicians no authority to tinker with the value of money. In Congress, Pennsylvania Democrat John L. Dawson said that by introducing legal tender, Chase had sacrificed "constitutional" currency. A serious charge in itself, but Democrats like Dawson believed that Chase's misdeeds went beyond merely violating the Constitution. Like the abolitionists he despised, Dawson saw the Constitution not merely as a political act by a sovereign people but also as an articulation of natural values and moral ethics established by God and not man. Unlike many abolitionists, he believed that the Constitution trusted the states to safeguard such natural values; to the extent that it massed political power in a central authority, the national government threatened nature. When Chase persuaded Congress to pass the Legal Tender Act, he misused national political power against the natural order, according to critics like Dawson. This issue went beyond money. Chase's critics understood that putting the federal government in charge of the nation's currency threatened to expand national power in every facet of life. Dawson feared there might be no stopping a government powerful enough to determine the value of money. He believed in a foundational racial order—also guarded by the states—just as much as he did in a financial order.[17]

Ironically, Chief Justice Chase, the same man who had circulated so much paper money as secretary of the treasury, presided over the Court that would decide the constitutionality of his own program. Even more ironically, although Chase never shared Dawson's racism, he essentially agreed that Congress's power should be curbed and Jeffersonian principles of small government reasserted. He knew that to do this he must roll back the expanded power he had advanced during the war. Chase's contemporaries were astounded by his apparent reversal, but his biography helps explain the true consistency in his thinking. His commitment to human rights reinforced a strong belief in small government. Chase's antebellum legal practice had largely consisted of fights against such federal laws as the fugitive slave acts and for the northern states' right to protect their citizens from a wrong-headed nationalism bent on violating the rights of black Americans. Even on those occasions when Chase advocated national power, as when he urged Congress to abolish the slave trade and end slavery in the District of Columbia, he did so on strict constructionist terms. He simply did not trust national power not based on some text he could put his finger on in the Constitution—the federal government has only enumerated powers, he said, and slavery had not been one of them. Therefore, Chase concluded, Congress must repeal laws tolerating slavery in the District of Columbia and in the territories—the Constitution did not authorize any national legislation on slavery.[18]

The case that Chase and his fellow justices chose to consider came out of Kentucky, where, in June 1860, Henry Griswold had loaned over eleven thousand dollars to Susan Hepburn, expecting to be paid back with gold and silver. Since the Legal Tender law forced creditors to accept devalued paper money instead of the gold and silver originally promised, Griswold went to court, arguing that the Constitution did not allow Congress to print money. It may have been necessary in wartime, he conceded, but by the time he got to court, the war was over.[19]

In 1865, Kentucky's Court of Appeals ruled for Griswold and declared the 1862 Legal Tender Act unconstitutional. To accomplish this, it struck at the heart of the intellectual foundation underlying expanded national power, the celebrated case of *McCulloch v. Maryland* (1819). Though decided long before the Civil War, *McCulloch v. Maryland* stood as the flagship for implied power, repeatedly denounced by antebellum Democrats and cited by wartime Republicans as authorizing expanded congressional power. As the Kentucky judges recognized, *McCulloch v. Maryland* gave an enlarged reading to the Constitution's necessary and proper clause. "Let the end be legitimate," Marshall's Court had declared, "and all means, which are appropriate, which are plainly adapted to that end, which are not prohibited, but consist within the letter and spirit of the Constitution, are constitutional."[20] Kentucky's Court of Appeals conceded that *McCulloch v. Maryland* had settled the question of whether Congress could incorporate a bank. Although the Constitution did not explicitly state that Congress could charter a bank, it implied the power. Not daring to overturn such a monument as *McCulloch v. Maryland*, the Kentuckians distinguished it from *Hepburn v. Griswold*. The power to create a bank was merely incidental to other powers, the Kentuckians maintained.[21] The power to make and regulate money, by contrast, was the "highest and most essential attribute of national sovereignty." Such sovereign powers could never be implied, the Kentucky court declared. The Kentuckians avoided declaring unconstitutional an icon of the Marshall era, but, in effect, they sought to blunt and limit the implied-powers argument that lay at the heart of *McCulloch v. Maryland*. By circumscribing *McCulloch v. Maryland*, the Kentucky Court of Appeals sought to reverse the Republicans' wartime efforts to expand federal power.

The Kentucky judges looked skeptically at the influence of politics on constitutional law. Gold and silver had a "universal standard of value," they said, while paper money had no intrinsic value; its worth was upheld only by "an uncertain and vibrating public opinion."[22] Although they wrote well after emancipation (but before the Thirteenth Amendment had been ratified by the states), the Kentucky judges defended states' rights by insisting that under the Constitution, regardless of popular will, Congress had no power over slavery, a "domestic institution of the states."[23] To defend such conservative values, the Kentucky court pushed for more robust judicial review. Temporary popular agitations to usurp authority, the judges said, would sooner or later be defeated by the Constitution, acting through an independent judiciary, righting the wrong. "Nothing inconsistent with the Constitution can be implied as constitutional," the Kentuckians declared. Leading congressional Democrats had said the same thing when they argued against the Civil Rights Act of 1866 and the Fourteenth Amendment.[24]

On February 7, 1870, Chase issued his opinion in the case, endorsing Kentucky's call for more vigorous judicial review and declaring the Legal Tender Act unconstitutional. Chase explained that the Court had to decide whether a law making legal tender in payments of debts contracted prior to its passage was constitutional. He did not see requiring creditors to take a loss on their loans as incidental to the war effort. "Not every act of Congress," Chase said, "is to be regarded as the supreme law of the land"; that distinction applies only to acts genuinely made in pursuance of the Constitution. Congress could pass laws that impaired the obligation of contracts,

Chase conceded, but only under powers expressly—not implicitly—stated in the Constitution. The argument for the Legal Tender Act proved too much, Chase complained. Claims that the federal government had the power to command creditors to accept greenbacks as an incident to its authority to coin money alarmed the chief justice. "Is there any power which does not involve the use of money?" he asked. Congressional power had to be kept within bounds. Chase wanted to make sure that Congress, and all Americans, understood that federal power had limits and that the Supreme Court would police those limits. This decision dealt a staggering blow to the prospect of continuing a strong national government beyond the Civil War.[25]

To all of this, Justice Samuel Miller dissented, taking the side of national power. Yes, the Civil War had required a massive expansion of congressional power, suggesting a need for powers to preserve the Union only implied in the Constitution. Unlike Chase, Miller thought this expansion should be made permanent, but his commitment to expanded national power was far from certain. Before joining the Court, he had led Iowa Republicans, small-town capitalists invested heavily in land speculation and railroad development. When the 1857 economic recession hit, these small-timers blamed eastern banks and financiers for their financial difficulties. They formed a western wing of the Republican Party that conceived a free-labor/producer ideology so hostile to eastern capitalists that it considered them little better than slave owners. Most Republicans went a different way, but Lincoln was evidently oblivious to Miller's divergence from the majority view when he appointed him to the Court in 1862. Miller came to Washington out of step with many of his fellow Republicans, ambivalent about industrialization and a bitter critic of eastern capitalism. He questioned government's partnership with corporations even though Union success in the Civil War depended, at least in part, on cooperation between government and business.[26]

Historians have generally described Miller as more or less supportive of Reconstruction. Charles Fairman, an early biographer, characterizes Miller as "least out of sympathy" with congressional Republicans' aggressive use of military power to remake the South.[27] The historians Harold Hyman and William Wiecek describe Miller as very nearly a Radical, a term bandied about the halls of Congress often as a slur denigrating those most committed to civil rights.[28] Miller's most recent biographer compares his desire to punish leading Confederates with views held by the most extreme Radical Republicans. Michael Ross charges that Fairman's personal bias against Reconstruction led him to underestimate Miller's commitment to reform. None of these writers has fully come to grips with the recent widespread scholarly recognition that many in Congress did expect to incorporate the Bill of Rights into the Fourteenth Amendment. Miller's picayune view of privileges and immunities is congruent with support for a generous Reconstruction policy only if Republican Reconstructionists never intended the Fourteenth Amendment to enforce citizens' rights listed in the Bill of Rights, but we now understand that they did.[29]

Miller's confidence in the ultimate wisdom of the people led him to favor policies that would encourage sectional reconciliation and to doubt those that looked broadly punitive. Miller also felt constrained by American federalism; he wanted to preserve states' powers. Although he sympathized with freed people's rights, he did so within this context. Miller's thinking can be best reconstructed from the detailed record of his ideas about judges and judging that he left when lecturing law students at National University (now George Washington University Law School) in Washington, D.C., in the winter of 1889 and the spring of 1890. Miller delivered ten lectures, reading from prepared texts. After he died in 1890, J. C. Bancroft Davis edited the lectures for publication, along with two other speeches, finding that Miller had prepared his lectures so carefully that he could publish them "as they came" to him. Miller's lectures reflect his generation's acceptance of the old Jacksonian idea that the Court took a welcome democratic turn with the death of Marshall. When Marshall died, his supporters had praised his commitment to principle and his resistance to the "public clamor" and questioned whether Taney's political enthusiasms and party work did not make him unfit for the Court.[30] Not everyone agreed. Even in its notice of Marshall's death, usually a place for respectful eulogies for the departed, at least one Democratic newspaper could not resist denouncing Marshall as an aristocrat who had distrusted the people's virtue and intelligence. By 1838, Marshall had become too much a figure of veneration for the *United States Magazine and Democratic Review* to criticize him so directly, but it disparaged the "blind veneration" once directed toward "that sacro-sanct tribunal," the Supreme Court. The Court had long acted on false premises, entirely omitting its responsibility to public opinion, the magazine charged. With Marshall gone, the Court could finally achieve "purity" through a better deference to public opinion and steer away from the centralization of power that had so often poisoned the Marshall Court, according to the

United States Magazine and Democratic Review.[31] Democrats did not stop distrusting the judiciary until the 1850s, when they converted it into a backstop for their political game against the Republicans. Still more years had to pass before they began using constitutional doctrine to justify their longstanding attachment to states' rights, a turn hardly consistent with their traditional reliance on majority rule.[32]

Miller embraced the Jacksonian view of how the Court should function. In his version, though, the Court, even under Marshall, had always deferred to the people. Miller manufactured continuity. At National University, he set the theme for his course on the first day when he urged his students to consider public opinion when evaluating court cases. He began with a cliché: "the wisdom of the nation" produced the 1787 Constitution, he said, but then quickly came to his real point, warning that the Constitution did not represent such genius that it could stand on its own, unchallenged. "No amount of wisdom in a constitution," he said, "can produce wise government, unless there is a suitable response in the spirit of the people." The framers of the Constitution did not desire a pure democracy, Miller acknowledged, but they nonetheless determined that "the people should be felt in the direction of public affairs." Miller believed that a written constitution alone could not guarantee the safety or perpetuity of any government. That required "a due reverence" from the people. He paraphrased Alexander Hamilton to describe the judiciary as "the feeblest branch" of government, reliant "upon the confidence and respect of the public for its just weight or influence." Miller examined the canon of great Supreme Court cases in his lectures, focusing on some but hurrying over others as useful only for establishing practical rules. In his discussion of *Marbury v. Madison* (1803), for example, he praised the decision as valuable but never assessed the public's reaction to it and mentioned it only three times. He passed over the *Passenger Cases* (1849) and *Cooley v. Board of Wardens* (1852) in the same fashion, considering them technically valuable for making workable rules but not really a matter of public debate. When it came to property, Miller departed from his usual course and approved checks on any leveling tendencies that the public might support. In John Marshall's contract cases, he found a valuable brake on an impassioned public's challenge to private property. For the leading cases he chose to discuss most often, though, he focused on their power to reflect or shape the public mind. *McCulloch v. Maryland* came up on eight pages of his published lectures, sometimes quoted at length. According to Miller, Marshall wrote *McCulloch v. Maryland* at a time when the "prevailing sentiment of the country and especially of its leading statesmen" favored a central bank. Marshall's decision in favor of the bank succeeded because it had the public on its side.[33]

Similarly, Miller presented *Cherokee Nation v. Georgia* (1831) and *Worcester v. Georgia* (1832) as success stories. The Court's judgments, he said, "influenced the course of legislation by Congress" and in the states as well, suggesting that the Court achieved political success with its opinions. In fact, the Cherokee cases actually stirred up far more political controversy than Miller acknowledged. By ruling in favor of Cherokee sovereignty, Marshall and his Court ran against a strong current of anti-Indian public opinion. Coming near the end of his life, Marshall's work in *Cherokee Nation v. Georgia* was not his best, hesitant with arguments not fully developed, and it failed to unite the Court. A year later, Marshall did much better with *Worcester v. Georgia*, a long and detailed opinion showing that the old man was still in command of his faculties, ordering Georgia to release a missionary it had illegally jailed in violation of Cherokee sovereignty. Jacksonians hated the decision, and Jackson himself remained silent as his followers blasted Marshall and his opinion. In contrast to Miller's positive assessment of Marshall's influence, in reality the Cherokees saw the opinion as "worth no more than the paper it was written on" according to a recent Marshall biographer.[34]

When he got to *Dred Scott v. Sandford*, Miller parted company with the preceding generation of Republicans. In 1857, Republicans had recognized its political dimensions, as did Miller. Abraham Lincoln charged the Supreme Court with following "the necessities of the present policy of the Democratic Party" in its decision.[35] The central pincer in the Republican attack singled out Taney's history, often using Curtis's dissent as a roadmap for criticism, as Lincoln did in his debates with Douglas. "The entire records of the world" offered not one single affirmation that the Declaration of Independence did not include blacks, Lincoln said in Galesburg, Illinois. No living man on earth ever said such a thing—until Taney's opinion, Lincoln asserted.[36] He then focused his attack not on Taney's logic but on the premises underlying that logic. Taney claimed that the Constitution "distinctly and expressly affirmed" slavery, Lincoln pointed out. From this falsehood, Taney reasoned that no law could ever deprive a slave owner of his property.[37]

Both Lincoln and Miller saw the politics in *Dred Scott*. But while Lincoln thought Taney successfully carried out his party's will, Miller saw Taney's decision as a political failure. The case came shortly after Congress had already violated the Missouri Compromise, angering a majority of Americans by recognizing slavery in Kansas and Nebraska, Miller explained. The Missouri Compromise, Miller said, had happily calmed public controversy by dividing the western lands between free soil and slavery along the parallel of 36° 30′ north latitude. Miller believed Taney should have mitigated the controversy that Congress had ignited. Instead, Taney added fuel to the flame. What Miller found most despicable in Taney was his failure to assuage public opinion. Miller himself would not make that mistake, he implicitly assured his students. Had Miller written *Dred Scott*, he would have done so in the spirit of sectional compromise, much like Webster or Clay. Looking back, he criticized Taney for exciting the public's emotions; at the time, Lincoln had been one of the emotionalists.[38]

Miller's view that the Supreme Court should sometimes accommodate or ameliorate public opinion required that he explain the southern public's support for secession and the Civil War. As Oliver Wendell Holmes would later demonstrate, it was certainly possible to defer to public opinion while holding the public—"the thick fingered clowns we call the people"—in contempt.[39] But Miller never showed a hint of such cynicism, even when writing about rebellious white Southerners. He expressed confidence at the outset of Reconstruction that sensible people could agree across sectional lines. He felt "the sentiment of the South was one of acquiescence in the political & constitutional results of the war."[40] Far from anticipating Holmes's cynicism, Miller expected ordinary white Southerners to assess their situation rationally and act for the good of the Union. Somehow, though, Miller had to explain how such reasonable people could go so wrong as to plunge the nation into a bloody civil war in the first place. To solve this problem, Miller followed the lead of congressional opponents of Reconstruction, blaming the Civil War not on ordinary Southerners but rather on their demagogic leaders.

The evidence for this comes from his lifelong friendship with a proslavery white Southerner. In 1842, while still living in Kentucky, Miller had married Lucy Ballinger and befriended her brother, the slave-owning lawyer William Pitt Ballinger. Miller moved to Iowa in 1850, at least in part to find a place free of slavery. William Pitt Ballinger also left Kentucky, but he took his slaves to Texas. During the war, Miller lost contact with Ballinger, but in 1865, the pair resumed both their friendship and correspondence. In their first letters, the two swapped theories about the Civil War. Writing only a few months after Appomattox, Miller still feared the war might resume and emphasized that such a cataclysmic bloodbath must not be repeated. Miller loved his brother-in-law, whom he continually referred to as "brother" even though Lucy Ballinger Miller had died in 1854 and he had married Eliza Winter Reeves in 1856. Nonetheless, his continuing affection did not keep Miller from frankly saying that he favored executing the most prominent and wicked Confederate leaders to prevent further war. He told his "brother," "If you had been the most eminent in guilt of all the rebels," then "you should suffer the highest punishment which the law provides for all."[41]

Miller's enthusiasm for hanging Confederate leaders hardly makes him a Radical Republican. In 1865, real anger at Confederate leaders pulsed through the grassroots, commonly voiced in northern neighborhoods, where residents circulated petitions demanding the death of Jefferson Davis.[42] It is true that some Republicans devoted to reconstructing the South, such as George Washington Julian, favored hanging Confederates. But so did congressmen like Edgar Cowan, a leading opponent of Reconstruction. While Julian wanted to punish Confederate leaders as part of a larger program aimed at reforming the entire South, Cowan *only* wanted to punish those leaders *instead* of reforming the entire South and claimed that most white Southerners had committed no crime at all. Cowan did not agree that secession gave Congress authority to intervene in southern affairs. Former Confederates like Augustus R. Wright of Georgia favored hanging Confederate leaders— rather than punishing the entire South with black voting.[43]

What truly marked the champions of civil rights was their determination to put the whole South under the control of Congress. This notion coursed through the ranks of all Republicans dedicated to civil rights, from the leadership to the backbench. Indiana backbencher Ralph Hill scoffed at the idea of individual responsibility for secession. "There are some crimes which individuals cannot commit," Hill said, adding, "You cannot look to the individual liability of each man engaged in the rebellion for responsibility and punishment, but must look to the stupendous facts of this organized resistance to your authority."[44] Illinois Republican Samuel Moulton blamed "the great mass of the people in the southern States" not only for secession but for continuing disloyalty. White Southerners, he said, still hate Northerners and "are as much rebels and disloyal to-day as they were at any time during the war." For proof Moulton cited vigilante violence, "constant and barbarous outrages."[45] New Yorker Roswell Hart traced the problem of the South to all "the people who [were] within the boundaries of their respective States." Those people overthrew and destroyed their government.[46]

Miller's most recent biographer defends him against charges that he opposed Reconstruction in part by arguing that the justice opposed "sweeping amnesty and pardons for Confederate leaders."[47] Scholars have long criticized Andrew Johnson's pardon policy as the keystone of his effort to
restore old-line white Southerners to power. His "amazing leniency" "reinforced" his image as the white South's "champion," Eric Foner writes.[48]
For Miller's attitudes about Johnson's pardon policy, biographers again rely
on his letters to Ballinger. Charles Fairman quotes Miller's August 31, 1865,
letter at such great length that it hardly seems necessary to go to the original document.[49] But the portions Fairman left out document the justice's
lawyering on behalf of pardons for Ballinger and his friends.

> I fear also you will not succeed in obtaining early action in your cases. I
> think I can discern very clearly in the President's course a determination,
> not to enter in the business of executing pardons or of *considering* ordinary
> cases until he is better advised of the general feeling of the southern people,
> in this I think he is wise.[50]

The Republicans most committed to civil rights had not yet broken with
Johnson in the summer of 1865, but they had their suspicions. Johnson announced his pardon policy on May 29, 1865. Initially it seemed aimed at
breaking the grip of wealthy men on the South, the "slaveocracy": auto-
matic pardons went only to white Southerners with no rank in the Confederate government and holding less than twenty thousand dollars in property. That impression lasted weeks, not months. By mid-June, newspapers
reported that so many leading Confederates had filed petitions for individual pardons that the paperwork overwhelmed the government's clerks. The
most prominent Confederates, including Robert E. Lee and Alexander Ste-
phens, lined up for pardons. On July 4, George S. Boutwell of Massachusetts
assailed Johnson's pardoning as excessive.[51]

Miller, though, resisted such doubts. As late as January 11, 1866, he still
hoped that Johnson would not break with the Republican majority in Congress. He put great faith, he said, in Johnson and in those congressional
Republicans dedicated both to protecting the civil rights of blacks and to
avoiding a rupture with the president. Probably because he shared Johnson's
qualms about black suffrage, Miller considered Johnson's initially negative
reaction to his overtures entirely reasonable.[52] Miller thought Johnson wise
to delay action on pardons to better ascertain public opinion, but his January 11 letter shows the justice willing to personally go to the White House on

behalf of his southern friends. Fairman once again quotes this letter at un-usual length but again excises the portions showing Miller's lobbying. Miller enlisted a friend from Iowa, former congressman Green Adams, on behalf of his clients, but Adams realized that Miller himself would have to put his prestige, name, and reputation on the line to overcome the president's re-sistance. In January Miller wrote Ballinger, "Last Friday, now a week ago, Judge Adams procured the papers in both cases from the office of the At-torney General and said he thought if I would carry them in person to the President that he would grant the pardons."[53]

This Miller would do. When he met Johnson late in the day on January 5, he found the president "jaded and tired," complaining about the "clamor" for pardons. Pardons, Johnson told Miller, could wait. There was no hurry. Miller responded as a lawyer for his clients: "I replied as best I could, with such commonplaces no doubt as he had often heard before. But I told him I was quite willing to share the responsibility of [illegible]. That I was a northern man, and one who would by no means be suspected of too much tenderness for rebels. Next I asked these pardons as a personal favor, and should feel the obligation if granted."[54]

Johnson relented and asked Miller to leave his papers, saying that "he would do the best he could for [him]."[55] So the picture that emerges from the portions of Miller's letters not previously published is one of Miller pressing a reluctant Johnson for pardons.

By March 4, 1866, two months after he had met with the president, Miller recognized that Johnson had broken with congressional Republicans and that the breach could not be healed. Miller nonetheless continued his pur-suit of pardons for his Texas friends, especially Confederate general James Edward Harrison, formerly commander of the Fifteenth Texas Infantry. On March 30, he reported to Ballinger that Green Adams had spoken with Johnson about Harrison's pardon. He told Ballinger that he had not been able to learn more about the pardon because there had been other men present when he met Adams. If Miller had found a chance for a private word with Adams, he would have learned that Johnson had pardoned Har-rison the previous day based on the justice's recommendation.[56]

If Miller's pardon work at least raises questions about his commitment to Reconstruction, his support for legal tender seemingly put him on the side of the Reconstructionists. To sustain paper money, he positioned him-self behind a strong nation-state, exactly where he needed to be to sup-port expanded national power. But Miller would not do this without again affirming the importance of public opinion. He strongly disagreed with the Kentucky court's notion that money had an intrinsic value that should be placed safely beyond the reach of politicians and public opinion. While the Kentucky court had praised universal values and criticized "vibrating public opinion," Miller said it would have been "unwise" for the authors of the Constitution to write "immutable rules" and noted that the 1862 Legal Tender Act had received "almost universal acquiescence" and that a "strong concurrence of opinion" supported it. Miller took a more feeble view of judicial review than that advocated by the Kentuckians. In the face of widespread public approval, Miller asked whether the Court should reverse a law merely because its necessity seemed less clear now than it had in 1862. "Such is not my idea of the relative functions of the legislative," Miller said.[57]

Although Miller rooted his dissent in his reading of public opinion, many newspapers nonetheless hailed it as a true reflection of constitutional principle, ironically misreading it as less political than Chase's majority opinion. The *New York Times* accused Chase of violating strictures laid down by Chief Justice John Marshall in *McCulloch v. Maryland*. Some scholars now argue that given the opportunity, the Taney Court would have overturned *McCulloch v. Maryland*, thus proving the provisional and political nature of even the greatest Supreme Court decisions. The evidence for this theory seems unconvincing. After Chase's Legal Tender decision, the *New York Times* hailed *McCulloch v. Maryland* as a landmark of the Marshall era and berated Chase for daring to contradict its ruling. Marshall, the *Times* pointedly observed, had acted outside politics, with no hint of personal ambition. In those days, the *Times* wrote, with a needling use of the past tense, the Supreme Court "was . . . an august tribunal."[58] In that great decision, the *Times* said, Marshall had found that nothing confined congressional power within narrow limits, but rather Congress could enact "*any*" measure appropriate to a more perfect Union. In this spirit, patriots had approved the Legal Tender law as necessary to save the Union, the *Times* stated. Now Democrats, members of the party of treason, after all, wanted to reverse all of this. Chase upheld "the tone of Kentucky, and of the Democracy which assimilates with that State . . . reversing that of nearly every loyal state."[59]

Miller's chief rival was not Chase but Joseph Bradley, nominated on February 7, 1870, the same day the Court announced its decision in *Hepburn v. Griswold*. On that day, President Ulysses S. Grant appointed two men to the Court who were more unreservedly nationalistic than either Chase or Miller. The significance of Bradley's appointment for national power excited controversy at the time and for decades afterward, primarily because Grant's critics charged that he had "packed" the Court in favor of legal tender. The evidence for assessing this criticism involves Grant's attorney general, Ebenezer Hoar, who later claimed credit for selecting both Bradley and William Strong. There seems little reason to doubt his claim. Years later Charles Francis Adams remembered that Grant took Hoar's advice on judicial appointments "in every instance, but one or two." Grant habitually delegated authority to his cabinet, and Hoar owned up to the choices after receiving severe criticism from his political opponents. Since his enemies charged him with "packing" the Court, he could have quite reasonably defended himself by saying Grant, not he, made the nominations. Instead, he admitted making the choices, pointing out that the timing of the Court's Legal Tender decision and the selection process made the "packing" charge preposterous. Congress passed a law enlarging the size of the Court in April 1869, months before the Court's February 7, 1870, decision. Hoar crafted his recommendations for the Court weeks before Grant made the nominations. Hoar conceded that the Court had privately decided the Legal Tender case in conferences on November 27, 1869, and January 29, 1870, but plausibly insisted he knew nothing of these secret deliberations and that no word of the Court's decisions had leaked to the press. When Chase announced the decision on February 7, Hoar said, it came as a complete surprise.[60]

Hoar had been eager to remake the Court for at least six years, well before he joined the Grant administration. In 1864, he so anxiously awaited Roger B. Taney's demise that he received reports of the chief justice's continued good health with "disgust."[61] When Taney finally did die, Hoar maneuvered to get his cousin William Evarts appointed as chief justice. The two had been talking politics at least since 1852, when they had traded copies of Cicero's writings and gossip about Emerson, a mutual friend.[62] Hoar trusted Evarts to carry out the two principles he thought most vital for a renewed Court. First, the rights of everyone under the Emancipation Proclamation had to be held "sacred." Second, the Confederate states should be welcomed back into the Union only when northern Republicans committed to civil rights were ready. Hoar did not explain the implications of this second point, but Evarts would have understood. Hoar wanted to hold the southern states in a territorial status until their societies and their governments had been remolded by northern Republicans, in a word, reconstructed. Hoar did not think public opinion should constrain this work. In the long run, Hoar believed, the public would come to support a leader taking a strong and resolute stand.[63] Evarts's defense of Andrew Johnson during the president's impeachment trial surprised and offended Hoar, as did his subsequent decision to join Johnson's cabinet as attorney general. These actions raised questions about Evarts's suitability for the Court, Hoar believed, but they were also those of a good friend. He could rationalize his cousin's decision to defend Johnson: "Every criminal has a right to the aid of counsel on his trial," he maintained. Hoar had a harder time with Evarts as Johnson's attorney general. A lawyer had a duty to defend even guilty clients to the best of his ability, Hoar acknowledged, but after the acquittal, if the grateful client should invite his counsel to form a partnership, "some other considerations seem to apply."[64]

Hoar served as attorney general from March 5, 1869, until his dismissal on November 22, 1870. He quickly got into hot water when he defended the constitutionality of military trials of civilians authorized by the 1867 Reconstruction Act. White Southerners insisted that they had functioning civilian courts and resisted military trials, which, they pointed out, denied civilians the right to trial by jury. Hoar's first case came from Texas, where a military commission convicted James Weaver of murder and sentenced him to death. On May 31, 1869, Hoar reviewed the conviction and approved it because Texas had not yet been returned to the Union at the time of the trial; therefore, the military could—and should—supplant civilian courts.[65] In Mississippi a military commission convicted and sentenced to death Edward Yerger for killing an army officer. Protesting his conviction, Yerger filed for a writ of habeas corpus with the U.S. Supreme Court. Hoar again defended military commissions and again insisted that military trials must continue until this most recalcitrant of southern states had been sufficiently reconstructed so that civil authority could safely be restored.[66] In oral argument and in his opinion, Chief Justice Chase objected, saying that once hostilities end, civil authority must resume.[67]

Despite Hoar's stalwart defense of military Reconstruction, those Republicans at the hard core of their party's dedication to civil rights began criticizing Hoar for his supposed lack of commitment to Reconstruction. There was always at least a hint that something other than his opinions on Reconstruction stirred Hoar's fellow Republicans against him. Hoar found the spoils system distasteful and refused to make appointments based on the recommendations of Republican politicians, a position demonstrating integrity but not designed to win friends. Some newspapers disliked him because he threatened to delay construction of a transatlantic cable on the legal "technicality" that Congress must approve such a venture.[68] The carping he received from within his own party rankled Hoar, and he could not conceal his exasperation from the press, which led to a fresh round of criticism.[69] No doubt criticism from the other side was more welcome, and white Southerners obliged by dismissing him as a "Radical."[70] "To the Radicals he seems a conservative and to the conservatives a Radical," the *Milwaukee Daily Sentinel* observed.[71]

During Hoar's time as attorney general, Grant made four nominations to the Court to fill the vacancy following Justice Grier's resignation and the new opening created by Congress: Hoar himself (December 14, 1869; rejected); Edwin M. Stanton (December 20, 1869; Stanton died four days after nomination); and Bradley and Strong. All four nominations were of men committed to national power and distrustful of states' rights. Thereafter Roscoe Conkling, increasingly willing to subordinate his commitment to civil rights to machine politics, persuaded Grant that Hoar had become a political liability. Grant privately explained to Hamilton Fish that while he regarded Hoar as "a true man and friend," he had to go because he lacked the "faculty of making himself popular with politicians." Hoar could be clumsy. Journalists thought him unnecessarily quarrelsome, "cross and surly," according to the *Newark Advocate*. His disdain for public opinion was so obvious that he acted as if he had been "training to look upon mankind as something beneath him," the *Advocate* alleged. Incredibly, his distaste for mere mortals apparently extended even to the Supreme Court. The press snickered that while appearing before the Court, he once dared tell a justice not to interrupt his presentation with a question, an affront that earned him a stern rebuke.[72]

Hoar's departure from Grant's administration had enormous consequences. After Hoar left his cabinet, Grant's Supreme Court nominations went in a different direction, perhaps one more sensitive to public opinion but certainly more respectful of states' rights. It is hard to believe Hoar would have countenanced Morrison Waite as chief justice.

Joseph Bradley and William Strong could each be expected to vote with Miller if the Court should rehear the legal tender question and both exceeded Miller's fealty to national power on other issues. Strong had already upheld the Legal Tender Act while sitting on the Pennsylvania Supreme Court. For two decades, Bradley had been giving vigorous flag-waving speeches narrating American history as a long struggle for national strength against the states' enervating influence. While the defenders of states' rights pointed to the Revolutionary period as proof that state sovereignty had a long history, legitimately emerging from the colonies' conflict with England, Bradley argued that the English had tried to sabotage the colonists by deliberately planting many independent societies on the North American continent. The British, hoping to engineer a diversity of interests that would render each colony dependent on the mother country, had created an obstacle for patriotic Americans to overcome, according to Bradley. He noted that strong jealousies did arise between the colonies, rivalries that continued after independence. Those attending the 1787 Constitutional Convention, he said, had learned to fear the "infinite danger" of such "evils." The Constitution, Bradley believed, had implied great powers for the government, "the most ample powers to preserve, protect, and defend itself." Nonetheless, some political leaders—entirely misguided and mistaken, according to Bradley—contended that the federal government lacked the power to compel the states to obedience. Bradley denounced such "pestilent" heresies with distaste. The U.S. government is supreme, he proclaimed, "in all respects national" with "unlimited powers of self preservation." "So thought every true hearted lover of his Country," he continued, at least those with eyes "not blinded by a superstitious regard for the consideration and importance of the State Governments and the sacredness of state sovereignty."[73]

Hoar may have recommended Bradley for the Court in hopes that he would vote with Miller on any legal tender questions that might recur after *Hepburn v. Griswold*. He would have had to be extraordinarily naive to assume that Chase's decision, whatever its outcome, would be the final word, putting an end to all questions about paper money forever. He certainly considered Bradley a more reliable vote than Miller for a strong national government that increasingly could expect only wavering public support. When Ebenezer Hoar defended himself against charges that he had "packed" the Court, he did so by saying of Bradley: "I knew he was a Republican, and supposed, though I did not know, that he thought the Legal Tender Act constitutional." Hoar then added that he had no reason to believe Bradley more committed to that stance than Chase, who had done so much to pass the Legal Tender law in the first place. In fact, Hoar had every reason to believe Bradley more committed to legal tender than Chase, for exactly the reason he stated. Bradley *was* a Republican, dedicated to nationalism; Chase, in his heart of hearts, was really committed to Jeffersonian small-government principles. He was a Democrat.[74]

Perhaps the key difference between Chase and Bradley can be summarized in this way. Chase genuinely favored black civil rights but could not bring himself to support the national power necessary to enforce those rights. Bradley, by contrast, had little interest in black civil rights but supported national power. Unfortunately, the extant evidence does not allow easy confirmation of this hypothesis. Historians traditionally rely on a subject's letters and private writings to reconstruct personal feelings, and Bradley's extant letters reveal little about his views on slavery or race. His library, though, can be partially reconstructed, and this evidence suggests that, in fact, he did have considerable interest in race and civil rights. He must have been a member of the American Colonization Society, as he owned its annual reports from 1825 to 1849. He prepared for his own use a two-volume collection of twenty-three pamphlets related to colonization and slavery.[75]

Bradley puzzled over the question of black inferiority as a scientific issue. He had an enduring curiosity about all things scientific, but the opponents of civil rights may have convinced him that questions of civil rights turned on natural science more than anything else. To rebut claims that blacks had a natural right to vote and a natural claim to other rights, the opponents of civil rights depended on science. Nobody in Congress made the scientific argument more clearly than Republican congressman Thomas T. Davis, who cited learned texts "proving" a racial hierarchy with whites at the top and Africans at the bottom. Davis and his allies presented these scientific "realities" as timeless, but actually the path to racial distinctiveness was long and tortuous. For nineteenth-century scientists, the seemingly empirical reality of racial distinctiveness ran afoul not only of the Bible but also of such formidable eighteenth-century naturalists as Linnaeus (1707–78) and Samuel Stanhope Smith. Linnaeus and Smith agreed with the Bible: all humans belonged to the same species, and all had a common ancestry, however remote. This was the science behind the Declaration of Independence. Beginning in the 1830s, Dr. Samuel George Morton led a spirited scientific rebellion against this orthodoxy. Others had preceded Morton in this direction, but he seemed to have the evidence: a huge collection of skulls, all carefully measured to prove European superiority. The fruits of Morton's challenge to Linnaeus and Smith became the science behind political resistance to civil rights. Davis could point to such academic stars as Jeffries Wyman (1814–74), the Harvard anatomist, but also to leading academic texts, including Josiah Clark Nott and George R. Gliddon's *Types of Mankind* (1855); Louis Agassiz and Augustus A. Gould's *Principles of Zoology* (1870); William Lawrence's *Lectures on Physiology, Zoology and the Natural History of Man* (1828); and Charles Hamilton Smith's *Natural History of the Human Species* (1852).[76]

Bradley interested himself in the question and purchased two books that Davis had used to make his argument, Lawrence's *Lectures* and Nott and Gliddon's *Types*. He also found a book that Davis did not mention, Charles Pickering's *Races of Man and Their Geographical Distribution*. From 1838 to 1842, Pickering (1805–78) had accompanied the U.S. Exploring Expedition, studying over two hundred islands and the coasts of North and South America. Pickering developed a view strikingly contrary to the certainty of white superiority. Pickering thought he could identify at least eleven human races, but he followed Linnaeus and Smith in finding that all belonged to one species and further that the African and European races did not differ in their intellectual faculties. The closest student of Pickering's writings contends that the scientist muddled his message in the face of political hostility for his unorthodox views. For all its confused verbiage, however, *The Races of Man* nonetheless offered Bradley a challenge to the idea of white superiority.[77]

In similar fashion, he owned proslavery writings but also abolitionist books, including a collection of Henry Ward Beecher's sermons and a copy of *The Iron Furnace*, by John Aughey, a white Southerner who had fled the South because he hated slavery and loved the Union. In part due to his own outrageous declamations (made in Supreme Court opinions written after Miller's *Slaughterhouse* triumph), Bradley can seem a two-dimensional villain on civil rights. Women should stay home and out of the job market, and after three centuries of slavery black people should snap out of their doldrums and take care of themselves, expecting no special favors from the government, he declared in 1874 and 1883, respectively.[78] The journalist Charles Lane has recently argued that these views represented a consistent pattern of prejudice. Bradley had long tolerated or even supported slavery, Lane writes, suggesting that racism consistently controlled his thinking long before his unsavory remarks made after the *Slaughterhouse Cases*. This is supposedly proven by his efforts to amend the Constitution in 1860 as well as remarks made while campaigning for Congress in 1862. In 1860, Bradley wanted to avoid civil war by reversing the Supreme Court's *Dred Scott* decision, proposing an amendment that would have restored the Missouri Compromise. This indeed would have preserved slavery in a portion of the West, but Bradley later seemed troubled by his own appeasement, saying that at the time he would have done "anything in God's name" to avoid war, a sentiment shared by Miller and most other contemporary political leaders.[79] When running for Congress in 1862, he did indeed remind his audiences that he had never been an abolitionist, something so obvious that his listeners erupted in laughter. This sounds, though, like a politician currying favor with backward voters, and Lane omits Bradley's support for the Thirteenth Amendment, something he did in a way that paralleled positions taken by those Republicans most strongly committed to civil rights. Charles Sumner, Bradley said early in 1865, was right: states that seceded had no right to interfere with the loyal states' efforts to abolish slavery. Bradley took the "conquered provinces" approach so often associated with Sumner and his fellow "Radicals." If a state secedes, he said, "the general Government has a right to occupy the obnoxious territory" and "to impose such condition of habitancy therein as it sees fit to do . . . as it would have a right to do in relation to any conquered or purchased territory."[80] No doubt Bradley was not as attached to the antislavery movement as Chase, but his library as well as his support for the Thirteenth Amendment suggest he could at least consider some level of civil rights.[81] While Bradley did not neatly reverse Chase's distrust of national power and support for civil rights, he definitely came to the Court supporting national power and did not reflexively embrace racial antipathy.

Hoar understood that any justice, once on the Court, might well be swayed by some new argument that overcame his predispositions. But justices do not only hear arguments in court. Their closest friends wield considerable influence. Bradley's confidant Frederick Frelinghuysen served as an influence to keep him on track, reinforcing his ideas about expanded national power and progressive thinking. Frelinghuysen had been New Jersey's Republican senator until 1869, when the Democrats regained control of the state legislature and ousted him. As a private citizen, he lobbied for Bradley's confirmation, no doubt wanting a Jersey man on the Court. Frelinghuysen's support, though, went beyond such provincialism. He and Bradley had attended Rutgers together. Bradley had come from poverty and wore homespun clothing made by his mother. Frelinghuysen appeared in clothing that was anything but homespun; he had an elite background and was part of a political dynasty. Frelinghuysen was the nephew and adopted son of Theodore Frelinghuysen, New Jersey senator from 1829 to 1835. The elder Frelinghuysen so fervently supported Indian rights against Andrew Jackson's Indian removal program that contemporaries called him the "Christian Statesman." Like his adopted son, he became president of the American Bible Society. Although Bradley and Frelinghuysen came from dramatically different backgrounds, their shared commitment to Christianity drew them together, across the class divide. They became fast friends.[82]

In addition to his friendship with Bradley, Frelinghuysen believed that getting Bradley on the Court might reverse the Court's decision on legal tender. His extant letters during the confirmation effort make no reference to the legal tender question, but afterward he confided to his friend his hope that he would overturn Chase's decision.[83] Frelinghuysen was a rich man, a creditor who stood to lose money through the Legal Tender law. This seems a paradox, but Frelinghuysen's elite background actually helps explain why he would favor soft money to the advantage of debtors and disadvantage of his own creditor class. Although he profited from industrialization, its pace alarmed Frelinghuysen's religious sensitivities. Frelinghuysen could see that industrialization created a new generation of capitalists who did not share his sense of national mission and brotherhood with the working classes. This actually threatened the class structure that God had sanctioned. Since Frelinghuysen could all too easily imagine class warfare leading to an apocalyptic meltdown of the whole capitalistic system, this development especially worried him.[84]

On March 21, the Senate confirmed Bradley, and the next day the new justice picked up his commission from the attorney general; he took his seat on the Court on March 23.[85] Almost immediately the government moved the Court to reopen the legal tender question. In their secret conferences, the justices quarreled bitterly. Miller accused Chase of using "all the strategies of the court" and "trickery" to prevent a rehearing of the issue. Miller wrote that he had to marshal his forces against Chase and keep up their courage. It was an exhausting effort, he confided to Ballinger.[86] Anyone arguing that Bradley's nomination and confirmation had nothing to do with reopening the legal tender question must contend with the sequence of events that played out through the week of March 21, 1870 (see table 4.2). The conclusion seems inescapable: Hoar saw the confirmation of his picks for the Court as an opportunity to be exploited—an opening to rebuild the national power that Chase had demolished—and moved with almost indecent haste.[87]

No wonder white Southerners, so protective of their states' sovereignty, chafed at the two nominations. They recognized what the legal tender case meant for national power and with good reason feared that Strong and Bradley intended to restore congressional authority, amounting to a "radical" effort to turn the Court away from the Constitution's guarantees of

TABLE 4.2 Calendar of events for reopening the legal tender cases

Monday March 21	Tuesday March 22	Wednesday March 23	Thursday March 24	Friday March 25	Saturday March 26
Bradley confirmed by the U.S. Senate.	Bradley meets Hoar and picks up his commission.	Bradley sworn in and takes his seat on the Court.		Hoar asks the Supreme Court to reconsider its legal tender decision.	In conference, the Court agrees to reconsider its legal tender decision.

states' rights. The *Daily Arkansas Gazette* called Strong more a "radical artisan" than an "impartial judge."[88] In South Carolina, the *Charleston Courier* approved Chase's original decision and thought that with Strong and Bradley the Supreme Court "ceased to be the organ of, or the authority for law."[89] There were opponents of continued national power outside the South as well. The *San Francisco Daily Evening Bulletin* thought the appointment of Strong and Bradley, coming simultaneously with the decision, was "calculated to weaken popular confidence" in the Court. The *Bulletin* added that rumors circulated that Bradley had advised the directors of the Camden and Amboy Railroad to hold off acting under *Hepburn v. Griswold*. This was a "scandalous intimation," the *Bulletin* fumed.[90] The *New York Tribune* found "universal" "alarm concerning the purity of [the nation's] judiciary."[91] The *Nation* blamed the appointments on "a few politicians and moneyed corporations" and called the affair a "political intrigue" and an "outrage on all the national ideas of respect for law."[92]

Bradley, more than Strong, emerged as the leading challenger to Miller. Miller saw himself as striving to keep the Court on course, to make it, as he said, "a court of law, and of justice."[93] Miller certainly wanted to dominate the Court, keeping it on his course, with a proper appreciation for public opinion. Bradley, between 1870 and 1874, pressed Miller for control of the Court, basing his challenge at least in part on his conviction that nature defined rights apart from the political process. Religion offered Bradley one alternative to Miller's reliance on popular approval; a judge convinced that his judicial reasoning followed religious principles could, somewhat, set aside public reactions to his rulings, confident he had the higher power on his side. Miller was not an irreligious man; he had converted to Unitarianism when he moved to Iowa, but he did not follow Unitarianism beyond its limits as had some Boston intellectuals. Unitarianism had become popular

in Boston early in the nineteenth century before spreading outward, rejecting dogma and emotionalism for a more rational—and skeptical—reading
of the Bible, and offering a rationale for questioning all authoritative texts.
Unlike previous Massachusetts religious leaders, early nineteenth-century
Bostonian Unitarians looked within themselves not for original sin but for
an innate moral sense common in all individuals.[94]

Bradley was no Unitarian; he had united with the Dutch Reformed tradition early in life, but he joined the Supreme Court at a time when American
culture had reified Ralph Waldo Emerson, the Unitarian minister who had
famously exploded the boundaries of Unitarianism. Emerson alone did not
move American culture, but he became the icon for individualism, personal
reflection, and a commitment to higher law. Emerson served as pastor of a
Unitarian church from 1829 to 1832, preaching 164 sermons that increasingly questioned standard Unitarian principles.[95] For Bradley the universe
of ideas that Emerson came to represent eventually roughly paralleled his
own thinking in a way they never did for Miller.

Neither judge could possibly have been oblivious to the ideas associated with Emerson. By the end of the Civil War, Emerson's thinking had
become pervasive in American culture, at least among the educated and
literate. He gave lectures across the country, his name appeared in newspapers thousands of times, and the press printed columns of his aphorisms.
The first collected edition of his writings appeared in 1866, a second, *The
Prose Works of Ralph Waldo Emerson*, came out in 1869, and publishers
produced numerous collections throughout the 1870s. Hardly any thinking
person or even a casual reader of newspapers and magazines could escape
his influence.[96]

Emerson championed individual rights. Rights came from nature, he
said, which meant they could not be conferred by institutions or authorities but only recognized and enforced. Emerson developed a deep skepticism about the Bible or any other existing path to moral truth, but he never
abandoned his faith in absolute truth. Every individual must search for "the
law of the soul," a quest necessarily pursued without maps or markers, according to Emerson, but one with a single destination nonetheless. He told
one audience, "You cannot conceive yourself as existing . . . absolved from
this law which you carry within you." Emerson cautioned his followers to
be wary of the state; every individual must define his personhood apart
from any group, and he sometimes measured each individual's worth by his
or her opposition to the group. Some scholars have emphasized Emerson's

commitment to the democratic potential inherent in the Declaration of Independence, but others, especially Judith Shklar, have observed that Emerson struggled to reconcile his belief in an intellectual hierarchy—only a few special people had minds capable of finding higher law—with democracy. "Men who make themselves felt in the world," he wrote, know how to use "a certain fate in their constitution." The few people equipped with this "fate" can see and hold "the central reality." "Good men" have good visions, Emerson believed, but he worried about everyone else, those with "the undisciplined will that is whipped with bad thoughts and bad fortunes." In his darker moods, and Emerson could be quite moody, he had real contempt for the masses and condemned anyone relying on the brute force of numbers for truth. Just because most people favored something did not make it right, Emerson believed. In that sense, Emerson sharply broke with a tradition dating back to the medieval era, when the poet William Langland's text *Piers Plowman* urged the king to seek "the commons' help." Emerson had a deeper skepticism for "commons," meaning common people. Those people capable of finding truth, he said, did so alone, in private reflection. There was no wisdom in crowds. Truth did not emerge from the tumult of public debate.[97]

Nothing in Emerson's distrust of politics could possibly have appealed to Miller, while Bradley, on the other hand, may have been particularly receptive. Though he grew up on a hardscrabble farm, his parents encouraged reading, and Bradley made "frequent explorations into the town library," his mind running more toward the practical and the mathematical than the philosophical. He taught himself algebra and surveying with borrowed books. A college friend remembered him as "eccentric," "a most peculiar man," "a man who did his own thinking," all suitable descriptions for Emerson as well.[98] For an energetic reader with a curious mind known for independent thought—even one who favored algebra over literature—Emerson's influence would have been hard to avoid, and although Bradley appears not to have purchased any of Emerson's books, he did own works that summarized Emerson, including the *Concord Lectures on Philosophy*, a commemoration of transcendentalism and Emerson.[99] He also read the *Atlantic Monthly*, founded in 1857 by Francis Underwood and a group of New England writers that included Emerson. Emerson had expected the *Atlantic Monthly* to defy the public and majority rule, leading and not following cultural trends. The articles he contributed articulated the major points from his oeuvre: the need for solitude, his support for abolition, and his confidence in a "central reality" visible to "good men."[100] The *Atlantic Monthly* confidently reported that the United States had made steady progress toward "a broad ideal of national authority." States' rights did survive, the magazine conceded in a spate of overoptimistic enthusiasm, but the principle was no longer a living force.[101]

By the 1850s, one biographer has written, Emerson had become "dangerously famous," such "a conspicuous part of the literary landscape" that his fame threatened to take on a life of its own, distinct from the reality of his accomplishments. One scholar states that Emerson was "as inescapable a presence in America's intellectual and cultural life as Lincoln was in its politics," comparable to Shakespeare. Like very few intellectuals, Emerson insinuated his insights into the language. "All life is an experiment," he said in words a later member of the Supreme Court would find compelling.[102] In the 1830s, Emerson had been avant-garde; in the 1870s, his insights had become commonplace. During the Civil War, he had put himself on the right side of history, joining the abolitionists, supporting the war effort against slavery, and favoring Reconstruction. Frederick Douglass's writings show some familiarity with Emerson, though Douglass espoused a self-reliance more down-to-earth than transcendental. When Kentucky's Senator Garrett Davis said, "The creator placed man on earth not for perfection of the individual but for the perfection of the race," he clearly had Emerson in mind as his foil.[103]

Emerson's influence seems apparent when Bradley urged his son, "Adhere to God's law which will guide us into the true way," but he nonetheless confided his doubts about the common maxim that all wisdom comes from the Bible. Bradley had studied the Bible carefully; he owned forty-one editions and commentaries, 2 percent of the titles in his personal library. "There is a great deal there certainly," Bradley admitted, adding, "If a man wants to find [wisdom] there, by ingenious construction he can make it out." Bradley, then, shared Emerson's doubts that the Bible had a monopoly on wisdom. "There is much in the profound reflections of the thoughtful in every age," Bradley said and urged his son to peruse the newspapers looking for wisdom, "pithy things—things that have wisdom in them." Bradley and Emerson shared faith in higher law and an agnosticism about traditional methods of finding it.[104]

Emerson made a name for himself promoting universal truths higher than American law or even the U.S. Constitution, becoming a spokesperson for an American individualism so cosmopolitan that, according to one writer, it anticipated globalization. Emerson, in the words of the scholar

Gregg Crane, rejected "law as a tribal inheritance." Unlike Daniel Webster, who believed the national identity produced justice, Emerson searched for ethical norms outside the United States, outside Christianity.[105] So did Bradley. He owned the Koran, the Book of Mormon, James Legge's *Life and Teachings of Confucius*, and the British Museum's facsimile of the Egyptian *Book of the Dead*. He collected dictionaries and grammars of Sanskrit, Latin, Greek, Russian, Hebrew, Italian, Arabic, French, Dutch, and Gaelic. Holding court on the borderlands between the United States and Mexico, he confronted unfamiliar legal systems, land disputes involving Spanish land grants and law from Spain, Mexico, and the United States, truly terra incognita for a New Jersey lawyer. Bradley labored over the unfamiliar principles, but he gloried in the work, delighting in the collision between cultural worlds. According to one theory, Bradley lived at a time when borderlands had effectively become "bordered lands," but he could still sentimentalize the mingling of diverse traditions and look forward to a rejuvenation of law based on cultural exchange rather than national identity.[106]

Bradley was hardly the first judge to find foreign law helpful. American judges have relied on foreign law since the very beginnings of the nation. John Marshall used foreign law, citing the French theorist Montesquieu, the Dutch legal scholar Cornelis van Bynkershoek, the Swiss legal scholar Emmerich von Vattel, and the English scholar Joseph D. Chitty.[107] Taney had used foreign law and concepts when he wrote *Dred Scott v. Sandford*. But although Bradley did not introduce foreign law into American jurisprudence, in his most private moments, he really luxuriated in the work of understanding foreign legal concepts, which he easily reconciled with his fervent nationalism. "What a great country ours is," Bradley exulted to his son, "lying at the breasts of so many traditions and grand histories, and making the milk of political wisdom form so many fountains."[108] To his students, Bradley said that the same "uniform and permanent principles" govern all law in every society, in any nation. For this reason, no person in any community need become learned in local law to live a peaceful life. Echoing Emerson, he believed the individual could look within himself for transcendent legal values: "All he has to do is follow the dictates of his conscience and endeavor to do right." Law is not arbitrary but immutable, Bradley asserted, visible to anyone willing to "gaze profoundly into its depths" and gain that insight only available through "deep study and reflection." By this standard, all law comes from nature. All rights are natural.[109]

In his writings, Bradley loved to cite not Emerson but the ancient writers, especially the Roman lawyer Cicero (106–43 BC). Charles Fairman has

plausibly suggested that Bradley first came to his conclusions and then orna-
mented what he had already decided with quotations from Roman sources.
This suggests the real influence must have come from sources more commonly available than Cicero, someone like Emerson, for example, but Bradley did use Roman writers to instruct his son. In his private writings, he referred to Cicero, analyzed Cicero, reflected on Cicero, and urged friends
and kin to read Cicero. He admired a passage from Cicero saying there
is only one true law, and it is "conformable to nature." Cicero saw Julius
Caesar defy the Roman Senate to invade Italy after campaigning in Gaul.
Knowing the Republic needed a single, coherent law not only to unite its
expanding territories but to control wayward generals as well, Cicero favored higher law. "Neither the Senate nor the People can absolve private
dictates," Cicero said. The "private dictates," of course, were the voice of
conscience, where natural law found its lair. This natural law is the same
everywhere; "it is not one thing at Rome, another at Athens." Since it comes
from within, "he who would refuse its obedience must fly from himself,"
Bradley quoted Cicero as saying. "A splendid passage," Bradley told his
son.[110] Bradley used Cicero to promote nationalism over states' rights. Cicero, as Bradley used him, served as a classical proponent of cosmopolitan ideas about rights that many Americans had come to associate with
Emerson by 1870.

Bradley came to the Court ready to defend the power that Congress had
gained during the Civil War. Some of Bradley's earliest writings suggest he
harbored progressive views, even as he had labored on behalf of New Jersey railroad corporations. In 1864, he lamented to his daughter that "the
practices of society offer but little opportunity for a woman to earn her
bread alone, and occupy an independent position." Despite this grim assessment, Bradley held out hope for the future, writing that "the times are
gradually improving in that respect, and I hope to live to see the day when
an industrious woman can earn a livelihood as well and as honorably as an
industrious man."[111]

In 1867, Bradley had traveled through New Orleans on his way to Cuba
for a vacation. This was his first foray into the South, and the letter he wrote
his daughter offers at least a hint of his attitudes toward the South and race.
Conversations with well-to-do white Southerners whom he found in and
around the St. Charles Hotel fascinated Bradley, and he wanted to share
what he had learned with his daughter. Even two years after the war, the
white people he met still seemed "secesh," or prosecession, Bradley ob-

served. "They look upon themselves as a conquered people," he told his daughter and then added one of the few observations he made based on his own thinking: "And I fear [they] will have to suffer still more before they will give up their cherished notions of a great Southern Confederacy." When he looked beyond politics, Bradley's conversations with white Southerners gave him some reason for optimism. The soil was rich and valuable, he reported before telling his daughter that the planters had warned him that if labor became too expensive it would leave southern plantations idle, "a desert waste." The economic consequences of emancipation have yet to be understood in the North, Bradley wrote, again clearly echoing what he had heard property-owning Louisiana whites say. Bradley formulated the problem white landowners faced entirely on white terms: how to keep freed people on the plantations. The answer, Bradley offered, was to pay them proper wages. Bradley also reported that "the people here" disliked the Freedmen's Bureau because they thought it interfered with their labor, but again Bradley did not offer his own view.[112]

In May 1870, Bradley headed south to take up his circuit duties, meeting Circuit Judge William B. Woods for the first time. Born in Ohio, Woods had fought in the Civil War on the Union side under Sherman, became a general, and then settled in Alabama. Appointed to the Fifth Circuit in 1869, he had been holding court across the South for a year when Bradley joined him. The two faced the most contentious issues of Reconstruction.[113]

During his first tour of the Fifth Circuit, Bradley heard the case that would prove crucial to the Supreme Court's determination of civil rights after the Civil War. In 1869, Louisiana's Republican-dominated legislature passed a law monopolizing all slaughtering operations in New Orleans in a single slaughterhouse. The numerous independent butchers, accustomed to operating in small shops scattered around the city, sued under the Fourteenth Amendment. Their lead attorney, John A. Campbell, argued that the Fourteenth Amendment's privileges and immunities clause protected workers from onerous state legislation. The law had been passed by Louisiana's Republican-dominated legislature, and John A. Campbell led the butchers' legal team. He used litigation politically, to attack Republicans and the whole idea of Reconstruction. Campbell confided to his daughter, "We have the African in place all about us." Blacks served as jurors, Campbell told his daughter, and confided that he wanted to put a stop to such public service by former slaves, "by any means necessary."[114] Campbell's political motives initially repelled both Bradley and William Woods.[115]

Bradley and Woods nonetheless set aside their distaste for Campbell and did what he asked. Bradley's opinion began by identifying the question to be answered: "whether the fourteenth amendment to the Constitution is intended to secure to the citizens of the United States of all classes merely equal rights; or whether it is intended to secure to them any absolute rights." Bradley argued for a broad reading of privileges and immunities. The privileges and immunities clause, he said, "embraces much more" than the rights protected by Article IV. It is possible, Bradley speculated, that the Fourteenth Amendment means more than its authors intended:

> If the amendment, as framed and expressed, does in fact bear a broader meaning, and does extend its protecting shield over those who were never thought of when it was conceived and put in form, and does reach social evils which were never before prohibited by constitutional enactment, it is to be presumed that the American people, in giving it their imprimatur, understood what they were doing, and meant to decree what has in fact been decreed.[116]

Bradley then asked, "What, then, are the essential privileges which belong to a citizen?" Answering his own question, Bradley stated that it would be "difficult to enumerate or define them" and cited the Supreme Court as saying it would be unwise to do so. Bradley did not explain this in his opinion, but he and Woods must have realized that a federally protected right to labor, while useful to white Democrats in the short term, would be helpful to freed people far more often and in the longer term.[117] Bradley's opinion, though aimed at a state law, makes little of state action; he is more concerned with *not* setting limits on the rights that Congress could protect than with defining limits of such new powers.

While on circuit each summer, Bradley wrote letters home to his family and to Frelinghuysen, who returned to the Senate in 1871. During the rest of the year, he corresponded with Woods, who looked to him for advice and help in understanding just how the Fourteenth Amendment had, or had not, expanded the powers of Congress to protect individuals' rights. Woods's greatest concerns came from a case in Alabama, where the U.S. district judge was Richard Busteed, a Lincoln appointee. Beginning in 1865, Busteed rotated between Mobile, Montgomery, and Huntsville, trying to teach grand juries that congressional laws enforcing the Fourteenth Amendment really were constitutional. Conservative white Southerners called him a carpetbagger, pointing out that he had no permanent home in Alabama and seemed corrupt as well as incompetent. Assassins tried to kill him in 1867. Every lawyer not working for the government insisted that the enforcement acts violated state sovereignty. By the time he resigned his seat and fled the state to avoid impeachment, Busteed had compromised his principles, denying before Congress that Alabama vigilantes presented any special problem in his jurisdiction. He apparently faced such violent resistance to civil rights enforcement that he found it easier to agree with his opponents that the problem did not exist than risk the peace and his personal safety.[118] Throughout the fall of 1870, as white Democrats threatened and harassed Republicans, the Republican member of Congress from western Alabama's Fourth Congressional District, though a former Confederate army officer, would not publicly acknowledge Klan violence for fear of assassination. Witnesses daring to testify in federal court faced brutal beatings or even death.[119] The Ku Klux Klan was so active in the western counties that Republicans hardly dared pass unescorted through that part of the state. In Greene County, the Klan took a black Republican leader named Gilford Coleman from his home, murdered him, and mutilated his body. Soon afterward another black leader perished. The climax to the violence came on October 25, when Republicans scheduled a political rally in Eutaw, the county seat of Greene County. Some 2,000 blacks attended, but some 160 armed white belligerents showed up as well. Whites began their harassment with taunting catcalls and then escalated to gunfire, shooting 54 people, including 4 mortally. White youths then took the train home, hooting in triumph.[120]

When the Eutaw riot occurred, Amos Akerman had been attorney general since the previous June, replacing Hoar. A former Confederate soldier from Georgia, Akerman nonetheless proved a stalwart foe of the Ku Klux Klan and an enforcer of civil rights laws. He believed in "a sternly just God" and in the rule of law. "Our cause is either right or wrong," he wrote. "If right, we should adhere to it fearlessly and never abandon it."[121] Akerman complained that Northerners did not really grasp the depth of the southern problem, in part because their minds assumed progress and fled from the past. "Even such atrocities as Ku Kluxing do not hold their attention, as long and as earnestly, as we should expect," he said. Akerman brought up the Klan so often at cabinet meetings that the Northerners on Grant's cabinet thought him obsessed. Columbus Delano, the secretary of the interior from Ohio and a former congressman, began maneuvering for Akerman's removal. Despite such machinations, Akerman campaigned for clean elections throughout the fall of 1870. The press reported that this time the government's lawyers "mean business."[122]

Akerman's determination to prosecute violence of the sort whites used in Eutaw probably does not fully explain the prompt federal reaction to the riot. A Eutaw man named Samuel B. Brown traveled to Demopolis, where he met Woods and filed a complaint. Brown was apparently not a leading Republican. He was not on the speakers' platform, and Democrats identified him only as a "radical Republican." As U.S. attorney, John P. Southworth might have taken Brown's complaint, but his name does not appear on the document; instead, Woods transcribed the narrative himself, in his own hand (see fig. 4.1).[123]

Woods translated Brown's narrative into a complaint that made two charges. First, he accused fourteen white men with violating the First Amendment free-speech rights of William H. Smith, Lewis E. Parsons, Willard Warner, and Charles Hays. He then accused the white Democrats of conspiring with intent to prevent himself, Isaac Clark, Samuel W. Cockrell, William Miller, A. L. Davis, Lewis E. Parsons, and Charles Hays "from exercising and enjoying the right or privilege granted or secured to them by the Constitution" (see fig. 4.2). Woods's version of Brown's narrative assumed that the Fourteenth Amendment had incorporated the Bill of Rights and accepted the Enforcement Act approved by Congress approved on May 30, 1870, as applicable in Eutaw. The U.S. commissioner at Demopolis, James Gillette, issued warrants for the arrest of the men whom Brown accused and summonses for the witnesses he named.[124]

Election day, November 8, passed quietly as large numbers of African Americans either did not vote or voted Democratic out of fear and intimidation. State officials did nothing toward charging the whites with criminal offenses, although officers did arrest some of the black victims for trying to defend themselves.[125] Federal officers moved ahead with Brown's complaint. A week after the election, Gillette began putting the defendants on four-thousand-dollar bonds to guarantee their appearance in court.[126]

On December 24, 1870, two days before a federal grand jury indicted twenty Eutaw rioters, Woods wrote Bradley asking if federal law, specifically the May 31, 1870, act, could be invoked against the white terrorists.[127] Perhaps Busteed or Southworth had questioned his thinking, or perhaps he just wanted to soften up the Supreme Court, knowing that the defendants would certainly challenge their indictments through an immediate appeal. Woods told Bradley that he thought Section 6 particularly relevant:

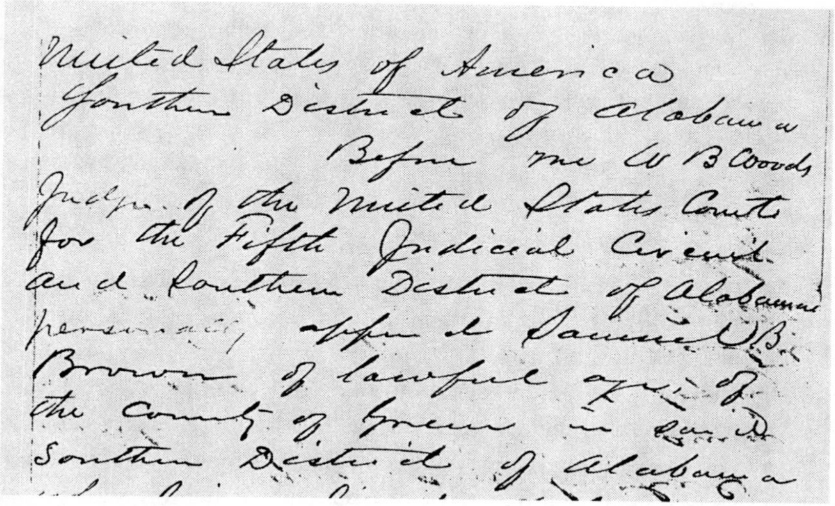

FIGURE 4.1. Circuit Judge William B. Woods listened to Samuel B. Brown's account of the Eutaw violence and converted it into a legal document, a complaint based on Woods's assumption that the Fourteenth Amendment had incorporated the Bill of Rights.

Source: Samuel B. Brown, complaint, October 28, 1870, case no. 62, *United States v. John J. Jolly, et al.*, Criminal Case Files, U.S. Circuit Court, Southern District of Alabama, Mobile Term, Records of the United States District Courts, RG 21, National Archives Southeast Region, Atlanta.

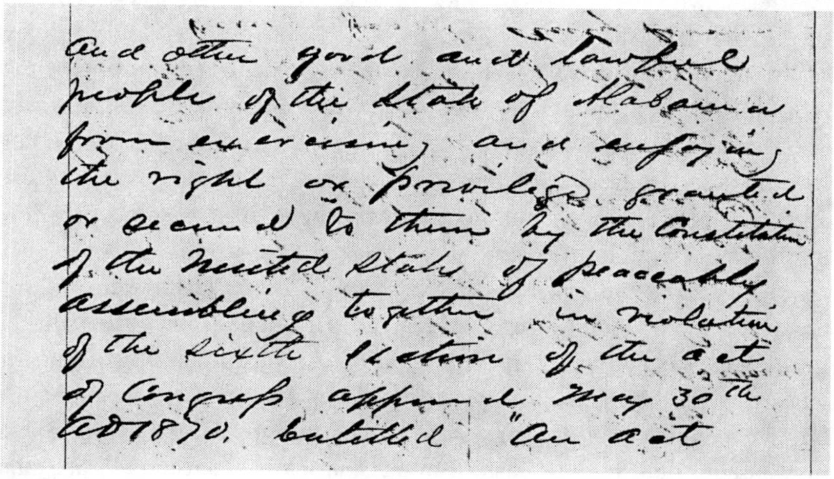

FIGURE 4.2. Woods accused the white rioters with threatening their victims' "right or privilege" to enjoy their constitutional rights.

Source: Samuel B. Brown, complaint, October 28, 1870, case no. 62, *United States v. John J. Jolly, et al.*, Criminal Case Files, U.S. Circuit Court, Southern District of Alabama, Mobile Term, Records of the United States District Courts, RG 21, National Archives Southeast Region, Atlanta.

That if two or more persons shall band or conspire together, or go in dis-
guise upon the public highway, or upon the premises of another, with intent
to violate any provision of this act, or to injure, oppress, threaten, or intimidate any citizen with intent to prevent or hinder his free exercise and enjoyment of any right or privilege granted or secured to him by the Constitution
or laws of the United States, or because of his having exercised the same,
such persons shall be held guilty of a felony.[128]

On January 3, 1871, Bradley responded to Woods's letter, summarizing
the question: "Whether the breaking up of a peaceable political meeting
by violence, is a preventing or hindering the free exercise or enjoyment of
a right granted or secured by the Constitution or laws of U.S.?" Bradley already understood that the real question was whether the Eutaw rioters had
violated the constitutional rights of their victims by shooting at them. Bradley considered the right of the people to assemble together "one of the most
sacred rights of citizenship," but he recognized that both the Fourteenth
and the Fifteenth Amendments only protected against state action. And in
Eutaw, private individuals, acting without state authority, had broken up the
meeting, not the State of Alabama. Neither the Constitution nor the federal
laws, Bradley wrote, have any provision securing the right to assemble for
political discussion. "They only contain a prohibition against a state from
interfering with such a right, included as one of the privileges and immunities belonging to all citizens."[129]

Even as Bradley puzzled over the Fourteenth Amendment's meaning, the
political landscape shifted. In 1868, when Grant had first run for president
as a Republican and a war hero, he faced Horatio Seymour, a New Yorker
seemingly less dedicated to patriotic Unionism. The contrast seemed clear
and the Republicans won, but they carried some critical states by only a few
hundred votes; Ohio voted Republican by a smaller margin than it had during the war, and the key states of New York and New Jersey went Democratic.[130] Despite such warnings of danger, the Republicans forged ahead.
Leading Republicans committed their party to a constitutional amendment
ending racial discrimination in voting, applicable not only in the South
but in the North as well. Democrats charged that the Republicans did this
to maintain their hold on power through black votes, but the Republicans
knew that they put at peril greater numbers of white votes. Through the
early months of 1870, the last of the southern states excluded from Congress
regained representation. On March 30, the secretary of state announced that
enough states had ratified the Fifteenth Amendment to make it part of the

Constitution. In the 1870 midterm elections, Republicans had hoped that the mere existence of enforcement acts would protect black voters. Grant's administration enforced election laws in New York City, but despite Akerman's pronouncements did little in the South, where violent whites had a free hand. "The presumption," James G. Blaine wrote in his memoirs, "was that these States would be obedient to the Constitution and laws." In August 1870, Tennessee, North Carolina, and Kentucky held elections, blasting the Republicans' presumptions to pieces. The first reports arrived on August 6, bringing news that Republican judicial candidates had gone down in Tennessee.[131] A week later came more devastating news. North Carolina Democrats had won by ten thousand votes, taking five of seven congressional districts. One defeated Republican was James H. Harris, "the ablest colored man in the country," swamped in the Democrats' electoral "avalanche." It soon became clear that the Democrats had not won these elections by playing fair. At the end of August, the *Daily Cleveland Herald*'s black correspondent in the South acknowledged that black out-migration had contributed to the defeats but charged that white violence played a more important role. More reports of Klan violence confirmed the Democrats' willingness to openly flout the laws in their campaign to regain power.[132] A few days after the gloomy news from North Carolina, the press reported that in Kentucky, Democrats had triumphed at all points, again carrying the day through nefarious means. Things did not improve when more states voted in the fall. The Republicans hung on to control of the Congress but lost fifty seats in the House, including fifteen turnovers in the South.[133]

Such political setbacks left Bradley unmoved, or perhaps they actually hardened his determination to apply the law against violent white Southerners. Despite his party's defeats and the rise of a new generation of Republicans not dedicated to civil rights, Bradley remained committed to the idea that the privileges and immunities clause incorporated the Bill of Rights. On January 3, 1871, he wrote:

> By the 1st Amendment to the Constitution it is declared that *Congress* shall make no law abridging the right of the people peaceably to assemble, and to petition the Government for a redress of grievances.
>
> By the 14th Amendment, *No State* shall make or enforce any law which shall abridge the privileges or immunities of Citizens of the U.S. [134]

That neither Congress nor Alabama carried out or authorized the Eutaw violence did not deter Bradley. "But suppose the state authorities are inactive," he asked, "and will do nothing to punish the crime?" Normally, murder and riot are crimes only policed by the states, he observed, but in this case, the white men shooting into the political rally did not have the right to prevent persons from exercising the right of suffrage, secured by the Fifteenth Amendment. This violated Section 4 of the 1870 law, which made it a crime for any person "by force" to "hinder, delay, or obstruct any citizen from doing any act required to be done to qualify him to vote or from voting at any election."[135] Bradley added that the white gunmen also violated Section 6, which prohibited banding and confederating together, and Section 5, making it a crime for anyone to prevent someone from exercising the right of suffrage under the Fifteenth Amendment.[136]

In March, Bradley considered the crucial matter of proof. This would turn out to be the most important point of all when the Court considered its power to influence state jury selection practices. The shooting could be easily proven, Woods fretted in a letter written February 7, but what the rioters had in mind as they shot into the crowd was another matter. On March 12, Bradley answered: "You ask whether the breaking up of a peaceable political meeting by riot and murder when committed simply for that purpose, without any definite intent to prevent the exercise of the right of suffrage, is a felony . . . in view of the First amendment."[137]

In contrast to his January letter, which asked whether free speech was a right protected by the Fourteenth Amendment, in March Bradley's main concern was whether the federal authorities could effectively police rights under the language of the Fourteenth Amendment. If the Court set the level of proof required to prosecute a violent violator of constitutional rights too high, then, in fact, federal prosecutors would be unable to pursue such crimes in practice, even if they had the authority in theory. Prosecutors could turn away victims like Samuel B. Brown by asking if they knew that their assailants had intended to violate some constitutional right. It was a question that would determine just how active federal officers could really be in their pursuit of crime. As Bradley noted, the question was exactly what Congress had debated but never resolved: "Where Congress is prohibited from *interfering with* a right by legislation, does that authorize Congress to *protect* that right by legislation?" Before the Fourteenth Amendment, Bradley reminded Woods, there was no question but that only the states could protect the people's rights. Bradley refined his question: "Does the XIVth Amendment in giving Congress power to enforce its provisions by appropriate legislation, make any alteration in this respect?"[138]

Bingham's success at getting the privileges and immunities clause into the Fourteenth Amendment dictated the answer: yes. Americans' privileges and immunities "undoubtedly" included fundamental rights, Bradley said, echoing Bingham. For this Bradley cited without comment a case that had repeatedly come up during congressional debates over the privileges and immunities clause, *Corfield v. Coryell*. Among the fundamental rights that Congress had the power to protect, "I suppose we are safe in including those which {in the Constitution} are expressly secured to the people, either as against the action of the Federal Government or the State Governments."[139] And so, Bradley concluded, Congress had the right to protect through appropriate legislation such fundamental rights: "undoubtedly." If the states refused to protect their citizens' rights, then Congress could. This last was an especially important point in Alabama and every other southern state, for that matter. State authorities had done nothing to prosecute the Eutaw rioters. When the state prosecutor (called a solicitor in Alabama) had tried to investigate an earlier incident, the Ku Klux Klan killed him. Thereafter, efforts by state authorities to investigate and prosecute racial violence in Greene County ended. In such a lawless environment, Bradley wrote, the law authorized federal prosecution, "and the law is within the legislative power of Congress."[140] No lawyer in Alabama not employed by the U.S. government agreed. In a Eutaw riot case titled *United States v. Hall, et al.*, attorneys for the defendants filed a demurrer claiming that the indictment of their clients failed to identify "any right or privilege granted or secured by the constitution of the United States" violated by the Eutaw rioters. In May 1871, Busteed and Woods rendered their decision, borrowing language from Bradley's letters to sustain the indictment.[141]

Bradley continued to fight reassertions of state power in 1872 and 1873. In Georgia the notorious scalawag Henry P. Farrow drew from Bradley his most detailed resistance to reassertions of state power. Democrats called Farrow a "scalawag," a southern-born Republican. Originally from South Carolina, he came from a family with a long history of unionism; his father had opposed South Carolina nullifiers' efforts to overturn federal tariff law in the 1830s.[142] In Georgia, Farrow helped found the Republican Party and joined the "Georgia Ring," criticized by Democrats as operating "a regular Federal office brokerage in Washington."[143] In 1872, Farrow served as United States attorney in Georgia. His letters reveal a vigorous determination to enforce civil rights and frustration that the rules of his court limited jury service to white men; the federal courts used jurors selected by state clerks, and those clerks chose only white Democrats. Such "packed" juries thwarted justice, Farrow fumed. By the end of the year, he had persuaded federal judges William B. Woods and John Erskine to adopt new rules whereby U.S. commissioners—and not state officers—would select the jurors.[144]

The stakes were high. With black jurors investigating and deciding election cases, Georgia might have fair elections, which in turn meant that black voters could oust white conservatives from office. "The Radicals adopt singular means to aid in carrying the elections their way," the *Georgia Weekly Telegraph and Georgia Journal & Messenger* grumbled, adding, "There is some curiosity to see how far they will proceed with this new movement."[145] In October whites attacked three hundred blacks lined up to vote in Macon; with a sympathetic grand jury that included blacks, Farrow investigated and ordered arrests. Whites fought back, denouncing Farrow in the press and filing motions in court against the new, "illegal" process of picking jurors. The Macon newspaper charged that Farrow, "the pious prosecutor of our people," organized a "packed, illegally-drawn and subservient grand jury" to carry out "malicious provisions of the Enforcement act."[146] The arrests "insulted" state authority, the *Georgia Weekly Telegraph and Georgia Journal & Messenger* reported, citing "eminent gentlemen of the bar."[147] Lawyers for one of the arrested men, Appleton P. Collins, alleged that the U.S. commissioners did not choose jurors randomly. Instead, "they were so selected & designated as to be composed as nearly as the appointees of this Court could arrange, to consist of about an equal number of white & black persons each."[148]

In 1873, Bradley heard these complaints and rejected them. He had little patience for assertions of state power against congressional acts authorized by the Fourteenth Amendment. Bradley berated state efforts to retain control of jury selection. He denied that any "fundamental principle" required the federal courts to follow state law when picking jurors. Nothing in federal law required "slavish or minute adherence" to state laws, he insisted. The federal method of jury selection adhered to the "spirit" of the Fourteenth and Fifteenth Amendments, Bradley added. So far, so good: Bradley had used strong language to resist state efforts to oust blacks from federal jury service. Bradley, though, then revealed the cracks in the facade of his certainty. He observed that the case probably would not go to the Supreme Court but stated, "I shall avail myself on the first opportunity of consulting the views of my associates on the supreme bench, and if any different result should be arrived at, this court will cheerfully modify its rules." Bradley knew that the *Slaughterhouse Cases* were pending and that his brethren would soon speak authoritatively on the states' authority under the Fourteenth Amendment. He was not sure he could thwart Miller when the two men inevitably collided.[149]

When the *Slaughterhouse Cases* reached Washington, Bradley pressed his expansive reading of the Fourteenth Amendment's privileges and immunities clause. As the Supreme Court deliberated, his views collided with Miller's. Exactly what passed between the two justices in the Court's secret conferences cannot be known, but Miller organized a five-man majority against Bradley's broad reading of privileges and immunities. On April 14, 1873, Miller announced the Court's opinion in the *Slaughterhouse Cases*. On one level, Miller's opinion addressed a public health law from Louisiana requiring all New Orleans butchers to ply their trade at a single state-sanctioned facility. Miller did not share Campbell's antipathy to blacks. Not long after writing his *Slaughterhouse* opinion, Miller chastised his "brother" for his racial attitudes: "I am very sorry to find that you retain more of the bitterness inbred by the past than I had supposed." Miller found Ballinger's continued complaints about Reconstruction frustrating: "No measure adopted by the republican party for reconstruction of the rebel states has met your approval, scarcely your acquiescence."[150] Miller's flashes of irritation with Ballinger's recalcitrance may explain his support for the Republican legislature in Louisiana. Ballinger's thinking offered evidence of continued white resistance. His persistent racism repulsed Miller, but it did not lead him to support the intellectual core of the Reconstruction effort, privileges and immunities.

Focusing on the Fourteenth Amendment's privileges and immunities clause, he issued an interpretation that continues as law today. Miller cited *Corfield v. Coryell*, as well as other Court rulings that addressed the meaning of privileges and immunities, but he significantly narrowed the term's meaning so much that privileges and immunities ceased to have much constitutional significance. Bradley's intuition that privileges and immunities might bring a host of natural rights under the care of the federal government came to naught.[151] (Table 4.3 plots the rights cited in *Corfield v. Coryell* against those listed in the *Slaughterhouse Cases*.) Miller correctly described *Corfield v. Coryell* as "the leading case" on privileges and immunities. But while Bradley and many others understood *Corfield v. Coryell* generously, as protecting many national rights, Miller read it parsimoniously, as putting few rights under the care of Congress. Miller's biographer doubts that he

TABLE 4.3 Comparison of the meaning of privileges and immunities in *Corfield v. Coryell* and the *Slaughterhouse Cases*

Corfield v. Coryell (1823)	*Slaughterhouse Cases* (1873)
Protection by the government.	To demand the care and protection of the federal government over his life, liberty, and property when on the high seas or within the jurisdiction of a foreign government.
	Right of free access to its seaports, through which all operations of foreign commerce are conducted, to the subtreasuries, land offices, and courts of justice in the several States.
The enjoyment of life and liberty, with the right to acquire and possess property of every kind, and to pursue and obtain happiness and safety.	
	The right to peaceably assemble and petition for redress of grievances.
To pass through, or to reside in any other state for the purposes of trade, agriculture, professional pursuits, or otherwise.	To come to the seat of government to assert any claim he may have upon that government, to transact any business he may have with it, to seek its protection, to share its offices, to engage in administering its functions.
	The right to use the navigable waters of the United States, however they may penetrate the territory of the several states.
To claim the benefit of the writ of habeas corpus.	The privilege of the writ of habeas corpus.
To institute and maintain actions of any kind in the courts of the state.	
To take, hold, and dispose of property, either real or personal.	
An exemption from higher taxes or impositions than are paid by the other citizens of the state.	
The elective franchise, as regulated and established by the laws or constitution of the state in which it is to be exercised.	

Source: *Corfield v. Coryell*, 6 F. Cas. 546 (1823); the *Slaughterhouse Cases*, 83 U.S. 36 (1873).

really put much stock in precedent, and his concern with managing public opinion is evident throughout the text of his decision. He wrote that founders of the country had disagreed over where to draw the line between federal and state authority, and the question remained undecided.[152] Miller appealed to public opinion while asserting the Court's role as a steadying influence. Public opinion, he said, fluctuates on this subject, but "we think it will be found that this court . . . has always held with a steady and an even hand the balance between State and Federal power." Miller trusted that the Court would continue that function.[153]

Miller effectively neutralized the privileges and immunities clause, rejecting Bradley's hope that it might have placed citizens' natural rights under the protection of Congress. The public's response to his opinion measured its success, Miller believed. His *Slaughterhouse* opinion won public sentiment "with great unanimity," he told his students.[154]

Bradley fought back with a vigorous dissenting opinion.[155] But his confidence in privileges and immunities wavered after his defeat in the *Slaughterhouse Cases*. In the first days of 1874, Frederick Frelinghuysen still hoped Congress could enforce the Fourteenth Amendment, with powers both implied and enumerated. Where those rights might be uncertain, Frelinghuysen suggested, Congress had as much authority as the states to enforce them. Bradley responded sympathetically, telling his old friend that his theory had much force before adding two observations of his own. If the framers of the Constitution had defined citizenship in 1789, Bradley said, there would be little doubt that the title to all citizenship, state and national, would be seen as flowing from the U.S. Constitution and not dependent on any state or local regulation. Bradley's second point raised a problem for Frelinghuysen's argument. "Has it not always been the fact that the Constitution implicitly conferred citizenship?" Bradley then asked, "And has any such power as that now claimed ever been asserted or pretended?" If Congress had always had power to protect rights, then some Congress should have asserted that power at some point in the past. No Congress ever had. For Bradley this undermined assertions of such a power now. Bradley dismissed concerns about conflict between national and state jurisdictions— if the rights Congress could protect were circumscribed. Such conflicts did not present insurmountable problems, he believed, thinking that the nation could find the answer to the question of how much power Congress had to protect rights in the Fourteenth Amendment's text, most particularly the clause protecting citizens' privileges and immunities.[156]

Bradley had begun to reverse course, seeing privileges and immunities as limited, not covering all natural rights. If privileges and immunities meant the natural rights (in this letter Bradley called them "private") that all citizens enjoy regardless of their government, then Congress could legislate on any subject whatsoever. Bradley rejected this possibility because it would allow the federal government to duplicate state authority for all purposes,

creating a structure with the states and the federal government performing the same tasks and assuming the same responsibilities. No sensible man
would contemplate such a monstrosity, Bradley now believed.[157] "I do not
think," Bradley said, "that the rights, privileges and immunities of a citizen
embrace all private rights."[158]

Citizens got the means to protect their private rights through the political process, from government; individual rights came from nature. The
right to go to court was politically determined; the rights fought for in
court came from nature. Bradley believed rights were naturally determined;
the right to enforce those rights depended on the political process, on
public opinion.[159]

As his earlier commitment to a broad reading of privileges and immunities deflated, he told Frelinghuysen that his mind was "rather in the condition of *seeking the truth*." In April 1874, while riding on circuit, he returned
to the question of privileges and immunities in *United States v. Cruikshank*.
Cruikshank had joined a group of whites in an attack on African American
Republicans in Colfax, Grant Parish, Louisiana, murdering hundreds of
blacks. The U.S. attorney in New Orleans, James R. Beckwith, worked hard
to indict and then convict the killers. From the beginning, he worried that
Miller's defeat of Bradley's position in the *Slaughterhouse Cases* might ham-
string efforts to enforce civil rights laws. On April 18, 1873, Beckwith ur-
gently telegraphed Washington, asking for a copy of Miller's opinion because, he said, "It is believed here to limit the criminal jurisdiction of federal
courts under recent acts."[160] Despite his concerns over the Court's *Slaughterhouse* decision, Beckwith went to trial, where he encountered Bradley, who
joined Woods on the bench. A jury convicted three of the whites under the
same May 31, 1870, Enforcement Act that Bradley had approved in 1871.
Only convicting three men frustrated Beckwith. It was a "beggarly verdict,"
he fumed.[161]

It was questionable whether even such a "beggarly verdict" would stand.
Cruikshank's lawyers attacked the Enforcement Act as unconstitutional,
"municipal in character, operating directly on the conduct of individuals."
They knew they could not budge Woods from his confidence in the law and
the verdict, but if they could sway Bradley, the two judges would certify
their disagreement to the Supreme Court. At this time, criminal verdicts
could be appealed only when the presiding judges disagreed over the law.
Beckwith initially expressed confidence that the verdicts could not be overturned, wanting only to ensure that the men went to a prison strong enough

to withstand efforts to break them out.[162] By June 20, 1874, Beckwith realized that Bradley probably intended to follow the *Slaughterhouse* decision and not defy it. "Bradley will to what end God only knows decide the enforcement act unconstitutional," Beckwith predicted on June 25, 1874, and warned that hundreds would die if the federal courts lost jurisdiction over violent civil rights cases.[163] Bradley did not have to attend the trial and could have let it proceed with Woods sitting alone. Beckwith passionately wished he would stay away. "His presence in the district was to me a nightmare," he said.[164] But Bradley was determined to continue his nightmare presence and showed up in court. For Bradley the facts of this case were not unfamiliar; they closely resembled the Eutaw riot. This was Alabama again, but with Bradley now on the other side.[165]

Bradley began by addressing an issue he had seen as central at least since 1871 and which Congress had so vigorously debated in 1866: Did Congress have the power to enforce privileges and immunities? Bradley used *Prigg v. Pennsylvania* (1842) to say, "It seems to be firmly established by the unanimous opinion of the judges . . . that congress has the power to enforce . . . every right and privilege given or guarantied by the Constitution."[166] That sounded expansive, but he actually limited congressional power to protect rights to those rights and privileges specifically assigned it by the political process that created the Constitution and its amendments. It was the job of judges to police Congress, making sure it did not protect too many rights.

When he distinguished the rights guarded by the states from those assigned to Congress for protection, Bradley adopted the same states' rights arguments he once despised, arguments based on a history quite different from what he himself had once taught. Some rights and privileges derive from the mother country, "challenged and vindicated by centuries of stubborn resistance to arbitrary power," and belong to all citizens as part of their birthright. These rights predate the Constitution. When the Constitution declared them, "it [was] understood that they [were] not created or conferred by the Constitution" but recognized as existing rights originally won by the states from the British. Bradley said that enforcement of these rights was therefore the job of each state, "as a part of its residuary sovereignty."[167]

This understanding would seem to leave the federal government with very few rights to protect, but Bradley refused to entirely yield on the question of federal power. He singled out trial by jury as a federal right. Citizens have "a constitutional security against arbitrary and unjust legislation." If states proceed against their citizens "without benefit of those time-honored forms of proceeding in open court and trial by jury," then the federal government can act. The Congress can legislate, Bradley said, only when states misbehave. "The duty and power of enforcement take their inception from the moment that the state fails to comply with the duty enjoined." The manner of enforcing these rights depends on the character of the privilege and immunity in question. He concluded that "there can be no constitutional legislation of Congress for directly enforcing the privileges and immunities of citizens of the United States by original proceedings in the courts of the United States." Bradley agreed with the defense lawyers: Congress cannot create a "municipal code" against ordinary crimes, like murder.[168]

Bradley's decision heartened white Southerners and alarmed anyone dedicated to civil rights. One Louisiana Republican predicted a racial bloodbath, "thanks to Justice Bradley," shortly before dying himself in the bloodbath he predicted, killed by white vigilantes.[169] The *Chicago Inter-Ocean*, always friendly to civil rights, quoted senators as calling the ruling "worse than the Dred Scott decision."[170] For white Southerners, the winking and nodding began. According to Bradley's reasoning, killing black people was not a federal crime, the *Georgia Weekly Telegraph and Messenger* explained, only killing them on account of their color, race, or previous condition of servitude. Such cases "can hardly ever arise," the Georgia paper gloated, apparently confident that whites could evade federal justice by keeping mum about their motivation.[171]

Having moved away from his original commitment to privileges and immunities, documented in the private letters he wrote in 1871 and 1874, Bradley prepared for his files an undated note saying that his views had been "much modified by subsequent reflection so far as relates to the power of Congress to pass laws for enforcing social equality between the races" (see fig. 4.3).[172] Defending his brother from charges that he had "packed" the Court with his selection of Bradley, George Frisbie Hoar pointed to the justice's *Cruikshank* decision as proof. Hoar said that with *Cruikshank*, Bradley, not Miller, broke the back of the Republican effort to reconstruct the South. Ebenezer Hoar never intended such an outcome and would not have "packed" the Court to devastate his own dream of protecting the rights of freed people as "sacred." Ebenezer Hoar, in fact, did the best he could, picking a man he thought truly dedicated to national power, not fully realizing that Bradley had a more complicated relationship to higher-law doctrines than Hoar himself had. Hoar, after all, knew Emerson; Bradley only read

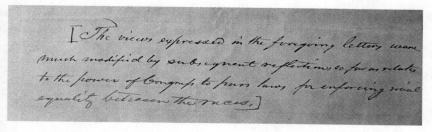

FIGURE 4.3. Bradley penned an undated note for his files saying that he had changed his mind about the power of Congress over "social equality between the races."

Source: Box 18, Bradley Papers, New Jersey Historical Society, Newark.

him in the *Atlantic Monthly.*[173] Hoar could not know that Bradley would be overpowered by Miller. Miller's determination to both respect and manage public opinion turned him and the Court away from the influence of the most powerful intellectual figure in postbellum American culture. Ralph Waldo Emerson's higher law doctrines made little headway on the Court, even as Emerson became a national icon. Miller's concern for public opinion shielded him from the public's increasing respect for higher law. It was a strange and ironic kind of autonomy for the law.

CHAPTER FIVE

The Jury Cases

TO ENFORCE ITS RULES IN THE SOUTH, *the Supreme Court had to contend with the wall of resistance that white Southerners built against federal "interference." The Court most candidly acknowledged the limits of its power after Alabama's 1901 state constitutional convention openly ousted blacks from the state's voter rolls. To this frank insult to the Fifteenth Amendment's protection of voting rights, Oliver Wendell Holmes responded that he lacked the "practical power to deal with the people of the State in a body" even when they voted to violate the Constitution. Better to resolve such affronts politically, Holmes wrote.*[1]

Yet Holmes made his extraordinary confessions of limited power in a case involving political action by a state constitutional convention. In other cases, the Court did not so easily yield its authority—for good reason. In criminal trials, white Southerners' power was more vulnerable to the Supreme Court's reach than in cases involving elections and legislative action. There were white Southerners dedicated to the rule of law. John Cashman is a hard person for modern academics to like: a conservative, a racist, a Confederate, a champion of the Lost Cause, and a stalwart opponent of labor unions and Populists. Nonetheless, Cashman urged law and apolitical constitutionalism. Rather than represent public opinion, Cashman battled to shape it, believing that law had to surmount public passion. His hopes that ordinary white Mississippians could embrace the rule of law waxed and waned throughout his life. He struggled, not with inner demons, but with demons more tangible, his neighbors, his readers, his friends, his state, and his region.

Cashman edited the Vicksburg Evening Post from 1883 until 1914. His newspaper followed white journalistic conventions; blacks charged with crimes were "maniacs," "brutes," "beasts," "wretches," and "fiends."[2] Yet while Cashman used the jargon of his trade, he would not follow his fellow editors when they excused mob law. Cashman first published the Evening Post on May 4, 1883, and swiftly laid out his position on mobbing. White Mississippians, Cashman explained, no longer needed the violence they had used against the Republicans after the Civil War. "There is no danger of a return to Radical rule—circumstances and changes render it almost impossible." Instead, "these are happy times when peaceful methods, wise counsels, and sagacious statesmanship can supplant the measures that were rendered necessary to gain control of the government of the State in 1875."[3]

Many southern newspaper editors mouthed such platitudes only to find ways to justify particular lynchings. Specific incidents tested general principles. On September 3, 1883, a Hinds County mob hanged Jim King and gunned down George Gaddis for grave robbery. Many whites blamed King and Gaddis rather than the mob. Since one of the dead men had been a "conjure doctor," John R. Chapman urged the legislature to treat the lynching problem by outlawing conjuring. Several newspapers considered this as a serious proposal.[4] Not Cashman. He knew better than to go hunting for the source of Mississippi's lynching problem in the black community. Cashman observed that it had not even occurred to Chapman "that laws should be passed or enforced to protect the lives of prisoners in custody of officers of the law." Mississippi, Cashman pointed out, had the worst record for protecting prisoners of any state in the Union.[5]

For a year after he launched his paper, Cashman maintained an almost sunny optimism that most white Southerners, a silent majority, really did not support extralegal violence. But Cashman could not maintain this view against the string of lynching reports that crossed his desk. He was particularly troubled that so many of his fellow editors supported mob law. By the fall of 1884, Cashman's good cheer had faltered. In contrast to his earlier confidence in public opinion, he now wrote that lynching, that "great outrage upon civilization," a "horrible state of affairs," a "stain upon the good name of the State," happened because "communities . . . allow these horrible and cowardly murders." White Mississippians' "apathy . . . is a sad feature," Cashman glumly wrote.[6] As Cashman lost heart that Mississippi could ever really be governed through the rule of law, the Supreme Court continued its retreat from the aggressive assertion of national power. The Court increasingly insisted it had to defer to the states. Two parallel narratives developed: in Mississippi, Cash-

man's increasing lack of confidence in Mississippi governance; in Washington, the Supreme Court's increasing insistence that Mississippi whites must be allowed to govern themselves, largely free of federal oversight.

Bradley's failure to dislodge Miller from his constricted reading of the Fourteenth Amendment's privileges and immunities clause meant that the Court would be deciding the crucial question of federal power over state juries having already conceded the major point to the states. Privileges and immunities, which some members of Congress and Bradley himself had once thought would be a mighty sword against state sovereignty, had been retired from the battlefield before the fight over all-white juries had even begun.

At the moment this happened, as the Supreme Court deliberated the *Slaughterhouse Cases*, real racial progress seemed possible. In 1872, the Mississippi attorney general told a congressional committee that by law county officials had to put the names of every voter in their jury boxes as possible jurors. This was not true everywhere. A Georgia lawyer told the same committee that he had never seen a black juror. In Mississippi, however, black access to law could be measured by the swelling numbers of blacks serving on juries. In 1873, blacks made up two-thirds of Warren County grand jurors. This was the same year that Mississippi's legislature passed a civil rights law that outlawed segregated seating in public accommodations. In Vicksburg a former slave, Peter Crosby, became Warren County sheriff, replacing the white Union Army veteran whom General Ord had selected.[7]

A black man as sheriff seemed truly revolutionary. In part because they controlled the collection of taxes and other fees, Mississippi sheriffs traditionally served as the political bosses of their counties. This zenith of black political power launched whites on a ruthless crusade to regain control of local government. For a hundred years after they took back power, white Mississippians regaled themselves with stories of their fight to oust blacks from the political culture; the first publications of the Mississippi Historical Society documented the memories of unreconstructed white men candidly detailing the tricky ways they stole elections. In Vicksburg they turned to violence. On December 7, 1874, rioting whites ejected Crosby from office. Blacks and whites fought a pitched battle on old Civil War battlefields before Crosby could regain his office. Although once again sheriff, he and the Republicans never fully gained the power they had once enjoyed. Black participation in Warren County juries followed the downward path of

Republican power and influence. In 1875, only nine of twenty-three grand jurors who can be identified by race were black. In 1878, that number fell to five of twenty-seven (18.5 percent).[8]

Northerners' ideas about jury selection hobbled their ability to impose a new regime on the South. Northern whites had trouble understanding why the emancipation of black people should change the way they picked juries. They still thought it more important to have competent jurors than representative ones. On the Supreme Court, Joseph Bradley told an inquiring Norwegian lawyer that how courts selected jurors mattered greatly and that the American method required that county officers randomly select jurors from "the whole mass of male citizens, without regard to character." Bradley preferred the old method of limiting jury service to freeholders, though he admitted property qualification had been an arbitrary standard. "Still it is a distinction which had the effect of getting a better class of men," he observed. If trial by jury seemed less satisfactory, Bradley believed, it was because the quality of jurors had declined.[9]

Attorney General Amos Akerman favored vigorously reconstructing the South more than Bradley, but even he thought most blacks unqualified for jury duty. Challenged by a New Jersey Republican warning that blacks might abandon the party if federal officers did not take care to include them on juries, Akerman reacted indignantly. The attorney general warned that seating unqualified blacks on juries would strengthen the enemies of equal rights, giving them valid grounds for criticism. Excluding blacks from juries, on the other hand, carried no political cost, Akerman said. He doubted blacks could be so thoroughly depraved as to abandon the Republican Party for the Democrats on the issue of jury service.[10]

Nonetheless, some northern jurisdictions did seat black jurors. Massachusetts began accepting black jurors in 1860, when three Worcester aldermen selected William H. Jankins and Francis A. Clough, property-owning "colored barbers, doing a very good business," as jurors. However intelligent and wealthy Jankins and Clough may have been, even the suggestion that they might sit with whites as jurors upset other white Northerners. An Indiana congressman promptly confirmed the accuracy of Akerman's acuity when he denounced the whole idea as a characteristic example of "negro equality" and its evils.[11]

Most northern legislatures retained the same requirements for good character that they always had. Statutes almost universally limited jury duty to voters and gave city officials or sheriffs discretion to select from their ranks "sober and judicious persons" or "persons of good moral character" or "such persons as they judge[d] best qualified."[12] Antebellum Pennsylvania law had exhorted sheriffs and county commissioners to choose only jurors from the taxable citizens of their counties, "sober, intelligent, and judicious persons," a stricture the new law, "An Act for the Better and More Impartial Selection of Persons to Serve as Jurors," retained.[13] Only a very rare sheriff indeed would have dared judge any black male voter more sober, intelligent, or judicious than a white man.

Under pressure from the federal government, some southern states did revise their qualifications for jury service. Such changes did not happen on the border, where slave states had not seceded and the national government had little leverage. Kentucky, West Virginia, and Missouri still limited jury service to white males by law into the 1870s. Until 1871, Virginia law required that jurors be white males, but in that year the legislature enacted a new jury statute that deleted the word "white." In North Carolina, blacks distrusted a legal system that very often served the needs of white elites, perpetuating racial violence, until army generals Daniel E. Sickles and Edwin R. S. Canby required black jury service. In May 1867, Sickles opened jury service to all taxpayers, while Canby, his successor, changed all taxpayers to all voters. Some whites resisted, but at least two North Carolina state judges not only refused to obstruct the military orders; they pressed for quicker implementation. Robert Ballard Gilliam, a native of North Carolina with a long record of service in the state legislature before becoming a superior court judge, found a way for a few blacks to serve as jurors even after Sickles delayed implementation of his order. Those already chosen could not be removed, he decided. In August, Judge Daniel Gould Fowle, also a native of North Carolina, a Confederate veteran, and soon a defense attorney for Ku Klux Klansmen, decided that once slavery had ended, existing laws did not allow exclusion of blacks from jury service.[14] North Carolina's 1868 constitutional convention, attended by U.S. Army officers, implicitly confirmed black jury service by eliminating racial restrictions on suffrage and officeholding. A minority bitterly protested that voting was not a natural right and that Congress had no authority to prescribe voting rights.[15]

Tennessee and Louisiana in 1868 and South Carolina in 1869 passed laws expressly forbidding racial discrimination in the selection of jurors. Tennessee had been restored to the Union in 1866, after it enfranchised black voters and ratified the Fourteenth Amendment. In 1867, blacks made up nearly half of Tennessee voters, and both Conservatives and Republicans competed for their votes in an election season marred by violence and bloodshed. The Republicans triumphed and so dominated the state legislature that they could pass a law forbidding jury discrimination.[16] The Louisiana legislature that forbade jury discrimination had been elected in April 1868, when Republican candidates faced some violence, fraud, and intimidation. By the time they enacted their jury law, however, Louisiana Republicans had begun to realize that their opponents would stop at nothing to unseat them. No act of violence, however perverse or sadistic, seemed out of bounds to the Knights of the White Camellia, the Ku Klux Klan, the Swamp Fox Rangers, and other paramilitary groups fighting for white supremacy. Republicans responded to such lawlessness by outlawing discrimination against black jurors. White jurors could not be trusted to convict the vigilantes, they realized.[17]

In South Carolina, the state's 1868 constitution allowed the black majority population a fairer representation in the state legislature than had ever been the case before or would be the case again once Reconstruction ended. As a result, African Americans filled 84 of 157 seats in the 1868 legislature. In 1932, a pair of deeply racist historians complained that "an alien people and a former subject race were placed in control against the will of a majority of the white people." White newspapers ranted so much against the legislature that their editors appeared insane or "obsessed with some fearful mania," the same two historians admitted. Despite the battering it took from the press, the South Carolina legislature wrote a law requiring that the proportion of white to black jurors match the proportion of white to black voters.[18]

As electoral politics failed to build momentum behind reform, some civil rights advocates held out hope for the more principled environs of the Supreme Court. Republicans despised Chief Justice Taney's *Dred Scott v. Sandford* decision for betraying the nation's principles, but they still valued the Supreme Court as an institution and planned to use it for their own ends. Charged with illegal voting after she cast a ballot in the 1872 presidential election, Susan B. Anthony hoped to vindicate herself with the Fourteenth Amendment's privileges and immunities clause. Before she could be put on trial in June 1873, Miller issued his rulings in the *Slaughterhouse Cases* and the less well-known *State v. Myra Bradwell*, an opinion denying that women had a constitutional right against state gender discrimination. Both cases severely limited the reach of the Fourteenth Amendment's privileges and immunities clause. Anthony's lawyer had planned to use the

Fourteenth Amendment to claim that state voting officers had denied his client her privileges and immunities. He went ahead with his argument, just as planned, but Judge Ward Hunt ruled against Anthony so swiftly that she assumed he must have written his opinion before hearing the arguments, perhaps even before listening to the testimony. Anthony could not persuade the Supreme Court to hear her case.[19]

Hunt's reading of the constitutional situation did not mean that all hope that the Supreme Court might yet take a stronger stand for civil rights had been extinguished. The death of Salmon Chase in 1873 provided an opportunity for the Republicans to make a decisive statement at a time when many awaited judicial consideration of the new federal civil rights laws. Grant's earlier appointments of Strong and Bradley suggested that the president favored strong nationalists for the Court. This time, though, Grant chose Morrison Waite. That venerable champion of civil rights from Massachusetts Charles Sumner disliked the nomination, but the more moderate *New York Times* printed an article from Waite's hometown paper, the *Toledo Commercial*, expressing satisfaction with Waite for supporting Lincoln without becoming a "radical."[20] White Southerners reacted with caution. In Macon, Georgia, the *Weekly Telegraph* anticipated a contest between law and politics and could only hope for a judge dedicated to law and not the "Radical Party."[21] Southern whites could draw some measure of reassurance from reports that Secretary of the Interior Columbus Delano and not the "Radical" Ebenezer Hoar had engineered Waite's nomination, the same Columbus Delano who had plotted against Amos Akerman when the attorney general seemed overly interested in the Ku Klux Klan.[22]

As chief justice, Waite quickly moved to protect states' powers to choose their jurors. A few months after Waite joined the Court, the justices unanimously held that the Seventh Amendment applied only to federal trials. New Jersey law allowed seizure of ships for debt, without a trial by jury. The owners of a seized ship complained that when New Jersey took their property without due process of law, it violated their Fifth Amendment rights and denied them their right to a trial by jury protected by the Seventh Amendment. They took their case to the Supreme Court on November 24, 1874; counsel for New Jersey relied on the *Slaughterhouse Cases* to argue that trial by jury was neither a privilege nor an immunity.[23] Waite was predisposed to agree, finding the state law constitutional, but political developments probably hardened his resolve. Even before the November elections, Congress had showed signs of moving away from civil rights. On

May 27, 1874, the House easily passed legislation requiring a literacy test for federal jurors. Introduced by New York Democrat Clarkson Nott Potter (1825–82), the bill required that all jurors in federal courts be able to read and write the English language. A Michigan Republican, Omar Conger, objected to Potter's bill, but the Republicans clearly found it hard to oppose a bill that supposedly only aimed at improving jurors' competence. The white southern press understood the bill's deeper significance. "The ignorant blacks, who hang around the petty courts, waiting for a chance to serve on juries," the *Galveston News* happily observed, "will have to go to school or go to work." The hopes of the *Galveston News* faded when Senate Republicans killed the bill in committee, but that such a bill could pass the House suggested that congressional support for civil rights had waned.[24]

Waite was confirmed in November, when the cause of states' rights triumphed at the polls, handing the Republicans heavy losses. Democrats could scarcely contain their joy at the prospect of controlling both the House and the Senate for the first time in fifteen years. "The people in the grand majestic voice in November commanded you to halt," one Democrat lectured the Republicans. "We represent the people," Georgia Democrat James H. Blount, a former lieutenant colonel in the Confederate army, exulted.[25] As chief justice, Waite could decide who wrote the Court's opinion in the New Jersey ship case, and he chose Nathan Clifford, the senior member of the Court, a Democrat, and an old "doughface"—a northern man with southern (states' rights) principles. The election results meant that when Clifford rejected the shipowners' arguments, he could do so confident that he too spoke for the people. Since the Seventh Amendment issue had not been raised in the lower courts, Clifford could have avoided that question; instead he declared that the states, insofar as the Bill of Rights is concerned, are free to regulate trials in their own courts any way they please.[26]

Meeting in a lame-duck session, Congress considered whether to endorse the Court's course. Not only had the Republicans suffered serious losses in the elections, but their foremost champion for civil rights, Massachusetts Senator Charles Sumner, had died. Sumner had been pressing for a civil rights bill outlawing discrimination for years, but he died before he could see it enacted. Bradley's friend and confidant Frederick Frelinghuysen took up Sumner's bill. He particularly singled out its fourth section, forbidding jury discrimination. "In the name of Justice," he orated, "let us now take our depressing hand from long wronged people." He condemned the "rapacity of our fathers that brought them here." Citizens have no right to be jurors, Frelinghuysen conceded, but they do have a right not to be discriminated against by the officers selecting jurors. He assured his fellow senators that states could continue to set qualifications for jurors, but under his bill they would no longer be able to discriminate racially. Despite the *Slaughterhouse Cases* decision, Frelinghuysen still hoped Congress could use the privileges and immunities clause to protect rights. The question of which rights fell within privileges and immunities remained an open question, he thought. In the face of such uncertainty, Congress had as much right to enforce such rights as any state. Frelinghuysen consulted with Justice Bradley, who agreed that when states denied citizenship rights, the U.S. courts could intervene. A victim of discrimination had no choice but to look to the Supreme Court, Bradley observed, noting, "This is the only practical way in which he can vindicate his right to sue."[27]

Republicans, especially those defeated in November and presumably at the end of their political careers, nonetheless rallied behind the bill. Democrats recognized the Republicans' determination and considered resistance hopeless. In 1875, the bill first passed the House (where it lost its controversial prohibition against school segregation) and then went to the Senate, where Democrats promptly pounced on the provision outlawing state jury discrimination. The proposed law envisioned federal officers arresting state deputy sheriffs and other county officials caught picking only white jurors. Allan Thurman, an Ohio Democrat, while proposing to strike out such an affront to state sovereignty, acknowledged his recommendation had no chance, but nonetheless insisted that the Fourteenth Amendment did not authorize congressional interference in state juries. He cited the *Slaughterhouse Cases* as evidence that the Supreme Court had expressly decided that the privileges and immunities clause protected only those very few rights Americans had through their national citizenship. Most rights came by virtue of state citizenship.[28] Republicans repeated Frelinghuysen's denial that they planned to regulate state jury selection procedures. The states could still set age limits for jury duty, set property qualifications, and exclude women, they said, adding that the bill only forbade racial discrimination.[29]

The question, Congressman Augustus S. Merrimon of North Carolina protested, was not whether blacks ought to be allowed on juries. Rather the question was whether Congress had the power to pass a law interfering with state juries at all. To northern congressmen asking how southern whites would react if blacks came to political power and subjected them to all-black juries, Merrimon admitted there would be an outcry. It would be wrong, Merrimon continued, because whites are the more intelligent race and therefore better qualified to sit on juries, but it would be constitutional. Do the states have the constitutional right to restrict jury service to black men, if a majority of their voters want to discriminate in that way, Merrimon asked. "I answer yes, they have such power." Merrimon concluded by accusing northern whites of "falling down and worshipping at [blacks'] . . . feet with a view to get their votes." That, Merrimon said, was "infamous hypocrisy" and the "the worst sort of demagoguism."[30] Despite his bigotry, Merrimon made a consistent constitutional argument. Regardless of the wisdom of state jury discrimination, the federal government had no power to stamp it out, he believed. The Constitution protected trial by jury, not the right to be on a jury.

Not all the Southerners would admit their discrimination as readily as Merrimon. In fact, some denied that their states had even violated the Fourteenth Amendment, as New York Congressman Robert S. Hale discovered when he argued that Congress had not only the authority but the duty to protect citizens' rights in the states. Mississippi Congressman Lucius C. Lamar interrupted to demand the name of any state that had violated the Fourteenth Amendment. An architect of Mississippi's secession ordinance, Lamar had been a Confederate diplomat, a close friend of Jefferson Davis, and a Confederate army officer. After Appomattox he represented Ku Klux Klansmen in court so energetically that he once punched a U.S. marshal in the face. He won his seat in Congress representing northeast Mississippi after the Republican-controlled state legislature reapportioned the state in the face of a resurgent Democratic Party. To secure five of the state's six congressional seats, the legislature conceded one district to the Democrats, gerrymandering it so that white voters had a three to one advantage over blacks. This made Lamar Mississippi's sole Democrat in Congress; it took a special act of Congress to erase his treasonous past and seat him. In his mind, he and not the Republicans truly represented the South. He never conceded a hint of legitimacy to Republican representatives. Although Lamar at first said little, his power grew with his tenure in Washington. For the first time in his life, he learned to lead rather than follow, becoming the foremost opponent of civil rights legislation. According to an early biographer, he saw the civil rights bill as a "calamity," the "irretrievable ruin of the whole structure of his later life." Not only white Southerners found logic in Lamar's arguments for white supremacy. By 1875, some Northerners had begun to appreciate his "honest indignation" at excessive federal power.[31]

While doggedly opposed to civil rights legislation, Lamar made a name for himself as a new kind of white Southerner, one who did not dispute the legitimacy of the Civil War amendments to the Constitution. Nonetheless, his demand that Hale name a state that violated the Fourteenth Amendment confused the New Yorker, since other southern members of Congress had been arguing for the right to discriminate when selecting jurors.

"I did not suppose any gentleman disputed it," Hale responded.

"I do dispute it," Lamar shot back.[32]

Lamar denied that southern whites discriminated through their state laws against blacks at all. He said, "*Throughout the length and breadth of the southern section there does not exist in law* one single trace of privilege of discrimination against the black race. If there is, I know nothing of it."[33] George McKee, a native of Illinois and a Union army veteran also representing Mississippi, tried to explain Lamar's contentions by distinguishing between practical and legal discrimination, but Lamar refused to yield even on that point. He insisted again that no discrimination existed at all, in fact or in law.[34]

Congress passed the 1875 Civil Rights Act, with its provision requiring that states seat black jurors:

> That no citizen possessing all other qualifications which are or may be pre-scribed by law shall be disqualified for service as grand or petit juror in any court of the United States, or of any State, on account of race, color, or pre-vious condition of servitude; and any officer or other person charged with any duty in the selection or summoning of jurors who shall exclude or fail to summon any citizen for the cause aforesaid shall, on conviction thereof, be deemed guilty of a misdemeanor, and be fined not more than five thou-sand dollars.[35]

Historians have struggled ever since to understand how this could happen. Some have emphasized that removing the stricture against school segregation "gutted" the bill even though white Southerners hated and feared the requirement that they end jury discrimination. Eric Foner has called the 1875 Civil Rights Act "an unprecedented exercise of national authority" but one that nonetheless reflected divisions in the Republican Party. According to William Gillette, Republicans showed their ambivalence through their absences, abstentions, or outright opposition.[36]

These doubts in Congress might have prepared Frelinghuysen and other idealists somewhat, if not for what the Supreme Court did, then at least for the resistance itself, the shock of continued judicial support for state sovereignty over equal rights. The case that would bring the Supreme Court to its judgment on the 1875 law's prohibition of jury discrimination began in 1872, when Taylor Strauder took a hatchet in his right hand and drove it into his wife's left temple in West Virginia, a state that mandated all-white juries by law. He fled to Philadelphia, where police found him working as a carpenter, still using the blood-stained hatchet as a tool in his trade. It would be nine years before his case reached the Supreme Court.[37] In the meantime, the Court had two opportunities to reconsider its position on state juries in light of the 1875 law, as Strauder's case worked its way to Washington.

The first jury case came from Louisiana, always ready to test Republicans' commitment to Reconstruction. In 1868, Louisiana had elected as governor Henry Clay Warmoth, a moderate Illinois Republican transplant determined to win Whiggish Louisiana business leaders to his biracial coalition. To prove just how racially reasonable he could be, Warmoth vetoed a strong civil rights law in 1868 (passed only to embarrass him, Warmoth said later) before signing a weaker version a year later. In 1872, when Warmoth's term ended, he supported John McEnery, a fusion candidate supported by Democrats against the regular Republican, William Kellogg. The campaign ended with both McEnery and Kellogg claiming victory. The Kellogg side impeached Warmoth, making Pinckney Benton Stewart Pinchback the first black governor in America. Warmoth refused to surrender power and on December 3 appointed John Kennard as a justice on the Louisiana Supreme Court. Pinchback countered by appointing Philip H. Morgan to the same position. When Kennard refused to vacate his office, the pro-Pinchback legislature passed a law allowing for the removal of judges in a summary proceeding, with no trial by jury. Kennard protested his ouster to the U.S. Supreme Court.[38]

At the Supreme Court, his lawyers essayed to invoke the Fourteenth Amendment:

> The sole question then is, whether the State of Louisiana, acting under this law, through her judiciary, has deprived Kennard of his office without due process of law, contrary to the Fourteenth Amendment of the Constitution of the United States.
>
> We are not aware that this Court has passed upon the meaning of "due process of law," as contained in the Fourteenth Amendment, but, can discover no difference in the meaning of the phrase, from that which has been by frequent adjudications given to the same expression in the Fifth Amend-

ment, except that the former applies to the States, whilst the latter is confined to the United States.

We are therefore at liberty to seek for the true definition. . . .

The term as used in the Constitution doubtless had a fixed meaning. It
was borrowed from our English ancestry.[39]

If due process "doubtless had a fixed meaning," then there really were
limits on the states, limits enforceable in federal court. For Waite due process had no fixed meaning except in the most general terms possible. Kennard had a trial, where he presented his case, and had had an opportunity
to appeal his loss to Louisiana's highest court. "Mere errors" at the trial can
be corrected within the state system, Waite wrote, adding, "Our authority
does not extend beyond an examination of the power of the courts below
to proceed at all." Waite ignored the invitation that Kennard's lawyers had
extended to address the Fourteenth Amendment directly. He did, however,
approve the Louisiana court's declaration that the Fourteenth Amendment
had made no change in state power over trial by jury, and he did not dispute Louisiana's argument that privileges and immunities had not enlarged
federal power over state trials. By the time Waite wrote the Court's opinion,
Louisiana had moved on to fresher controversies, and a decision sustaining
the state yielded no practical benefits to Pinchback or Morgan, but it did
score another victory for state power over trial by jury.[40]

A few months later, the Supreme Court revisited Louisiana and again
ruled for state sovereignty over trial by jury. The case involved two Louisiana laws, its 1869 civil rights law and a statute passed in 1871 that allowed
judges to decide cases when juries deadlocked. In his memoirs, Governor
Henry Clay Warmoth remembered signing the 1869 law because it did not
violate the Constitution, but considered it a harmless dead letter; "colored
men and women never attempted to avail themselves of its provisions," he
said. They did not dare, because to do so went too much against public
opinion, he added.[41] In fact, though, public opinion prevented neither black
people from using the law nor courts from ruling in their favor. On March
1, 1871, Joseph A. Walker, operator of a New Orleans coffeehouse that refused to serve Charles S. Sauvinet because of his color, found himself in
court, convicted by the judge after his jury could not agree on a verdict.
Walker's lawyers, like Kennard's, invoked the Fourteenth Amendment's
privileges and immunities clause to claim their right to a jury, but it did
no good. Waite ruled the law constitutional—not the civil rights law, but

the law abridging trial by jury.[42] Although the Court only indirectly gave its support to the Louisiana civil rights law, by upholding the conviction of a segregating coffeehouse owner, this decision still defied Louisiana public opinion, according to Warmoth's assessment.

In part the Court used cases arising out of the commerce clause to reconsider how to balance neutral constitutional principles against public opinion. In 1877, five years after Strauder killed his wife and three years before the Supreme Court would decide his case, Waite wrote the most important decision of his career, one that sided with state law and became emblematic of his thinking. He sanctioned state regulation of Chicago grain elevators. Illinois had passed a law that dictated the price elevator operators could charge for storing grain: two cents a bushel for the first thirty days and a half cent thereafter. If Waite's biographer is to be believed, even this seemingly race-neutral opinion had a racial component; Waite acted for the state law in part because he saw it as a better alternative to the natural-rights arguments that he associated with the abolitionists he so disliked.[43]

Just a year after deciding that Illinois could regulate interstate commerce flowing through its grain elevators, Waite decided that Louisiana could not regulate interstate commerce passing through its borders by protecting the rights of black passengers on steamboats. The case began when Josephine DeCuir sought passage on the steamboat *Governor Allen* to her plantation. DeCuir was well educated, had lived in Paris, and owned a plantation, but because of her color the *Governor Allen*'s captain refused her a stateroom or even a place at the ship's dinner table. DeCuir sued, asserting that her equal rights had been violated. Arbitrary rules requiring equal treatment should be avoided, Waite wrote; far better to decide each case "upon a view of the particular rights involved." Waite's most prominent scholarly defender on this point explains that Waite only wanted to halt state "burdens" on interstate commerce. Most passengers on steamboats were white, and white people might not buy tickets if they had to associate with black passengers. Louisiana's desegregation law was a "burden" on interstate commerce in that it threatened the profits of steamboat operators. The lawyers attacking Louisiana's civil rights law made precisely this point when they urged the justices to consider public opinion:

> It is to no purpose to say that the unwillingness of most white people to occupy the same apartments with colored people, and to eat at the same table with them on steamboats and at hotels, is a prejudice. We must deal with

things as they are, not as we may imagine they ought to be. Laws cannot change human nature. This feeling exists; it is almost universal; it is natural; and the master of the steamboat, on the Western and Southern waters, who should attempt to place white and colored passengers promiscuously in the same apartments . . . would incur the risk of constant disorder and conflicts, and drive from his boat the greater part of the traveling community, to the ruin of his business.[44]

Scholars have criticized Louisiana's supreme court for failing to adequately defend its state's law against charges that it burdened commerce. Louisiana's court simply asserted that the legislation meant no interference with interstate commerce and legislators had enacted the law "solely to protect the newly enfranchised citizens of the United States" within the state from prejudice, not to affect any commercial interest. This terse denial was not enough, Charles Lofgren has alleged. The Louisiana court argued that because the act involved civil rights, "it simply did not regulate commerce." According to Lofgren, the Louisiana judges "sidestepped" an "opportunity" to say that "the law pertained only to commerce *within* Louisiana."[45]

This argument fails because the Illinois Supreme Court had issued a similarly skimpy and terse denial in the grain-elevators case: "The statute is not a regulation of commerce within the purview of the Constitution." So, in fact, both states' highest courts disclaimed any attempt to burden interstate commerce, and neither built a detailed argument supporting its assertions. The legal scholar Joseph R. Palmore has pointed out that ship captains testified at DeCuir's trial, one saying that the boats were segregated "to protect a man in his business." He continued, "If a man started on a steamboat out of this port or any other port and allowed negroes to occupy rooms in the main cabin, . . . I don't think he would carry many other people." This statement shows that one important element in the argument against DeCuir's suit was that segregation protected commerce. Making a profit *is* commerce.[46] But none of the testimony could predict with certainty that whites definitely would boycott steamboats if they had to ride with blacks. The Louisiana law was a burden because it *might* infringe on the steamboat operators' ability to make a profit; whether it might or not represented judicial speculation about how the public might react. By dictating a price— two cents a bushel for the first thirty days—the Illinois law *definitely* impinged on the grain-elevator operators' ability to turn a profit. Lawyers for the elevator operators contended that the principle of the law threatened not only the warehousemen but their customers as well. If the state had a right to impose a low price, then it also had the right to impose a high price. Waite sided with what he saw as the majority of the public in both cases; by its apparent approval, public opinion lightened the burden inherent in the Illinois law and by its disapproval created the burden in Louisiana. If the majority of white steamboat passengers had not objected to civil rights, there would have been no burden. In this instance, public opinion mattered more to Waite than his commitment to states' rights.[47]

In 1880, when the Supreme Court finally reached its most important jury discrimination cases, Waite's indifference to civil rights and his approval of states' rights converged. Even as Mississippi's Lamar had challenged congressional Republicans to name even one discriminating statute in the South, West Virginia "singled out and denied its black citizens the right and privilege of participating in the administration of the law, as jurors."[48] West Virginia's law, still in force in 1875, had been enacted by the legislature in 1873: "All white male persons who are twenty-one years of age and not over sixty, who are citizens of this State, shall be liable to serve as jurors."[49]

West Virginia officials followed this law when an all-white Ohio County grand jury charged Taylor Strauder with murdering his wife. Strauder's lawyers, Blackburn Barrett Dovener and George D. Davenport, complained to the state judge trying his case that because West Virginia does not allow black men to serve on juries, "he cannot have the full and equal benefit of all laws and proceedings of the State of West Virginia . . . as is enjoyed by white citizens." Dovener and Davenport's motion began by explaining that Strauder was "a person of color," formerly a slave. They continued:

> Your petitioner avers that under the laws of Virginia and West Virginia the relation of Husband and wife was not recognized between slaves and that an impression is general in this county and the adjacent ones, and throughout the whole state that colored men are not entitled to the same protection in their marital relations as white men.[50]

After making this claim—no doubt entirely accurate—Dovener and Davenport proceeded to complain that West Virginia did not allow black men on its juries. One element of their argument logically followed the other. White men charged with murder in circumstances similar to Taylor Strauder routinely escaped punishment. Strauder had come home to find a white man escaping from his house, evidently having just had sex with his wife. The white men on juries expected white husbands, fathers, brothers, sons, and fiancés to react violently in such a situation. They expected the white man to kill the man, not the woman, but they did expect violence, and they sympathized with a white man so enraged by another man's invasion of his marital bed that he could not control himself. White male jurors routinely excused such white men as temporarily insane. Contemporary observers doubted the juries really thought the men insane but acquitted them anyway because an unwritten law tolerated such violence. In fact, defense lawyers could call on nineteenth-century science to argue that their clients suffered "moral insanity" or fell victim to an "irresistible impulse," maddened by the sight of "their" woman in bed with another man. A good lawyer could make a plausible case. There were at least ten well-known instances of men acquitted after killing their wives' lovers, the most famous being a congressman, Daniel Sickles. Sickles not only escaped punishment for killing Philip Barton Key, the U.S. attorney for New York; he went on to become a Union army general, the same general who required that Texas blacks be admitted to jury service. Dovener and Davenport implied that Strauder, a black man, could expect no similar sympathy with an all-white jury and that was discrimination. Black male jurors would sympathize with Strauder's rage and even understand why a black man might turn on his wife rather than her white lover. In fact, a jury of both black and white men might be perfect: the blacks could empathize with the husband's rage and the whites with a former slave too subservient to kill a white man.[51]

Since West Virginia would not treat him equally, Strauder petitioned the state court to transfer his case to federal court. He based his request on the Civil Rights Act of 1866, which conferred exclusive jurisdiction on U.S. courts in all cases affecting persons who cannot enforce their rights in state courts. Judge Thayer Melvin ruled that Strauder was not entitled to have his case removed to federal court and the trial proceeded in May 1873. Convicted, Strauder appealed to the West Virginia Supreme Court of Appeals, meeting in Wheeling. W. S. Haymond, president of the court, mulled over Strauder's conviction and the record of his trial. As he considered the case, Haymond jotted his thoughts on a legal pad. In selecting Strauder's jury, the trial court followed West Virginia law, Haymond noted, reviewing the details: "Sect. 3 ch 159 is still the law now having been repealed and the jury is taken from the 24 required by Code 1873 p. 103 sec 3 to be summoned— From the 24—20 shall be taken & the accused shall strike off eight names." Haymond knew full well that as he considered Strauder's conviction, Congress was debating a federal civil rights law, one very likely to pass. But it had not passed yet: "If the laws now require negroes to be summoned" for jury duty, Haymond reasoned, "there would be no necessity for the passage of the civil rights bill now pending."[52] Haymond rejected Strauder's discrimination argument but still overturned his conviction because he had not been properly examined in county court before being tried in circuit court, as West Virginia law required.[53]

One month before Lamar's speech claiming that no state violated the Fourteenth Amendment, on January 9, 1875, a second all-white West Virginia jury again convicted Taylor Strauder of murder. Strauder and his lawyers then returned to court "pray[ing] that judgment may be arrested" for a variety of reasons, including the judge's refusal to transfer his case to a court that did not discriminate in the selection of jurors. Rejecting defense motions for a new trial, Melvin sentenced Strauder to be hanged on March 26, 1875, and urged him to give up any hope of winning a new trial.[54]

Through his lawyers, Strauder once again appealed to the Supreme Court of Appeals of West Virginia, meeting in Wheeling. The lawyers alleged that Melvin had erred in not granting their petition to have Strauder's case removed to federal court. On November 17, 1877, the West Virginia court again ruled against Strauder, this time directly confronting Strauder's constitutional claims. Judge William Green (1806–80) considered "the true meaning" of the Thirteenth and Fourteenth Amendments as well as the 1866 Civil Rights Act. Green returned to the Supreme Court's proslavery ruling in *Dred Scott v. Sandford*, which, he explained, found that black people were not and never could be citizens, "except by amendment to the Constitution." "Though disapproved by many lawyers," Green observed, *Dred Scott v. Sandford* had never been reversed. Green believed that the Fourteenth Amendment had overruled *Dred Scott v. Sandford* only in a few, very particular ways. The Fourteenth Amendment conferred no new rights, privileges, or immunities, he said. It merely replicated Article IV, Section 2. The West Virginia judge announced "with great confidence" that the language of the Fourteenth Amendment had no effect whatever on any person's rights, but merely protected the rights of travelers across state lines.[55]

Green also found solace in the Supreme Court's ruling against Myra Bradwell, decided on the same day as the *Slaughterhouse Cases*. If the Constitution allowed Illinois to prevent women from becoming lawyers, Green reasoned, then it should also permit states to keep blacks from becoming jurors. "The mere prohibition of negroes to sit upon the jury which tried him cannot be regarded as a denial of equal protection," Green said. Blacks have no more right to jury service than "a Chinaman or a woman." Green

denied that West Virginia deprived blacks equal protection of law by refusing to seat them as jurors. "It is doubtful," he said, "whether in the future,
any action of a State is likely to occur, which will ever be held to come
within the purview" of the Fourteenth Amendment's prohibition against
denial of due process. No state law passed since the Fourteenth Amendment had ever discriminated against blacks, Green said. According to West
Virginia's highest court, the state's jury law did not contradict Congressman
Lamar at all because restricting jury service to white men did not deny the
equal protection of the law to anyone. Green concluded that Judge Thayer
Melvin had not erred in refusing to transfer Strauder's case to federal court
and ordered Ohio County to hang Strauder.[56]

As Strauder's lawyers pondered their next move, other lawyers challenged the South's all-white jury system, as happened after January 29, 1878,
when an all-white grand jury in Patrick County, Virginia, indicted two
black teenage brothers, Burwell and Lee Reynolds, for murdering Aaron C.
Shelton, a white man. In Virginia at this time the black minority voted and
served in the state legislature, but whites, in the words of one English visitor,
"systematically" excluded them from juries, saying, "They have got votes,
and we cannot give them everything."[57] Nonetheless, the policy of keeping
blacks off juries was not so settled that white lawyers with political ambitions could not challenge all-white juries. Two Confederate army veterans,
Andrew Murray Lybrook and William Martin, represented the Reynolds
brothers. Lybrook took the case, and pressed for black jurors, while serving
in the Virginia State Senate and presumably anticipated continuing his political career after representing two black men charged with killing a white
man. His wife was the daughter of Hardin Reynolds, a slave owner, and
in 1970 one Virginia scholar speculated that Hardin Reynolds might have
owned the Reynolds brothers' mother. Perhaps the two lawyers asked for a
jury that included some black men because Lybrook felt a family obligation
to his wife's family's slaves. Such an explanation denies that the two former
Confederate army officers could have been anything other than paternal-
ists. In fact, few leading Virginia army officers came from the ranks of the
state's large-scale planters. Army officers in the South, as in the North, more
often had engineering or mechanical training, and they led the Confederacy toward greater centralized power, just as did their counterparts in the
North. Their paternalism cannot be assumed.[58]

When the trial judge rejected their request for black jurors, Lybrook and
Martin asked to have their cases transferred to a federal circuit court. Denied that as well, they then had little choice but to go to trial, where an

all-white jury convicted Lee Reynolds. The Supreme Court of Virginia reversed Lee Reynolds's conviction and awarded him a new trial. In October
another all-white jury convicted Lee Reynolds. Lybrook and Martin now
applied to federal Judge Alexander Rives for a writ of habeas corpus, alleg-
ing "that the right secured to them by the law providing for equal civil rights
of all the citizens of the United States [was] denied to them" by Virginia.[59]

With its connotations of liberty and personal freedom, the great writ had
long threatened state sovereignty. In 1833 and 1842, Congress had passed habeas corpus laws that encroached on state power, protecting federal officers
from punishment by state judges. The 1842 law promised "remedial justice
in the courts of the United States," suggesting that state courts' procedures
sometimes needed remedying.[60] In 1863, Congress approved Lincoln's sus-
pension of habeas corpus, but it also looked forward, again freeing federal officers held in state jails and authorizing federal judges to take cases
from state courts. Later, in 1866 and 1867, Congress further expanded federal habeas corpus at the expense of the states. These expansions of federal
power alarmed Pennsylvanian Edgar Cowan, the stalwart defender of state
sovereignty. He produced the familiar argument—"this Government of
the United States is a Government of delegated powers"—an argument that
antebellum defenders of states' rights had used for decades, but now the
argument provoked laughter from Wisconsin Republican Senator Timothy
Howe: "I should like to see the authority for that."[61]

"I know such gentlemen sneer," Cowan shot back. "I know they snigger
at this doctrine; and I know that a man has a right to snigger at his own disgrace, at his own ignorance."[62]

Ignorance was hardly the problem. Every member of Congress knew that
Thomas Jefferson had made an enumerated-powers argument, holding that
the federal government only had the specific powers listed in the Constitution and no more, nothing implied. The Supreme Court had contradicted
that argument with its *McCulloch v. Maryland* decision, and by 1867 some
Republicans thought it moribund. Cowan and the Democrats defended it,
but their efforts seemed hopeless against the rising tide of federal power and
did no good; Congress authorized lawyers like Lybrook and Martin to approach federal judges for the writs of habeas corpus that would force state
judges to justify themselves, to prove that they really had not violated their
prisoners' constitutional rights.[63]

Lybrook and Martin must have expected a sympathetic response from
Rives. Rives had been using black jurors in his court since 1871 and even

claimed that the lawyers he knew preferred them. Descended from a prestigious slaveholding Virginia family, Rives was best known as the brother of a well-respected Virginia politician opposed to the plantation oligarchy, William Cabell Rives. In the Jacksonian era, William Cabell Rives had transformed Virginia politics by leading business-minded Democrats into the Whig Party, much to the disgust of states' rights–oriented planters who associated business and industrialization with the centralized power they so feared as a threat to their human-property rights.[64] Alexander Rives never achieved the fame of his brother, but like his brother he also favored the Union and opposed planter interests. In 1866, Governor Francis Harrison Pierpont appointed Alexander Rives to Virginia's Court of Appeals, an appointment hailed from one end of the state to the other, the *Washington Daily Intelligencer* enthused. This seems quite improbable. In 1865, Virginians had elected a reactionary state legislature that rejected the Fourteenth Amendment, forbade black voting, and enacted a Black Code designed to perpetuate slavery through vagrancy laws and other legal stratagems. Four years after, when Alexander Rives ran unsuccessfully for Congress as a Republican—a "Radical" Republican, according to his enemies—most white Virginians had turned away from both the Democrats and the Republicans, electing Conservative Party candidate Gilbert C. Walker as governor in 1869.[65] In power for more than a decade, the Conservative Party ratified the Fourteenth Amendment, allowing Virginia to regain its place in Congress, but retained white Virginia's traditional hostility toward blacks' rights while still appealing for their votes. In acknowledging that blacks could vote, one Conservative newspaper guilelessly expected that blacks would want to vote with their employers: "It is the most natural thing in the world," the *Richmond Daily Dispatch* explained, for "the superior race" to tell a black voter how he "ought" to vote. Conservatives forbade marriage across racial lines, and although they did not require formal segregation, one Conservative congressman exclaimed, "Never! Never! Never!" when asked about "social equality" between the races. Conservative judges summoned only white men for jury service.[66]

In attacking this practice, Rives confronted a problem more complex than in West Virginia, with its obviously discriminatory law. Under Governor Pierpont, Virginia whites had first tried to overtly reassert antebellum values but ran into determined opposition from African American men and women using rallies, popular celebrations, and mass rescues of police prisoners to assert themselves, forcing Virginia Conservatives to eliminate racial discrimination from the text of the law. "The state law is not at fault here," Rives conceded and focused his attention instead on the county officials picking the jurors, observing that an all-white jury could not "be imputed to chance." This fact could not be overlooked, Rives believed. To allow blacks to be tried for their lives, liberty, and property by white men hostile to them, Rives said, would be to deny them the guarantees secured by the Sixth Amendment. Rives decided that Burwell and Lee Reynolds had been denied the fair trial promised by the laws of Virginia and ordered that their trials be docketed in his court. He ordered federal marshals to take them into custody and to secure a jury, chosen without distinction as to race or color.[67]

Virginians rushed to defend their state's sovereignty. Newspapers howled in protest. The *Richmond Daily Dispatch* dismissed Rives's opinion as "puerile" and "too absurd for comment."[68] Virginia's attorney general denied that keeping juries all-white violated black defendants' rights.[69] A resident of Patrick County, where the murder had occurred, reported "great dissatisfaction" with Rives and asked if his decision might not be "a fatal stab at the doctrine of State rights."[70] The state government asked the U.S. Supreme Court to issue a mandamus ordering Rives to return the prisoners to its custody. In the meantime, the state continued its legal processes against the two brothers. In November 1878, the state tried both Burwell and Lee Reynolds again. The all-white jury trying Lee Reynolds reached a guilty verdict, while the all-white jury hearing Burwell Reynolds's case could not agree on a verdict.

In his answer to the state's petition, Rives repeated his argument that the absence of blacks in Virginia juries proved discrimination: "I humbly submit, it matters not whether it be done by the State by commission or omission, by law or want of law, by administration of its executive or judicial departments, the mischief is equal and the remedy as much needed."[71] Virginia lawyers responded by quoting the Constitution's Article III, giving the Supreme Court jurisdiction "in all cases . . . in which a State shall be a party." Virginia insisted this meant exclusive jurisdiction; in no circumstance can an inferior court decide questions involving state sovereignty. Virginia's lawyers also cited the Declaration of Independence, which, they explained, said that to secure the natural rights of life and personal liberty "governments are instituted among men." Those governments were the state governments, and to protect the natural rights of life and liberty, sovereignty rests alone with the states. Like their counterparts in West Virginia, the Virginia lawyers resolutely held that their state had never denied equal protection of the laws to anyone. They did not believe that having a mixed-race jury guaranteed equal protection.

> With much more propriety could it be claimed that civil rights had been denied where *judges* were not taken in equal proportion from all races and colors without reference to previous condition of servitude. We do not believe there is a State in the Union the bench of which is adorned by judges selected from the colored race.[72]

Rives did not stop with seizing control of the state's case against Burwell and Lee Reynolds. He told a grand jury that by choosing only white jurors Virginia state judges neglected their own state's laws, which did not discriminate, and their obligation to the supreme law. Rives read the text of the 1875 Civil Rights Act's Section 4 and added, "If it should appear to you that by a long and systematic course" a judge "has never admitted to his list the names of colored men duly qualified, you would be compelled to infer his guilt and indict him." Rives lectured the jurors that he meant to "assert the just supremacy of the Constitution and laws of the United States," and he rejected "shallow disquisitions" on the constitutionality of the 1875 law. The grand jury proceeded to collect evidence that Franklin County had never had a black juror since the county had been organized in 1785. The same could be said for Patrick and Charlotte counties. Pittsylvania County had never had a black juror since the current judge took office. In Henry County jurors found that the judge had said, "No nigger shall ever sit on a jury in my court!" Newspapers as far away as St. Louis and New York published the news that Rives had launched an investigation into his state's jury system.[73]

On February 27, 1879, the federal grand jury indicted the county court judge in Pittsylvania County, James Doddridge Coles, and thirteen other state judges. In March a deputy U.S. marshal led a posse to arrest Coles and take him before Rives. Coles responded with a petition for habeas corpus with the U.S. Supreme Court. To make sure the Supreme Court had original jurisdiction, the state of Virginia filed for the writ on Coles's behalf. In their petition, Virginia's lawyers pressed the Supreme Court to declare Section 4 of the 1875 Civil Rights Act unconstitutional. Virginia's attorney general and his cocounsel charged that the 1875 Civil Rights Act threatened to turn the government into "a consolidated despotism, the despot being the congressional majority of the day."[74]

All three cases attracted national attention as they made their way to the U.S. Supreme Court. In April 1879, when the Court postponed argument on the Commonwealth of Virginia's case against Rives, the *Washington Post* told its readers that the case raised questions both interesting and important. In fact, the *Post* explained, the issues were too important to be heard in the hurry and confusion at the end of the term. The justices postponed argument until they next met, in October.[75] African Americans followed the proceedings and crowded into the Supreme Court to hear arguments in the cases.[76]

At precisely the moment that Rives ordered the Virginia judges arrested, and the case made its way to the Supreme Court, the strength of Democrats' challenges to the Republican defense of integrated juries became apparent in Congress. In the words of Drew Kershen, Democratic congressmen attacked federal jury selection "with the fervor of a tent revival," charging that Republican marshals kept Democrats off federal juries, seating Republicans and blacks instead, to the detriment of Democratic litigants. After the 1874 elections, Democrats controlled the House by nearly eighty votes and had made inroads in the Senate, reducing the Republican majority. They could change the law, and they did. The new law required federal judges to appoint a jury commission that would put at least three hundred names in a box to be drawn at random. In theory the new system should have led to juries half Republican and half Democrat since the law specified that both parties had to be represented on the new commissions. As one Democrat said, "If they are to be packed at all, I prefer that they be packed half and half." In fact, though, Kershen's research in Louisiana shows that after 1879 white Democrats increasingly dominated jury pools and blacks disappeared. Before 1879, one-third of jurors had been black; afterward, 7 percent. This shift must have occurred because Democratic commissioners unabashedly pursued their partisan agenda while Republicans flinched in the face of changing public opinion.[77]

On June 30, 1879, Republican President Rutherford B. Hayes signed into law the bill passed by congressional Democrats. Despite its nefarious purpose, the new law did reiterate the 1875 rule against racial discrimination in jury selection. On the question of state discrimination, Hayes sided with Rives and argued for the constitutionality of the 1875 Civil Rights Act. In 1876, Hayes had campaigned for office promising to reconcile with the South, but as the 1878 off-year election season progressed, disturbing reports reached the White House that white Southerners had renewed their violence against blacks. Hayes had responded by ordering the Department of Justice to enforce election laws. He also wanted Rives's action on behalf of black jurors defended at the Supreme Court. In October 1879, Hayes's attorney general, Charles Devens (1820–91), a Massachusetts lawyer and former Union army general, argued before the Supreme Court for Rives and on behalf of the 1875 law. A courageous but indifferent general who at Chancellorsville had disastrously left his flank exposed to enemy attack, Devens had barely survived the war: slightly injured at Ball's Bluff, more seriously wounded at Chickahominy, and wounded a third time at Chancellorsville before being struck down with severe rheumatism. After the war, he adhered to the position favored by the Fourteenth Amendment's strongest proponents, seeing it as a logical and necessary result of the war that realized "the immortal truths of the Declaration of Independence." Now Devens took those immortal truths to the Supreme Court, arguing that although the U.S. Army had destroyed the southern states' Black Codes, in fact, they actually continued them off the books.[78]

As Devens trampled out the vintage where the grapes of wrath were stored, Justice Stephen J. Field loosed what he thought was his own terrible swift sword. A native of Connecticut who had migrated to California in the 1849 gold rush, Field joined the Court in 1863, appointed by Lincoln when Congress added a tenth seat to the Court. Lincoln chose Field to better cement California to the Union and because of Field's strong Unionist credentials and capable work on California's state supreme court. That Field was a Democrat apparently had not troubled Lincoln, but now he challenged Devens with the same small-government arguments that Democrats had pressed in Congress: Many segments of the population could not sit on juries but nonetheless received fair trials, he said. Foreigners, for example, could not serve on American juries, yet few would suggest that they were not equally protected by the law. Devens acknowledged the point but answered that as citizens of the country, blacks were therefore entitled to take part in the administration of the laws.[79]

Field then asked how a state legislator could be punished for enacting a law that contradicted a federal statute. Field hoped to trip up Devens with his question, but instead he misstepped. In the Civil War, Devens had been defeated when he had not known enough about his opponent, but Chancellorsville had been a lesson, and Devens was finished leaving his flanks exposed. Only one month earlier, Field had given an interview to the *Washington Post* explaining why he had ruled against a San Francisco city ordinance that called for cutting the hair of Chinese prisoners. Field, hearing the case while on circuit in California, had favored punishing the sheriff who cut the hair, not the lawmakers who had originally written the ordinance that the sheriff enforced with his clippers. Devens reminded Field of this fact and added that he expected to prosecute the people who actually discriminated, not the lawmakers—exactly as Field had authorized in California.[80] Whatever the logic of his argument, Devens had no chance of winning the irascible Field to his side, but the other justices could not have missed the spectacle of Field caught in a contradiction by the attorney general.

On March 1, 1880, the Supreme Court decided all three cases in decisions written by William Strong.[81] West Virginia's conviction of Taylor Strauder posed the fewest complications. Strong said that by singling out "colored persons" for discrimination, West Virginia affixed a brand upon its black population, asserting their inferiority and stimulating race prejudice. This clearly violated the Fourteenth Amendment, Strong wrote, which had necessarily implied a positive immunity or right, the right being the exemption from unfriendly legislation. West Virginia lost its case; explicit discrimination actually written into the statute would not be tolerated. In the end, while Strauder walked out of jail a free man, never to be tried again, nine years in prison awaiting his day before the Supreme Court had broken his health.[82]

Virginia, lacking a state law against black jury service, fared better. The Court decided that Rives should not have taken the Reynolds brothers from state authorities. Strong wrote:

> If, as was alleged in the argument, though it does not appear in the petition or record, the officer to whom was intrusted the selection of the persons from whom the juries for the indictment and trial of the petitions were drawn, disregarding the statute of the State, confined his selection to white persons, and refused to select any persons of the colored race, solely because of their color, his action was a gross violation of the spirit of the State's laws, as well as of federal law.[83]

The key phrase was "though it does not appear in the petition or record." With those words, the Supreme Court ruled that discrimination would have to be proved in the petition, or the record before the Court would act against it. Moreover, since Strong believed discriminating county officers violated their own state's law, he presumed that Virginia's appeals process would right the wrong. Only if the appeals state's highest court ratified a proved discrimination, bias documented with testimony, could the federal courts intervene.[84] The Court denied federal courts the ability to intervene in cases of jury discrimination until the states' highest courts had spoken. So Strong required two things: proof of discrimination in the petition or record and approval of the discrimination by the states' highest courts. Federal judges could not rush in at the first sign of trouble, as Rives had done.

Strong's requirement of proof was explicit. He rejected Rives's argument that the appearance of discrimination proved the prejudice, emphasizing that the Reynolds brothers had not proved discrimination by the state officers. Strong referred to "the assertions in the opinion for removal" and declared that such assertions fell "short of showing that any civil right was denied."[85] The Court's decision in *Virginia v. Rives*, then, provided a road map for black defendants charged in state courts by all-white juries: They would have to produce positive proof of the discrimination. Mere assertions and allegations would not be sufficient, nor would the appearance of discrimination; under Strong's formulation, federal courts could intervene when states seated white-only juries, but only if state authorities confessed their prejudice and the highest state court endorsed the discrimination.[86]

In the case of Judge Coles, Strong ruled for the United States. The great purpose of the Thirteenth and Fourteenth Amendments, Strong wrote, was to raise black people from a condition of inferiority and servitude to perfect equality of civil rights with all other people within the jurisdiction of the states. The amendments intended to "take away all possibility of oppression by law because of race or color." Strong frankly said that the amendments shrank the power of the states and enlarged the power of Congress. He reiterated what he had already said in *Strauder v. West Virginia*: black people have a right to an impartial jury trial by jurors chosen without discrimination. His words exactly echoed those of Frederick Frelinghuysen as he shepherded the 1875 jury discrimination law through Congress. In his discussion of the 1875 law, Strong repeated what Frelinghuysen and other Republican proponents had said, that it did not interfere with states' powers to select jurors. It did prevent them from discriminating as they did so. State officers had no immunity from federal prosecution, Strong wrote and found that Coles was "correctly held to answer for" his actions.[87]

Field and Clifford dissented, taking the side of southern white Democrats, who claimed the 1875 law's juror provision unconstitutionally interfered with state juries, menacing the independence and autonomy of the states, rendering them dependent on the central government. The authors of the Thirteenth and Fourteenth Amendments did not intend to alter the constitutional structure of the nation, the balance of power between the states and the national government, Field wrote. Finally, he alleged that Strong assumed white people cannot be fair and honest jurors when black people are involved, a doctrine Field repudiated. He also seemed to reject his own reasoning in the Chinese haircutting case that he had decided only a few months earlier. In the Chinese case, Field said, a national question involving the whole country could not be left to San Francisco or California. How San Francisco jailers treated their prisoners was not just a local problem and could not be left to local authorities. Angering China by mistreating its citizens risked a military confrontation and raised diplomatic questions beyond the provenance of local police. Field apparently calculated that African Americans could be mistreated because no African country had, or could have, sufficient military power to threaten American national security. Field's reasoning suggested that American constitutional rights depended on the power of the victim's country of origin.[88]

Republicans welcomed Strong's opinions. There is some evidence that the decisions pleased African Americans as much as they outraged Field. Boston blacks published a letter thanking Devens for his work on their behalf. The "good fruits" of the war had finally begun to ripen with black people protected in their rights, a Vermont paper opined.[89] The *New York Times* defended the Supreme Court from criticism and charged that critics had not yet accepted the fundamental changes wrought by the war.[90]

Other papers sided with Field. The editor of the *Nation*, Edwin Lawrence Godkin, had once studied law under David Dudley Field (Stephen's brother) and now pronounced Stephen Field's dissent "very lucid" and "able." Godkin warned that Strong's opinion threatened to carry the nation a long way toward an unhealthy centralization of authority.[91] The *Washington Post* saw the jury decisions as "partisan" and headlined its story "The States Rights Cases Decided for the Republicans." The *Post* noted that both Democrats on the Court filed a "vigorous dissent."[92] The *San Francisco Daily Evening Bulletin* headlined its story "Federal Supremacy."[93] The *St. Louis Globe-Democrat* agreed, calling the decisions "Judgments against Democracy," meaning against the Democratic Party. The *Globe-Democrat* explained to its readers that Democrats in Congress had been trying to roll back the results of the Civil War, working night and day to do so. The paper observed that the two Democrats on the Supreme Court took the same position as their Democratic allies in Congress, standing against their Republican associates.[94] In Virginia the legislature prepared resolutions instructing the state's congressional delegation to seek repeal of all laws based on implied powers. The Supreme Court threatened "the very existence of state government," the Virginians charged.[95]

By its ruling, the Supreme Court stabilized uncertainty about the balance of power between federal authorities and state officers picking juries. It had taken steps toward resolving issues that the political process could not settle. Despite newspaper claims that the Supreme Court had followed a Republican agenda, what the Court did was actually far more subtle. Black defendants had a right to hold discriminating state officers accountable, but they did not have a right to have blacks on their juries. Every defendant had a right to a jury selected without racial discrimination by the state. Contrary to what Rives had claimed, the mere absence of blacks did not prove that a civil right had been violated; evidence of deliberate discrimination by a state officer did.[96] Defendants would have to prove, not merely allege or assert, that state officers had discriminated by selecting only whites for their juries.

One week after the jury cases, the Supreme Court rendered its decision in another case involving state power. *Ex Parte Siebold* did not involve juries, but it tested the element in the 1875 Civil Rights Act that so concerned Field, the provision punishing state officers who violated citizens' federal rights while carrying out state law. The *Washington Post* condemned *Siebold* as the final step in an unholy quartet of decisions reaching "as far as the most arrogant advocate of a consolidated government and central omnipotence can possibly demand." Albert Siebold, Walter Tucker, Martin C. Burns, Lewis Coleman, and Henry Bowers had served as election judges at various Baltimore voting precincts. The federal court in Baltimore indicted, arrested, and convicted all five for preventing federal officers from inspecting the voting and for stuffing their ballot boxes in violation of federal law. At the Supreme Court, the five men made a historical argument, showing that constitutional safeguards of property and liberty against a despotic centralized power had emerged from medieval England. In America this tradition continued as men had established institutions in separate political societies to protect their rights. The colonies and then the states tried all felonies except treason by courts of their own creation. Americans knew that concentrating power in one center would "inevitably and speedily destroy all liberty," Siebold and his fellows alleged.[97]

Bradley wrote the Court's opinion. Much of the argument that Siebold and his fellows made seemed perfectly designed to challenge decades of his own thinking that states' rights had threatened the establishment of a genuine American nation. In a passage that clearly represented Bradley's personal beliefs, the justice lectured the defendants that they failed to recognize that the nation had adopted a national constitution, one that established a real government therein, operating upon persons and territory and things. This Constitution, Bradley said, should be as dear to every American citizen as his state government. He warned against jealousy of the federal power and insisted no one should regard the federal government "as a hostile organization." The federal law authorized prosecution of state officers carrying out state laws when doing so violated federal law, and when state laws come into conflict with federal law, they become void. But Bradley did believe that American history had given the states powers to protect their citizens' natural-law rights. Limiting himself to federal elections, Bradley decided that federal courts could prosecute state officers and denied Siebold's application for a writ of habeas corpus.[98]

The effervescent Frederick Frelinghuysen could hardly contain his joy. Frelinghuysen thought Bradley's opinion, allowing for federal punishment of discriminating state officers, not only right but "calculated to do great good to the nation." Bradley had apparently cleared the way for the Supreme Court to hold state officers who chose only white jurors responsible for their discrimination.[99]

Subsequent decisions reaffirmed but did not materially alter the decisions Strong issued on March 1, 1880. Not long after the Supreme Court issued its decisions in the three jury cases, officials in New Castle County, Delaware, gathered to select persons to serve as grand jurors and petit jurors for the coming year. As they had always done, they chose only white men as jurors, deliberately excluding all blacks. On May 10, New Castle County's court of oyer and terminer seated its grand jury, made up entirely of white men. The next day the jurors indicted William Neal, a black man, for the rape of Margaret E. Gosser. Neal filed a motion protesting the grand jury and the trial jury. Neal's attorney, Anthony Higgins (1840–1912), explained that in Delaware jurors came from the voting rolls, and Delaware's constitution limited voting to white men. Since the laws of Delaware prevented Neal from getting a fair trial, Higgins asked to have his client's case transferred to the Circuit Court of the United States for the District of Delaware. Higgins, a Republican Union army veteran, had been the U.S. attorney for Delaware under Andrew Johnson. Although he represented a black man charged with rape, Higgins had political ambitions that would soon land him a seat in the U.S. Senate.[100]

In Delaware five judges composed all the courts in the state, one from each county in the state, each appointed by the governor for life. Joseph P. Comegys (1813–93) had been sitting as chief justice since 1876.[101] Comegys harbored no sympathy for a black man accused of rape or for a Republican lawyer seeking to transfer a Delaware case to U.S. Circuit Court. The son of a governor, Comegys had begun his political life as a Whig but shifted to the Democratic Party. In 1870 he urged organization of a white man's political party to counter African Americans' influence, believing white men had to overcome their party loyalties to organize along racial lines to counter rising black political activism.[102] His court rejected Higgins's motion, saying that no law in Delaware prevented the selection of black jurors. Although the juries were made up entirely of white men, Comegys asserted that "it did not appear" that they had been chosen because of their color. Higgins took this ruling as a challenge to produce evidence of discrimination and asked to be allowed to call witnesses proving that New Castle County officials deliberately chose only white men. Higgins wanted to call the court's commissioners, clerk, and the bailiff so that he could interrogate them.

Delaware's attorney general objected. George Gray opposed allowing any such investigation, and the chief justice of Delaware agreed with Gray. Comegys said that there had been "full time" to produce such witnesses before making the motion. On May 25 an all-white jury convicted Neal of rape. Two days later, the court sentenced Neal to hang on August 27. Higgins appealed to John Marshall Harlan, the associate justice of the Supreme Court assigned to the circuit that included Delaware, for a hearing before the Supreme Court.[103]

Appointed to the Court in 1877 by President Hayes, Harlan has long seemed an enigma, a former slave owner and opponent of emancipation who came to champion equal rights for African Americans. Harlan's most penetrating biographer uses his wife's memoirs to argue that the Harlans created an identity for themselves as humane patriarchs. John Harlan's insistence on equal rights for black people emerged from his paternalism, which also set limits on his belief in civil rights. In 1866 he positively despised Sumner and Stevens. When Garrett Davis and other border-state members of Congress complained that they had not fought secession to see a Republican-dominated Congress violate the nation's foundational principles, they spoke for Harlan. But Garrett Davis migrated from the Whigs to the American Party to the Unionists. Harlan, also an old Whig, hated Democrats too much to become one; he gravitated to the Republican Party instead. Harlan sometimes joked that he feared death because he might have to spend eternity among Democrats, who would all be in hell. His distaste for the Democrats, and his paternalism, naturally inclined him to criticize them for abusing former slaves.[104]

Like Miller, Harlan delivered lectures to law students in Washington while serving on the Court. Unlike Miller, Harlan did not lace his lectures with bromides to public opinion. Miller fled Kentucky for the more hospitable climes of Iowa because Kentucky public opinion proved itself staunchly proslavery in the 1850 elections. Harlan stuck it out and became more cynical about the shifting currents of public opinion in his native Kentucky. Miller congratulated himself that the public approved his work in the *Slaughterhouse Cases*. When lecturing to his students, Harlan sometimes explained a decision where he had dissented and got a laugh by adding, "But of course I was wrong." Harlan's faith in his country's Christian mission, his love of the Constitution, his old-fashioned formalism, all meant that he possessed the confidence to joke about being out of step with public opinion. He knew he was right.[105]

Since he had most of the justices on his side, Harlan did not joke about *Neal v. Delaware*, an opinion that cut no new ground but merely applied the existing law, written just a year before by the now-retired William Strong. He began by first reviewing *Strauder v. West Virginia*, *Virginia v. Rives*, and *Ex Parte Virginia*, three cases that had sustained the removal law authorizing the transfer of cases from discriminating state courts to federal courts, and the jury protections in Section 4 of the 1875 Civil Rights Act. States are perfectly free to limit jury service to males and property holders and to set age restrictions and educational qualifications. But the nation, through its Constitution, had decided that states could not racially discriminate in the selection of jurors. The rule was very particular: defendants could object to their juries and ask for a transfer to federal court only before the trial commenced. Once the state trial began, defendants had to seek remedy for any state misconduct through the higher courts of the states and, ultimately, the U.S. Supreme Court, through the appeals process.[106]

Harlan acknowledged that Delaware's 1831 constitution restricted voting to white males and that Delaware law based jury service on voting. But Harlan accepted the arguments of Delaware state lawyers that the Fourteenth and Fifteenth Amendments had abrogated those racial restrictions, even if the state had not formally rewritten its laws. Under Strong's rule, Neal needed proof that Delaware officers actually discriminated in the selection of its jurors. The laws of the state would not serve as that proof. "Our conclusion," Harlan wrote, "is that the alleged discrimination in the state of Delaware, against citizens of the African race, in the matter of service on juries, does not result from her Constitution and laws." Harlan was willing to assume that Delaware obeyed and did not defy the Civil War amendments, even if all the jurors were white, a generous concession to the state.[107]

This meant that Neal was not entitled to have his case removed to the U.S. Circuit Court based on the mere language of the state constitution or laws of the state, written long before passage of the Fourteenth Amendment. If those old laws justified removal, then every case in Delaware could be transferred into the federal courts. "We cannot believe," Harlan said, that the framers of the removal act intended such far-reaching results. If Delaware had passed a discriminatory law after the Fourteenth Amendment had become part of the Constitution or if its courts had repudiated the amendment, then defendants would be entitled to transfer their state cases into federal court. Since Delaware had not openly defied the Fourteenth Amendment or any other part of the Constitution, transfer to federal court could not be justified. If discriminatory practices became evident as the trial proceeded, defendants could seek a remedy through the normal appeals process.[108]

Harlan, however, noted that Joseph P. Comegys, the chief justice of Delaware, had first conceded that no black person had ever sat on a Delaware jury with the remark, "[This] is in nowise remarkable in view of the fact— too notorious to be ignored—that the great body of black men residing in this State are utterly unqualified by want of intelligence, experience, or moral integrity to sit on juries." Harlan understood that a majority of the justices believed that a black defendant had no right to claim, as a matter of right, that other black people should be on his jury, but they did have a right against blanket discrimination of the sort that Comegys articulated.[109]

Harlan chastised Delaware for not allowing Neal to call the commissioners, clerks, and bailiff of the court to seek evidence of discrimination. "With entire respect for the court below," Harlan wrote, "the circumstances, in our judgment, warranted more indulgence, in the matter of time, than was granted to the prisoner whose life was at stake." Harlan pointed out that the allegations of discrimination in Neal's affidavit stood uncontradicted by the prosecution. The state failed to offer "any suggestion or intimation" that it objected to Neal's claims.[110] An action by the officer of the state, Harlan said, "is to be deemed the act of the State." Harlan again relied on Strong, quoting *Ex Parte Virginia*: "A State acts by its legislative, its executive, or its judicial authorities. It can act no other way." No agency of the state, Harlan declared, can discriminate against black people without violating the Fourteenth Amendment. When the chief justice of Delaware confessed his prejudice, he spoke for his state, and his was the final word for Delaware, leaving the wronged defendant no option other than federal law and federal courts. The Court overturned Neal's conviction and ordered a new trial.[111]

Neal v. Delaware reiterated Strong's rule of the previous year. When they could prove discrimination, defendants had a right to a new trial. Mere allegations, unsupported by testimony, were not enough to overturn an array of jurors. Like Strong, Harlan had also made it clear that county officers could be held responsible if they chose only white jurors—if the defendant could prove they did so deliberately and if the state's highest court approved.

Two justices dissented. Field objected to Harlan's assumption that a defendant's allegations, unsupported by evidence, can be taken as true if the prosecution fails to specifically contradict them. The mere absence of black people from a jury did not prove discrimination, he said. Like Harlan, Field quoted Comegys's statement that the great body of black men are utterly unqualified, but unlike Harlan, Field did not disapprove. To Field, Comegys correctly stated the obvious: Many blacks were not qualified, and their absence from jury panels did not automatically prove discrimination. The blacks might just not be worthy of jury duty. More importantly, Field did not think the state should have to contradict such claims. Acknowledging that he merely repeated what he had stated the previous term, Field said that he had carefully reconsidered Strong's opinions and still rejected them. Nothing in the Fourteenth Amendment justified federal interference with state jury selection procedures. States could achieve equal justice under the laws without selecting women, children, old or young people, and they did not have to seat blacks either.[112]

Since becoming chief justice, Waite had shown that he could never match Bradley, Miller, or Field as a presence on the Court. He filed only a brief dissent in *Neal v. Delaware*. He believed defendants had to produce real proof when making an allegation of jury discrimination. Neal had never done that, Waite believed, so he did not deserve a new trial.[113]

The nature of that proof remained an open question. In 1883, the Supreme Court indicated that it might look suspiciously at state denials of discrimination. In that year Harlan, now the Court's expert on jury discrimination cases, kept the majority he had organized in *Neal v. Delaware* to find against Kentucky. Kentucky lawmakers had twice reaffirmed their commitment to all-white juries after ratification of the Fourteenth Amendment, in 1873 and 1877. Three months after the three 1880 jury cases, Kentucky's Court of Appeals declared the state's racial requirement unconstitutional. In 1882, the laggardly legislature finally followed suit, formally striking the word "white" from Kentucky's jury selection laws. The case Harlan and his brethren considered came as Kentucky revised its laws.[114]

On January 13, 1879, John Bush of Fayette County shot Anna Vanmeter, who subsequently died, either from the gunshot wound to her thigh or, more probably, from sharing a bed with her sister, infected with scarlet fever. An all-white grand jury indicted Bush, but the all-white trial jury could not reach a verdict. In May a second all-white jury pronounced Bush guilty. Kentucky's Court of Appeals reversed this verdict and ordered a new trial. By the time Fayette County was ready to put Bush on trial for the third time, the Supreme Court had ruled in the three 1880 jury cases. Bush and his court-appointed lawyer asked that his case be transferred to U.S. Circuit Court, pointing out—accurately—that Kentucky law still required all-white juries. The trial judge rejected this motion, and another all-white jury found Bush guilty.[115]

Bush asked for a writ of habeas corpus from the U.S. Circuit Court for Kentucky. In October the federal court found Kentucky's jury selection laws so flawed that no fair trial was possible and quashed the indictment against Bush. The federal court, however, clearly hesitated to turn loose an accused murderer merely because he had been indicted and convicted by white jurors. The federal judge directed marshals to escort Bush back to Fayette County and to notify state authorities in writing that he had been released. State officers in Fayette County got the hint and promptly rearrested Bush, reindicted him, and on December 20, 1880, again called his case for trial. After several continuances, the prosecution was ready to proceed in May 1881. To make sure they would not again run afoul of the Fourteenth Amendment, Fayette County officers directed the sheriff to summon jurors without regard to their race or color. The panel selected by the sheriff turned out to be entirely white, just as in the past. So Bush was again indicted and convicted by all-white juries. Kentucky's Court of Appeals affirmed his death sentence.[116]

In 1882, the Supreme Court heard Bush's case. For the first time, a state did not directly make the sovereignty arguments the Democrats had advanced in Congress and that Virginia and West Virginia had made in court. Kentucky's lawyers instead argued that Bush had failed to produce any proof of discrimination and quoted a line from *Virginia v. Rives* where Strong found that the mere fact that all the jurors were white did not prove discrimination in their selection: "The fact may have been as stated, and yet the jury which indicted them, and the panel summoned to try them may have been impartially selected."[117]

Bush's lawyer countered with the same argument that Alexander Rives had advanced:

> There is no way to enter the inner consciousness of those officers whose
> duty it was to select and summon these jurors and find out why they passed
> one, two, three, aye, a dozen colored men, eligible and qualified to be sum-
> moned, and to perform such service, only to select and summon the thir-
> teenth man, who happened to be a white man. That this should be done
> once in a trial might indicate nothing, but that it should be done until per-
> haps five hundred such colored men should have been passed and not one
> summoned, and ninety-three white men met and all summoned, presents
> a *prima facie* case of denial—by those officers charged with the selection of
> that jury.[118]

The defenders of states' rights had hoped that such questions of proof would never reach the federal judiciary. They wanted the Court to say that a black defendant could be fairly tried by white jurors chosen by officers unwilling to seat black men as jurors. Those hopes had been dashed by the three 1880 jury cases. Black people did have a right to trial by jury where their fellow blacks had not been systematically excluded from jury service. The question then became a matter of evidence. On questions of evidence, lawyers on both sides of the Atlantic looked to the English barrister William Mawdesley Best, author of *The Principles of the Law of Evidence* or *Best on Evidence*, a treatise that went through twelve editions from 1849 to 1922. Best identified two kinds of evidence: knowledge and judgment. Strictly speaking, he wrote, knowledge can only be actual perception. Judgment is inferior to knowledge, resting, as it does, on the "*probability* or likelihood" of truth, "*presumed* from its conformity or repugnancy to our knowledge, observation, and experience."[119]

Best's distinction between knowledge and judgment carried at least an echo of the medieval moralists' struggle with conscience and duty. For Christians conscience came from God, an inner moral voice warning against sin. The word "conscience" is ambiguous. It can mean revulsion to sin, a moral sensitivity, not factual information but something more inchoate, feelings. Such feelings are a kind of knowledge, though, reflecting what the individual (or his community) "knows" about right and wrong, about sin. The historian James Q. Whitman writes that it can also mean something more concrete, "awareness of certain facts" or "private knowledge." Since conscience offers knowledge that comes not from legal evidence but from personal or community knowledge gained outside court, it can conflict with law. What happens, these moralists asked, when a judge or a juror "knows" something not adequately proven in court? The 1680 writer Sir John Hawles worried that conscience threatened the rule of law. Legal doctrine seeking to set aside conscience in favor of legally established evidence had the effect of easing moral concerns about judging; it allowed Christian jurors and judges to say they did not condemn; they simply carried out the law. In Mississippi, where every white person certainly knew full well that deputies and bailiffs discriminated against blacks when selecting jurors, putting law ahead of conscience allowed judges and jurors to permit discrimination. Hearing a discriminating official confess his prejudice was knowledge; deducing discrimination based on the absence of black jurors was a judgment. Judges and jurors could forget what they "knew" and "follow the law" simply by demanding the best evidence, testimony by the discriminators. This, in fact, was what the U.S. Supreme Court demanded that they do. The Supreme Court required proof at the highest level, knowledge, not judgment.[120]

In 1883, Harlan wrote the Court's opinion on Bush's case, overturning his conviction. Harlan began by reviewing the 1880 cases and announcing that he planned to follow their principles. The question was whether anything in the action of the state required the Supreme Court to find that Kentucky had restricted grand jury service to white men. Harlan observed that Kentucky's 1852 law had limited jury service to white men, and in 1873 the legislature reiterated the discrimination. The Kentucky legislature, Harlan pointed out, confirmed its prejudice after the

Fourteenth Amendment had been ratified in 1868. In 1880, Kentucky's highest court recognized that its law was unconstitutional, but not until January 26, 1882, did the Kentucky legislature open its juries to black men. "It was not until after the grand jurors who returned the indictment against Bush had been selected that the highest court of Kentucky . . . declared that the local statutes . . . were in conflict with the national Constitution," Harlan wrote. So in this case there was the best evidence of all that the state had discriminated: statutes passed by its legislature. Harlan pioneered no new ground, following the 1880 cases exactly. Only Field and Waite objected, with Waite complaining that Kentucky's courts should be trusted to follow the Fourteenth Amendment. Harlan was too skeptical of the Kentuckians, Waite alleged.[121]

For defenders of the states' right to seat all-white juries, the scorecard after *Bush v. Kentucky* was mixed. They could take considerable satisfaction that privileges and immunities, from their point of view, the most dangerous part of the Fourteenth Amendment, had been taken off the table. Harlan had not interpreted the equal protection clause as they had hoped, but even there the situation was not entirely bleak. The Court found that the absence of black men from a jury did not necessarily treat black litigants unfairly, and state judges and prosecutors could insist that defendants produce the highest level of proof to show discrimination.

One part of the Fourteenth Amendment remained: due process. A year after Harlan's decision in *Bush v. Kentucky*, the Court reviewed California's conviction of Joseph Hurtado for murder. Lawyers for Hurtado understood that the Supreme Court had moved away from privileges and immunities and focused on due process. California's 1879 constitution allowed the state to prosecute defendants based on a grand jury indictment *or* an "information." An information involves no jury at all; in 1882 Sacramento County's district attorney simply filed a short document accusing Joseph Hurtado of murder, a procedure the California Supreme Court approved. Hurtado's lawyers complained to the U.S. Supreme Court that California authorities had denied Hurtado the right to a grand jury protected by the Fifth Amendment and applied to the states through the Fourteenth Amendment's due process clause. Hurtado did not complain that the jurors had been chosen by prejudiced state officials; he complained that he had been denied any grand jury at all. His argument invited the federal government to intervene in state trial procedures:

> The words "due process of law," as used in the Fourteenth Amendment, embrace the right to be indicted by a grand jury . . . and that amendment deprives the States of the power which they possessed before its adoption, to provide any system by which an individual may be prosecuted for a felony until he has been examined and indicted by twelve of his peers.[122]

Hurtado's lawyers continued with a lengthy historical argument claiming that trial by jury was an ancient right, celebrated and protected by the common law. The thrust of their argument held that the Fourteenth Amendment's guarantee of due process empowered the federal government to require that the states follow traditional due process standards of trial by jury. To attach such an ancient and rich tradition of rights to the due process clause would have essentially made that part of the Fourteenth Amendment do the work that Bradley had once envisioned for the privileges and immunities clause.

Hurtado contended that the phrase "due process" enacted a portion of the Magna Carta and that it had a "fixed, definite, and technical meaning" separating it from political consideration. To support their argument, Hurtado's lawyers invoked a landmark on the constitutional landscape, *Murray's Lessee v. Hoboken Land & Improvement Company*, the opinion Benjamin R. Curtis had written in 1856. Curtis had sought to separate constitutional principle from politics: "It is manifest," he wrote, that the Constitution did not leave "the legislative power [free] to enact any process which might be devised." Due process of law cannot be left to the "mere will" of politicians representing public opinion. Thus, Hurtado's lawyers confronted the Waite Court with Curtis's effort to guard due process rights against political considerations, the tumult of popular opinion.[123] Although their case came from Sacramento, California, they made it clear that the Court's decision might well endanger the rights of black Southerners. A flexible reading of the due process clause, they warned, would render the Fourteenth Amendment worthless

> because any of the late Confederate States, by general laws, might, under such circumstances, confer upon judges, in criminal cases, the discretionary power to grant or refuse a trial according to any of the methods mentioned in the 5th and 6th amendments; and if, under such a general law, a judge would regularly grant to white men, and refuse to negroes, the right of trial by indictment, the right to trial by jury, the right to confront their witnesses,

&c., there could be no power in the United States Government that could correct the abuse.[124]

In 1881, Stanley Mathews had taken the aging Noah Swayne's seat, and in 1884 he wrote the Court's opinion rejecting Hurtado's expansive reading of due process. It is a measure of the respect that Curtis's work had achieved that Mathews could not ignore or overturn *Murray's Lessee v. Hoboken Land & Improvement Company*. Curtis had offered two ways of determining the meaning of due process: the text of the Constitution and "those settled usages and modes of proceeding existing in the common and statute law of England before the emigration of our ancestors." Mathews proceeded to remake the meaning of Curtis's words. He began by saying that the "real syllabus of the passage" holds that "a process of law, which is not otherwise forbidden, must be taken to be due process of law." Mathews urged deference to the legislature. Any "process of law" popular enough among voters to win legislative approval passed muster, so long as it did not explicitly violate something expressly forbidden. Mathews continued, "But it by no means follows that nothing else can be due process of law." Mathews engineered maximum space for political maneuver. Even as he urged his brethren toward greater deference for the political, Mathews had a political purpose himself. His language reveals that he saw himself as correcting widely held "misunderstandings" about due process. In his heart, he had to know that he was making law, not finding it.[125] Mathews's opinion in *Hurtado* made it difficult if not impossible for defense lawyers to challenge state jury procedures with the Fourteenth Amendment's due process clause.

By the time Chief Justice Waite died in 1888, the Supreme Court had taken great strides toward restoring power to the states. Nevertheless, President Grover Cleveland took the opportunity of Waite's death to name as chief justice his fellow conservative and Democrat Melville Weston Fuller, a committed Jeffersonian, convinced that the pendulum of power had swung too far from the states. "It is perhaps time for the pendulum to swing the other way," he wrote in 1883.[126] Like Miller, he doubted that abstract constitutional theories could prevail against the popular will, "those for whom the Constitution was framed."[127]

Just a year after Fuller joined the Court, President Benjamin Harrison appointed David Brewer of Kansas to replace Stanley Matthews. Unlike his uncle, Stephen J. Field, Brewer quickly emerged as the intellectual leader of the Fuller Court. Brewer is best known for valuing individual liberty over the state, a position he had adopted before his nomination to the Supreme Court and therefore probably represented Harrison's ambition for the appointment. Brewer despised labor unions and defended property rights. He favored natural law and pronounced himself fully prepared to "rule squarely against public sentiment."[128] Brewer gave numerous speeches and published scores of magazine articles. Defending the jury system became a theme, something he thought best accomplished by improving the character of jurors. Jurors should represent the highest intelligence of the community or at least the average, he believed.[129]

Brewer's ideas about race certainly colored his ideas about whether black people could ever qualify for jury service. At the end of the Civil War, several thousand people freed from slavery migrated to Leavenworth, where Brewer lived. Brewer had helped open a school for these migrants, though their bare feet, ragged clothing, and disorderly manner offended him. It made an impression when Brewer returned later and found the black Kansans who had once seemed so disorderly and dirty neatly dressed and intelligent in appearance. Despite that experience, or because of it, Brewer scorned charity or paternalism. He urged blacks to uplift themselves and said, "The Caucasian cannot put knowledge in the negro's brain, nor transform his heart by any application of outside force."[130] Speaking to white audiences, Brewer candidly conceded the shortcomings he found in the black race, "the most inferior of God's creatures." But he also asked if black people, "grateful to the nation for their liberty," might one day "prove themselves a mighty force, upholding law, order and the supremacy of the nation." He added, "Stranger things have happened."[131] A profoundly religious man, Brewer told an audience of missionaries that he hoped that one day blacks, whites, and other races would realize the full brotherhood of man. Brewer, himself the son of a missionary, thought that achievement would be magnificent.[132] Brewer, then, believed blacks might one day qualify to serve their country as voters and jurors, but the state should do nothing to help them. They had to improve themselves.

Though wary, Brewer had a healthy respect for the power of public opinion, a force that "exceedingly" influences individuals and governments alike. The year Brewer graduated from Yale, 1856, the *Yale Literary Magazine* published an unsigned article titled "Public Opinion." Its anonymous author, almost certainly Brewer, complained that public opinion threatened individual autonomy and independence of character. The author observed that universal sentiment, an almost irresistible power, came from persons in authority, individuals "of the noisier sort," and sometimes, but not always, through sensible discussion led by the press and orators. Brewer, if he was the author, recognized that who counted as the public mattered. He also thought that less advanced societies had more primitive and superficial publics; among the most savage peoples, the public could be nothing more than a small tribe. To guard against the unconscious influence of public opinion, Brewer urged his readers to be alert to such threats to individual thinking.[133]

Under Fuller's leadership and Brewer's influence, the Court resolutely and repeatedly refused to apply the Bill of Rights to the states. The Fuller Court wanted to leave the states' procedures for jury selection alone, but on that point the justices hardly needed to innovate; in 1880 Strong had written rules they found satisfactory.[134] In 1896 and 1898, an African American attorney named Cornelius J. Jones took three cases to the U.S. Supreme Court from Mississippi, each charging state officers with racial discrimination in the selection of jurors. In *Gibson v. Mississippi*, Jones complained that Washington County officials could not find a single black qualified for jury service in a population of seven thousand African Americans theoretically eligible for jury duty and only fifteen hundred whites.[135] Alexander Rives had unsuccessfully made the same argument sixteen years earlier, and Jones also lost; the Court complained that Jones had collected no testimony from county officials admitting that they only picked whites. Jones could only ask the Supreme Court to reason from the statistics, and the justices spurned the invitation, declaring instead that a mixed jury was not "always or absolutely necessary to the enjoyment of the equal protection of the laws." In order for the federal courts to intervene, Mississippi would have to overtly discriminate through its constitution or its laws, as interpreted by its supreme court.[136]

In *Smith v. Mississippi*, Jones had no more luck, though he pointed out that Mississippi law said defendants could challenge grand juries only before they had been impaneled. This effectively meant that Charles Smith could not question the racial makeup of his grand jury since he sat in an iron cell unrepresented by counsel at the time his grand jurors took their oaths.[137] Two years later, Jones argued that since Mississippi officials chose jurors from voter rolls, and whites had designed the state's 1890 constitution to keep blacks off the voting rolls, the state effectively had legislated against black jury service. The Court rejected that argument as well, insisting once again that Jones had to prove his case with direct evidence that the deputies picking jurors consciously discriminated.[138] Jones's arguments did not disturb the consensus that the Court had achieved in 1880 and which persisted through the Fuller era.

The Court's consensus on jury discrimination simplified its handling of habeas corpus petitions. The writ of habeas corpus had long been a theater of conflict between state sovereignty and national power. In his private notes, Bradley observed that habeas corpus law gave the Supreme Court a "general power . . . *in all cases* of ~~alleged~~ unlawful imprisonment." The Supreme Court's power was, however, appellate, meaning it reviewed denials or grants of habeas corpus writs by U.S. circuit courts. Thus, habeas corpus became another independent means by which the Supreme Court exercised its authority to review the work of lower courts.[139]

Defense lawyers began seeking writs of habeas corpus for clients convicted in state courts by all-white juries. In a typical case, Joseph Wood alleged that the New York courts used all-white juries to try him for murder. Harlan wrote the opinion rejecting Wood's appeal. The mere fact that no blacks served on the jury constituted no federal claim, he said, repeating Strong's old rejection of Rives's argument. Harlan and the other justices had decided to trust state appellate courts to right such wrongs. The trial court that heard the case against Wood, Harlan said, "was competent to guard and enforce every right secured to him" by the Constitution.[140]

Sometimes the justices had to educate local lawyers who were slow to catch on, as happened in the case of Aleck Richardson, condemned to death in South Carolina. Apparently convinced that Harlan might be receptive to the plight of a black man condemned to death by an all-white jury in South Carolina, Richardson's lawyer wrote the old Kentuckian, asking for an appeal from the South Carolina Circuit Court of the United States after that court denied his application for a writ of habeas corpus. Richardson's lawyer, C. P. Barrett, argued that his client should be tried by a jury composed, in part, of black men. Harlan at once recognized that Barrett did not know the law, had apparently not read the earlier jury cases setting out the law, and furthermore did not understand that custom dictated that he apply to the justice assigned to his circuit, Fuller. Harlan patiently explained the facts of life, which had nothing to do with his personal feelings toward blacks. Barrett had not claimed that the jury had been all white due to any statute of the state excluding blacks from serving on juries. If any black man had been excluded from the jury, the error was made by the trial court and would have to be remedied by a writ of error, through the normal appeals process, and not by a habeas corpus petition. Harlan said that the Constitution does not secure to either a black or a white man the right to be tried by a jury made up in part or in whole of men of his race. The Constitution secures to each person the right to be tried by a jury chosen without discrimination. Harlan provided citations to the case law. He then lectured Barrett that "the careless allowance of appeals in such cases has no other effect than to interfere with the ordinary administration of the criminal laws of the State." The only hint that Harlan might have any sympathy for Richardson's plight came when he observed that he might favor a writ of habeas corpus "if [he] could perceive that there was any possibility whatever that the Supreme Court would entertain jurisdiction of the case and consider it upon its merits." There was, however, no possibility of that; the law was clear.[141]

In 1900, Fuller's Court again followed Strong's rules when it considered *Carter v. Texas*. In 1897, Galveston County, Texas, had indicted Seth Carter for the murder of a black woman. He had shot Alberta Brantley five times in the head after she rebuffed his romantic advances; Carter then slashed his own throat in a failed suicide attempt.[142] Wilford H. Smith, later a confidant of Booker T. Washington, represented Carter. He proved to be a tenacious litigator in a state where the law did not overtly limit jury service to whites ("wisely" according to the Texas Court of Appeals in 1883) but which nonetheless kept blacks off its juries.[143] Lawmakers trusted their state's jury commissioners to make the right choices. "A very large discretion is confided in the commissioners by the law," the court of appeals observed in a surprising moment of candor.[144] Texas law also limited challenges to jurors: "The defendant may challenge the array for the following causes only: That the officer summoning the jury has acted corruptly, and has willfully summoned persons upon the jury known to be prejudiced."[145] That statute applied only to sheriffs and not to jury commissioners. In the case of jury commissioners, Texas law held that "no challenge to the array [was] allowed."[146] In 1875, the Texas Supreme Court specifically ruled that the absence of black men from a jury did not justify a challenge to the array.[147]

Smith challenged the all-white grand jury that indicted Carter. The trial court spurned his complaint. Smith then protested the all-white trial jury, and again the court rebuffed him. On March 18, 1898, the court convicted Carter of murder after one of the quickest murder trials in the history of Galveston, according to the local paper. Smith moved for a new trial and then filed a bill of exceptions. Thereafter, the Court of Criminal Appeals affirmed the conviction without commenting on the Fourteenth Amendment issues that Smith had raised.[148] Smith demanded a rehearing.

The Court of Criminal Appeals gave him one, revisiting the case in December. The Texas judges began by examining Smith's complaints about the all-white grand jury, scrambling to reconcile their own law with the Supreme Court's rulings. The Texans acknowledged that their law only allowed challenges to the array filed before the grand jurors took their oaths. Obviously, anyone not under indictment would have no reason to challenge the array until the grand jury acted, and under Texas law, it was then too late. A person under arrest, awaiting indictment, could in theory challenge the grand jury, but for a poor person sitting in jail without a lawyer, such a right was theoretical indeed. Nonetheless, the judges stubbornly insisted that "where practicable" defendants should follow the law and put their objections in the form of a challenge to the array. "In this particular case," they acknowledged that this was impossible. When Smith filed his motion to quash the indictment, he acted at his first opportunity and followed the proper practice outlined by the U.S. Supreme Court but not by Texas law. The Texas judges had essentially conceded every point to Smith, but they could not resist raising a technical objection: "We think . . . this question should have been raised in a motion to set aside the indictment or in the form of a special plea." But even then they had to admit that the Texas Code of Criminal Procedure did not allow for that challenge either.

The Texas court understood that Smith had no complaint about Texas law on jury selection, which was race neutral. The problem involved the administration of the law. Citing the Supreme Court's jury cases, the Texans recognized that if the state officers had discriminated, and if the appeals court approved the fruits of their discrimination, the Supreme Court would overturn their work. Fortunately, in *Virginia v. Rives*, the Court had said that the mere absence of blacks from a jury proved nothing. That was helpful, the Texans thought, but they also took time to praise the "strong" dissenting opinions filed by Field and Waite, which they clearly liked even better. The Texans then suggested that all these federal cases might be moot because Seth Carter had killed another black person. The cases the Supreme Court had decided all involved crimes across racial lines. The Texans thought race prejudice could hardly play a role when the white jurors judged one black person charged with killing another black person.

On the question of the all-white trial jury, the Texas court noted that Smith filed his motion with no supporting evidence whatsoever. The judges acknowledged that Smith had wanted to call witnesses to prove his claim, and the trial judge had refused to permit any such testimony but complained that Smith's motion to call witnesses was too vague and general, not naming the witnesses to be summoned or what he hoped to prove by their evidence. The Texas court asserted that all courts require more than "a bare proposition to prove certain facts . . . to invoke the action of the court." The judges knew full well, and admitted, that any inquiry attempting to prove discrimination by state officers faced formidable obstacles. The Texans really and truly hoped that the Supreme Court would not see this as a reason to loosen enforcement of the rules of evidence. Such difficulties, the judges opined, "instead of relieving him of the necessity of pointing out the means of proof, it occurs to us, would require a greater strictness in naming the witnesses by whom the allegations could be established." Since it was difficult to prove discrimination, the Texans reasoned that judges should make it more difficult. The Texas Court of Criminal Appeals once again affirmed Carter's conviction.[149]

A few months before it decided *Carter v. Texas*, the Supreme Court upheld the conviction of Charles L. Maxwell by an eight-man jury with no grand jury in Utah. Maxwell's lawyers foolishly tried to resurrect the privileges and immunities clause, arguing that it had incorporated the Bill of Rights' protections of trial by jury.[150] In his opinion for the Court, Justice Rufus Peckham took the opportunity to embrace politics over principle. The Utah constitution allowed prosecution by information and eight-man trial juries in cases not capital. Public will, expressed through the political process, had to be respected, Peckham wrote. He said "emphatically" that the people can provide for their own affairs, adding, "We are of opinion they are much better judges of what they ought to have in these respects than anyone else can be." Controlling crime, Peckham wrote, "is a case of self-protection, and the people can be trusted to look out and care for themselves." Peckham's opinion must have delighted the Texans as they prepared to argue their own case before the justices. The Court seemed ready to defer to the people, speaking through state law.[151] Texas wanted the same deference.

Nevertheless, the Supreme Court clearly considered *Carter v. Texas* an easy case—easy to overturn. Unlike Maxwell's lawyers, Smith had not relied on privileges and immunities. The words "privilege" and "immunity" do not even appear in his brief. He wisely focused on equal protection, recognized as a federally protected right in jury-discrimination cases. No doubt a majority of Fuller's Court agreed with Peckham on the need for self-protection against crime; Fuller and his brethren stood as a bulwark against criminality and anarchism, but the justices may not have seen Seth Carter as a threat on the same level as the Haymarket bombers.[152] Their decision for Carter was unanimous; Fuller assigned the job of writing the opinion to Horace Gray.

Fuller obviously believed that the Texas effort to dilute Strong's rulings required an opinion by a nationalist dedicated to precedent, and Gray had that reputation, though perhaps not entirely deserved. His had been a family of wealth and privilege, but in his youth natural science held more appeal for him than business. He joined the Free Soilers before becoming a judge, and his previous opinions had sometimes seemed overtly nationalistic, affirming legal tender and favoring federal over state authority to regulate resident aliens. Just two years before *Carter v. Texas*, he had led the Court in deciding that birthright trumped race under the Fourteenth Amendment's citizenship clause.[153] The income tax tested his commitment to precedent; he apparently waffled before finally voting with property and against the tax in a decision that hardly rested on precedent at all. On trial by jury, though, he and the rest of the Court would not innovate. In 1899, when writing the Court's opinion in *Capital Traction Company v. Hof*, he gave full vent to his love of research, precedent, and history, producing a seventeen-thousand-word historical essay on juries. His language shows determination to protect the Seventh Amendment's guarantee of trial by jury by using history and the common law against state law and state precedent:

> A comparison of the language of the Seventh Amendment, as finally made part of the Constitution of the United States, with the Declaration of Rights of 1774, with the Ordinance of 1787, with the essays of Mr. Hamilton in 1788, and with the amendments introduced by Mr. Madison in Congress in 1789, strongly tends to the conclusion that the Seventh Amendment, in declaring that "no fact tried by a jury shall be otherwise reexamined, in any court of the United States, than according to the rules of the common law," had in view the rules of the common law of England, and not the rules of that law as modified by local statute or usage in any of the States.
>
> This conclusion has been established, and "the rules of the common law" in this respect clearly stated and defined, by judicial decisions.[154]

In 1900, Fuller and the other justices expected him to slap down Texas for trying to use legal inanities to thwart the Fourteenth Amendment and the 1875 jury law. Gray set aside his penchant for long, historical essays and turned in a brief effort that was not only short but well organized and to the point. Apparently, no justice was inclined to do any original thinking: "The rules of law which must govern this case are clearly established by previous

decisions of this court," Gray wrote. That was what made the decision "easy."
If the Court, or any faction of the Court, had accepted Texas's invitation to
loosen federal oversight of the states' crime-control efforts for political reasons, it would have been a "hard" decision.[155]

The first part of Gray's opinion reviewed the Texas laws that limited defendants' options for challenging all-white juries. Clearly, Texas had created
a structure designed to prevent blacks from gaining access to the jury box.
Gray told the Texans that they could not forbid defendants from challenging grand juries by limiting those challenges to the time before the grand jurors took their oaths. Gray also observed that Smith had tried to introduce
witnesses to prove discrimination, and the trial judge had not allowed him
to gather such testimony. Such a denial took away a right set by the Constitution. The Court reversed Carter's conviction.[156]

In a decision that extended beyond the fate of Seth Carter, the Supreme
Court had made a rule for every defense lawyer in the country. Although
historians often describe the 1875 Civil Rights Act as a dead letter, the Court
left its provision making jury discrimination illegal very much alive; it is
still the law today: 18 U.S.C. § 243 (1964). Defendants have a right, the Court
said, to introduce witnesses to prove discrimination in the selection of jurors. States cannot disallow challenges to their grand juries on the grounds
that they come too late. At the time Gray penned his *Carter* decision, several states still had laws forbidding challenges to a seated grand jury. One of
those states was Mississippi.

CHAPTER SIX

Getting Blacks on Mississippi Juries

AFTER SHOOTING AND KILLING Rufus Tilford Dinkins, Dabney Marshall entered Mississippi's infamous penal system. In this time before Mississippi had constructed its Parchman archipelago, Dabney Marshall's imprisonment first took him to the state's downtown Jackson prison (a space now occupied by the state capitol building), built in 1840 and known as "The Walls." Yet, while the state had not yet purchased Parchman Plantation, Mississippi already took its prisoners—both black and white—to plantations, where it routinely violated its own constitution by leasing black convicts to Delta planters who literally considered the prisoners "slaves." One scholar has called Mississippi's prison system "a story of endless brutality and neglect," where plantation managers whipped convicts for "slow hoeing" or "sorry planting" until the blood ran down their legs. On December 27, 1898, after he had served three years of his sentence, Marshall wrote that he had not yet been able to harden himself to the "constant heart-breaking suffering" all around him.[1]

He had, however, found some "Vicksburg negroes" at the prison and shared his Christmas dinner with these black men from his hometown. Even in prison, Marshall kept his hometown patriotism, describing the black prisoners as coming from "our dear old town."[2] Only someone entirely unfamiliar with the South could imagine that Marshall's contact with the black prisoners forged any kind of common bond based on a shared hometown. Marshall's Vicksburg was not black Vicksburg. Marshall's family had used black labor to construct a place of privilege for themselves, and their reliance on blacks for their advantages meant that they had deep reasons to fear black criminality. Marshall's family had once owned black men and women, but even now—long after emancipation—black labor continued to elevate the Marshalls. Marshall and his family still owned farmland, which meant they relied on African Americans to plant and harvest their crops. Black labor created the wealth that had allowed Marshall to practice law or take a break from law to run for political office, as he chose. The black Vicksburgers whom Marshall met in prison came from places in Vicksburg that Marshall could hardly imagine and lived lives he could scarcely envision. They were people he pitied, not his friends.

Marshall shared his dinner with the black prisoners from feelings of paternalism, the charitable instincts commonly felt by white elites toward what they saw as the lower orders. Rich white men were supposed to extend kindnesses to poor black men; such generous impulses helped separate them from the rougher, cruder classes of whites. At the same time, serving time alongside black prisoners challenged Marshall's paternalistic pretenses. If prison did not entirely erase the distance that separated benevolent white Southerners from their beneficiaries, it shocked his confidence in the certainty of the distinction. Just like every other prisoner, black or white, Marshall needed paternalistic largesse himself. He now understood that "the one star in the night of a prisoner's sorrow is the hope of a pardon." No matter how remote the possibility, he wrote, every prisoner clings to the chance of a pardon as to life itself. "For when they lose it they either risk life in an attempt to escape under fire of the guns, they commit suicide or go insane." Many prisoners' minds tottered on the edge of madness. Transferred out of The Walls, Marshall spent most of his sentence at Oakley Plantation, a 2,700-acre plantation in Hinds County, which the state had only recently purchased for its prisoners. The guards kept the prisoners rigidly segregated, and once Marshall went to Oakley Plantation, he seldom saw a black prisoner. Nonetheless, the white prisoners suffered fates not entirely different from the black prisoners, marched out to the fields under armed guard. A driver rode up and down the rows of prisoners laboring over the crop, scolding and whipping those moving too slowly. Bloodhounds patrolled as well. Captain J. Q. Mays ran the white camp, and Marshall judged him as essentially a humane person. But that was just luck; Marshall heard troubling stories of other, less merciful, captains.

Marshall himself did not work in the fields; he was too weak for that labor. He tended the commissary, ordering and dispensing the food and handling the mail. In one letter to a friend, Marshall suggested that his experience had challenged his faith. Although he thanked Alice Shannon for offering to send him Christian Science books, he continued, "I do not believe they would help me just at this juncture. Maybe some day I will be in a frame of mind more suited to such reading." A Methodist preacher came to the prison farm to hold services once a month. Marshall doubted this did the prisoners much good, but he thought it probably helped their parents, imagining their sons were getting religious instruction.[3]

Marshall did his best writing in prison. In a short story titled "The Escape," he keeps the race of his inmate-protagonist obscure, but by depicting his main character at work hoeing cotton, many readers must have assumed him to be black. His story sympathizes with the cotton-hoeing prisoners by describing their treatment as slavelike. Driven by cursing, armed overseers, they worked the cotton "from the time it was light enough [for the guards] to see how to shoot." Prisoners received whippings laid on "with the dexterity of long practice and the skill of an artist who delights in his work." Like few other white men, Marshall learned in prison that only a porous boundary separated the admired from the loathed. Marshall considered himself and his fellow prisoners to be the "hated, despised, scorned of the world," adding, "They had lost liberty, and in losing it had lost everything. N[either] time, nor toil, nor tears could here give them back what once was theirs, and sweep disgrace from their names."[4] His empathetic tone was clear in a letter that he wrote a friend; while acknowledging that his fellow prisoners included "the vilest of the earth," he confessed, "Somehow when I see their misery, I can't remember their crimes."[5]

By killing a man to defend his honor, Marshall had embraced Mississippi's gendered system of honor, and even prison did not convince him he had been wrong. From prison, he wrote, "I stand acquitted in my own mind of all blame. Had I not thought I was doing right, I would not have acted as I did." He added that he had received letters "from all over the South, nearly all of them not only sympathetic but expressing also their approval of [his] action."[6] By joining the prohibitionists, he had toyed with standing apart from public opinion. His aristocratic upbringing no doubt also encouraged him to separate himself from ordinary people. Imprisoned on Oakley Plantation, he received special treatment, working in the commissary, checking in the mail, but he had nonetheless crossed the line between scorn and respect.

Like all other prisoners, Marshall hoped for a pardon, but unlike almost every other inmate, he had the connections to make his dream plausible. The *Vicksburg Evening Post* stood by him even in prison. In 1896, Cashman opined that impartial observers must admit that Marshall was innocent. Cashman obviously understood that Marshall had shot Dinkins, but he had been convicted of first-degree murder, and Marshall insisted he had not premeditated the shooting. In 1901, the *Post* reported that some Vicksburgers had been calling for a pardon. Their persistence finally paid off that year, when Andrew H. Longino succeeded McLaurin as governor. Longino clearly understood that releasing a man in jail for defending his honor would cost him few votes, if any.[7] Marshall himself believed that his release resulted from his popularity. Just after he left prison, his friends in Vicksburg even maneuvered to restart his political career. These efforts went so far as to lead Warren County's election commission to put his name on the ballot—briefly—as a candidate for the legislature. A clue to the tactical approach Marshall would soon adopt as a litigator came at the beginning of the brief he wrote arguing for his right to run for office. Fresh out of prison, resuming the practice of law, he announced in one of his first briefs, "The Constitution is the law of the land."[8]

Many Mississippi whites did not think so. They demonstrated this in spectacular fashion three years after Marshall left prison when Luther Holbert murdered a white planter named James Eastland and a black man named Albert Carr on Wednesday, February 3, 1904. According to the February 4 *Memphis Commercial Appeal*, the trouble began when Holbert, a "ginger cake colored negro" with sideburns and a good education, quarreled with another African American over a woman. After killing Eastland, Holbert and a female companion fled.[9]

James's older brother Woods C. Eastland quickly took control of the effort to find James Eastland's killers. From the start, it was clear that law had nothing to do with this manhunt; the sheriff played no role in organizing the posse. There would be no trial by jury for this murder, no question of blacks on the jury. Woods C. Eastland almost immediately shot a black man named John Winters as Winters tried to flee from Eastland's posse. There was no investigation, no prosecution, no jury, no inquiry by the courts or by law enforcement. In Mississippi white public opinion sided with Eastland, so much so that no officer of the law, not the sheriff, not the governor, dared interfere.[10] It was also shortly after the murder that Eastland told the press how Holbert would die: Luther Holbert was going to burn.[11]

On Friday, Eastland's posse searched the county. While telephone lines buzzed with calls for whites all over the area to watch for Holbert, their prey seemed to have vanished. By Saturday, February 6, the posse men began to lose hope. Then, late Saturday afternoon, a sixteen-year-old boy named Luther Lloyd came into the store where Victor Lavender worked as a clerk to report that he had seen two suspicious-looking Negroes east of Sheppardstown. Lavender, a plantation manager named E. I. O'Neal, and the boy raced to this site and captured both Holbert and his companion. O'Neal and Lavender escorted their prisoners to O'Neal's house. Holbert spent the night in the house, though he tried to escape only to be shot twice by Lavender. Newspapers never identified Holbert's female companion by name, and they disagreed over whether she was actually married to Holbert. In an authentic-sounding dispatch, the *Commercial Appeal* reported that she wore men's clothing and had cut her hair short and covered it with a large cap.[12]

Early on Sunday morning, February 7, word circulated that the killers of James Eastland had been captured and would be burned at the stake near the scene of the original crime. By noon hundreds had gathered, including a reporter for the *Greenwood Commonwealth*, the author of the most detailed account of Holbert's death. Founded by James K. Vardaman in December 1896, the *Commonwealth* had historically supported murderous racial violence to help advance Vardaman's political career. Vardaman served in Mississippi's House of Representatives from 1890 to 1896 and ran for governor unsuccessfully in 1895 and 1899, becoming increasingly combative and bitterly racist, urging that rapes committed by Negroes justified murderous racial violence. In 1903, Vardaman ran for governor and won. He served one term as governor (1904–8) before winning a seat in the U.S. Senate, where he served from 1913 to 1919. As governor, Vardaman retreated from his earlier advocacy of lawlessness and actually worked to suppress racial violence, though he did little or nothing to stop the Doddsville lynchings. He urged local officials to arrest and try those charged with burning Holbert, offering the state militia "if needed" to restore order. No white person around Doddsville thought it needed. The *Greenwood Commonwealth* covered the lynching, but it was no longer his newspaper. By the time the mob gathered at Doddsville, Vardaman had sold the *Commonwealth*. Frank R. Birdsall now owned the paper; Edgar O. Harris served as associate editor, and Otis C. Blow acted as local editor and manager. There is no way of knowing whether Birdsall or Harris or Blow attended the burning. Perhaps they all did or perhaps Blow went alone as part of his duties as "local editor." It is tempting to assume that such an event attracted all three. In any case, the paper placed no byline on its detailed and vivid story, so it is not possible to know who actually attended the burning and wrote the article.[13]

By three o'clock over a thousand persons watched as wagonloads of firewood arrived and workers kindled a blazing fire. Civic leaders mounted stumps and tried to dissuade the mob. The *Commonwealth*'s editors may well have been among those urging that Holbert be put on trial and not murdered. In any case, the crowd drowned out their voices, chanting, "Burn them!"[14] The crowd decided to cremate the woman first though she may well have been innocent of any crime; even some newspapers acknowledged she had nothing to do with killing Eastland and Carr, while other papers claimed Holbert's son had fingered her as an accomplice. The *Greenwood Commonwealth* never accused her of the murder. Perhaps her innocence won her a modicum of sympathy; someone asked her if she wanted to pray, and she replied that she had already done that. According to the *Greenwood Commonwealth*, "She was then bound in chains and cast into the flames. She tugged at the chains for a few seconds and then swooned. It was all over with her." She died quickly, certainly the best outcome she could have hoped for at that point. Things did not go so well for Holbert. He had already been tortured. "Bruised and battered almost beyond recognition; bleeding from a hundred tortures, with ears shorn from his head; with palsied limbs and fingerless hands—more dead than alive—John Holbert was then led to his doom." The whites forced two strong Negroes to chain Holbert and drag him through the flames. Holbert screamed at first but soon writhed in silence, his throat too burnt to make a sound. The *Commonwealth*'s account is grisly, all the more so when one realizes that this story was too routine to attract the level of attention won by Cashman's account of the lynching. The *Commonwealth* story did not reach the iconic status writers have accorded Cashman's version of events.[15]

On Saturday, February 13, 1904, the *Vicksburg Evening Post* published a gruesome article detailing the lynching as part of its campaign against mob violence. Cashman hoped to shock his readers with vivid imagery.

When the two negroes were captured they were tied to trees and while the funeral pyres were being prepared they were forced to suffer the most fiendish tortures. The blacks were forced to hold out their hands while one finger at a time was chopped off. The fingers were distributed as souvenirs. The ears of the murderers were cut off. Holbert was severely beaten, his skull was fractured, and one of his eyes knocked out with a stick, hung by a shred from the socket. Neither the man nor woman begged for mercy, nor made a groan or plea. When the executioners came forward to lop off fingers, Holbert extended his hand without being asked. The most excruciating form of punishment, consisted in the use of a large corkscrew in the hands of some of the mob. This instrument was bored into the flesh of the man and the woman, in the arms, legs and body, and then pulled out, the spirals tearing out big pieces of raw, quivering flesh, every time it was withdrawn[.] Even this devilish torture did not make the poor brutes cry out. When finally they were thrown on the fire and allowed to be burned to death, this came as a relief to the maimed and suffering victims.[16]

Mississippi's gendered system of honor required that public men challenge anyone questioning their masculinity. For Woods Eastland, this meant hunting down and killing the black man who had killed his brother. In the case of Dabney Marshall, this system led him to murder the man who had defiled his reputation. When he went to prison for the murder, he came to identify with the slavelike status under which blacks were forced to live. His ability to empathize with his fellow prisoners seems to have led him to take up the cause of black Mississippians, redirecting the ambition he had once devoted to politics. Once he realized he could no longer pursue political office or meaningfully ally himself with Mississippi's political elite, he decided to fight for the civil rights of blacks by challenging Mississippi's all-white jury system.

He teamed up with Willis Mollison, Mississippi's foremost civil rights leader. No letters that might have passed between the two men survived. Whatever they said to each other went unrecorded. Yet there is no doubt that they acted as a team: Mollison wanted blacks on juries; Marshall went to work to make it happen. On some level, the black man and the white man must have shared some common understanding about race and the plight of black Mississippians. Unfortunately, the bits of evidence about Marshall that survive reveal little about his racial attitudes. Mollison's son, however, interviewed his father and published an article that described the older man's thinking about race. Mollison blamed Mississippi's deteriorating racial situation on Vardaman. While Vardaman, as governor, sometimes resisted lynching, it is a measure of the depth of his hatred of blacks that while Vardaman campaigned against capital punishment, he spoke in favor of lynching black "brutes." Vardaman denounced Booker T. Washington's self-help strategy. He denied that education could salvage blacks. He thought blacks incapable of self-government, not just in the short run but always and forever. His biographer calls him a "hard-shelled racist" but explains that he reflected his time and circumstances. Mollison did not think so. Vardaman's racism had plunged Mississippi into a new hell after he became governor in 1903, Mollison said.[17]

Mollison believed in racial uplift, an idea that dated at least to the 1860s, when a young Richard R. Wright supposedly urged General O. O. Howard to tell northern whites, "We're rising." In 1901, George H. White, the last African American congressman of his era, proclaimed in a farewell speech that blacks were a "rising people—full of potential force." The uplift movement reacted against white racial stereotypes, demeaning images that saturated popular music, journalism, and literature. Thomas Dixon Jr. emerged as a preeminent force in whites' cultural war on African American character, publishing *The Leopard's Spots* in 1902 soon followed by *The Clansman*, which became a theatrical production, and then *Birth of a Nation*, a movie created by the foremost director of the day, D. W. Griffith. Dixon wrote fiction, but the history he popularized came from William A. Dunning, the nation's top historian.[18]

Although Dunning is known today chiefly for his racial prejudice, his scholarship included values some now still find appealing, contempt for idealism, idealists, and higher-law principles as a source for governmental reform programs. It was this skepticism that led him to look behind reformers for their true motivations. Scholars have compared him to William Graham Sumner, the famous proponent of laissez-faire. Like Sumner, Dunning trusted facts as weapons he could use against sentimentalism. His mentor, John W. Burgess, tried to pass onto his student a Hegelian confidence in higher law and the Constitution, but Dunning repudiated the old man's optimism in favor of Sumner's doubts that government could ever overcome cultural practices. Dunning published two seminal books on Reconstruction, a period Sumner identified as proving government impotence in the face of culture. Dunning silently rejected Lincoln's argument that the Civil War gave the nation an opportunity for "a new birth of freedom" rooted in its original founding "dedicated to the proposition that all men are created equal."[19]

Proponents of racial uplift rejected Dunning's history and his theory of state helplessness. Their optimism pitted a black middle-class—dignified, capable, and professional—against white racialism that denied any class distinctions among blacks. Mollison never hinted at any hidden doubts about the middle-class values he hoped to share with whites. According to

W. E. B. Du Bois, though, he must have had a second consciousness, an ambivalent hunger for a black identity not dependent on whites' standards of success. The danger in Mollison's class-based approach to racial uplift was that it put a burden on blacks to prove themselves when the real drag on black achievement came from the constant threat of white violence—lynching—not some internal shortcoming that could be cured through better schooling or improved manners. One modern critic of uplift theory writes that such an approach "forgot" that the state hindered black progress, implying that the state always hindered progress, never resolving on "a new birth of freedom" unless forced into it by a protesting segment of the public.[20]

That criticism ignores the optimism about government characteristic of the Progressive Era. Early in the twentieth century, reformers expected to harness the state against all sorts of evils to engineer genuine improvement in the human condition.[21] Christianity infused reformers with a holy zeal and a moral outrage that made change seem not just possible but imperative, essential for the survival of the nation's soul. Muckraking journalists sought out sin, which they used to outrage the reading public, not for mere titillation but to make reform happen. Evangelicals did not doubt the propriety of converting institutional structures to their cause; they used the Bible's higher law—"preconceived evangelical morality" in the words of one critic—for modern ends. William Jennings Bryan may have been no more than another politician, but he imagined himself a Christian soldier, carrying out God's work through politics.[22] Women could build public careers in part on their faith, their ability to define policy still circumscribed by their gender, but boosted by the greater acceptance of interest group power vis-à-vis traditional electoral politicking.[23] The reformer Frederick Howe said that American reformers could not be understood apart from their "evangelical psychology."[24]

For a dedicated proponent of racial uplift like Mollison, hopeful he could mobilize national power on his behalf, jury duty seemed a good place to start. It was a lawful and entirely dignified way to challenge not only whites' racism but the state's institutional support of that prejudice. Arguing for black jury service implied that government could be legitimate without sponsoring white supremacy; in fact, Mollison went further than that, suggesting that government could be legitimate only if it did not sponsor white supremacy. Mollison faced white opposition organized in violent and frightening proportions, but he could imagine, at least, that he did so with the highest law of the land on his side. The Supreme Court had ruled against jury discrimination, after all. Mollison personally appeared before the Warren County Board of Supervisors to plead his case. The supervisors listened and then dismissed him with an empty promise to "take the matter under advisement," prompting snickers from neighboring Hinds County. No black man would have the nerve to present such a petition in Hinds County, an anonymous writer implied. "There has not been a Negro on the juries in Hinds county [sic] for several years. . . . Hinds county found out years ago that Mr. Negro did not make a good juryman, and she has none of them any more."[25]

Whites' increasingly brazen assaults on the dignity of blacks tested Mollison's commitments to lawful resistance. Shortly after Vardaman took office, the Mississippi legislature passed a new segregation law, one that required streetcar companies to separate black people from white people riding on their trolley cars. The law took effect June 1, 1904, and based on past experience whites anticipated that blacks would boycott the segregated cars. The Vicksburg Street Railway readied its cars for the big day by building screens for seat backs to make separate compartments. The expected boycott began on June 1 and lasted for three months, but in September Mollison urged black Vicksburgers to call it off.[26] Boycotting the streetcars did not fit with his strategy of presenting his race as respectable and earnest. Better to protest in a way that promoted the talents and abilities of the best men whom the black race had to offer, Mollison believed.

Mollison's strategy would directly and boldly challenge whites' prejudices in court. He doubted he could aggressively cross-examine white men in power without sacrificing his carefully crafted persona; he presented himself as quietly competent, educated, and professional. He could be dogged in his pursuits, but he never insulted white sensitivities. Mollison turned to Dabney Marshall as his point man in the fight to get worthy black men seated on juries. Mollison must have recognized Marshall's unusual talent for empathy. Marshall believed Christianity made all people equal, and his time in prison had not robbed him of his faith in law or progress. About law Marshall wrote:

> law abides and shapes
> The whole of life, and makes us what we are.
> As are its laws, the nation is. It stands a dream
> Of right incarnate made. It takes and binds
> The scattered might of weakling men to powers
> That topple down a tyrants throne, and makes
> The babe, with justice armed, a Caesar's peer.[27]

Mollison recognized that joining with Marshall meant taking Marshall's friend and ally John G. Cashman as well. Cashman advocated law over lynching in a way that Mollison approved, but he also favored Mississippi's discriminatory 1890 constitution, specifically designed to keep blacks from voting. Cashman thought law and order "absolutely indispensable to the material development and progress of the South" and extolled the 1890 constitution for—he hoped—delivering Mississippi from its lawless past. In other words, Marshall's friend and booster thought that excluding blacks from voting made lynching and vigilantism unnecessary.[28] Cashman assumed that the rule of law could be reconciled with racial prejudice. Perhaps Marshall did as well, but we do know that he believed law represented "the scattered might of weakling men" able to "topple down a tyrants throne." Mollison certainly saw racial prejudice as tyranny; so did Marshall. Cashman saw the public's support for lynching as a positively intolerable despotism. Cashman anthropomorphized lynching as an overbearing dictator: "the Prince of all the hosts of merciless tyrants, JUDGE LYNCH . . . the most conspicuously commanding and majestic personage in the State of Mississippi." His words dripping with sarcasm, Cashman ridiculed JUDGE LYNCH as too "jealous of his power" to be bothered with pardons, "too infallible in judgment to tolerate an appeal." "Fearful and appalling SILENCE surrounds our King," Cashman wrote. Does "our King" hide like a murderous criminal, slinking in the shadows? Cashman asked. Of course not, "like a King, that he is, he walks with head erect and face uncovered, in the broad light of day."[29]

Marshall's belief in law carried him closer to equal rights across racial lines than most white men in Mississippi. Once released from prison, he regularly tangled with local law enforcement on behalf of black citizens, fights that were approvingly documented by Cashman's *Vicksburg Evening Post*. It seemed Marshall's clients were mainly black after 1901.[30] In 1905, Marshall complained that Vicksburg police, as well as private security guards employed by railroad companies, regularly violated Mississippi law by arresting persons—black persons—charged only with misdemeanors.[31] He later filed a lawsuit against the county for mistreating a black prisoner named Jules Monroe. When a police officer arrested Monroe, Marshall swore out a warrant accusing the officer of planning to spirit his client away so he could not be present for his civil trial. Marshall, in fact, personally confronted the officer on the street, standing shoulder to shoulder with Monroe. The officer insisted that he had been ordered by his chief to take Monroe in for questioning. "I then warned Policeman McKee not to touch either Monroe or myself, even if the chief did want to talk to Monroe," Marshall recalled.[32] Later, in another case, Marshall clashed with the police chief on behalf of his black client in what the *Post* called "a pyrotechnical display."[33] Marshall lectured the chief that he should leave law to the lawyers. The newspaper's account of his quarrel with the police chief makes it sound as if Marshall dominated the courtroom, teaching law not only to the police chief but to the judge as well. In still another case, Marshall scored the police for mistreating black suspects, claiming one officer had actually dared to kick his client while marching him to jail.[34] In other cases, he alleged that the police denied black prisoners access to counsel and sometimes tortured them into confessing.[35]

The *Post's* articles about Marshall and the police were comedies. This may have been literally true, with white Vicksburgers shaking their heads at Marshall's continuing battles with the police, but comedy has a more profound meaning. At its deepest and most abstract level of meaning, comedy expects seemingly inalterably opposed elements in the world to discover shared interests and harmony. In any comedy, the ultimate joke is always that apparently irreconcilable forces are not so different after all.[36] At this time, some of the most prominent white Southerners understood the Civil War, and perhaps life generally, as comedy. In the Civil War, white men had fought other white men over slavery—race. By the twentieth century, this seemed "comic" in the sense that white men, though divided by region, obviously shared a common racial heritage and interests. A classic statement of this can be found in Vardaman's speeches. The governor seemed genuinely puzzled that white Northerners and white Southerners—men "of the same flesh"— could war with each other over African slavery. "It must have been," he decided, "because the North and the South did not know each other."[37]

Marshall's comedy differed from Vardaman's racist variety. A few months after the *Post* ran a headline that read "Dabney Marshall Has Policeman Arrested," it ran another article, "T. D. Marshall Says the Police are Efficient."[38] One article did not contradict the other. The comedy was that while the police sometimes broke the law and needed correction when they did, they, like all Americans, really understood the necessity of obeying the law and adhering to constitutional principles. In early twentieth-century Mississippi, this notion was a howling legal fiction to be sure, but one not without its uses. Marshall hoped that by calling the police law abiding, he could make them obey the law. He just needed to educate them so that they could better understand the law and equal rights.

He schemed to win cases with all-white juries and judges. He won an acquittal for a black woman accused of prostitution even after a judge openly sided with the state. Marshall had objected when the prosecutor asked for a continuance, successfully reminding the judge that since the state had set the case for trial, the state had a responsibility to prove its case on the spot. This legal technicality freed a woman of questionable character, but Marshall had underscored that nagging necessity of obeying the law and adhering to constitutional principles. The judge disliked ruling for Marshall's client, grumbling to her, "It is evident you are not a very hard-working woman," but Marshall's vigorous legal arguments and the prosecutor's sloppy work left him no room to rule against her.[39] In 1902, Marshall persuaded the Supreme Court of Mississippi to throw out a conviction based on a confession "sweated" from Edward Ammons, an accused burglar. The police, Marshall revealed, softened up black suspects for questioning in a five-by-six-foot box, or "apartment," covered in blankets to deprive inmates of even a stray ray of light or a breath of fresh air.[40]

By questioning Ammons, accused of stealing a pistol, Marshall already knew about the sweatbox when he cross-examined the chief of police. His client had confessed, and Marshall needed to get the confession thrown out if he had any chance at all of winning his case.

"Had he been put in the sweat box?" Marshall asked. The police chief answered, "Yes sir, what we call the sweat box."

On cross-examination, Marshall could lead the witness, so he described the box. The police chief agreed with Marshall's description but soon had second thoughts about so readily agreeing to use the term "sweat box." The transcript does not record body language or other nonverbal communications, but he must have seen the negative reaction that the term "sweat box" stirred in the courtroom. The very word "sweat box" strongly implies coercion, "sweating" a confession from an unwilling prisoner. Under the common law, a valid confession must be entirely voluntary, not forced. No one doubted torture occurred, but everyone realized the importance of keeping it off the official transcript, the record of the trial. Realizing his mistake, the police chief started calling the sweatbox a "cell" instead of a "box."

The switch came too late. The judge interrupted Marshall's examination. "Tell us, what is, that sweat box?" he asked.

The police chief changed the subject so fast he barely answered the court's question. "They call it a sweat box, but it is nothing but a dark cell; I heard about this pistol being lost, and it was several days that we were engaged in getting up the stolen property."

The judge did not pursue further details, but Marshall did, using the correct vocabulary.

"How long had he been in that sweat box, before he acknowledged to taking these things?"

"I don't remember."

"Do you know whether he had been in there previous to that?"

"He had been in that little dark room."

"How long?"

"I don't know."

Marshall wanted to show that the police had kept Ammons isolated: "Had he any communication with anyone?"

"I don't know."

Many white lawyers, appointed to defend black men, put in only a perfunctory performance; Marshall had gotten to know his client's family: "Do you know whether his mother or aunt or any of them had been there to see him?"

The chief professed not to know that either, so Marshall raised another issue: "Did you tell him that he did not have to answer these questions?"

"No sir, I did not."

Before the Civil War, Mississippi's highest court had required that black prisoners be warned that if they confessed their words might be used against them in court. Under the slavery regime, white racism prompted extra protection for black prisoners. Mississippi's supreme court thought slaves so easily intimidated that it ruled that just the presence of an authority figure spoiled any confession made by a slave, a rule that did not apply to whites. A white man did not need to be coddled with warnings that his confession might be used against him in court, whites reasoned.[41] Marshall must have had those earlier decisions in mind when he showed that the Vicksburg police used the threat of lynching to extract confessions from their prisoners.

"Did you not tell him if he did not quit breaking in houses around here that these white people would come in here and hang him?"

The chief confessed to that charge: "I told him he was liable to be hung about stealing things."[42]

The police chief insisted that Ammons's confession had been "free and voluntary," but after the Mississippi Supreme Court reviewed the case— and the chief justice's testimony—it did not agree. "Such proceedings as this record disclosed cannot be too strongly denounced" for violating "every principle of law, reason, humanity, and personal right." The court then reiterated that every officer not only should refrain from torture but actually had a duty to warn prisoners that their confessions might be used against them in court. This was 1902. One day the U.S. Supreme Court would agree.[43]

Mollison's name does not appear on the documents connected with the sweatbox case, but a white lawyer willing to doggedly question the police chief on behalf of a black man must have caught his eye. Mollison had worked with white lawyers many times. Once Vardaman became governor and began encouraging white supremacy anew with the weight of the state, this kind of cooperation became more difficult but could still happen. Mollison also knew that to defeat Mississippi's unconstitutional all-white jury system would require a defense lawyer who would be willing and able to aggressively cross-examine the county sheriff and his deputies, the men who picked the jurors. The Supreme Court demanded evidence of discrimination, actual confessions by the discriminators. The cross-examination would have to be relentless, the questions asked without regard for racial etiquette. Judges and court officers in Vicksburg tolerated black lawyers far more readily than county officers in the more rural parts of Mississippi. In some places, deputies would not allow black lawyers to even enter the courtroom and required that they sit in the balcony with other black spectators. Some allowed them in the courtroom but not behind the bar, with the white lawyers.[44] Vicksburg was not that inhospitable, but Mollison must have figured that even in Vicksburg Marshall could get a confession of discrimination more easily than could a black man.

On October 28, 1905, a black laborer named Joe Hill confronted Matilda Davis as she sat eating pecans with her children and friends. Hill, who had been drinking whiskey, quarreled with Davis, grabbed a Winchester rifle, and shot the woman, killing her. The killing seemingly occurred in a momentary instant of rage. Hill had been boarding with Davis for four years. Making no attempt to hide his crime, he instead carried it out in front of a roomful of witnesses. "Did you see it?" authorities asked Adeline Davis, Matilda's daughter. "Yes sir I certainly did see it." She then described what happened: "Mr. Joe called my mama to his room and she says, 'What do you want Joe?'" He wanted whiskey. When he drank half the whiskey offered, Matilda complained. Hill responded by shooting the woman.[45]

On the first Monday of December 1905, the Circuit Court of Warren County, Mississippi, opened its December term. Court officials had written the names of fifty potential grand jurors, all white men, on slips of paper. They distributed the names in five boxes. The court appointed J. K. Hirsch to reach into the boxes and select twenty names, the Warren County grand jury. The next day, which was December 6, 1905, the grand jurors indicted Joseph Hill for the murder of Matilda Davis. District Attorney James D. Thames then signed the indictment. Two days afterward, the court appointed Dabney Marshall and H. H. Coleman attorneys for Hill.

Dabney Marshall filed a motion to quash the indictment. He accused the Warren County Board of Supervisors of deliberately excluding "all duly qualified electors of the African race, and descent, though otherwise duly qualified" and preventing them from sitting as either grand or petit jurors. Marshall reminded the court that Willis Mollison and others, being fully qualified for jury service, "tax payers and property holders, of good moral character," had petitioned the Board of Supervisors requesting that qualified black people be made jurors. The board had rejected the petition solely because the petitioners were black, Marshall charged. And the board continued to pick only white men as jurors. Marshall also pointed out that since Hill had been jailed immediately after Matilda Davis had died and had been denied access to a lawyer, there was no way he could have challenged the grand jury until after the grand jurors had indicted him, and the court had appointed his lawyers. Marshall wanted to call witnesses and produce evidence to prove his allegations, but the court ruled that he had failed to make his motion in time—Mississippi permitted challenges to grand jurors only before they were sworn.

Marshall also tried to persuade the court to quash the trial jury. He made this motion before the jurors had been sworn, so the court allowed a hearing and Marshall called his witnesses. He was looking for the kind of confession that had decided the case of *Neal v. Delaware*, where Delaware's chief justice had said:

> That none but white men were selected is in no wise remarkable in view of the fact—too notorious to be ignored—that the great body of black men residing in this State are utterly unqualified by want of intelligence, experience, or moral integrity to sit on juries. Exceptions there are, unquestionably; but they are rare.[46]

Harlan, speaking for the Court, had called this "a violent presumption" and had ruled against Delaware, awarding Neal a new trial.[47]

Marshall knew full well that very nearly every white person in Mississippi, and certainly all those who selected jurors, completely agreed with the chief justice of Delaware. If he could persuade the county officers selecting the juries to simply say what they believed, admitting prejudices similar to those expressed by Delaware's chief justice, he could then place Mississippi's supreme court in an awkward position. It could either overturn Hill's conviction or ratify the trial court's racism and invite reversal by the U.S. Supreme Court. In Mississippi county boards of supervisors prepared jury lists, but judges sometimes ordered the sheriff and his deputies to summon trial jurors from bystanders, ordinary people whom the officers found on the street. In Hill's case, the judge had ordered just such a bystander jury.

Francis Wellman, a leading expert on cross-examination at the time, cautioned that any witness will feel a loyalty to one side or the other and will fear becoming disloyal to "his" side. Marshall understood that the county officers he called as witnesses would be especially hostile to his effort; he was, after all, trying to get them to admit their prejudices and misconduct in picking jurors. This did not mean that Marshall would try to break them down by an obviously brutal examination. By 1906, many lawyers had abandoned the old-fashioned stormy style of oratory common to the nineteenth century. They no longer tried to "grasp the thunderbolt," as Wellman put it. Instead, their approach had become more scientific. In his treatise on cross-examination, Wellman disapproved of "a shouting, brow-beating style," urging lawyers instead to appear courteous and conciliatory, inducing even the most hostile witness into "a discussion of his testimony in a fair-minded spirit."[48]

Regardless of the style a lawyer adopted, all authorities on cross-examination warned of its dangers. One expert cautioned that cross-examination was "inherently the most dangerous branch" because the wrong question could easily unleash "a flood" of unhelpful evidence. Richard Harris likened cross-examination to fighting a naval battle: like a ship captain in combat, a lawyer should never loiter too long in one place. Harris advised: "You must circumvent a good deal, firing a shot here and a shot there, until, maybe, you can catch your adversary unawares and leap on board."[49]

For Marshall the dangers may have been less than for many advocates: he could have no doubt that the sheriff and his deputies really did choose white men as jurors and only white men as a matter of policy, perhaps unstated, but as a policy nonetheless. It seems unlikely that any "flood of evidence" existed that could explain away the fact that only white men served as jurors. The only question was whether he could catch his enemy unawares and "leap aboard."

Marshall called the sheriff first. Sheriff John Leigh Hyland fell into that category of witnesses who make up the majority of all witnesses, according to William Mawdesley Best, the leading expert on evidence. Best—like Francis Wellman and many other authorities—knew that almost any witness had an interest in one side or the other; few people came to court genuinely neutral. Unlike the "hardened villains" prepared to swear an outright falsehood, most biased witnesses had a way of "compounding with their consciences" by concealing the truth or keeping back a portion of it. Not fully explaining an answer was not really lying, such people believed.[50]

"Did you summon the jurors that are serving this week?" Marshall asked. Hyland explained that he did not very often personally summon jurors, leaving that job to his deputy, T. C. Childs.

"Did you give any instructions who to summon, whether to have all white or colored people?"

"No sir, I did not give Mr. Childs instructions."

Marshall asked Hyland if he had ever summoned even one black juror since he had been first elected sheriff. The sheriff had not.

"Why?"

"I had no special reason for it. It was not necessary. There was always some white men sitting around."

Marshall questioned that response, wanting to know why he preferred white men over blacks.

"Because they are generally not eligible." Hyland was on safe ground with this point. Mississippi law, like the law in many other states, still restricted jury service to men registered to vote. Mississippi's 1890 constitution had eliminated almost all black men from the voting lists. The U.S. Supreme Court had approved this action. In Warren County, barely a handful of black men remained registered to vote.[51]

Marshall asked Hyland what he would do if, as he searched for jurors, he found a black man equal to a white man.

"I would summon a white man."

"If you could possibly get a jury made up of all white people you would get it rather than get a negro?"

Hyland was not sure he wanted to agree to that: "I don't know about that." But he admitted: "I would give the white man the preference."

"If you could possibly get a jury of white people you would get them," Marshall asked again and this time Hyland agreed.

"You would exclude the negro because they were negroes?"

Hyland quibbled a bit and then allowed, "I would not go hunt him."

"Just because he was a negro?"

"Yes sir just because he was a negro. Because they are generally not eligible."

At this point the district attorney interrupted, asking if the number of blacks eligible for jury duty was large or small.

"They are small."

Thames also wanted to make sure that the record showed that no county official had instructed anyone to pick only white men as jurors. "In the selection of this particular jury you never instructed any of your bailiffs to summon men because they where white men, or left them out because they were negroes?"

"No sir." Thames knew he was getting things back onto safer ground; he just wanted to nail down the fact that no discrimination had occurred, and so he asked Hyland if he had ever instructed his bailiffs to pick only white men as jurors, in the entire time he had served as sheriff.

"No sir."

Marshall resumed his questioning. "Is it not tacitly understood by your deputies" to select only white men, he asked. Hyland, an experienced witness, easily evaded that question: "I can't say what they understand."

Marshall next called the circuit clerk. J. W. Collier testified that he had between 1,700 and 2,100 names on the voting lists. Less evasive than the sheriff, he readily admitted that some black men had registered to vote. Marshall asked Collier if he personally knew the black voters, and the clerk acknowledged that he knew many of them.

"Are they pretty respectable . . . people?" Marshall asked, and Collier admitted that they were, adding, "As far as darkies go. As far as I know some of them are respectable darkies."

Marshall started reading the names of specific black people, forcing Collier to acknowledge that none had been convicted of any crime, and all had paid their taxes and registered to vote. Marshall then prompted Collier to produce poll books and list blacks registered to vote and eligible for jury service. By the time Collier left the stand, it was clear that very few, but some, black men eligible for jury service lived in Warren County.

Marshall next called Deputy Sheriff T. C. Childs.

"Did you summon this jury out there that is trying Joe Hill?" Childs agreed that he had. "Did you try to get any negroes on there?"

"I did not."

"Why?"

"Well I don't know as I had any reason for it at all. I could not give you any; I just followed the usual custom that they are not qualified jurors."

For Marshall, Childs' confession that the sheriff's office had a "usual custom" was a huge step in the right direction, but he did not immediately pounce. Instead, he asked how long Childs had served as deputy. Six years, the deputy answered. Marshall then asked if during that entire time he had ever tried to find even one qualified black man to serve as a juror.

"No sir."

Marshall asked Childs if he would summon a black man as a juror if he knew there were qualified blacks available.

"It has never come down to that," Childs answered and then added, "I have never given it a thought."

"Now be fair with me," Marshall insisted. "Don't you know that you would not summon a negro on the jury if you could get out of it just because he was a negro."

Childs weaseled: "Oh, I don't know, I have not hatred towards the negro; I rather like them." Marshall brushed that aside: "Do you like them as jurors?" The deputy answered that he had never seen a black juror, so he really did not see how he could be expected to have an opinion on that.[52] Marshall was relentless. "Be fair," he insisted again, "would you summon a negro to sit on the jury if you could get a white man." Childs answered that he could not see any reason to pick a black man as a juror.

"Would you do it?

"I don't know."

"You never have done it?"

"No sir."

So, Marshall concluded, "You fail to summon negroes simply because they are negroes."

"I have never given it a thought."

"You never even think about it," Marshall accused.

"Never do," Childs retorted.

Marshall knew he had him. "You never even think about it," he said again. Childs testily agreed. Marshall continued, "The policy is so settled in this court to summon white men solely you don't even think about summoning a Negro?" Childs, sounding nettled, snapped that it was "settled with me; I never give it a thought."[53]

This was getting dangerously out of hand, so Judge Oliver Catchings, perhaps casting a wary glance at his court stenographer mindlessly transcribing every word as Deputy Childs marched deeper into territory already pioneered by the chief justice of Delaware, intervened. Catchings got the witness to reiterate that no one had ever instructed him to select only white jurors. The deputy, in turn, had never told his helpers to choose only white people as jurors. It just happened to work out that way. "Did you summon this jury simply because they were white people?" Catchings asked, getting things firmly back on track. It was a leading question and even a Warren County deputy sheriff could figure out what he was supposed to say: "No, sir."[54]

In the next moment, it must have seemed to the deputy that everyone in the courtroom was hurling questions at him. The district attorney asked that he reiterate that he never chose jurors solely because they were white men. Marshall then demanded to know who was responsible: "The selection of these people was left solely with you?" A good opportunity to implicate his superiors, but Childs would not take the bait; he agreed it was all on him. Marshall gave him a second chance: "You summoned all these persons yourself?" Childs agreed that he had. Marshall's cousin and partner, Harry Coleman, asked which bailiffs had helped him pick jurors—showing that, in fact, Childs had not acted alone in picking the jurors—but the deputy claimed he could not remember which bailiffs had helped with this particular jury.[55]

Marshall then called Willis Mollison as a witness. Since no documents or other writings survive to show the exact relationship between the two lawyers, Mollison's testimony is the best evidence of their collaboration. Mollison had initiated his plan to get blacks on juries by petitioning the board of supervisors. Now Marshall carried his fight into court, calling the black man to prove that competent black men, eligible for jury duty, lived in Warren County. Mollison had himself never been called for jury duty, yet he told the court he was an attorney, practicing for thirteen years. He added that he knew other black voters of good intelligence. "Most of them are good citizens." One had served as chairman of a committee during a recent quarantine. "Didn't he seem to have the respect and consideration of the fellow citizens here generally?" Marshall wanted to know, and Mollison agreed that he did, so Marshall next asked: "Wouldn't you think him in every way suitable to make a juror?" Mollison thought that was true as well.[56] Marshall's questioning of Mollison followed the logic of Mollison's forthcoming book, *The Leading Afro-Americans of Vicksburg, Mississippi, Their Enterprises, Churches, Schools, Lodges, and Societies* (1908). Mollison's book was a who's who of intelligent and capable black people in Vicksburg, prepared in the tradition of Booker T. Washington to prove the racism of bigots like James K. Vardaman wrong. In fact, Mollison wanted to prove wrong every white man convinced that no black man could benefit from schooling. In Vicksburg there were highly intelligent and honest African Americans, entrepreneurial men with property who voted and paid their taxes. By calling Mollison as a witness, Marshall helped him make the same point in court.[57]

Then the hearing on Marshall's challenge to the trial jury ended. The court rejected Marshall's challenge to the trial jury just as it had his objection to the grand jury. Hill went on trial December 13.

After the all-white jury, "good and lawful men" according to the transcript, found his client guilty, Marshall filed a motion for new trial. His motion listed six grounds for granting a new trial. Three concerned the judge's instructions to the jury and evidence admitted or not admitted, but Marshall summarized the main thrust of his argument in three steps:

1. The court erred in overruling the defendant's motion to quash the indictment;
2. the court erred in overruling the defendant's motions to quash the various petit juries tendered by the state and the jury by which he was tried;
3. the court erred in not sustaining the defendant's challenge to the panels of the petit juries tendered by the state, and the jury which tried him.[58]

The court overruled and denied Marshall's motion for a new trial. On December 21, the court sentenced Hill to be hanged on January 26, 1906.[59]

Despite the judge's intervention, Marshall left court confident that, as he put it in his brief to the Mississippi Supreme Court, "the cat is out of the bag."[60] Marshall argued that state officers had admitted their discrimination against potential black jurors, not only violating the Fourteenth Amendment but doing so overtly, making comments about the general lack of qualification among blacks that sounded similar to remarks made by the Delaware chief justice. Marshall felt that he had forced a Mississippi court to document its own discrimination. Not only that, but the judge rejecting his challenge to the grand jury said that he did so because it had been filed too late. This was Marshall's strongest argument, rooted in *Carter v. Texas*, but for Marshall to win on that basis meant that the Mississippi Supreme Court would have to overrule both itself and the law of Mississippi. "The American judicial system vests considerable discretion in lower-court judges," Gerald Rosenberg has observed, adding that the biased judge "has a myriad of tools with which to abuse discretion."[61] As recently as April 1905, the Mississippi Supreme Court had insisted, in two cases not involving race, that once impaneled, a sitting grand jury could not be challenged, even by a defendant unaware that the grand jury might indict him. Challenges had to come before the grand jury was sworn. To follow Mississippi statute law, they defied the Supreme Court.[62]

In those cases, the Mississippi judges apparently felt comfortable that their rulings would not be reviewed by the U.S. Supreme Court. When Marshall appealed Hill's conviction to Mississippi's supreme court, he seemed tenacious, a man on a mission to embarrass the power structure; the judges could not be so sure that he would not go to the U.S. Supreme Court.

The Mississippi Supreme Court consisted of three judges, selected by the governor, with the advice and consent of the state senate. In 1906, Robert Burns Mayes, Albert Hall Whitfield, and Solomon Saladin Calhoon sat on Mississippi's highest court, with Whitfield as chief justice. The oldest of the three, Calhoon, wrote the court's opinion in *Hill v. State of Mississippi*. Marshall knew Calhoon well. Before he became a judge, Calhoon had served on Marshall's defense team after he shot Dinkins. Calhoon (1838–1908) had been a newspaper editor before the Civil War; he joined the Confederate army when the war started and rose to the rank of lieutenant colonel. He played a leading role in promoting Mississippi's 1890 constitution and, in fact, became president of the convention, where he pursued his agenda of disfranchising black voters. Calhoon outlined his racial views in a pamphlet titled *Negro Suffrage*, published in 1890 and intended to build public support for the convention and the new constitution. To properly understand black people, Calhoon urged his readers to look to Africa, where, he averred, there is "no advancement, no invention, no progress, no civilization, no education, no history, no literature, no governmental polity. We see only ignorance, slavery, cannibalism, no respect for women, no respect for anything save the strong hand." Calhoon insisted he felt "affection for the negro, and esteem[ed] highly many of his characteristics. As a rule he is docile, good-natured, hospitable, charitable, faithful in his friendships, but not inventive, not progressive, not resourceful, not energetic." Calhoon wrote about black voting in 1890, but his comments no doubt captured his feelings about black jury service as well when he wrote that "Negro suffrage is an evil, and an evil to both races. Its necessary outcome is that conflicting aspirations and apprehensions must produce continual jars and frequent hostile collisions, which do not occur with homogeneous races." Calhoon acknowledged that some whites believed that education and Christianization could remedy blacks' shortcomings. "This is a grave mistake," he said. Black inferiority, Calhoon believed, followed "God's own laws" and could not be remedied by the hand of man.[63]

As president of the 1890 convention, Calhoon explained that "two distinct and opposite types of mankind" found themselves together in Mississippi. Rule by one meant economic ruin; rule by the other meant prosperity and happiness. Calhoon had to choose his words carefully; he knew that what he said went into an official record that would be litigated before the U.S. Supreme Court. Any kind of overt bigotry of the sort he had published in his own pamphlet must not be repeated on the official record of the convention, he understood. Alluding to the Civil War Amendments forbidding discrimination by the states, Calhoon told his fellow delegates that they must never pass any discriminatory ordinance. Every law must benefit all citizens of this state. "That is the great problem for which we are called together," Calhoon said. The "problem" was how to oust black people from the voting rolls and do so without seeming to treat them differently from everyone else. Mississippi had been debating the problem in its press for months. The solution came in the form of a poll tax, which white people expected black people not to pay, and a literacy test, which white people expected county officials would apply with great prejudice against black applicants. Removing blacks from the voting rolls would remove them from juries as well. In fact, within a few years of the 1890 convention, a small number of blacks remained on the voting rolls, but none served as jurors.[64]

Thereafter, Calhoon became one of the leading criminal lawyers in the state and had joined other leading lawyers to defend Dabney Marshall in 1895. Five years after that, as a judge he joined Mississippi's highest court, where he wrote most of the court's opinions on criminal cases.[65]

Judges are limited not only by their own prejudices but also by the culture they inhabit. As a resident of Mississippi, Calhoon lived in a society that tolerated and even encouraged every possible discrimination against black Americans, from segregated cemeteries to lynching. Nonetheless, the U.S. Supreme Court had ruled that state judges had to allow criminal defendants to at least try to prove discrimination in jury selection. Hill's trial judge had blocked Hill's effort to attack his grand jury much as Texas had disallowed Seth Carter's effort to prove discrimination in Texas. It took ten months for Calhoon to write 1,007 words in five paragraphs. As the *Vicksburg Evening Post* observed, "It is evident that the members of the bench tried to reach some other conclusion, but in the face of the Federal decisions, it was impossible to do so."[66] On December 18, 1906, Calhoon finally issued his opinion. He began by acknowledging that the trial-court judge had followed Mississippi law and precedent when he rejected Marshall's challenge to the grand jury:

> The court below refused to consider the motion to quash the indictment solely on the ground that the objection to the constitution of the grand jury should have been made before the grand jurors were sworn and impaneled. Sec. 2375, Code of 1892, making the impaneling of the grand jury conclusive evidence of its competency and qualifications, has been often considered by this court, and has been held applicable even to a defendant who was not advised that any accusation against him was being considered by that body.[67]

Then, in his customary crisp manner, Calhoon explained that the state of Mississippi had no choice but to follow the Supreme Court's rulings:

> However, the objection to the grand jury presented by the motion to quash in this case is based on a right claimed under the federal constitution, and it has been held by the supreme court of the United States that the question whether a right arising under the constitution or laws of the United States is sufficiently pleaded or brought to the notice of a state court is itself a federal question. It has also been held by that court that, when a defendant has had no opportunity to challenge the grand jury which found the indictment against him, objection to its constitution may be taken either by plea in abatement or motion to quash the indictment before pleading in bar. Whatever application we may give to the statute in cases not involving a federal question reviewable by the supreme court of the United States, we are bound by the above rulings of that tribunal. Since the motion to quash clearly presented a federal question, we must hold in this case that it was error to refuse to consider the motion to quash on the ground that it was presented after the grand jury was impaneled.[68]

Calhoon reversed Hill's conviction and awarded him a new trial. He did not say that blacks could or should serve on juries—the U.S. Supreme Court had ruled that he did not have to say that—but he did say that the U.S. Supreme Court would not permit Mississippi to block defense lawyers' inquiries into all-white juries. At his new trial, a jury convicted Joseph Hill again, but this time he was not sentenced to death. He went to prison instead. Always ready to praise Dabney Marshall, Cashman commented that the lawyer's able defense had saved Hill's life.[69]

More important than Calhoon's grudging reversal of Hill's conviction or Hill's fate was what John Cashman made of the opinion. The *Vicksburg Evening Post* pronounced the Hill opinion important and far reaching, one likely to permanently return blacks to Mississippi juries. The *Post* warned that failure to admit blacks to jury service would allow defense attorneys with black clients to tie up the courts with constant inquiries into jury selection procedures. Cashman never said so explicitly, but he obviously knew that repeated searching inquiries into how Warren County deputies chose jurors would expose rampant and deliberate discrimination. The issue in every criminal trial with a black defendant would shift from the defendant's guilt to the court's discrimination. This would "defeat the ends of justice, regardless of the merits of their cases." The following January, the *Vicksburg Evening Post* announced that the county's board of supervisors was busily at work adding African Americans' names to the county's jury lists. Pinkard Dowans served on a jury in April, apparently without much incident. In May a panel of white jurors protested the presence of blacks in their midst, and the circuit judge had to quiet their protests before proceeding. But quiet them he did, and the trial proceeded, with black jurors.[70]

Local authorities in Vicksburg resented judicial power. Several scholars have stressed the obstacles that confronted any federal judge if he tried to enforce decrees in the face of determined local opposition. Missing from this analysis is a recognition that judges wielded considerable power in criminal cases: they could free felons convicted of dangerous and violent crimes. Public safety demanded that even rules contradicting Mississippi law, rules emanating from the federal government, must be obeyed. Judges could make it easier for defense attorneys to challenge every conviction of a black defendant. Courts had the power to release prisoners. Hordes of black thieves and murderers could be unleashed on the city if local authorities refused to cooperate with Supreme Court rules. For that reason, in matters of criminal procedure, the Supreme Court had considerable structural power over provincial authorities.

The system did depend on energetic and capable defense attorneys to vigorously defend the rights of African Americans who ran afoul of the law. Dabney Marshall was clearly an unusual person; few white defense attorneys so boldly challenged white power and the all-white jury system. In

explaining the brief break in Mississippi's all-white jury system, he was—
in part—what Marc Bloch would call an exceptional rather than a general
cause. In one sense, obviously, he confounded his context and baffles our
expectations. But he also represented his context: He served time in prison
because of a characteristically southern "affair of honor," and then from the
ashes of his own thwarted ambitions, he demonstrated his talents on behalf
of black defendants. He was an exception to his culture but also a product
of it. His honor-bound, hypermasculinized culture freed him from its con-
straints by sending him to prison. Perhaps more importantly, the judges
of Mississippi's supreme court, where racism ran amok, and the Warren
County Board of Supervisors, dared not violate the determined rules of the
U.S. Supreme Court, when clearly articulated. Mississippi's brief experiment with integrated juries had a systemic cause too.

In October 1907, the supreme court of Mississippi handed down its decision in *George Lewis v. State of Mississippi*. This time Robert Burns Mayes
and not Calhoon wrote the opinion of the court, affirming Lewis's conviction by an all-white jury. Through his lawyers, Lewis had borrowed Marshall's strategy, objecting to the discrimination, but Mayes wrote, "The testimony shows conclusively that the laws of the state have been complied with
strictly, and that no person was put on the jury simply because he belonged
to the white race." A few lines later, Mayes got to his larger purpose, which
was to correct the damage he felt that his court had done a year earlier when
it reversed Hill's murder conviction. "It is a mistaken impression," Mayes
said, "which seems to have become prevalent, that in order to constitute a
valid jury there must be some Negroes in the jury list." Mayes assured his
readers, "Such is not the case."[71] He neatly and expertly summarized the law
articulated by the U.S. Supreme Court: "There is nothing in the law which
permits [court officials] to discriminate and refuse to take a negro on a jury
simply because he is a negro; neither are they required to take him on the
jury because he is a negro."[72] Juries could be entirely white, and Mayes assured white Mississippians that the U.S. Supreme Court had fully and completely approved the state's jury-selection procedures:

> In the case of *Dixon v. State*, 74 Miss. 271; 20 So. 839, and *Gibson v. State*, 162
> U.S. 565; 16 S. Ct. 904; 40 L. Ed. 1075, all the provisions of our law with ref-
> erence to the selection of jurors, both by the statute and the Constitution,
> are reviewed and elaborately discussed, and held not to be violative of any
> clause or section of the Constitution of the United States.[73]

Mayes revealed that, rather than a knife at the throat of Mississippi discrimination, the U.S. Supreme Court was an ally and legitimizer of all-white juries. Mississippi had once again affirmed that its juries would be entirely white. Mayes exactly followed U.S. Supreme Court rulings. He said nothing in *Lewis v. Mississippi* that challenged or contradicted anything said by the justices. Rather, he followed the road map they had laid out in their jury decisions.

Willis Mollison's plan to use jury service to prove black men capable, competent, and dignified had succeeded, even if only briefly. In that brief moment, though, his campaign for black jurors laid bare the U.S. Supreme Court's rules governing jury selection, taking them as far as they would go. A few years after the Hill case, as the racial situation in Mississippi grew more hopeless, he left Vicksburg for Chicago. Soon black newspapers in Chicago reported his "masterful" arguments to juries in sensational cases. He died in 1924.[74] His son became a federal judge.[75]

In its decision calling an end to Mollison's plan, the Mississippi Supreme Court implicitly rebuked Cashman and the *Vicksburg Evening Post* for misinterpreting its decision in *Hill v. State.* This might seem one more piece of evidence that Cashman's lonely crusade against lynching and for law put him too far outside the mainstream of white thinking to matter. Before dismissing Cashman as simply a historical loser, however, we must consider his paper's bitter battle for survival against the *Vicksburg Herald* (sometimes known as the *Vicksburg Commercial Herald*). In contrast to the *Post*, the *Vicksburg Herald* did not adamantly oppose lynching and had nothing much to say about Dabney Marshall. In 1883, it approved when the Copiah County Democrats resolved to use violence against black voters and killed one man. Rather than denounce the murder, the *Herald* explained that the murdered man, Print Matthews, "was such an extreme, desperate negro leader, that there was danger of a race conflict at every election. The people preferred to remove the devil rather than endure his hell."[76] The *Herald* said that "when it became necessary, the negro leader, P. Matthews, stopped a few leaden messengers."[77] Reviewing the Copiah County violence, the *Post* boasted that it had been the first paper in the state to denounce the murder and had maintained its position in the face of criticism from several Mississippi papers, including the *Herald.*[78] In 1888, the *Herald* "regretted" "the necessity for lynch law" but added that when the necessity existed "there should be no hesitation about resorting to it [lynch law]."[79]

Cashman's *Evening Post* began as an upstart challenger against this pro-lynching voice; in 1883, the *Herald*, a morning paper, tried to destroy the *Post* by publishing an evening edition for ten cents a week, far cheaper than Cashman could afford. Like Babe Ruth pointing to where he would hit a home run before he came to bat, the *Herald's* editor, Charles E. Wright, announced plans to destroy the *Vicksburg Evening Post*. Wright proclaimed Vicksburg a one-newspaper town and said that the *Herald* would be that one paper, a voice criticizing the courts and juries and favoring mob law when necessary.[80] The *Herald* had every advantage over the *Post*. For a time, national advertisers patronized the *Herald* but not the *Post*. The *Herald* could afford to lease a wire that gave its readers access to national and international news unavailable to the *Evening Post* and its readers.[81]

It would be foolish to argue that the *Evening Post* ultimately triumphed over the *Herald* because Cashman took such a hard-nosed position for law and against mob violence. Cashman and his son won, it seems more likely, because they ultimately published a more lively, modern-looking paper than the *Herald*. No doubt it helped that a fire destroyed the *Herald* offices. But Cashman took the most uncompromising position possible for law and against mob law, publishing a gut-wrenching description of a lynching designed to make the coldest bigot squirm; he began as an upstart challenger to a well-established pro-lynching paper and ended up not just defeating the *Herald* but owning it. In 1925, the Cashman family finally bought the *Vicksburg Herald* and continued printing it as Vicksburg's morning paper. And then there were two newspapers in Vicksburg adamantly opposed to lynching. In the Deep South newspaper market, it certainly was possible to make a law-and-order attack on lynching and win. It was possible to support integrated juries and win. Perhaps no other mode of attack, no other rhetoric outside the constitutional approach that Cashman favored, would have survived that market.

Conclusion

WILLIS MOLLISON AND DABNEY MARSHALL'S campaign against Mississippi's all-white jury system provides an opportunity to examine the connections that run through the American criminal justice system. First, and most obviously, the tendrils of racial prejudice reached into American courts and their juries. Considerable scholarly ink has been spilled on efforts to keep blacks away from the ballot box and segregate their access to public accommodations. At the end of the nineteenth century, state legislatures passed segregation laws and enacted the grandfather clauses, poll taxes, and literacy tests, which removed most blacks from the voting rolls. At this historical moment, the states also whitened their juries. All-white juries played an essential role in guaranteeing that blacks could be intimidated and harassed if they dared challenge their discrimination.

Mollison and Marshall's challenge to Mississippi jury procedures tested the ligaments binding the state courts to rules articulated by the U.S. Supreme Court. Recent scholars have emphasized the ability of lower courts to resist supervision by the U.S. Supreme Court, but Marshall's campaign complicates this picture. Mississippi's highest court did not, in fact, dare challenge the U.S. Supreme Court's rules, but it is also true that the Court seemed to make it a point not to do anything that would make state judges want to challenge its rules. The Court decided that the appearance of discrimination did not prove the discrimination. It was not enough to show that only white men served as jurors in majority-black counties and had done so for years. The discriminators had to confess. Setting the bar so high discouraged defense attorneys from challenging all-white juries and signaled court officials that they had only to keep quiet about their prejudices, and the juries could remain white. In short, it invited continued discrimination.

This willingness to accede to local bias tested the connections between jury mythology and courtroom realities. Over centuries a powerful tradition evolved holding that criminal defendants were entitled to a jury of their peers. It requires no great feat of investigation to prove that Americans did not always or even often live up to this ideal. Between the 1787 Constitutional Convention and the Civil War, whites with power successfully denied trial by jury to almost all black Americans. They made sure that women almost never got juries composed of their peers. Yet it goes too far to simply dismiss the fair-jury-trial ideal as entirely toothless. Lawyers sympathetic to the plight of black Americans and black Americans themselves agitated for fairer trials and fairly picked juries. They built an archive of arguments for fairly selected juries. They could then go into court with long-established arguments, seemingly legitimate for their durability, but they made their own contributions to this canon as well.

In 1866, Congress hosted a battle between those wanting to finally enforce such idealism and those determined to protect their interests through the existing structure, the balance of power between the states and the national government and between white and black Americans, a balance of power that decidedly favored the local and the white. In the end, Congress could not decide the most fundamental question of all: could all-white juries give black defendants a fair trial? That question came to the Supreme Court, where champions of natural-law rights—the idea that some rights are so fundamental that government must protect them—clashed with a rival faction, led by Samuel Miller. A majority of justices decided that they must defer to public opinion. And so they compromised. Juries could be all white, but those white jurors had to be chosen without documented bias. It is revealing that the justices thought it possible for unbiased officials to fairly choose only whites as jurors.

Finally, the history of jury discrimination also reveals the problems inherent in connecting justice with public opinion. Congress struggled to know what the public wanted, and in 1866—a transitional moment in American history—several members confessed that they found the public's will unknowable. The Supreme Court did not automatically yield to public opinion. Justices Joseph Bradley and Miller quarreled over the role that natural law and politics should play in the Supreme Court's thinking. In the end, the Court did follow "the shifting currents of Northern public opinion." The critical point is that it consciously chose to follow a particular kind of public opinion. There were other currents available, streams less prone to shifting, transcendent values with roots deep in history: the ideal of a mixed jury, truly representative of a landscape populated with many different peoples, some excluded from the "public opinion" privileged by the Congress and the Supreme Court.

One way nineteenth-century government leaders kept track of public opinion was by reading newspapers. Newspapers often seemed to represent the public, especially before the advent of the public-opinion poll. For Mollison and Marshall, it mattered greatly that they had a friendly newspaper supporting their efforts. John Cashman interpreted the Mississippi Supreme Court's *Joseph Hill v. Mississippi* decision in ways that made black jury service seem inevitable and essential. Cashman had consistently campaigned for the rule of law in Mississippi. He struggled with public opinion, wanting to believe that ordinary white Mississippians could be persuaded to follow the law and not the tyranny of "King Lynch," but in this endeavor he found continual frustration. In the end, Cashman triumphed; his newspaper defeated its competition and continues as Vicksburg's newspaper today. Cashman's story demonstrates the power he wielded by representing court decisions to the public. In much the same vein, Dabney Marshall tried to get excluded people onto Mississippi's juries. He did so against impossible odds in a game rigged against him. That he succeeded at all is remarkable.

Appendix 1

States Discriminating by Property and Race in Their Statutes

State	Constitution	Constitution	Jury statute
Alabama	1819, art. III, § 5: Every white male person of the age of twenty-one years.	1865, art. VIII, § 1: Every white male person, of the age of twenty-one years.	*Code of Alabama* (1852), 613: The sheriff of the several counties in this state must obtain, biennially, a list of the *householders and freeholders* . . . and the sheriff, judge of the probate court, and clerk of the circuit court . . . meet . . . and select from such list the names of such persons as may be thought competent to discharge the duties of grand and petit jurors with honest, impartiality and intelligence.
Arkansas	1836 and 1864, art. IV, § 2: Every free white male citizen of the United States, who shall have attained the age of twenty-one years.	1868, art. VIII, § 2: Every male citizen born in the United States, and every male person who has been naturalized, or has legally declared his intention to become a citizen . . . who is 21.	*Revised Statutes* (1838), 482–83: Every grand juror shall be a free *white* male citizen. . . . A householder or a freeholder. . . . Every petit juror shall be a free *white* male citizen.

State	Constitution	Constitution	Jury statute
Florida	1838 and 1865, art. VI, § 1: Every free white male person of the age of twenty-one.		*Acts and Resolutions* (1846), 26: [T]he sheriffs . . . shall obtain biennially, a list of all the *house-holders* . . . to serve as jurors taken from the tax list, or which may otherwise come to his knowledge; and it shall also be the duty of the County Commissioners . . . to examine the list so returned by the Sheriff, and add to it such name and names as each of them may know of subject to serve as jurors; and it shall be the duty of said board of County Com-missioners to select from the list aforesaid, the names of such person as may be adjudged competent to discharge the duties of Grand and Petit Jurors with honesty, impartial-ity and intelligence.
Georgia	1789 and 1798, art. IV, § 1: [C]itizens and inhabitants of this state . . . [who are] 21 years [old], and have paid tax for the year preceding the election.	1865, art. V, § 1: The electors or members of the general assembly shall be free white male citizens . . . [who are] 21 years [old], and have paid all taxes which may have been required of them.	*Codification of the Statute Law* (1845), 578: All free male *white* citizens.
Illinois	1818, art. II, § 27: All white male inhabitants above the age of 21.		*Public and General Statute Laws* (1839), 395: [A]ll free *white* male taxable inhabitants.
Indiana	1816, art. VI, § 1: [E]very white male citizen of the United States . . . 21 years [old].	1851, art. II, § 2: [E]very male citizen of the United States, of the age of 21.	*Revised Statutes* (1843), 951: [G]ood reputable *freeholders or householders*, residents of the county in which they are selected and taxable therein.
Kansas	1855, art. II, § 2: Every white male person, and every civilized male Indian who has adopted the habits of the white man, of the age of 21.	1857, art. VIII, § 1: Every male citizen of the United States, above the age of 21.	*Statutes* (1855), 444–45: Every grand juror shall be a free *white* citizen . . . a *householder* . . . . Every petit juror shall be a free *white* male citizen.

State	Constitution	Constitution	Jury statute
Kentucky	1799, art. II, § 8: [E]very free male citizen (negroes, mulattoes, and Indians excepted) . . . the age of 21.	1850, art. II, § 8: Every free white male citizen of the age of 21.	*Revised Statutes* (1852), 426: No person shall be qualified to serve as a grand juryman, unless he shall be a citizen and a *house-keeper* . . . . No person shall be a competent juryman for trial of criminal, penal, or civil cases, in the circuit court, unless he be a free *white* citizen . . . a *house-keeper* . . . sober, temperate, discreet, and of good demeanor.
Louisiana	1812, art. II, § 8: [E]very free white male citizen . . . 21 years [old].	1845 and 1852, art. II, § 10 (§ 14 in 1864): [E]very free white male . . . 21 years [old].	*Consolidation and Revision of the Statutes* (1852), 361: [A] free *white* male citizen of the State.
Mississippi	1817 and 1832, art. III, § 1: Every free white male person of the age of 21.	1868, art. VII, § 2: [A]ll male inhabitants of this State, except idiots and insane persons, and Indians not taxed . . . 21 [years old].	*Revised Code* (1857), 497: All persons being *freeholders or householders*.
Missouri	1820, art. III, § 10: Every free white male citizen of the United States, who shall have attained the age of 21 years.	1865, art. II, § 18: Every white male citizen of the United States, and every white male person of foreign birth who may have declared his intention to become a citizen.	*Revised Statutes* (1856), 910: [A] free *white* citizen of this State . . . sober and judicious, of good reputation.
New Jersey	1776, art. IV: That all inhabitants of this Colony, of full age, who are worth fifty pounds proclamation money, clear estate in the same, and have resided within the county in which they claim a vote for twelve months immediately preceding the election, shall be entitled to vote for Representatives in Council and Assembly; and also for all other public offices.	1844, art. IV: Every male citizen of the united States, of the age of twenty-one years, who shall have been a resident of this State one year.	*Laws* (1821), 340: [A] citizen of the state, and resident of the county, above the age of twenty-one and under the age of sixty-five years, and having a *freehold* in lands . . . or tenements.

State	Constitution	Constitution	Jury statute
New York	1821 and 1846, art. II: No man of colour, unless he shall have been for three years a citizen of this state, and for one year next preceding any election, shall be seized and possessed of a freehold estate of the value of $250, over and above all debts and incumbrances charged thereon; and shall have been actually rated, and paid a tax thereon, shall be entitled to vote at such election.		*Revised Statutes* (1851), 656: 1. Male inhabitant of the town. 2. of the age of twenty-one years and upwards. 3. who are at the time assessed for personal *property* belonging to them in their own right . . . or in the right of their wives, to the value of one hundred and fifty dollars; 4. In the possession of their natural faculties. 5. Free from all legal exceptions, of fair characters, or approved integrity and well informed.
North Carolina	1776, art. VII: That all freemen, of the age of 21 years, who have been inhabitants of any one county within the State twelve months immediately preceding the day of any election, and possessed of a freehold within the same county of fifty acres of land . . . shall be entitled to vote for member of the Senate. Art. VIII: That all freemen, of the age of 21 years, who have been inhabitants of any one county within the State twelve months immediately preceding the day of any election, and shall have paid public taxes . . . shall be entitled to vote for member of the House of Commons.	1868, art. VI: Every male person born in the United States, and every male persons who has been naturalized, 21 years old or upward, who shall have resided in this State twelve months next preceding the election, and thirty days in the county in which he offers to vote, shall be deemed an elector.	*Revised Code* (1855), 161: [F]reeholders.
Oregon	1857, art. II, § 6: No negro, Chinaman, or mulatto shall have the right of suffrage.		*Organic and other General Laws* (1866), 377: [A] *white* male inhabitant of the county . . . in the possession of his natural faculties and of sound mind.

State	Constitution	Constitution	Jury statute
South Carolina	1790, art. I, § 4 (art. IV in 1865): Every free white man, of the age of 21.	1868, art. VIII, § 2: Every male citizen of the United States, of the age of 21 . . . without distinction of race, color, or former condition.	*Statutes at Large* (1838), 274: [F]rom the *tax list* . . . the name of every person who shall have paid the sum of twenty shillings current money or upwards for his tax list preceding, and out of the persons who shall have paid the sum of five pounds . . . they shall make a list of grand jurors.
Tennessee	1796, art. III, § 1: Every freeman of the age of 21 years and upwards, possessing a freehold in the county wherein he may vote.	1834, art. IV, § 1: Every free white man of the age of 21.	*Code of Tennessee* (1858), § 4009: Every *white* male citizen, who is a freeholder, or householder.
Virginia	1830, art. III, § 14: Every white male citizen.	1850, art. III, § 1: Every white male citizen.	*Code* (1860), 688: The county court of each county . . . shall . . . prepare a list of such inhabitants . . . as they shall think well qualified to serve as jurors, being persons of sound judgment and free from legal exception, which list shall include at least twenty persons for every thousand *white* inhabitants.

Note: Emphasis added.

Appendix 2

States Linking Jury Service to Constitutional
Suffrage Requirements

State	Constitution	Constitution	Jury statute
California	1849, art. II, § 1: Every *white* male citizen of the United States, and every *white* male citizen of Mexico, who shall have elected to become a citizen of the United States.		*Laws* (1852), 107–11: A person shall not be competent to act as a juror, unless he be, First, a citizen of the United States; Second, an *elector* . . . in possession of his natural faculties.
Connecticut	1818, art. VI, § 2: Every *white* male citizen of the united States . . . 21 years [old].		*Statutes* (1854), 86: [A]ble and judicious *electors*.
Delaware	1792 and 1831, art. IV, § 1: [E]very *white* free man of the age of 21.		*Revised Statutes* (1852), 384: All persons *qualified to vote* . . . sober and judicious persons.
Iowa	1846, art. II, § 1: Every *white* male citizen . . . of the age of 21 years.	1868: Every male citizen . . . of the age of 21 years.	*Revision of 1860*, 475: All qualified *electors* of the state, of good moral character, sound judgment, and in full possession of the senses of hearing and seeing are competent jurors.
Maine	1819, art. II, § 1: Every male citizen . . . 21 years [old].		*Revised Statutes* (1857), 619: The municipal officers . . . constitute a board for preparing lists of jurors to be laid before the town for their approval . . . in legal town meeting[s], by a majority of the legal voters assembled . . . of such persons, of good moral character, and *qualified to vote* as the constitution directs, for representatives.
Massachusetts	1780, chap. 1, § II, art. I: [E]very male inhabitant of 21 years of age.		*General Statutes* (1859), 679: All persons who are *qualified to vote* in the choice of representatives in the general court shall be liable to be drawn and serve as jurors. . . . [S]electmen of each town shall choose inhabitants they think well qualified to serve as jurors . . . persons of good moral character, or sound judgment.

Michigan	1835, art. II, § 1: [E]very *white* male citizen above the age of 21.	*Laws* (1806–30), 653: Judicious persons having the qualifications of *electors*.... [C]lerk of the county courts shall determine the number to be selected.... [S]heriff selects.
Minnesota	1857, art. VII, § 1: Every male person of the age of 21.	*Public Statutes* (1859), 149: All persons who are qualified *electors*.
Ohio	1802, art. IV: [A]ll *white* male inhabitants above the age of 21, having resided in the State one year next preceding the election, and who have paid, or are charged with, a State or county tax, shall enjoy the right of an elector.	*Statutes* (1788–1833), 175: [G]ood, judicious persons, having the qualifications of *electors*.
Texas	1845 and 1866, art. III, § 1: All free male persons over the age of 21 (Indians not taxed, *Africans and descendants of Africans excepted*).	*Laws* (1846), 170: [P]ersons of good moral character and qualified *electors*.
Vermont	1793, chap. 2, § 21: Every man of the full age of 21 years ... and is of a quiet and peaceable behavior, and will take the following oath or affirmation, shall be entitled to all the privileges of a freeman of this state.	*Revised Statutes* (1839), 94, 208: At town meetings, board of civil authority nominates jurors, and chosen by the inhabitants present; Sheriff shall draw out of the box, containing the names of the persons nominated by the authority of such town to serve as grand or petit jurors.
Wisconsin	1848, art. III, § 1: Every male person.	*Revised Statutes* (1849), 510: All persons who are citizens of the United States and qualified *electors* of this state.

Note: Emphasis added.

Appendix 3

States Relying on Local Discrimination

State	Constitution	Constitution	Jury statute
Maryland	1851, art. I, § 1: Every white male person of 21 years of age.	1864, art. I, § 1: [E]very white male citizen of the United States of the age of 21.	*General Public Statutory Law* (1840), 1:19. [T]he several sheriffs . . . shall cause to come before the justices of the several and respective county courts, a competent and sufficient number of good and lawful men of the last and most understanding freeholders . . . to serve as jurors.
New Hampshire	1792, § 28: [E]very male inhabitant . . . of 21 years of age and upward, excepting paupers and persons excused from paying taxes.		*Laws* (1821–28), 636: Selectmen of each town . . . [are] to make a list annually . . . of such persons . . . of good moral character, and having a freehold of the value of one hundred and fifty dollars, or other estate of the value of two hundred dollars, as they shall judge most suitable and best qualified to serve as jurors.
Pennsylvania	1790, art. III, § 1: [E]very freeman of the age of 21 years, having resided in the State two years next before the election, and within that time paid a State or county tax, which shall have been assessed at least six months before the election, shall enjoy the rights of an elector; Provided, That the sons of persons qualified as aforesaid, between the ages of 21 and 22 years, shall be entitled to vote, although they shall not have paid taxes.	1838, art. III, § 1: [E]very white freeman of the age of twenty-one years, having resided in this state one year, and in the election-district where he offers to vote ten days immediately preceding such election, and within two years paid a State or county tax, which shall have been assessed at least ten days before the election, shall enjoy the rights of an elector. . . . Provided, That white freemen, citizens of the United States, between the ages of 21 and 22 years, and having resided in the State one year and in the election-district ten days as aforesaid, shall be entitled to vote, although they shall not have paid taxes.	*Laws* (1834), 557: The sheriff and at least two of the commissioners of every county, shall . . . select . . . sober, intelligent, and judicious persons, to serve as jurors.

Rhode Island   1842, art. II, § 1:
               Every male citizen of the United States, of the age
               of 21.

               Public Laws (1822), 137:
               [E]ach town-council . . . shall annually make a list
               of all persons . . . whom they shall judge to be
               qualified as jurors.

West Virginia 1863, art. III, § 1:
               The white male citizens of the State.

               Acts (1863), 106:
               The board of supervisors of each county shall . . .
               prepare a list of such inhabitants of the county . . .
               as they shall think well qualified to serve as
               jurors, being persons of sound judgment and free
               from legal exception, which list shall include at
               least twenty persons for every thousand
               inhabitants in such county.

Appendix 4

*Members of the House of Representatives
for and against the Fourteenth Amendment,
Thirty-ninth Congress, First Session*

FOR THE TABLES IN THIS APPENDIX, I searched the *Congressional Globe*, reading every speech made by a member of the House of Representatives on civil rights or Reconstruction in the Thirty-ninth Congress, First Session. Although I examined their speeches carefully, I did not include senators in the charts because this book concerns congressional attachment to public opinion and in 1866 the House of Representatives was the only branch directly elected by the people. Facing election every two years kept House members close to the public pulse.

More than their votes, the quotes in the tables reflect members' feelings about Reconstruction and civil rights in the manner of their own choosing. The quotes represent my best judgment as to the members' true understanding of their authority.

Those representatives opposed to the Fourteenth Amendment often explained their votes on frankly racist grounds (table A4.1). Some of these members cited the law of nature as justifying racial hierarchy, and some cited states' rights. Several accused the Republicans of extending special privileges to African Americans, but all sought to preserve the racial hierarchy of slavery.

Those voting for the Fourteenth Amendment cited public opinion (table A4.2) or the Constitution (table A4.3). Those who based their votes on public opinion sometimes spoke with as much candor as those who voted against the amendment. Some of those members most adamantly committed to civil rights felt the wind of public opinion at their backs: James M. Ashley did not look backward to the framing but instead insisted that Congress should be guided by "the great anti-slavery revolution, which ha[d] swept over the country."

Some constitutionalists invoked higher law or explicitly cited God as a source of rights. John H. D. Henderson did this most clearly: the object of government, he explained, is to secure the rights that citizens receive from God. Government does not make or invent rights; it simply enforces those already existing in nature. Others presented themselves as finishing or correcting the work of the 1787 Constitutional Convention. Reader W. Clarke wanted to "amend [the] Constitution, not destroy it . . . but to make it strong in its weak places." Ignatius Donnelly said that the South had fooled the framers, leading them to think that slavery would peacefully die out on its own; we must not repeat that error, he declared.

Some members voting for the Fourteenth Amendment said nothing at all. They are listed here: John B. Alley (Mass.), William Allison (Iowa), Oakes Ames (Mass.), Andrews Barker (Pa.), Portus Baxter (Vt.), John Bidwell (Calif.), Henry T. Blow (Mo.), Amasa Cobb (Wis.), Nathan F. Dixon (R.I.), William E. Dodge (N.Y.), John F. Driggs (Mich.), Benjamin Eggleston (Ohio), Thomas W. Ferry (Mich.), John A. Griswold (N.Y.), Rutherford B. Hayes (Ohio), Samuel Hooper (Mass.), Giles W. Hotchkiss (N.Y.), Asahel W. Hubbard (Iowa), Demas Hubbard (Conn.), Calvin T. Hulburd (N.Y.), James Humphrey (N.Y.; died June 16, 1866), James M. Humphrey (N.Y.), John H. Ketcham (N.Y.), Addison Laflin (N.Y.), Benjamin Loan (Mo.), John Lynch (Maine), Gilman Marston (N.H.), Joseph W. McClurg (Mo.), Walter D. McIndoe (Wis.), Donald C. McRuer (Calif.), Ulysses Mercur (Pa.), Justin Morrill (Vt.), George F. Miller (Pa.), Charles O'Neill (Pa.), William H. Randall (Ky.), Alexander H. Rice (Mass.), John H. Rice (Maine), Edward H. Rollins (N.H.), Philetus Sawyer (Wis.), Francis Thomas (Md.), Rowland Trowbridge (Mich.), Charles Upson (Mich.), Robert T. Van Horn (Mo.), Samuel L. Warner (Conn.), Elihu B. Washburne (Ill.).

Member of Congress	State, party, and district	Percentage of vote in 1864	Comments on civil rights taken from *Congressional Globe*	Percentage of vote in 1866
Benjamin Boyer	Pa. Democrat 6th	57.08%	[2465] Southern states have atoned and should be allowed back in Congress.	55.03%
John W. Chanler	N.Y. Democrat 7th	67.13%	[48] [W]e have had enough of this love and zeal for the black race, it is an epidemic akin to the black vomit.	63.04%
John L. Dawson	Pa. Democrat 21st	50.29%	[541] [N]egro equality does not exist in nature. The African is without a history. He has never shown himself capable of self-government.	Not a candidate; Rep. win (50.69%)
Charles Denison	Pa. Democrat 12th	51.25%	[547] In . . . the Declaration of Independence . . . we find [this proposition] "that all men are created equal"; but they did not state that as the reason for their independence, or they would have enunciated the fact, and claimed by virtue thereof the right to be free; nor did they regard this abstract proposition as the basis of government, excepting so far as it applied to themselves and the white people whom they represented.	53.51%
Charles Eldridge	Wis. Democrat 4th	58.93%	[1156] I depreciate all these [civil rights] measures because of the implication they carry upon their face that the people who have heretofore owned slaves intend to do them wrong. I do not believe it.	56.57%
William E. Finck	Ohio Democrat 12th	53.49%	[2262] A State may . . . believe it necessary for the best interest of its people, in relation to certain crimes committed by a colored man, to impose upon him a "different" punishment from that imposed upon a white citizen; but here also this law steps in and rudely thrusts aside the State law.	Not a candidate; Dem. win (56.20%)
Henry Grider	Ky. Democrat 3d	57.27%	[appendix, 173] I fear we did not consider the consequences of this exclusive policy, this policy that assumes so much righteousness for the majority and so little of principle and patriotism for the minority; I fear this rigid, unrelenting, unforgiving feeling in the majority is pregnant with much wrong and error.	Not a candidate; Dem. win (86.59%)
Aaron Harding	Ky. Democrat 4th	72.10	[2256] [T]hese pestilent agitators [for civil rights] seize on the fact that slavery is abolished, and make that the basis of a new conflict. They are now everywhere striking for negro equality, warring against the laws of nature, seeking to blot out all distinctions, and crush down the white race to political and social equality with the blacks.	Not a candidate; Dem. win (74.64%)

Member of Congress	State, party, and district	Percentage of vote in 1864	Comments on civil rights taken from *Congressional Globe*	Percentage of vote in 1866
John Hogan	Mo. Democrat 1st	43.15%	[appendix, 62] [T]he fanaticism of the Republican having made an idol of the African, determined to give him a monopoly of all good qualities; and the more effectually to do so degrade the character, the intelligence, and the manhood of the foreign-born whites.	49.18%; defeated by Rep.
Michael Kerr	Ind. Democrat 2d	55.61%	[623] [T]he regulation of the ordinary civil relations of the negro to the society in which he lives, by the enactment of laws of a local and merely municipal character to control his contracts, and bestow upon him civil privileges having no necessary connection with his personal freedom, are wholly unauthorized by any warrant in any part of the Constitution.	53.47%
Francis Le Blond	Ohio Democrat 5th	55.15%	[1829] [Sumner] is the acknowledged leader of the present revolutionary party . . . has attained that eminence by offering more revolutionary measures, and saying more for the colored man and less for the white man than any of his party.	Not a candidate; Dem. win (55.44%)
Samuel S. Marshall	Ill. Democrat 11th	60.96%	[630] [W]hen the people . . . understand that this whole Government is in the power and control to-day of the manufacturers of Pennsylvania and New England, and the capitalists of Wall Street . . . and that the leading measures before this Congress are being put through in that interest, and in the interest of the negro, to the utter ruin of the laboring white men of the country, they will rise up in indignation.	53.69%
William Niblack	Ind. Democrat 1st	53.86%	[3214] I refer now to the inequality and physical difference between the white and black races. I have always maintained . . . that in the grand scale of humanity the negro race is inferior to the white race, and that anything like social or political equality between the two races is neither practicable nor desirable. Our whole system of laws in relation to the negro . . . has been based on that theory.	52.04%
John A. Nicholson	Del. Democrat	51.50%	[435] I firmly believe that [the American people] will never consent to share the Government of this country with a race of beings whom the Almighty himself has declared shall be the "servant of servants," and upon whom He has stamped the indelible mark of their inferiority.	53.73%

Member of Congress	State, party, and district	Percentage of vote in 1864	Comments on civil rights taken from *Congressional Globe*	Percentage of vote in 1866
Samuel J. Randall	Pa. Democrat 1st	55.78%	[2530] The first section proposes to make an equality in every respect between the two races, notwithstanding the policy of discrimination which has heretofore been exclusively exercised by the States, which in my judgment should remain and continue. They relate to matters appertaining to State citizenship, and there is no occasion whatever for the Federal power to be exercised between the two races at variance with the wishes of the people of the States.	61.20%
Burwell Ritter	Ky. Democrat 2d	54.66%	[2100] [W]e are told that the negro will work better and produce more as a freeman than they have ever done as slaves. To ascertain what is true [we should look to St. Domingo] "when on the night of the 26th of August, 1791, the negro insurrection . . . at once broke forth and wrapped the whole northern part of the colony in flames. . . ." Here, sirs, we have the result of an attempt to put the negro on an equality with the white man. Sir, does it afford any consolation to those who are so persistently endeavoring to bring on an equality here?	8.9%; defeated by Dem.
Andrew J. Rogers	N.J. Democrat 4th	53.59%	[2538] [T]he American people believe that this Government was made for white men and white women. They do not believe, nor can you make them believe—the edict of God Almighty is stamped against—that there is a social quality between the black race and the white.	48.49%; defeated by Rep.
Lewis W. Ross	Ill. Democrat 5th	55.55%	[2699] I have no unkind feeling toward the unfortunate colored people; they are free; be it so. I hope it may prove to them a blessing, and am opposed to any law discriminating against them in the security and protection of life, liberty, person, and property, and the proceeds of their labor. These civil rights all should enjoy. Beyond that I am not prepared to go, and those pretended friends who urge political and social equality, and conferring special privileges . . . are, in my judgment, the worst enemies of the colored race.	51.28%
Charles Sitgreaves	N.J. Democrat 3d	58.38%	[appendix 244] I denounce the doctrine of the northern radical as equally damnable and leading to treason, rebellion, or revolution. . . . The southern traitor declares his repentance, the northern traitor never has.	54.90%

Member of Congress	State, party, and district	Percentage of vote in 1864	Comments on civil rights taken from *Congressional Globe*	Percentage of vote in 1866
Myer Strouse	Pa. Democrat 10th	51.09%	[870] We have now been in session nearly three months, and have done little else than legislate for the benefit of the negro. Constitutional amendments by the score for the benefit of the negro; universal suffrage for the benefit of the negro; Freedmen's Bureau for the negro; and so on, *ad nauseam*.	Not a candidate; Rep. win (50.41%)
Stephen Taber	N.Y. Democrat 1st	54.96%	[715] By the provisions of the homestead law all persons that are not able to take an oath that they have at no time taken part against the Government in the rebellion have no right to participate in the benefits of the homestead act. The consequence is that all those who have served in the rebel army, no matter whether voluntarily or otherwise, are precluded from the benefit of the act. My amendment proposes that those who have been pardoned, and those that may be pardoned, may be permitted to enter upon these lands.	52.76%
Nelson Taylor	N.Y. Democrat 5th	53.05%	[543] [T]he present proposed [Freedmen's Bureau] legislation is solely and entirely for the freedmen. . . . This, sir, is what I call class legislation—legislation for a particular class of the blacks to the exclusion of all whites.	36.21% (ran as Ind. Dem.); defeated by Dem.
Anthony Thornton	Ill. Democrat 10th	58.13%	[1157] [T]he States have certain rights, and those rights are absolutely necessary to the maintenance of our system of government. What are those rights? The right to determine and fix the legal *status* of the inhabitants of the respective States, the local powers of self-government . . . and home rights which are nearer and dearer to us than all others.	Not a candidate; Dem. win (53.72%)
Lawrence Trimble	Ky. Democrat 1st	61.89%	[387] [I]n 1860 and 1861 the . . . Union party took the ground . . . that neither Congress nor the people of the States, to interfere with slavery in the States where it existed; much less, sir, did they claim the power not only to destroy it, but to strike down the provisions of the Constitution that protected me and my constituents in our right to our property. Sir, there was an amendment submitted then for the purpose of peace [to protect slavery]. . . . It met at the time my hearty support.	84.61%
Edwin R. V. Wright	N.J. Democrat 5th	53.91%	[459] [T]his pretended love for the negro is all sheer hypocrisy.	Not a candidate; Rep. win (51.92%)

Sources: *Congressional Globe* (page citations appear in brackets); Dubin, *United States Congressional Elections*, 198–207.

TABLE A4.2 Representatives voting for the Fourteenth Amendment citing public opinion

Member of Congress	State	Comments on civil rights taken from the *Congressional Globe*
Delos R. Ashley	Nev.	[1316] You cannot force negro suffrage upon the States either by statutory enactment or constitutional amendment, and I do not believe in enforcing political penalties against those who took part in the rebellion any further than the law holds them personally responsible.
James M. Ashley	Ohio	[2882] I am desirous to know whether this Congress is going to attempt the work of staying the great anti-slavery revolution, which has swept over the country and obliterated all the pro-slavery landmarks erected by parties and men.
Jehu Baker	Ill.	[462] [T]he guarantee of a republican form of government . . . belongs to Congress to judge and determine. Will any one question that the loyal people of the whole country wish to have this guarantee executed before admitting the revolted States to political power? . . . [I]s that a republican government which signally fails to protect the great right of liberty which has been conferred upon one half of its people by the sovereign will of the nation?
Nathaniel Banks	Mass.	[2532] I have no doubt that the Government of the United States has authority [to extend the elective franchise to the black population] under the Constitution; but I do not think they have the power. The distinction I make between authority and power is this: we have, in the nature of our Government, the right to do it; but the public opinion of the country is such at this precise moment as to make it impossible we should do it.
Fernando Beaman	Mich.	[1016] [T]hey threaten us with the indignation of the people, who they say are clamorous to have these seats lately vacated by traitors once more filled with occupants of the same stock. . . . Think you, sir, that the widowed wife or the bereaved father, who nightly dreams of seeing the famished husband or son lying in the filth of Andersonville prison, and who is ever and anon startled into wakefulness by the fancied cry for feed or pure water, is sighing for the speedy return to this Hall of the demon who connived at his death by the slow but sure and torturing process of starvation?
John F. Benjamin	Mo.	[1841] The people from the beginning have been in advance of authorities. They continually called upon Congress to make further demands on their purses and patriotism, and every such call was promptly responded to. They were determined the rebellion should be suppressed, and now being suppressed they require the strongest guarantees against a similar occurrence in the future.
John Bingham	Ohio	[158] I propose, with the help of this Congress and of the American people, that hereafter there shall not be any disregard of that essential guarantee of your Constitution in any State of the Union. And how? By simply adding an amendment to the Constitution to operate on all the States of this Union alike, giving to Congress the power to pass all laws necessary and proper to secure to all persons—which includes every citizen of every State—their equal personal rights; and if the tribunals of South Carolina will not respect the rights of the citizens of Massachusetts under the Constitution of their common country, I desire to see the Federal judiciary clothed with the power to take cognizance of the question, and assert those rights by solemn judgment.

Member of Congress	State	Comments on civil rights taken from the *Congressional Globe*
James G. Blaine	Maine	[377] Do you suppose the upland districts of Georgia and South Carolina, inhabited largely by whites, will, in the event of the adoption of this amendment [reducing the congressional representation of states that disallow black voting], allow the distribution of Representatives to be made on the basis of the whole population? By no means. They will at once insist on the white basis within the State. Therefore you make it the imperative and most urgent interest of the late slave masters . . . to enfranchise the black man.
Hezekiah Bundy	Ohio	[appendix, 206] The popular heart had been touched, and the popular mind of the country had been instructed by the terrific incidents of the war, as waged by the enemy, and the patriotic efforts and utterances of the great leaders of the loyal hosts in civil life while [207] grappling with the monster treason. Not a patriotic heart felt a single emotion nor a patriotic voice uttered a single sentiment that did not fully accord, harmonize, and demand the assertion of the great principle "That the loyal people of the country must govern the country."
Sidney Clarke	Kans.	[1838] I shall insist that the reconstructed rebels of Mississippi respect the Constitution in their local laws, before I will even consider their claims to representation in Congress. . . . [1839] [M]y constituents will never consent to be governed by rebels and traitors.
Roscoe Conkling	N.Y.	[356] A moral earthquake has turned fractions into units, and units into ciphers. If a black man counts at all now, he counts five fifths of a man, not three fifths. . . . Did the framers of the Constitution ever dream of this? Never, very clearly. . . . [357] Shall one hundred and twenty-seven thousand white people in New York cast but one vote in this House, and have but one vote here, while the same number of white people in Mississippi have three votes and three voices?
William A. Darling	N.Y.	[278] It is well known that the sentiments of the people of this country on the proposed question of colored suffrage are as varied as the shades of the people themselves. I would ask what public necessity exists for the passage of this bill [enfranchising D.C. blacks].
Thomas T. Davis	N.Y.	[245] The right to vote is not a natural, but an artificial right, as well in our country as all others wherever it has been exercised; and in the countries where it has been most diffused it never was allowed to one fourth of the people.
Joseph H. Defrees	Ind.	[872] I believe if there is one sin more heinous than another that man can commit, either toward God or his country, it is the sin of treason. But I am in favor of rallying around and sustaining whatever loyalty may be found in those disorganized states.
James A. Garfield	Ohio	[2462] With almost every proposition in the report of the joint committee on reconstruction I am pleased. . . . We have at last a series of propositions which, in the main, will meet the approval of the American people. . . . I believe that the right to vote, if it be not indeed one of the natural rights of all men, is so necessary to the protection of their natural rights as to be indispensable, and therefore equal to natural rights. . . . I profoundly regret that we have not been enabled to write it and engrave it upon our institutions, and imbed it in the perishable bulwark of the Constitutions as a part of the fundamental law of the land.

Member of Congress	State	Comments on civil rights taken from the *Congressional Globe*
Sidney T. Holmes	N.Y.	[1317] The people under our Government are the court of last resort for the trial of all public men and public measures. They have passed upon his [the president's] loyalty and fidelity during that fearful struggle, and from that decision there is no appeal.
Chester D. Hubbard	W.Va.	[310] I believe that all history will sustain the position that only a homogeneous people can make a united nation. I further believe that the effort to introduce into the sovereignty of this country a race which cannot in the nature of things become homogenous—which fact every instinct of our humanity and the whole legislation of the country attest—can only be productive of contention and conflict.
James R. Hubbell	Ohio	[660] It was in this speech [Lincoln] gave in his quaint and happy style his solution of the question at the political *status* of the States, "that they were not in their proper relation to the General Government." It is a fact well understood, that no measure of Mr. Lincoln's administration, except the emancipation proclamation, was more thoroughly discussed and better understood by the people than this. At the time it was proposed, political parties were directing their attention to the approaching presidential election, and Mr. Lincoln was a candidate for reelection. This measure became the subject, among both political friends and foes, of discussion and criticism in oral controversy, and by the press, the feeble opposition to Mr. Lincoln among his political friends was hushed into silence by the unmistakable public voice demanding his renomination and reelection.
Thomas A. Jenckes	R.I.	[125] [F]rom the time of the passage of the ordinances of secession until the time of the surrender of Lee's army. During that period what were the relations which all that territory—I will not use the term States, but all that territory—between the Potomac and the Rio Grande sustained to the Government of the United States? Who could see States there for any purpose for which legislation was required by the Constitution of the United States? . . . [T]hose states were not destroyed in the technical language of the law—they simply died out.
George Washington Julian	Ind.	[3211] [I]t is said . . . that the people are not ready for so radical a policy. . . . I defend the people against this accusation against their intelligence and loyalty. My own experience is that politicians are generally, if not invariably, behind the people, and rather inclined to block up the path of popular progress than to clear the way. This was undoubtedly true during the war, and every intelligent man can recall proofs of it in abundance. The people were ready for a radical policy in the first year of the conflict. . . . A servant of the people needs to have faith in the people.
John A. Kasson	Iowa	[238] I believe that the people control this Government. I believe that if those people have not intelligence to understand the policy and principles of our Government to a reasonable extent, our institutions are unsafe and liable to be upset. I also believe in my heart and in my conscience that if you make suffrage universal in certain districts of the Union where ignorance actually predominates, you have no security in those districts that the institutions to which we are attached will regain their permanence.

Member of Congress	State	Comments on civil rights taken from the *Congressional Globe*
Andrew J. Kuykendall	Ill.	[1170] [W]hat is a State? The people composing it. What is the United States? The people composing them, in the sense of the Constitution, where it says, "We, the people of the United States"; and in that people is vested and merged the sovereignty of the people of the States, so far as it covers the powers granted in the Constitution. . . . [1171] Congress has no right to destroy the States. . . . Congress has no right to regulate the suffrage question in any State, that being a right guarantied to the people of the different States by the Constitution of the United States.
George V. Lawrence	Pa.	[2409] [M]y district that voted for him [President Johnson] was in favor of sustaining his Administration until by some of his own acts, and by means of the copperhead party all over the land, he succeeded in destroying that confidence which I desired to cultivate; and to-day I have the gratification to know, although I represent a doubtful district, that the President, by the removal of pure, honest, and patriotic men, and by pardoning men covered all over with crime, who have been guilty of treason . . . has made it necessary for the Union men to stand together in support of the general policy we sustain here. . . . They stand in opposition to the general policy of the President. . . . I stand with them.
John W. Longyear	Mich.	[2536] I believe [the power to reconstruct the South] is in Congress. The people believe it is in Congress, and the great masses of the loyal people both North and South are looking to Congress to-day for protection and security; and for one, I intend to do my duty toward them in that respect to the best of my ability.
James K. Moorhead	Pa.	[2256] The victory won by our brave soldiers must bear its fruits, and the vanquished must relinquish all the causes of the war. They must not only abandon slavery, but the principle of slavery, and must secure the rights of freemen to all the freedmen within their borders. . . . This much I am prepared to require, and I know in doing so I will be carrying out the views of the constituency who sent me here.
Samuel W. Moulton	Ill.	[1617] The question as to the *status* of the people of the rebel States is exclusively a political question, determinable by the executive and legislative branches of the Government, this has been repeatedly decided by the Supreme Court of the United States.
Leonard Myers	Pa.	[1619] When I speak of the people I mean the majority. The right of the majority to rule is the principle underlying all our institutions. The rebellion was a rebellion against this principle. The overthrow of the confederacy is its triumph and vindication.
Godlove Orth	Ind.	[1303] [T]he virtue and patriotism of the American people may so control and fashion the political elements of the country as to prevent a recurrence [of civil war]. . . . [1306] The press of the country has at all times been regarded as a fair exponent of the feelings and sentiments of the people in its immediate locality. . . . [1307] [T]he Constitution was made for the people, and not the people for the Constitution.
James W. Patterson	N.H.	[2692] [T]he people will not be lulled into security by any Circean form of speech. Nor will they long submit in patience to the narrow ambition and unthinking zeal which attributes to a question of temporary policy the importance of essential principles and stakes the permanent welfare of the country upon a personal triumph. . . . Justice and public safety are to [the people] the natural and supreme law, and by them they will test our work.

Member of Congress	State	Comments on civil rights taken from the *Congressional Globe*
Sidney Perham	Maine	[2082] During four long and bloody years the people of this country have struggled for life and the vindication of the imperishable truths of the Declaration of Independence. . . . We have been sent here by our constituents, charged with the important duty of reconstructing this Union in accordance with the enlightened and progressive spirit of the age, and on the basis of complete and impartial justice.
Frederick Pike	Maine	[407] [W]hat are these purposes we wish to accomplish? Of course there are but two. One is to lessen the political power of the South; the other is to protect the colored population of the country. . . . I am free to say that with the first of these purposes I have but comparatively little sympathy. I have the honor to represent a district which for the future will be much more intimately connected by social ties and by commercial relations with the South than the western sections of the country.
Tobias Plants	Ohio	[1011] I maintain that all things with which we are surrounded, our institutions and ourselves as well, are subject to the universal law of growth. . . . Our Constitution . . . has worked well with us in the main, because it was an outgrowth from the people. The great and good men who put it into form did not make it. They simply embodied the average outgrowth of the social and political life of the people in to the forms adapted to their then existing wants. But it was necessarily impossible for them to frame an instrument that would be adequate in all future time to the wants of an advancing people, this is demonstrated in the whole of our past history, which shows that a progressive people cannot be long confined within the rigid terms of a written constitution. No man reveres the memory of the fathers more than I do, and it is doing them no dishonor to say that they could not accomplish impossibilities.
Robert C. Schenck	Ohio	[2471] [M]y own decided conviction is, that so far from going beyond the popular judgment and demand there is no part of all this amendment that will more commend itself to the sense of justice and propriety of the people of this country than this very third section. Everywhere through the land, in all loyal minds and hearts, the conviction has settled and grown strong and taken deep and fast hold that those who sought to destroy the Government ought not to be called upon so shortly afterward to undertake to rule and carry on that Government.
Thomas N. Stilwell	Ind.	[668] [Congress] pledge[d] the national faith to everyone in arms, that when he should capitulate, the rights of his State and of self-government should be preserved to his children and kindred even though he might suffer the penalties of law.
John L. Thomas	Md.	[262] [T]he people of my State, at least that portion of them whom I have the honor to represent, and who have always been true to the Government . . . are opposed to this measure [for black suffrage in the District of Columbia]. They see in it, as I do, the first effort to confer political privileges on a class who, although emancipated from slavery, are not at this time competent, by reason of their ignorance, nor qualified, by reason of their former *status*, to exercise the high and exalted privileges of an elector . . . which all good men must deplore.

Member of Congress	State	Comments on civil rights taken from the *Congressional Globe*
Burt Van Horn	N.Y.	[283] [W]iping out all distinctions as to caste or color, is, in my judgment, both proper and necessary, and demanded by the loyal people of the country, who have a right to be heard in the solution of all matters or questions that may arise.
Elijah Ward	N.Y.	[434] The fact that one South Carolinian, whose hands are red with the blood of fallen patriots, and whose skirts are reeking with the odors of Columbia and Andersonville, will have a voice as potential in these Halls as two and a half Vermont soldiers who have come back from the grandest battle-fields in history maimed and scarred in the contest with South Carolina traitors in their efforts to destroy this Government, cries aloud for remedy.
Martin Welker	Ohio	[726] [O]ur fathers . . . proclaimed, as the broad foundation of the Government then about to be erected, that "all men are created equal. . . ." They declared, also, "that to secure these rights Governments are instituted among men." To maintain these bold propositions, these new ideas of equality of man, to establish a republican form of government . . . these men of the Revolution, with firmness undaunted and patriotism unchilled, fought out the battles that won for us these grand principles and established this great Republic. We . . . have a great work to do in order to preserve and perpetuate the priceless inheritance of our fathers.
Thomas Williams	Pa.	[784] The people are here again in the persons of their representatives who are the law-making power of the nation, not on invitation but by constitutional mandate, to inquire what has been attempted, and to decide for themselves what shall be done with the Territories that have been conquered by their arms. . . . [797] [T]here are other considerations that demand our care beyond the mere rehabilitation of the conquered States. It is for us to that in the execution of the guarantee the Federal Republic itself shall receive no detriment and undergo no change. There are symptoms unquestionably of an alarming nature, developed, of course, by the high stimulus under which it has just been working, that forebode a serious disturbance of its balances—a revolution equivalent to a change in its organic structure. . . . The time has now come to check those tendencies.
William Windom	Minn.	[3170] The people . . . see the existing injustice and the impending danger, and are determined to remedy the one and avoid the other.
Frederick Woodbridge	Vt.	[1088] I simply suggest that we submit the proposition [of amending the Constitution to guarantee citizens' privileges and immunities] to the people, that they may remove these objections by amending the instrument itself. . . . Sir, is there anything anti-republican in this? Is there anything wrong in this? Is there anything which interferes with the sovereign power of a State that adheres to a republican form of government? Is there not rather in this a tendency to keep the States within their orbits, and by . . . "the organic law," insure and secure forever to every citizen of the United States the privileges and blessings of a republican form of government?

Sources: *Congressional Globe* (page citations appear in brackets); Dubin, *United States Congressional Elections*, 198–207.

TABLE A4.3 Representatives voting for the Fourteenth Amendment citing constitutional principles

Member of Congress	State	Comments on civil rights taken from the *Congressional Globe*
George W. Anderson	Mo.	[1478] We are to-day interpreting the Constitution from a freedom and not from a slavery stand-point. The old interpretation of the Constitution was from a slavery stand-point. We called upon these people in the midst of a struggle for the existence of the nation to aid and assist us in preventing traitors from tearing down the emblem of our nationality. Shall we now turn the cold shoulder upon them, and say, "Though you have assisted us and done all that men could do to preserve the integrity and nationality of the Government, yet, now that the battle is won and the victory sure, you have no rights that a white man is bound to respect?"
John D. Baldwin	Mass.	[1826] Two things are constantly forgotten by the advocates of this traitorous doctrine of State sovereignty: first, that the Union was formed before any State was constituted; and second, that the Congress representing this Union changed the colonies into States. . . . [1828] In giving [the vote] to the colored freemen we should only return to what was established by the founders of the nation.
George Boutwell	Mass.	[308] [W]hen we emancipated the black people we not only relieved ourselves from the institution of slavery, we not only conferred upon them freedom, but we did more, we recognized their manhood. . . . [309] [Voting] may not be a natural right, like the right of locomotion, like the right to breathe, a natural personal right, still I think I can offer suggestions, deduced from the law of nature, which will show that it is a natural social right.
Henry P. H. Bromwell	Ill.	[2904] [T]he results achieved by the Revolution of 1776 fell short of what might have been attained, yet we still boast with pride that during a period of twenty years . . . more was done for freedom than during twenty centuries before. Therefore we may well look back and take a lesson from the past. . . . And now, when that element of wrong which was left in this Government has worked on until the terrible convulsion it has produced has destroyed the institutions of government in one third of the States . . . what do we hear? The self-same arguments, the same outcry, which rang in the years of the radicals of the Revolution. Centralism, radicalism, ultraism, despotism—these are the cries. The reserved [2905] rights of the States are brought up.
John M. Broomall	Pa.	[467] [I]f the power of the conqueror in war is abused the law of nations knows no remedy. . . . I am maintaining the right of the conqueror always in international wars to treat the conquered as it pleases, without responsibility to anybody but the Almighty. . . . [470] [C]an we intrust the negroes unaided to the rule of their late masters? If no new cause of disagreement had occurred between the two classes, what warrant have we for supposing that the dominant race would treat the servile one better than heretofore? . . . [I]f we leave all power in the hands of the dominant race, we will have done the negro race little kindness in abolishing slavery.
Ralph Buckland	Ohio	[1627] If the Constitution of the United States does not now confer upon the national Government the power to provide against such outrages upon the rights of American citizens, which I think it does, then I say it is the duty of Congress and the President to insist upon such an amendment as will confer that power.

Member of Congress	State	Comments on civil rights taken from the *Congressional Globe*
Reader W. Clarke	Ohio	[1010] Our Constitution, the great work of our fathers, we revere; it came from the hands of wise and good men; and with none but good men to control, it would need no improvement; but, unfortunately, there were those among us who sought out many inventions and have assumed to use that sacred instrument as authority for its own destruction, and thereby break down the Government for which it was made. As a guard against this in the future, now that we are advised of the needed improvements, we propose to amend that Constitution, not to destroy it . . . but to make it strong in its weak places.
Burton C. Cook	Ill.	[899] Every individual citizen of each State in the Union has rights in every other State—the right to acquire, possess, and dispose of property; the right to fix his domicile in any State, and to enjoy every civil and political right or privilege possessed by the citizens of such State. . . . And these rights he has, not by virtue of any State authority, but by virtue of the Constitution of the United States.
Shelby Cullom	Ill.	[appendix, 253] When our fathers proclaimed in the language of the Declaration of Independence that they held these truths to be self-evident, that all men are created equal . . . they spoke to the world the thrilling notes of truth which set the American republic high above all other Governments. . . . That principle forms the very life of this nation; smother it out and America dies. . . . [S]lavery . . . was in direct antagonism to the spirit and life of the vital principle of the Government.
Henry L. Dawes	Mass.	[3176] [T]he Constitution of the United States imposes this obligation upon the United States, not upon the House, not upon the Senate, not upon the Executive, but upon all three—"the United States" is the term used—namely to guaranty a republican form of government to each and every one of the States of this Union.
Columbus Delano	Ohio	[appendix, 156] It needs no law, in my estimation, to make citizens of these emancipated people, they are citizens by law now; and our enactment can only declare the rights and privileges in this respect which already belong to them. But, sir, notwithstanding this, notwithstanding I regard them as entitled to citizenship, I have serious difficulties in my own mind in reference to the power of Congress, under the Constitution as it is, to pass the bill which is before us. I shall vote for it, if possible. If I can be brought to believe that there is a reasonable probability of its constitutionality, so that I can justify my conscience in turning over the question of the power of Congress to pass this bill to the courts, I shall sustain it; but without some further light upon the question than I now have, I do feel that there are such difficulties in the way as call for careful examination of the provisions of this bill, in a constitutional point of view.
Henry C. Deming	Conn.	[330] [T]here is one fact which, in all the fog and bewilderment which surrounds present issues, looms out in prominent and startling relief. We have been for the last four years "in a state of war"; . . . [331] I [intend] to apply to the insurgent eleven the touch-stone of the Constitution, and see what powers it confers upon States as States . . . for the purpose of deducing the comforting conclusion that a State under the Constitution has no rights, and can exercise no power, which discharges no duty and spurns every obligation.

Member of Congress	State	Comments on civil rights taken from the *Congressional Globe*
Ignatius Donnelly	Minn.	[585] [W]e are told . . . we must "trust the South." . . . [586] The framers of the Constitution trusted that slavery would speedily perish from the land. . . . What has been the result? From a quarter of a million the slaves increased to four millions; from a weak and helpless evil, slavery grew into a powerful, warlike, and aggressive system. . . . The safety of the country, the public faith, the plainest dictates of common sense and common humanity all demand that we shall inaugurate sweeping measures of reform, and regenerate and rejuvenate the South.
Ebenezer Dumont	Ind.	[1475] Congress has almost uniformly specified the conditions upon which a Territory might become a State and be admitted into the Union. Congress has always taken upon itself the privilege to scan closely the constitution of a State applying for admission, to determine whether its provisions were republican.
Ephraim Eckley	Ohio	[2534] The revolution in our affairs, caused by the gigantic struggle through which we have passed, renders such a change absolutely necessary. Congress is the only organized power that can make it; and we should be craven in spirit if we shrunk from the responsibility. It is claimed that this presents questions entirely new in American politics. I do not think so. If we but follow the wise examples left us by our fathers we shall find in the footprints of the past a precedent for our action that will produce wise and salutary results.
Thomas D. Eliot	Mass.	[2511] [I]f, under the Constitution as it now stands, Congress has not the power to prohibit State legislation discriminating against classes of citizens or depriving any persons of life, liberty, or property without due process of law, or denying to any persons within the State the equal protection of the laws, then, in my judgment, such power should be distinctly conferred. I voted for the civil rights bill, and I did so under a conviction that we have ample power to enact into law the provisions of that bill. But I shall gladly do what I may to incorporate into the Constitution provisions which will settle the doubt which some gentlemen entertain.
John F. Farnsworth	Ill.	[204] I say our fathers made this Government for men; not for black men or white men, not for Anglo-Saxons, not for Irishmen, or Germans, or Americans merely, but they made it for men, I take issue with [the] assertion that blacks were not regarded at that time as citizens, and had no part nor lot in the Declaration of Independence.
Josiah B. Grinnell	Iowa	[222] [T]hese four million slaves have not only taken care of themselves amid all the ingenious impediments which tyrants could impose, but they have borne upon their stalwart shoulders their masters, millions of people for a century. . . . [T]hese men have achieved the world's wonder—coming out from the tortures of slavery, from the prison-house, untainted with dishonor or crime; and out of the war free, noble, brave, and more worthy of their friends, always true to the flag. [652] Our authority to take care of them is founded in the Constitution; else it is not worthy to be our great charter.
Abner C. Harding	Ill.	[1831] Emerging from an exhausting war of unparalleled magnitude and cost, in which we have expended more than $3,000,000,000, with a national life endeared to us by the previous blood poured out to save it, we find ourselves scheming to banish the national currency that has been the sinew of war that bore us up through the struggle! Sir, I confess to a feeling of love, of almost reverence for greenbacks!

Member of Congress	State	Comments on civil rights taken from the *Congressional Globe*
Roswell Hart	N.Y.	[1628] We cannot, in honor, restore these States to their full relations to the Union until the bondsman we have set free shall stand erect in all the rights of citizenship, protected in person, property, and liberty, and burdened by no restriction imposed because of race or color.
John H. D. Henderson	Ore.	[728] The object of government . . . I understand to be, not to confer rights and privileges upon men, but to secure to each and every inhabitant of the land the rights that God has bestowed upon him. Good government aims to secure, not the rights of a part of the citizens, but of each and every one.
William Higby	Calif.	[1054] I understand this joint resolution [HR 63] . . . will only have the effect to give vitality and life to portions of the Constitution that probably have intended from the beginning to have life and vitality, but which have received such a construction that they have been entirely ignored and have become as dead matter in that instrument.
Ebon C. Ingersoll	Ill.	[2405] I believe that it is one of the inherent powers of Government to protect the citizen in the enjoyment of his liberty and in the security of person and in the rights of property, independent of all constitutions. It is inherent in power, a power that dwells in government without any written law—that in the language of the Constitution, that instrument was framed by the people of the United States in order to "establish justice," "insure domestic tranquility," to "provide for the common defense" "promote the general welfare, and secure the blessings of liberty," &c. Will it be said that it must be written in express terms in the Constitution, otherwise the Congress has no power to protect its citizens, without respect to color or race, in the enjoyment of that liberty said to be the prime object in founding the Government? No sir, it is but the makeshift of the demagogue.
William D. Kelley	Pa.	[180] In preparing to begin the work of reconstructing the grandest of human governments, shuttered for a time by treason, and in endeavoring to ascertain what we should and how and when it should be done, I have consulted no popular impulse. Groping my way through the murky political atmosphere that has prevailed for more than thirty years, I have seated myself at the feet of the fathers of our country that I might as far as my suggestions would go make them in accordance with the principles of those who constructed our Government.
John R. Kelso	Mo.	[732] As a southern man, I speak in behalf of the loyal men of the South. Without a murmur we sacrificed all we possessed. We fought during four long years, and thousands of our bravest and best went down amid the thunder clouds of battle. . . . [733] If the negroes are men, they are entitled to the rights of men, if it be true that "all men" in regard to their rights "are born equal," then whatever is the inalienable right of one man or one race of men is undeniably the inalienable right of all men and all races. If it be true that we should do unto others as we would that they should do unto us, and if would not that the African race should deprive us of any of our inalienable rights, how dare we, as a Christian people, do so unto them?
William Lawrence	Ohio	[405] If gentlemen will overlook fundamental principles of rights, and be guided by considerations of temporary expediency or power, constitutional amendments can never be made. [1835] I maintain that Congress may by law secure the citizens of the nation in the enjoyment of their inherent right of life, liberty, and property, and the means essential to that end, by penal enactments to enforce the provisions of the Constitution, article four, section two, and the equal civil rights which it recognizes or by implication affirms to exist among citizens of the same state.

Member of Congress	State	Comments on civil rights taken from the *Congressional Globe*
Samuel McKee	Ky.	[452] I care not what my people indorse. Convince me that I am right—and you cannot convince me that I am wrong when I go against traitors—and I will go upon that line whether one, two, or one thousand stand by me in the State of Kentucky. . . . I am not afraid of social or political equality with any race.
Daniel Morris	N.Y.	[2692] [M]en die, principles never. The individual who orders his life and shapes his course for no purpose other than to secure the popular applause of to-day; the party that is actuated by no loftier impulses than expediency; the Government that ignores the cardinal principles of justice and truth, must expect an ignominious grave. States and philosophers pass away and they are forgotten, but principles live on.
William A. Newell	N.J.	[866] [L]ike all human instruments, [the Constitution] was imperfectly constructed, not because the theory was wrong, but because of the existence in the country of an institution so contrary to the genius of free government, and to the very principles upon which the Constitution itself was founded, that it was impossible to incorporate it into the organic law so that the latter could be preserved free from its contaminating influence. . . . [867] The result of this rebellion, then, having made the principles of the Constitution not only theoretically but practically true, it is our duty to see that the principles of the Constitution are now carried out to the fullest extent of the idea of the framers; to have them carried out so as to embrace "all men" as truly as the fathers embraced them ideally.
Halbert Paine	Wis.	[564] [T]he constitutional relation of these communities to the Federal Government is that of unorganized territories. But they sustain at the same time another relation; that of the conquered to the conqueror under the laws of war. If it would be the right and duty of the Government to maintain the authority of the Constitution and the integrity of the Republic, by crushing a claim to absolute sovereignty on the part of a State . . . still clearer would be the right . . . if the State herself first flies to arms.
Hiram Price	Iowa	[1067] I trust that the Constitution, upon which all our civil and religious institutions are based, will have given to it sufficient stability and solidity to bear any burden that may be placed upon it, and give to us what we propose to have—equal rights and equal privileges from one end of this continent to the other.
Henry J. Raymond	N.Y.	[483] I think, especially, that in its distribution of the powers among the different departments of the Government, that Constitution has proved its wisdom, and I think this is even still more clearly shown in its distribution of powers between the General Government and the several States. That document has proved that it was made not for days or for years, but for all time. . . I cannot but dread any change that shall touch any of its fundamental provisions.
Glenni W. Scofield	Pa.	[180] I know that the prejudices, erroneous sentiments, and even vices of the people should be somewhat regarded in legislation, and that vested wrongs supposed to be vested rights should be divested very slowly. . . . In the Continental Congress they asserted that "all men are created free and equal." They subsequently made the Constitution in accord with this sentiment, and for forty years, and as long as they lived to administer it, negroes were allowed to vote in all the old States except, perhaps South Carolina. Both the precept and practice of our fathers refute the allegation that this is exclusively a white man's government.

Member of Congress	State	Comments on civil rights taken from the *Congressional Globe*
Samuel Shella-barger	Ohio	[2106] These monuments of the nation's origin are now covered with the gray mosses of near a hundred years, and three generations of the nation's children have passed to the dead beneath their shade. And still they stand there to-day, their foundations resting upon the granites, justice and law, upon which lie, in eternal repose, the deep foundations of the Republic itself.
Rufus Spalding	Ohio	[131] [T]he framers of the Constitution contemplated the creation "by the people of the United States," of a national Government, and not a Confederacy of States.
Thaddeus Stevens	Pa.	[73] Who is the United States? Not the judiciary; not the President; but the sovereign power of the people. . . . [74] Our fathers repudiated the whole doctrine of the legal superiority of families or races, and proclaimed the equality of men before the law. Upon that they created a revolution and built the Republic. They were prevented by slavery from perfecting the superstructure whose foundation they had thus broadly laid. . . . It is our duty to complete their work. If this Republic is not now made to stand on their great principles, it has no honest foundation, and the Father of all men will still shake it to its center. If we have not yet been sufficiently scourged for our national sin to teach us to do justice to all God's creatures, without distinction of race or color, we must expect the still more heavy vengeance of an offended Father. . . . [75] How shameful that men of influence should mislead and miseducate the public mind! They proclaim "This is a white man's Government," and the whole coil of copperheads echo the same sentiment. . . . Is it any wonder ignorant foreigners and illiterate natives should learn this doctrine, and be led to despise and maltreat a whole race of their fellow-men?
Martin Thayer	Pa.	[1152] Does it not strike the mind of every man with wonder that the framers of the Constitution of the United States who made this great and wonderful fabric of human Government . . . should have framed a government which is incapable of protecting its citizens in these fundamental rights of citizenship?
Henry Van Aernam	N.Y.	[3068] [B]y their own acts, by the laws of war, by the great axioms of the universal law of right, the rebellious States have forfeited, abdicated, and lost their position, and all the rights and privileges which they held as governing members of the Union. . . . This is the common sense, practical view of the case.
James F. Wilson	Iowa	[173] No where in the Constitution do we find class distinctions applied to citizens of the United States. Its ample fields envelop all citizens alike. It in no way develops color of skin as a tenure to the rights and privileges of citizenship.

Sources: *Congressional Globe* (page citations appear in brackets); Dubin, *United States Congressional Elections*, 198–207.

TABLE A4.4 Representatives voting against the Fourteenth Amendment who made no substantive comments on civil rights issues

Member of Congress	State, party, and district	Percentage of vote in 1864	Percentage of vote in 1866
Sydenham E. Ancona	Pa. Democrat 8th	66.91%	Not a candidate; Dem. win (65.33%)
Tennis G. Bergen	N.Y. Democrat 2d	60.69%	Not a candidate; Dem. win (62.50%)
Alexander Coffroth	Pa. Democrat 16th	49.85%	Not a candidate; Rep. win (51.18%)
Adam J. Glossbrenner	Pa. Democrat 15th	55.86%	55.90%
Edwin N. Hubbell	N.Y. Democrat 13th	53.14%	Not a candidate; Rep. win (50.83%)
James M. Humphrey	N.Y. Union 3d	50.71%	Not a candidate; Dem. win (53.91%)
Charles Winfield	N.Y. Democrat 11th	50.61%	Not a candidate; Rep. win (50.65%)

Sources: *Congressional Globe*; Dubin, *United States Congressional Elections*, 198–207.

Notes

INTRODUCTION

1. Testimony of Pinkard C. Dowans, transcript of evidence, Grand Court of *Calanthe v. P. C. Downs*, case no. 14712, Mississippi Supreme Court Records, Mississippi Department of Archives and History, Jackson, hereafter cited as MDAH. Skocpol and Oser, "Organization Despite Adversity"; Camp and Kent, "What a Mighty Power We Can Be"; Clawson, *Constructing Brotherhood*.

2. For Fayssoux Scudder's account of her father's role in designing the flag, see Scudder, "History of Mississippi Flag." On Scudder's service in the legislature, see Rowland, *Official and Statistical Register*, 3:204. For Scudder's service in the Sons of Confederate Veterans, see *Confederate Veteran* 16 (August 1906): 346; 17 (August 1909): 372; 19 (May 1911): 262; 24 (March 1916): 134. Anne Lipscomb Webster did detailed research on the Mississippi state flag when the legislature proposed replacing Scudder's design in 2000. See Elbert R. Hilliard to Senator Robert H. "Rob" Smith, June 15, 2000, subject file Flag Legislation, MDAH.

3. *Merchants and Planters Packet Co. v. Wright Brothers*, case no. 2778, in Minute Book UU, pages 118, 121, 124, Warren County Circuit Court, Warren County Circuit Clerk's Office, Vicksburg, Mississippi.

4. Transcript of evidence, Grand Court of *Calanthe v. P. C. Downs*, case no. 14712, Mississippi Supreme Court Records, MDAH; Grand Court of *Colanthe v. P. C. Downs*, 98 Miss. 740 (1910).

5. *Powers v. Ohio*, 499 U.S. 400 (1991); Amar, "Jury Service as Political Participation."

6. Oldham, *Trial by Jury*, 174–75. The Supreme Court recognized Oldham's contention in 1968, explaining that a jury of the defendant's peers safeguards against the overzealous prosecutor and the eccentric or biased judge; *Duncan v. Louisiana*, 3912 U.S. 145 (1968).

7. *Nation* 10, March 10, 1870, 148.

8. *Account of the Proceedings*, 83; Ritter, "Jury Service and Women's Citizenship"; Kerber, *No Constitutional Right to Be Ladies*, 124–220.

9. For articles on this subject, see Forman, "Juries and Race"; Schmidt, "Juries, Jurisdiction, and Race Discrimination"; Coleman, "Evolution of Race"; Alschuler and Deiss, "Brief History." For an examination of jury discrimination in medieval England, see Constable, *Law of the Other*.

10. Rubin, "Ghosts of Emmett Till."

11. For this argument, see Dunning, *Essays on the Civil War*; Klarman, *From Jim Crow to Civil Rights*.

12. Foner, *Reconstruction*, 529.

13. The scholarship on memory is considerable, but see most especially Blight, *Race and Reunion*; for my own work on memory, see Waldrep, *Vicksburg's Long Shadow*.

14. In the twenty-first century, some authors have emphasized majority rule over constitutional principle, finding collective wisdom in crowds, as James Surowiecki put it in his well-known book *The Wisdom of Crowds*. Other lawyers, most especially Ronald Dworkin, have warned that while a crowd might be better at guessing some objective fact than an individual, there is no particular reason to trust moral judgments to a majority vote. In addition to Surowiecki, see Sunstein, *Constitution of Many Minds*; Dworkin, *Freedom's Law*.

ONE. Making the Fairy Tale

1. Barney, *Secessionist Impulse*, 193–268; *Jackson Daily Mississippian*, January 16, 1861.

2. Baker, *Introduction to English Legal History*, 86; Stenton, *William the Conqueror*, 457–501.

3. Donahue, "Proof by Witnesses," 143–48.

4. Hyams, *Rancor and Reconciliation*, 158–60; Groot, "Early-Thirteenth-Century Jury"; Levy, *Palladium of Justice*, 3–15.

5. Groot, "Jury of Presentment before 1215"; Green, *Verdict according to Conscience*, 3–12.

6. Breay, *Magna Carta*, 52.

7. Constable, *Law of the Other*, 16–25, 96.

8. Ibid., 9–27, 49–66.

9. Oldham, *Trial by Jury*, 220.

10. Fortescue, *Laws and Governance of England*, 36–48, 40 (quotation).

11. Lawson, "Lawless Juries?"; Cockburn, "Twelve Silly Men?"

12. Post, "Jury Lists," 67–68; Mulholland, "Jury in English Manorial Courts."

13. Oldham, *Trial by Jury*, 128–45.

14. Musson, *Medieval Law in Context*, 109–16; Stephen K. Roberts, "Juries and the Middling Sort," 205; Oldham, *Trial by Jury*, 80–114; appendix 4 in Oldham has a table of juror qualifications established by Parliament and statutes of the realm.

15. O'Brien, *God's Peace and King's Peace*, 87–88; Mulholland, "Jury in English Manorial Courts."

16. Elton, *Parliament of England*, 280–81; Palmer, "Litigiousness"; Seipp, "Jurors, Evidences and the Tempest."

17. Whitman, *Origins of Reasonable Doubt*, 461–62.

18. Green, *Verdict according to Conscience*, 105–52.

19. Ibid.

20. *Complete Juryman*, 28, 30; Brayley, Brewer, and Nightingale, *Topographical and Historical Description*, 1:299–302.

21. Green, *Verdict according to Conscience*, 160–65.

22. *People's Ancient and Just Liberties*.

23. Ibid.

24. Starling, *Answer*; for an account of the entire Penn affair, see Green, *Verdict according to Conscience*, 202–49.

25. Starling, *Answer*.

26. Hawles, *Englishman's Right*.

27. *Case of the Seven Bishops*, 87 E.R. 136; Green, *Verdict according to Conscience*, 262–63, 320–21.

28. Green, *Verdict according to Conscience*, 35–38; Herrup, *Common Peace*, 113–15.

29. Oldham, *Trial by Jury*, 27–29.

30. *Honest Jury*.

31. *Guide to English Juries*, 2, 6.

32. Herrup, *Common Peace*, 92.

33. Shoemaker, *London Mob*, 27–152. In contrast, E. P. Thompson argues that at the end of the eighteenth century people became more violent as they desperately fought to impose their moral economy on the free market (*Making of the English Working Class*, 55–76). See also Howsman, *Thief-Taker General*.

34. *Complete Juryman*, 20–47; Langbein, "Criminal Trial before the Lawyers," 274–75.

35. Beattie, "London Juries in the 1690s," 214–15.

36. Hulsebosch, *Constituting Empire*, 6–10; Murrin, "Magistrates, Sinners, and a Precarious Liberty."

37. Murrin, "Magistrates, Sinners, and a Precarious Liberty."

38. Quitrents originated as fees paid to one's lord to absolve or make quit some service. The amount involved ranged from the nominal to the substantial.

39. Moglen, "Considering Zenger."

40. Ibid.

41. Ibid.; Hulsebosch, *Constituting Empire*, 59–64; Finkelman, *Brief Narrative*.

42. Pole, "Reflections on American Law"; Stimson, *American Revolution in the Law*, 5–12, 49. For a more general review comparing jury service to voting, see Amar, "Jury Service as Political Participation."

43. Levy, *Palladium of Justice*, 66–86; Bailyn, *Ideological Origins of the American Revolution*, 74, 108.

44. Wood, *Creation of the American Republic*, 291–305.

45. John Adams, *Adams Papers*, 2:180, 200, 288–90.

46. Bogen, "Individual Liberties."

47. Ibid., 817–19.

48. Madison to Edmund Randolph, May 20, 1783, in Madison, *Papers of James Madison*, 7:59–60; Madison, *Letters and Other Writings*, 1:320–27.

49. Farrand, *Records of the Federal Convention*, 2:73–83. Wood cites this passage as evidence that American Whigs enforced their constitutional principles in ordinary courts of law (*Creation of the American Republic*, 305n76).

50. Farrand, *Records of the Federal Convention*, 2:587–88, 628.

51. Ibid., 3:101, 163, 167, 309.

52. Centinel, "To the Freemen of Pennsylvania," in Storing, *Complete Antifederalist*, 2:136; Centinel, "To the People of Pennsylvania," in Storing, *Complete Antifederalist*, 2:177, 192.

53. Brutus, February 28, 1788, in Storing, *Complete Antifederalist*, 2:432.

54. Letter from a Federal Farmer, October 9, 1787, in Storing, *Complete Antifederalist*, 2:231.

55. Lee, *Observations*.

56. Luther Martin, "Mr. Martin's Information to the General Assembly of the State of Maryland," in Storing, *Complete Antifederalist*, 2:70.

57. Brutus, March 6, 1788, in Storing, *Complete Antifederalist*, 2:435.

58. A Farmer, March 21, 1788, in Storing, *Complete Antifederalist*, 5:37.

59. Cincinnatus, November 1, 1787, in Storing, *Complete Antifederalist*, 6:9.

60. One of the Common People, December 3, 1787, in Storing, *Complete Antifederalist*, 4:122.

61. Alexander Hamilton, *Federalist* No. 83, in Pole, *Federalist*, 441–51.

62. Representative Madison of Virginia speaking on Amendments to the Constitution, 1st Cong., 1st sess., *Annals of Congress* (June 8, 1789): 448–52; Bowling, "Tub to the Whale"; Finkelman, "James Madison."

63. *United States v. Callender*, 25 F. Cas. 239 (1800).

64. Essay by a Farmer, June 6, 1788, in Storing, *Complete Antifederalist*, 4:214.

65. *Perpetual Laws of the Commonwealth of Massachusetts*, 165, 167.

66. *Laws of the State of Maine*, 1:378.

67. An Act Proportioning Each Town's Quota of Jurors to Attend the Several Courts of This State, and Directing the Method of Choosing Them, and Regulating Their Attendance at Said Courts, 2, 1798 *R.I. Laws* 181.

68. *N.C. Rev. Stat.* c. 31, 26–27 (Iredell & Battle 1837).

69. *Maryland Gazette and State Register*, September 21, 1826; *New York Herald*, July 24, 1843.

70. McDermott "Gentlemen of the Jury"; Wilson, "Of Juries."

71. Tucker, *Commentaries on the Laws of Virginia*, 2:282–83; Chitty, *Practical Treatise on the Criminal Law*, 1:536.

72. *State v. Benjamin Seaborn*, 15 NC305 (1833) at 309.

73. Graham, *Essay on New Trials*, 19–44.

74. Tucker, *Commentaries on the Laws of Virginia*, 2:282–83.

75. Fehrenbacher, *Dred Scott Case*, 11–27; Wilson, "Of Juries," 958. Paul Finkelman disputes Fehrenbacher; see *Slavery and the Founders*.

TWO.   The Discovery That Race Politicizes Due Process

1. J. C. Smith, *Emancipation*, 291–92.

2. W. E. Mollison, *Leading Afro-Americans*; Holmes, *White Chief*, 34–39; McCormick, "Discovery That Business Corrupts Politics"; I. C. Mollison, "Negro Lawyers in Mississippi." Mollison's article is a virtual oral history with his father, Willis Mollison.

3. *Vicksburg Evening Post*, May 30, June 4, 17, September 9, 1904.

4. Farrand, *Records of the Federal Convention of 1787*, 1:134–36; James Madison, *Federalist* No. 10, in Pole, *Federalist*, 48–54.

5. G. James Forten, Letter, *Philadelphia Columbian Courier*, January 20, 1800; [Forten], *Letters from a Man of Color*; Winch, "Making and Meaning"; Winch, *Gentleman of Color*.

6. *Friend to the Constitution*, 6.

7. Caines, *Summary*, 203.

8. "An American," *Observations on the Trial*, 12–3, 24–25, 2833–35; "Observations on the Trial by Jury," *Philadelphia Gazette of the United States*, October 14, 1804; *National Intelligencer and Washington Advertiser*, December 14, 1803.

9. Kershen, "Jury Selection Act of 1879," 730; *United States v. Richardson*, 28 F. 61 (C.C.D. Me. 1886); *United States v. Tallman*, 28 F. Cas. 9 (C.C.S.D.N.Y. 1872) (no. 16429).

10. *Judiciary Act of 1789*, 1 Stat. 73; Blinka, "This Germ of Rottedness," 135–89; J. M. Smith, *Freedom's Fetters*.

11. *Calder v. Bull*, 3 U.S. (3 Dall.) 386 (1798); *Dartmouth College v. Woodward*, 17 U.S. 518 (1819).

12. *John D. Hoke v. Lawson Henderson*, 15 N.C. 1 (1833) at 28.

13. 5 *Stat.* 394; "Trial by Jury," *Albany Evening Journal*, May 15, 1840, reprinted in Boston *Liberator*, June 5, 1840; "Thomas Corwin in Favor of Extending the Privileges of the Blacks in Ohio—Abolitionism—Breakers Ahead—Cause of Increased Insolence by the Blacks!" *Columbus Ohio Statesman*, June 17, 1840.

14. Morris, *Free Men All*, 73; U.S. Const. art. IV, sec. 3.

15. Edmund Randolph to President George Washington, July 20, 1791, in *American State Papers* 037 Miscellaneous vol. 1, 2d Cong., 1st sess., publication no. 22, p. 41.

16. Finkelman, "Kidnapping of John Davis."

17. *Annals of Congress*, 2d Cong., 1st sess. (October 26, 1791): 18; *Annals of Congress*, 2d Cong., 1st sess. (October 31, 1791): 148; *Annals of Congress*, 2d Cong., 2d sess. (February 4, 1793): 861.

18. *Wright, Otherwise called Hall, against Deacon, Keeper of the Prison*, 5 Serg. and Rawle 62 (1819); Roper, "In Quest of Judicial Objectivity," 538; on this point, see Fehrenbacher, *Slaveholding Republic*, 36.

19. *Prigg v. Pennsylvania*, 41 U.S. 539 (1842); Finkleman, "Story Telling on the Supreme Court."

20. [Candler], *Summary View of America*, 291.

21. Ga. Const. of 1789 and 1798, art. IV, sec. 1; Ga. Const. of 1865, art. V, sec. 1.

22. *Revised Statutes of the State of Maine*, 619.

23. Alschuler and Deiss, "Brief History."

24. Dorsey, *General Public Statutory Law*, 1:349.

25. Acts of the General Assembly of the Commonwealth of Pennsylvania (Harrisburg, 1826), 150–54.

26. Burin, *Slavery and the Peculiar Solution*, 1–35.

27. Castiglia, "Abolition's Racial Interiors."

28. Birney, *Letter on Colonization*, 4–10.

29. Goodell, *Views of American Constitutional Law*, 3–5, 8–9, 107–8; see Sorin, *New York Abolitionists*, 57–62, for a biographical sketch of Goodell. Perry documents Goodell's objections to Garrison (*Radical Abolitionism*, 190–91).

30. Lloyd, "Revising the Republic," 88–93; Douglass, *Frederick Douglass Papers*, 2:193–97; Martin, *Mind of Frederick Douglass*, 31–38; Blight, *Frederick Douglass' Civil War*, 30–35.

31. Douglass, *Frederick Douglass Papers*, 3:153.

32. Stewart, *Legal Argument*. Fehrenbacher makes essentially the same argument in *Slaveholding Republic*. For the outcome of the case, see *State v. Post*, 20 N.J.L. 368 (1845); Ernst, "Legal Positivism."

33. *Jack, a Negro Man v. Mary Martin*, 12 Wend. 311 (1835).

34. *Revised Statutes of the State of New York*, 2:164.

35. *Jack, a Negro Man v. Mary Martin*, 14 Wend. 507 (1835) at 530–39.

36. *Jack, a Negro Man*, 14 Wend. at 524–29. Morris has an excellent discussion of this case in *Free Men All* (65–70). There is also a useful narrative in the *Boston Liberator*, September 7, 1833.

37. Yates, *Rights of Colored Men*, 89.

38. J. Q. Adams, *Address of John Quincy Adams*, 50–51.

39. *Wharton Jones v. John Van Zandt*, 46 U.S. 215 (1847). Chase's biographers agree that this case played an important role in his life. Hart praises Chase for his "zeal" but notes that he did not hope to win (*Salmon Portland Chase*, 76–77). Blue writes that the case helped him "systematize his thinking" (*Salmon P. Chase*, 36–37). Niven emphasizes that

Chase used the case to attract attention to himself and his cause, becoming a political leader in Ohio (*Salmon P. Chase*, 77–83).

40. Spooner, *Essay on the Trial by Jury*.

41. *Remarks of Henry B. Stanton*, 12; Morris, *Free Men All*, 73; Stanton, "Ultraists—Conservatives—Reformers."

42. Alvord, "Trial by Jury"; "Biographical Sketch of James C. Alvord"; Pierce, *Memoir and Letters of Charles Sumner*, 3:304–5.

43. *New York Emancipator*, June 5, 1840; "Trial by Jury," *Albany Evening Journal*, May 15, 1940, reprinted in *Boston Liberator*, June 5, 1840.

44. "Thomas Corwin in Favor of Extending the Privileges of the Blacks in Ohio"; Morris, *Free Men All*, 88.

45. Morris, *Free Men All*, 86.

46. *Laws of the State of New York*, c. 225, 174.

47. Resolutions of the General Assembly of South Carolina in relation to the controversy between the States of New York and Virginia, on the subject of surrendering fugitives from justice," February 7, 1842, printed in 27th Congress, 2d sess., *Senate Report* 96, p. 2.

48. *Proceedings and Debates of the Virginia State Convention of 1829–30*, 25–27.

49. Ibid.; Wolf, *Race and Liberty in the New Nation*, 162–95.

50. Tucker, *Few Lectures on Natural Law*, 2–93.

51. Wilentz, *Rise of American Democracy*, 218–358; Grimsted, *American Mobbing*.

52. Carter, Stone, and Gould, *Reports*, 189–90; N.Y. Const. of 1822, art. II, sec. 1.

53. Dorr, *Address to the People of Rhode-Island*, 37–38; Dennison, *Dorr War*; Wiecek, "Popular Sovereignty in the Dorr War."

54. Dorr, *Address to the People of Rhode-Island*, 10, 26–32, 57–59.

55. An Act calling a convention of the People to Frame a Written Constitution for this State, in *Luther v. Borden*, 48 U.S. 1 (1849), transcript of record in *U.S. Supreme Court Records and Briefs*.

56. People's Constitution, in *Luther*, 48 U.S. 1, transcript of record in *U.S. Supreme Court Records and Briefs*.

57. *Report of the Trial of Thomas Wilson Dorr*, 21–100.

58. *Luther*, 48 U.S. 1, transcript of record, file date: March 1, 1844, 148 pp., in *U.S. Supreme Court Records and Briefs*; Dennison, *Dorr War*; Wiecek, "Popular Sovereignty in the Dorr War."

59. J. V. Smith, *Report*, 56–57. For William Sawyer, see Remini, who describes Sawyer as a clownish figure (*The House*, 131); Taylor describes Sawyer as highly respected in his county (*Ohio in Congress from 1803–1900*, 189).

60. Fowler, *Report*, 233, 238.

61. Calif. Const. of 1849, art. II, sec. 1; Browne, *Report*, 48–50, 137–52, 330–40.

62. *Proceedings of the Maryland State Convention*, 496–97.

63. *Cleveland Herald*, August 11, 1851; Boston *Liberator*, January 10, 1851.

64. Fowler, *Report*, 135–44, 161–88; *Report of the Proceedings and Debates in the Convention to Revise the Constitution of the State of Michigan*, 5158; J. V. Smith, *Report*, 2:328–30.

65. Cole, *Constitutional Debates of 1847*, 864.

66. Ibid.

67. Emerson, "Introductory Lecture," in his *Collected Works*, 1:176; Emerson, "Politics," in his *Early Lectures*, 2:69–82; Grodzins, *American Heretic*, 62–249.

68. Brown, *Works of Rufus Choate*, 1:430.

69. Gura, *American Transcendentalism*, 240–42; Rose, *Transcendentalism as a Social Movement*, 207–23.

70. Potter and Fehrenbacher, *Impending Crisis*, 90–120; Wilentz, *Rise of American Democracy*, 637–45.

71. Congress, Senate, Senator Henry Clay of Kentucky speaking on The Slavery Question, 31st Cong., 1st sess., *Congressional Globe* (January 29, 1850): 244.

72. Ibid., 246.

73. *Prigg*, 41 U.S. 539; Finkelman, "Prigg v. Pennsylvania and Northern State Courts."

74. Congress, Senate, Senator James Murray Mason speaking on The Slavery Question, 31st Cong., 1st sess., *Congressional Globe* (January 4, 1850): 103; *Philadelphia North American and United States Gazette*, January 26, 1850.

75. Congress, Senate, Senator William Henry Seward of New York speaking on the Surrender of Fugitive Slaves, 31st Cong., 1st sess., *Congressional Globe* (January 28, 1850): 236; Senator Henry Foote of Mississippi responding, ibid.

76. Emerson, "The Fugitive Slave Law," in *Complete Works of Ralph Waldo Emerson*, 11:179.

77. Remini, *Daniel Webster*, 315.

78. Webster to Samuel Kirkland Lothrop, February 12, 1850, in *Papers of Daniel Webster*, 7:9–10 (first and second quotations); Remini, *Daniel Webster*, 27 (third quotation), 665–68; Potter and Fehrenbacher, *Impending Crisis*, 97. Potter's discussion of the compromise has long been considered authoritative, but see also Wilentz, *Rise of American Democracy*, 637–45.

79. Remini, *Daniel Webster*, 664.

80. Congress, Senate, Senator Daniel Webster of Massachusetts speaking on The Compromise, 31st Cong., 1st sess., *Congressional Globe* (March 7, 1850): 476–84. Webster had defended trial by jury as one of "the plainest constitutional provisions" and the "great bulwark of the citizen" after the War of 1812. Congress, House of Representatives, Representative Daniel Webster of Massachusetts speaking on "Punishment of Treason," 13th Cong., 2d sess., *Annals of Congress*: 885.

81. Congress, Senate, Senator John Hale of New Hampshire speaking on Trial by Jury for Fugitive Slaves, 31st Cong., 1st sess., *Congressional Globe* (March 14, 1850): 524

82. Congress, Senate, Senate's Select Committee of Thirteen, *Report*, 31st Cong., 1st sess., May 8, 1850, 7–10.

83. Webster to Edward S. Rand and others, Citizens of Newburyport, in his *Writings and Speeches*, 12:225–37.

84. Webster to Edward S. Rand and others, Citizens of Newburyport, in his *Writings and Speeches*, 12:225–37; Morris, *Free Men All*, 137.

85. *Boston Courier*, quoted in *Boston Daily Atlas*, June 3, 1850.

86. Congress, Senate, Senator Webster speaking on Fugitive Slave Bill, 31st Cong., 1st sess., *Congressional Globe* (June 3, 1850): pt. 2:1111; Fehrenbacher, *Slaveholding Republic*, 228, 414n79.

87. Mann's letter to his constituents, *Boston Daily Atlas*, May 6, 1850.

88. Grant, "Representative Mann," 105–23.

89. Webster to Edward S. Rand and others, Citizens of Newburyport, 225.

90. *Boston Liberator*, June 14, 1850.

91. Ibid.

92. Ibid.

93. Ibid., June 21, 1850; *Cohens v. Virginia*, 19 U.S. 264 (1821); *Parsons v. Bedford, Breedlove and Robeson*, 3 Pet. (28 U.S.) 433 (1830).

94. Irwin, *A Charge to the Grand Jury by the District Judge of the United States for the Western District of Pennsylvania, Delivered at June Term, 1851*, reprinted in Finkelman, *Fugitive Slaves and American Courts* 1:671, 682.

95. *Speech of the Hon. James Cooper*, reprinted in Finkelman, *Fugitive Slaves and American Courts*, ser. 2, 2:163.

96. *U.S. v. Thomas Reid and Edward Clemens*, 53 U.S. 361 (1852) at 364–66.

97. *Boston Slave Riot*, 49, 50.

98. Ibid., 50.

99. Ibid., 54; Von Frank, *Trials of Anthony Burns*, 1–203; Finkelman, "Legal Ethics and Fugitive Slaves."

100. Von Frank, *Trials of Anthony Burns*, 116–17.

101. Streichler, *Justice Curtis*, 98–118.

102. *Dred Scott v. Sandford*, 19 How. (60 U.S.) 393 (1857).

103. Ibid.; Fehrenbacher, *Dred Scott Case*, 114–51; in "The Unlikely Hero of Dred Scott," Earl Maltz argues that Curtis did not change his position once on the Court.

104. Allen, *Origins of the Dred Scott Case*, 178–202.

105. Von Frank, *Trials of Anthony Burns*, 97–103; Martel, *Love Is a Sweet Chain*, 132–33.

THREE. How Revolutionary Was the Civil War?

1. Bailey, *Prohibition in Mississippi*, 64, 108.

2. *Vicksburg Evening Post*, April 27, 1886; *Lowell Daily Citizen and News*, March 8, December 22, 1869; Welch, *George Frisbie Hoar*.

3. Foldy, *Trials of Oscar Wilde*, 98–127.

4. Marshall, "God and the Working Man," 133–44.

5. Silbey, *American Political Nation*, 20, 33, 59–60, 75–127.

6. *Toledo Blade*, August 22, 1862.

7. Guelzo, *Lincoln's Emancipation Proclamation*, 38–75; Vorenberg, *Final Freedom*, 23–31; Burton, *Age of Lincoln*, 161–70.

8. C. R. Williams, *Life of Rutherford Birchard Hayes*, 1:277.

9. Congress, House, Representative Crisfield speaking on Army Appropriation Bill, 37th Cong., 2d sess., *Congressional Globe* (May 14, 1862): pt. 3:2130–2.

10. Congress, House, Representative Kelley, speaking on Prohibition of Slavery, 37th Cong., 2d sess., *Congressional Globe* (May 13, 1862): pt. 3:2049.

11. Congress, House, Representative Crisfield, speaking on Prohibition of Slavery, 37th Cong., 2d sess., *Congressional Globe* (May 13, 1862): pt. 3:2048.

12. Congress, House, Representative Eliot, speaking on Confiscation, 37th Cong., 2d sess., *Congressional Globe* (May 22, 1862): pt. 3:2232–40.

13. Siddali, *From Property to Person*, 70–250; Guelzo, *Lincoln's Emancipation Proclamation*, 38–75.

14. "Emancipation in the Border States," *New York Times*, July 19, 1862, p. 8; Lincoln to A. G. Hodges, April 4, 1864, in Lincoln, *Collected Works*, 7:281–83; Pinsker, "Lincoln's Summer of Emancipation," 79–99; Guelzo, *Lincoln's Emancipation Proclamation*, 112–13.

15. Fehrenbacher, *Slaveholding Republic*, 310–11.

16. "President Lincoln's Emancipation Policy—an Important Movement," *New York Times*, July 15, 1862, p. 4; Browning, *Diary*, 1:558–60.

17. *Toledo Blade*, September 30, October 7, 1862.

18. Ibid., July 5, 1862.

19. Ibid., October 7, 1862; Benedict, "James Ashley," 814–37; Horwitz, *Great Impeacher*, 1–3.

20. Lincoln, *Papers*, 2:1–43.

21. Salmon Chase to David Dudley Field, June 30, 1863, in Chase, *Papers*, 4:73–74. Numerous historians have examined the legal tender cases. See Cormack, "Legal Tender Cases"; Walsh, "Legal Tender Cases."

22. Salmon Chase to Edward Mansfield, October 18, 1863, in Chase, *Papers*, 4:155.

23. Salmon Chase to Cyrus W. Field, April 6, 1864, in Chase, *Papers*, 4:365.

24. *Boston Liberator*, March 24, 1865; Crouch, "Black Dreams and White Justice," 54–68; Waldrep, *Roots of Disorder*, 101–3; Foner, *Reconstruction*, 68–70.

25. *Vermont Watchman and State Journal*, April 7, 1865.

26. *Boston Daily Whig and Courier*, April 4, 1865.

27. "The War News—Time for a Peace Policy," *Milwaukee Daily Sentinel*, April 6, 1865.

28. "Peace," *Boston Daily Advertiser*, April 10, 1865.

29. "Another Washington Celebration—Speech of President Lincoln," *Daily Cleveland Herald*, April 12, 1865.

30. Donald, *Charles Sumner and the Rights of Man*, 54–55; "The Work of Reconstruction—What Is the True Policy," *New York Herald*, reprinted in the *Washington Daily National Intelligencer*, April 13, 1865.

31. Boutwell, "Reconstruction: Its True Basis," July 4, 1865, in Boutwell, *Speeches and Papers*, 372–407; Boutwell, "Equal Suffrage," December 1865, in *Speeches and Papers*, 408.

32. Simpson, *Reconstruction Presidents*, 67–130; Foner, *Reconstruction*, 176–84.

33. Browning, *Diary*, 2:70, 79.

34. An Act to Regulate the Relation of Master and Apprentice, as relates to Freedmen, Free Negroes, and Mulattoes, 1865 Miss. 86–90.

35. An Act to Establish County Courts, 1865 Miss. 66; An Act to Amend the Vagrant Laws of the State, 1865 Miss. 90; An Act to Punish Certain Offences Therein Named, and for Other Purposes, 1865 Miss. 165; An Act to Prevent the Hunting of Stock with Guns or Dogs in This State in Certain Cases, 1865 Miss. 199; An Act to Confer Civil Rights on Freedmen and for Other Purposes, 1865 Miss. 82.

36. Samuel Thomas to Major General Thomas J. Wood, November 23, 1865, letters received, box 2, Department of Mississippi, U.S. Army Continental Commands, RG 393, National Archives, Washington, D.C.

37. *Chicago Tribune*, December 1, 1865.

38. Williams, *Life of Rutherford Birchard Hayes*, 1:278.

39. Ibid.

40. Stevens confessed his desire to punish Southerners on January 24, in an exchange with Robert Schenck of Ohio. Congress, House, Representative Schenck of Ohio on the Basis of Representation, 39th Cong., 1st sess., *Congressional Globe* (January 24, 1866): pt. 5, app. 299.

41. Congress, House, Representative Stevens of Pennsylvania for Reconstruction, 39th Cong., 1st sess., *Congressional Globe* (December 18, 1865): pt. 1:72–75.

42. Congress, Senate, Senator Sumner of Massachusetts speaking for the Protection of Freedmen, S. no. 9, 39th Cong., 1st sess., *Congressional Globe* (December 20, 1865): pt. 1:90–92. Historians have disagreed over the influence of such "Radicals" as Stevens and Sumner. Perhaps because of his dramatic and challenging language—calling the

southern states "dead" and subject to the "absolute" control of Congress—Stevens is especially controversial. In 1907, William Archibald Dunning described the House as tamely submitting to Stevens's "aggressive leadership," voting for "every measure that his policy required" (*Reconstruction*, 64). More recently scholars have tried to correct the excesses inherent in Dunning's account, written with such evident distaste for Stevens and the whole idea of Reconstruction. "No man was oftener outvoted," one newspaper commented after his death, and historians have used this quote to note the limits of Stevens's influence. See Foner, *Reconstruction*, 229. Stevens's most recent and best biographer writes that Stevens was not the absolute ruler of Congress, but that he successfully piloted the Fourteenth Amendment through the House and foiled President Johnson's plans for Reconstruction. He was not, Hans Trefousse concludes, ineffective (*Thaddeus Stevens*, 187–88).

43. Congress, House, Representative Bromwell of Illinois, 39th Cong., 1st sess., *Congressional Globe* (February 24, 1866): pt. 2:1019–20.

44. Congress, House, Representative Ashley of Ohio, 39th Cong., 1st sess., *Congressional Globe* (May 22, 1866): pt. 4:2882.

45. Congress, House, Representative Wade of Ohio, on Representation of Southern States, 39th Cong., 1st sess., *Congressional Globe* (March 1, 1866): pt. 2:1114.

46. Congress, Senate, Senator Davis of Kentucky, 39th Cong., 1st sess., *Congressional Globe* (January 24, 1866): pt. 1:394.

47. Nicholas, "Report of the Joint Congressional Committee," 3:27.

48. *Nation* 2 (February 15, 1866): 195; Fisher, *Philadelphia Perspective*, 2, 367, 508, 510, 523–24.

49. Benedict, "Preserving Federalism," 39–79; Congress, House, *A Bill to Preserve the Right of Trial by Jury, by Securing Impartial Jurors, in the Courts of the United States*, 39th Cong., 1st sess.

50. R. P. L. Baber to John Sherman, March 12, 1866, vol. 96, Sherman Papers, Library of Congress, Washington, D.C.

51. C. W. Moulton to John Sherman, March 8, 1866, vol. 96; A. B. Buttles to Sherman, February 27, 1866, vol. 95, both in Sherman Papers, Library of Congress, Washington, D.C.

52. Congress, Senate, Senator Stewart of Nevada, 39th Cong., 1st sess., *Congressional Globe* (May 24, 1866): pt. 4:2798.

53. Congress, House, Representative Buckland of Ohio, on Reconstruction, Admission of Tennessee, 39th Cong., 1st sess., *Congressional Globe*, (March 24, 1866): pt. 2:1623.

54. Congress, Senate, Senator Davis of Kentucky, on Reconstruction, HR 127, 39th Cong., 1st sess., *Congressional Globe* (June 7, 1866): pt. 5, app. 238, 240.

55. Congress, Senate, Senator Davis of Kentucky, on Civil Rights, S. no. 61, 39th Cong., 1st sess., *Congressional Globe* (April 6, 1866): pt. 5, app. 185.

56. Congress, House, Representative Benjamin Boyer of Pennsylvania, 39th Cong., 1st sess., *Congressional Globe* (January 10, 1866): pt. 1:175.

57. Congress, House, Representative Bundy of Ohio, on Loyal Men Must Rule, 39th Cong., 1st sess., *Congressional Globe* (May 5, 1866): pt. 5, apps. 206–7. For dissent and division in the Civil War North, see Neely, *Union Divided*. Numerous historians have noted the phenomenon; the disagreement involves whether partisan quarrels boosted the North. Potter, in "Jefferson Davis," and many others argue it did. Neely disagrees.

58. Congress, House, Representative Lawrence of Pennsylvania, on Reconstruction, 39th Cong., 1st sess., *Congressional Globe* (May 5, 1866): pt. 5, app. 203.

59. Congress, House, Representative Kelley of Pennsylvania, 39th Cong., 1st sess., *Congressional Globe* (January 10, 1866): pt. 1:180.

60. Congress, House, Representative Clarke of Kansas on Suffrage in the District of Columbia, HR 1, 39th Cong., 1st sess., *Congressional Globe* (January 18, 1866): pt.1:303.

61. Congress, Senate, Senator Clark of New Hampshire on Apportionment of Representation, 39th Cong., 1st sess., *Congressional Globe* (February 14, 1866): pt. 1:832.

62. "The Strong Government Idea," *Atlantic Monthly* 45 (February 1880): 273. Michael Les Benedict has an excellent discussion of the difference between states' rights and state sovereignty in "Judicial Infamy," 60–61.

63. Congress, House, Representative Rogers of New Jersey on Rights of Citizens, HR 63, 39th Cong., 1st sess., *Congressional Globe* (February 26, 1866): pt. 5, app. 133.

64. Congress, Senate, Senator Davis on Protection of Civil Rights, S. no. 61, 39th Cong., 1st sess., *Congressional Globe* (January 31, 1866): pt. 1:528–30.

65. Congress, Senate, Senator Davis on Protection of Civil Rights, S. no. 61, 39th Cong., 1st sess., *Congressional Globe* (January 31, 1866): pt. 1:530.

66. Congress, Senate, Senator Wilson of Massachusetts speaking for the Protection of Freedmen, S. no. 9, 39th Cong., 1st sess. *Congressional Globe* (December 13, 1865): pt. 1:39.

67. Congress, Senate, Senator Sherman of Ohio, speaking on the Protection of Freedmen, S. no. 9, 39th Cong., 1st sess., *Congressional Globe* (December 13, 1865): pt. 1:41–42; O'Connor, "Time out of Mind," 659–735; David S. Bogen, "Individual Liberties"; D. G. Smith, "Privileges and Immunities Clause" 809–57; Olson, "Natural Law Foundation."

68. Usually called "The Negro Seaman Act," the actual title of the statute was "An Act for the Better Regulation and Government of Free Negroes and Persons of Color; and for other Purposes." McCord, *Statutes at Large of South Carolina*, 7:459–60.

69. Greeley, *American Conflict*, 178–85; "South Carolina on the Mission of Samuel Hoar," December 5, 1844, *Reports and Resolutions of South Carolina, 1844*, 160, in Ames, *State Documents on Foreign Relations*, 5:46.

70. Congress, Senate, Senator Sherman of Ohio speaking for the Protection of Freedmen, S. no. 9, 39th Cong, 1st sess, *Congressional Globe* (December 13, 1865): pt. 1:41–42. Bingham brought up the Hoar incident later. Congress, House, Representative Bingham of Ohio speaking on the Policy of the President, 39th Cong., 1st sess., *Congressional Globe*, (January 9, 1866): pt. 1:158.

71. Congress, Senate, Senator Wilson of Massachusetts speaking for the Protection of Freedmen, S. no. 9, 39th Cong, 1st sess, *Congressional Globe* (December 21, 1865): pt. 1:111.

72. Congress, Senate, Senator Sherman of Ohio speaking on the Freedmen's Bureau, SB 60, 39th Cong., 1st sess., *Congressional Globe* (February 8, 1866): pt. 1:744.

73. Congress, Senate, Senator Trumbull of Illinois speaking for the Protection of Civil Rights, SB 61, 39th Cong., 1st sess., *Congressional Globe* (January 12, 1866): pt. 1:211.

74. Congress, Senate, Senator Creswell of Maryland speaking for the Freedmen's Bureau bill, SB 60, 39th Cong., 1st sess., *Congressional Globe* (January 23, 1866): pt. 1:373.

75. Congress, House, Representative Rousseau of Kentucky on Freedmen's Bureau, SB 60, 39th Cong., 1st sess., *Congressional Globe* (February 3, 1866): pt. 5, app. 69.

76. Congress, Senate, 39th Cong., 1st sess., *Congressional Globe* (January 25, 1866): pt. 1:421; Benedict, *Compromise of Principle*, 162–63.

77. Congress, Senate, 39th Cong., 1st sess., *Congressional Globe* (February 2, 1866): pt. 1:606–7.

78. D. A. Dangler to John Sherman, February 27, 1866, vol. 95., Sherman Papers, Library of Congress, Washington, D.C.

79. R. P. L. Baber to John Sherman, March 12, 1866, vol. 96, Sherman Papers, Library of Congress, Washington, D.C.

80. Dr. M. B. Wright to John Sherman, February 27, 1866, vol. 95, Sherman Papers, Library of Congress, Washington, D.C.

81. A. B. Buttles to John Sherman, February 27, 1866, vol. 95, Sherman Papers, Library of Congress, Washington, D.C.

82. John Pease to John Sherman, March 14, 1866, vol. 96, Sherman Papers, Library of Congress, Washington, D.C.

83. J. B. Bloss to John Sherman, reprinted in unidentified newspaper, clipping in vol. 97, Sherman Papers, Library of Congress, Washington, D.C.

84. A. Stone Jr. to John Sherman, April 1, 1866, vol. 98, Sherman Papers, Library of Congress, Washington, D.C.

85. Congress, Senate, 39th Cong., 1st sess., *Congressional Globe* (February 20, 1866): pt. 1:934.

86. Congress, House, 39th Cong., 1st sess., *Congressional Globe* (February 20, 1866): pt. 1:943–48.

87. Congress, House, Representative Bingham of Ohio speaking on the "Policy of the President—Again," 39th Cong., 1st sess., *Congressional Globe* (January 9, 1866): pt. 1:156–59.

88. Congress, House, Representative Bingham of Ohio speaking for the Rights of Citizens, SB 61, 39th Cong., 1st sess., *Congressional Globe* (March 9, 1866): pt. 1:1290–92. Increasingly, scholars accept that leading Republicans intended to apply the Bill of Rights to the states through the privileges and immunities clause. Charles Fairman argues to the contrary, noting that since ratifying states had laws and constitutions inconsistent with the Bill of Rights but did not object to privileges and immunities, they apparently did not understand the Fourteenth Amendment as a threat ("Does the Fourteenth Amendment Incorporate the Bill of Rights?"). Earl Maltz points out that incorporation was one intent of the Fourteenth Amendment, not the sole or primary goal, a point, he argues, that weakens Fairman's argument (*Civil Rights, the Constitution, and Congress,* 107–9).

89. Congress, House, Representative Delano of Ohio speaking on the Rights of Citizens, S. no. 61, 39th Cong., 1st sess., *Congressional Globe* (March 8, 1866): pt. 5, app. 157.

90. Congress, House, Representative Bingham of Ohio speaking for the Rights of Citizens, HR 63, 39th Cong., 1st sess., *Congressional Globe* (February 26, 1866): pt. 1:1033.

91. Congress, House, Representative Bingham of Ohio speaking for Civil Rights, HR 63, 39th Cong., 1st sess., *Congressional Globe* (February 26, 1866): pt. 2:1034.

92. Congress, House, Representative Bingham of Ohio speaking for Rights of Citizens, HR 63, 39th Cong., 1st sess., *Congressional Globe* (February 28, 1866): pt. 2:1088–89.

93. Congress, House, Representative Price of Iowa speaking on Rights of Citizens, 39th Cong., 1st sess., *Congressional Globe* (February 27, 1866): pt. 2:1066–67.

94. Congress, House, 39th Cong., 1st sess., *Congressional Globe* (March 13, 1866): pt. 2:1366–67.

95. Willard Warner to John Sherman, March 28, 1866, vol. 97, Sherman Papers, Library of Congress, Washington, D.C.

96. A. Stone Jr. to John Sherman, April 1, 1866, vol. 98, Sherman Papers, Library of Congress, Washington, D.C.

97. Unidentified clipping enclosed in Willard Warner to John Sherman, March 28, 1866, vol. 97, Sherman Papers, Library of Congress, Washington, D.C.

98. Barry, "Charleston Riot and Its Aftermath"; Parkinson, "Bloody Spring"; *Philadelphia North American and United States Gazette*, November 8, 1866.

99. Frankel, "Predicament of Racial Knowledge"; Frankel, *States of Inquiry*, 204–33; Owen, "Political Results from the Varioloid"; Owen, *Wrong of Slavery*, 133–92, 203–8, 204 (quotation), 222–25.

100. Owen, "Political Results from the Varioloid," 662.

101. Kendrick, *Journal of the Joint Committee*, 60–61.

102. Ibid., 61.

103. Congress, House, Representative Rogers of New Jersey speaking on Rights of Citizens, HR 63, 39th Cong., 1st sess., *Congressional Globe* (February 26, 1866): pt. 5, app. 135–6.

104. Congress, House, 39th Cong., 1st sess., *Congressional Globe* (February 26, 1866): pt. 2:1034.

105. Congress, House, 39th Cong., 1st sess., *Congressional Globe* (February 28, 1866): pt. 2:1095.

106. Kendrick, *Journal of the Joint Committee*, 82–88, 97, 100–106.

107. Congress, House, Representative Stevens of Pennsylvania speaking on Reconstruction, HR 127, 39th Cong., 1st sess., *Congressional Globe* (April 30, 1866): pt. 3:2286.

108. Whittington, *Political Foundations of Judicial Supremacy*, xi, 15–16, 31–38.

109. Congress, House, Representative Rogers of Kentucky on Rights of Citizens, SB 61, 39th Cong., 1st sess., *Congressional Globe* (March 1, 1866): pt. 2:1122.

110. Congress, House, Representative Thornton of Illinois on Rights of Citizens, SB 61, 39th Cong., 1st sess., *Congressional Globe* (March 2, 1866): pt. 2:1157.

111. Congress, House, Representative Phelps of Maryland speaking on Reconstruction, HR 127, 39th Cong., 1st sess., *Congressional Globe* (May 5, 1866): pt. 3:2394–98.

112. Congress, House, Representative Rogers of New Jersey, speaking on Reconstruction, 39th Cong., 1st sess., *Congressional Globe* (May 10, 1866): pt. 3:2538.

113. Ibid. Maltz makes this point; see his *Civil Rights, the Constitution, and Congress*, 107–9.

114. Congress, House, Representative Wilson of Iowa on Rights of Citizens, SB 61, 39th Cong., 1st sess., *Congressional Globe* (March 1, 1866): pt. 2:1115–19.

115. Congress, House, Representative Windom of Minnesota speaking on Rights of Citizens, SB 61, 39th Cong., 1st sess., *Congressional Globe* (March 1, 1866): pt. 2:1159.

116. Congress, House, 39th Cong., 1st sess., *Congressional Globe* (May 10, 1866): pt. 3:2398.

117. Congress, Senate, Senator Howard of Michigan speaking on Reconstruction, HR 127, 39th Cong., 1st sess., *Congressional Globe* (May 23, 1866): pt. 3:2765.

118. Congress, House, Representative Bingham speaking on the "Policy of the President—Again," 39th Cong., 1st Sess., *Congressional Globe* (January 9, 1866): pt. 1:158.

119. Foner, *Reconstruction*, 267; Benedict, *Compromise of Principle*, 208–9.

120. Dubin, *United States Congressional Elections*, 204–7; Harrison and Klotter, *New History of Kentucky*, 241.

121. House, Representative Brandegee speaking on Government of Insurrectionary States, HR 1143, 39th Cong., 2d sess., *Congressional Globe* (February 7, 1867): pt. 2:1076.

122. Congress, House, Representative Raymond speaking on Government of Insurrectionary States, HR 1143, 39th Cong., 2d sess., *Congressional Globe* (February 9, 1867): pt. 2:1122.

123. Congress, Senate, Senator Doolittle speaking on Government of Insurrectionary States, HR 1143, 39th Cong., 2d sess., *Congressional Globe* (February 16, 1867): pt. 2:1440–43; Howe to Grace T. Howe, January 22, 1869, Timothy O. Howe Papers, Wisconsin Historical Society. Madison Howe believed that Doolittle sided with the president in hopes of getting a seat on the Supreme Court (undated letter fragment, Howe Papers). For Howe and slavery, see Howe to Horace Rublee, April 5, 1857, Howe Papers.

124. Congress, House, 39th Cong., 2d sess., *Congressional Globe* (February 8, 1867): pt. 2:1101.

125. Congress, House, Representative Raymond speaking on Government of Insurrectionary States, HR 1143, 39th Cong., 2d sess., *Congressional Globe* (February 8, 1867): pt. 2:1101; Joseph P. Bradley to William B. Woods, January 3, 1871, box 3; Bradley to Frederick Frelinghuysen, July 19, 1874, box 18, both in Bradley Papers, New Jersey Historical Society, Newark, hereafter cited as Bradley Papers.

FOUR.   Privileges and Immunities in the Supreme Court

1. *Vicksburg Evening Post*, August 9, 1895.

2. Wyatt-Brown, *Southern Honor*, 7.

3. *Vicksburg Evening Post*, August 13, 1895.

4. Ibid., August 12, 1895.

5. *Biographical and Historical Memoirs of Mississippi*, 1:486. Catchings's knowledge of the law was such that in 1906 he helped compile and annotate the Mississippi code. Whitfield, Catchings, and Hardy, *Mississippi Code of 1906*.

6. *Jackson Clarion-Ledger*, August 12, 1895.

7. *Vicksburg Evening Post*, November 14, 1895.

8. *Jackson Clarion-Ledger*, August 16, 1895.

9. Whittington, *Constitutional Interpretation*, 1–16.

10. E. McPherson, *Political History of the United States*, 317, 319, 323, 324.

11. *Flake's Bulletin*, quoted in *Washington Daily National Intelligencer*, May 10, 1867; Richter, *Army in Texas during Reconstruction*, 98–102; Moneyhon, *Republicanism in Reconstruction Texas*, 67–69; E. McPherson, *Political History of the United States*, 324.

12. Harris, *Day of the Carpetbagger*, 1.

13. E. O. C. Ord to O. O. Howard, February 22, 1867, Outgoing Letters, 1866–1867, box 1, CB 479, Edward Otho Cresap Ord Collection, Bancroft Library, University of California, Berkeley; Waldrep, *Roots of Disorder*, 130–34; for the text of the Reconstruction Act, see *An Act to Provide for the More Efficient Government of the Rebel States*, Statutes at Large of U.S.A. 14 (1867), c. 153, 428.

14. Ord to Howard, February 22, 1867.

15. *An Act to Authorize the Issue of United States Notes, and for the Redemption or Funding Thereof, and for Funding the Floating Debt of the United States*, Statutes at Large, vol. 12, 345 (1862), c. 33, 345; *An Act to Provide Ways and Means for the Support of the Government*, Statutes at Large, vol. 12, 710 (1863), c. 73, 710; Niven, *Salmon P. Chase*, 297–99.

16. *An Act to Provide a National Currency, Secured by a Pledge of the United States Stocks, and to Provide for the Circulation and Redemption Thereof*, Statutes at Large of U.S.A. 12 (1862), sec. 57, 680. Amos Akerman testimony, April 24, 1876, in Congress, House, Committee on Expenditures in the Department of Justice, *Disbursements under the Registration Act*, 44th Cong., 1st sess., 1876, H. Rep. 800, 62–74; Jeffreys-Jones, *FBI*,

17–38; Davis, "Craftiest of Men," 111–26; Johnson, *Illegal Tender*, 65–90. For local resistance to using photographs as an investigative technique, see Charles E. Anchisi to Major Elmer Washburn, September 15, 1875, Daily Reports of U.S. Secret Service Agents, 1875–1936, RG 87, microfilm roll 13, T915, National Archives, College Park, Maryland. For the murder investigation, see Anchisi to Washburn, July 19, 1875, ibid.

17. Congress, House, Representative Dawson of Pennsylvania speaking on the Freedmen's Bureau, SB 60, 39th Cong., 1st sess., *Congressional Globe* (January 31, 1866): pt. 1:539.

18. Benedict, *Preserving the Constitution*, 133–37.

19. Brief for Defendant in Error, *Susan P. Hepburn. et al., Plaintiffs in Error v. Henry A. Griswold*, no. 241, Supreme Court of the United States.

20. *McCulloch v. Maryland*, 4 Wheaton 316 (1819); Ellis, *Aggressive Nationalism*, 34–201; Killenbeck, *M'Culloch v. Maryland*, 110–83.

21. *Griswold v. Hepburn*, 63 Ky. 20 (1865) at 26. Kentucky had been a center of hostility toward *McCulloch v. Maryland* when Marshall originally wrote the decision. Ellis, *Aggressive Nationalism*, 197–201.

22. *Griswold*, 63 Ky. at 29–30.

23. *Griswold*, 63 Ky. at 27–28.

24. *Griswold*, 63 Ky. at 41.

25. *Hepburn v. Griswold*, 75 U.S. 603 (1870); Ross, *Justice of Shattered Dreams*, 177–86. In some ways, Chase's opinion had the force of history behind it. The Court spoke just two years after Michigan legal scholar Thomas McIntyre Cooley published *A Treatise on the Constitutional Limitations Which Rest upon the Legislative Power of the States of the American Union*. More concerned with state legislatures than Congress, Cooley nonetheless promoted judicial review, urging judges to seize more power for themselves by more readily declaring laws unconstitutional. The Civil War threatened to expand legislative power, and Cooley designed doctrines justifying more-vigorous judicial scrutiny of legislation. Judges, though not elected, should not shrink from covering the same ground as legislators, he wrote. To overrule the decision of a coordinate branch of government, Cooley said, should be done only with "reluctance and hesitation." Declaring a law made by the people's representatives is "a solemn act" and "a delicate one," but when legislators overreach their authority to usurp power, judges are "not at liberty to decline" the task of throwing out unconstitutional law (Cooley, *Treatise on the Constitutional Limitations*, 160–577).

26. Ross, *Justice of Shattered Dreams*, 7–157; Kens, *Justice Stephen Field*, 65–123.

27. Fairman, *Mr. Justice Miller*, 123–48, 124 (quotation).

28. Hyman and Wiecek, *Equal Justice under Law*, 362, 367.

29. Ross, *Justice of Shattered Dreams*, 107; Wildenthal, "Nationalizing the Bill of Rights." For Fairman's "classic" article on privileges and immunities, see Fairman, "Does the Fourteenth Amendment Incorporate the Bill of Rights?"

30. *Charlestown (W. Va.) Virginia Free Press*, July 16, 1835; *Washington Globe*, March 24, 1836.

31. *New York Evening Post*, August 7, 1835; "The Supreme Court of the United States: Its Justices and Jurisdiction," *United States Magazine and Democratic Review* 1 (January 1838): 143–46; Przybyszewski, *Republic according to John Marshall Harlan*, 44–72; Przybyszewski, "Judicial Conservatism and Protestant Faith."

32. Kutler, *Judicial Power and Reconstruction Politics*, 30–31.

33. Miller, *Lectures*, 16; Fairman, *Mr. Justice Miller*.

34. Newmyer, *John Marshall*, 445–58.

35. Holzer, *Lincoln-Douglas Debates*, 252.

36. Ibid.; *Dred Scott v. Sandford*, 60 U.S. 393 (1857).

37. Holzer, *Lincoln-Douglas Debates*, 262–63.

38. Miller, *Lectures*, 16, 32, 70, 86, 97, 388, 390, 394, 404, 405, 411.

39. Howe, *Touched with Fire*, 71.

40. Samuel Miller to William Pitt Ballinger, December 31, 1866, Miller Papers, Manuscript Division, Library of Congress, Washington, D.C., hereafter cited as Miller Papers.

41. Samuel Miller to William Pitt Ballinger, August 31, 1864, Miller Papers.

42. "A Plea for Justice," petition to Andrew Johnson, not dated, folder 7, box 1, Henry Pelham Holmes Bromwell Papers, Library of Congress, Washington, D.C.

43. Testimony of Augustus R. Wright, July 13, 1872, in Congress, Joint Select Committee to Inquire into the Condition of Affairs in the Late Insurrectionary States, *Georgia*, 42nd Cong., 2d sess., Rep. 41, pt. 6:113.

44. Congress, House, Representative Hill of Indiana speaking on Reconstruction, 39th Cong., 1st sess., *Congressional Globe* (March 17, 1866): pt. 2:1470.

45. Congress, House, Representative Moulton of Illinois, speaking on Reconstruction, 39th Cong., 1st sess., *Congressional Globe* (March 24, 1866): pt. 2:1617.

46. Congress, House, Representative Hart of New York, speaking on Reconstruction, 39th Cong., 1st sess., *Congressional Globe* (March 24, 1866): pt. 2:1627.

47. Ross, *Justice of Shattered Dreams*, 106–7.

48. Foner, *Reconstruction*, 190.

49. Fairman, *Mr. Justice Miller*, 123–31.

50. Samuel Miller to William Pitt Ballinger, August 31, 1865, Miller Papers.

51. Presidential Proclamation, May 29, 1865, in J. D. Richardson, *Compilation*, 6:310–12; Samuel Miller to William Pitt Ballinger, January 11, 1866, Miller Papers; "The Amnesty," *New Haven Daily Palladium*, May 30, 1865; "Exceptions to the President's Amnesty," *Montpelier, Vermont Watchman and State Journal*, June 9, 1865, p. 1; "Washington Items," *Daily Cleveland Herald*, June 14, 1865; *Washington Daily National Intelligencer*, June 16, 1865; George S. Boutwell, "Reconstruction: Its True Basis," July 4, 1865, in Boutwell, *Speeches and Papers*, 406.

52. Miller to Ballinger, January 11, 1866.

53. Ibid.

54. Ibid.

55. Ibid.

56. Samuel Miller to William Pitt Ballinger, March 4, 1866, and Miller to Ballinger, March 30, 1866, both in Miller Papers; U.S. Congress, House, Executive Document no. 31, in *Pardons by the President*, 12.

57. *Hepburn*, 75 U.S. at 638.

58. "Chief-Justice Chase and the Supreme Court," *New York Times*, March 26, 1870, p. 4. For modern views of *McCulloch v. Maryland*, see Magliocca, *Andrew Jackson and the Constitution*, 70–72; Graber, *Dred Scott*, 70–72; Killenbeck, *M'Culloch v. Maryland*, 176–83.

59. Legal Tender Act—Congress and the Supreme Court," *New York Times*, March 8, 1870, p. 4. Many newspapers marveled at Chase's reversal from the position he had taken as treasury secretary. The *Daily Cleveland Herald* could only explain Chase's "dishonesty" as resulting from "the taint of Presidential ambition." The *Herald* accused Chase

of angling for Democratic votes, though it acknowledged that Chase alone had not betrayed the Republican cause. Justice Samuel Nelson (1792–1873) and Nathan Clifford (1801–81), the *Herald* observed, "are anti-war fogies of the strictest sort" (February 8, 1870). Like the Cleveland paper, the *San Francisco Daily Evening Bulletin* suspected politics had influenced the Court. See *San Francisco Daily Evening Bulletin*, April 2, 1870.

60. Charles Francis Adams to George Frisbie Hoar, February 22, 1895, George Frisbie Hoar Papers, Massachusetts Historical Society, Boston; Hoar, *Charge against President Grant*, 45, 12.

61. Ebenezer Hoar to William Evarts, February 1864, Ebenezer Hoar Papers in Duane N. Diedrich Collection, Manuscript Division, William L. Clements Library, University of Michigan, Ann Arbor. Hereinafter cited as Hoar Papers.

62. Ebenezer Hoar to William Evarts, March 8, 1852; Hoar to Evarts, November 16, 1864, both in Hoar Papers.

63. Ebenezer Hoar to William Evarts, November 16, 1864; Hoar to Evarts, January 23, 1861, both in Hoar Papers.

64. Ebenezer Hoar to William Evarts, July 18, 1868, Hoar Papers.

65. "Texas," *Milwaukee Daily Sentinel*, June 11, 1869.

66. Hoar, "Points of the Attorney General," *Ex Parte Yerger*, in *U.S. Supreme Court Records and Briefs*; "By Telegraph," *Boston Daily Advertiser*, July 15, 1869.

67. "By Telegraph," *Boston Daily Advertiser*, July 15, 1869; *Ex Parte Yerger*, 75 U.S. 85 (1869).

68. *Worcester (Mass.) Gazette*, quoted in *Lowell (Mass.) Daily Citizen and News*, June 15, 1869. For Hoar's opinion, see "By Telegraph," *Boston Daily Advertiser*, July 13, 1869.

69. "Attorney General Hoar," *Washington Daily National Intelligencer and Washington Express*, October 30, 1869.

70. *New Orleans Times*, quoted in the *Natchez Courier*, September 8, 1869.

71. "Why Judge Hoar Was Not Confirmed," *Milwaukee Daily Sentinel*, January 10, 1870. At least one Grant biographer finds Hoar's "conservatism" distasteful but paradoxically acknowledges he was Sumner's man. McFeely seems strangely uninterested in the Supreme Court (*Grant*, 301–2, 364–65).

72. Hamilton Fish diary, June 17, 1870, Papers of Hamilton Fish, diaries, container 311, microfilm reel 1, Manuscript Division, Library of Congress, Washington, D.C.; Welch, *George Frisbie Hoar and the Half-Breed Republicans*, 38–40; *Newark Advocate*, May 22, 1869, August 20, 1869.

73. Paper Read before Lecture Association, Morristown, March 22, 1865, box 15, Bradley Papers.

74. Hoar, *Charge against President Grant*, 33.

75. Bradley's library, or a portion of it, still survives today, housed at Rutgers law library in Newark. There is also the *Catalogue of the Library of the Late Joseph P. Bradley, Justice of the Supreme Court of the United States* (New York: Bangs, 1892), in box 27, Bradley Papers. The *Catalogue* may also be incomplete, but it lists 1,700 titles and presumably includes the bulk of the collection.

76. Fredrickson, *Racism*, 52–58; Fredrickson, *Black Image in the White Mind*, 2–72; Stanton, *Leopard's Spots*, 2–101; *Catalogue of the Library of the Late Joseph P. Bradley*.

77. Stanton, *Leopard's Spots*, 92–101; Congress, House, Representative Davis of New York speaking on D.C. Suffrage, 39th Cong., 1st sess. *Congressional Globe* (January 16, 1866): pt. 1:245; Pickering, *Races of Man*.

78. *Bradwell v. The State*, 83 U.S. 130 (1874); *Civil Rights Cases*, 109 U.S. 3 (1883).

79. Lane, *Day Freedom Died*, 191–93; Bradley, *Miscellaneous Writings*, 97–102; "The Administration Meeting," *Newark Daily Advertiser*, in Bradley, *Miscellaneous Writings*, 130.

80. Joseph P. Bradley to Charles Knap, February 18, 1865, in Bradley, *Miscellaneous Writings*, 151–63.

81. Beecher, *Freedom and War*; Aughey, *Iron Furnace*.

82. Eells, *Forgotten Saint*; Eells, "Theodore Frelinghuysen"; Magliocca, *Andrew Jackson and the Constitution*, 25–26.

83. Frederick Frelinghuysen to Joseph P. Bradley, April 27, 1871, box 3, Bradley Papers.

84. Rollins, "Frederick Theodore Frelinghuysen," 20–23.

85. Joseph P. Bradley, diary, March 21, 22, 23, 1870, box 1, Bradley Papers.

86. Samuel Miller to William Pitt Ballinger, April 21, 1870, Miller Papers.

87. Miller drafted a brief arguing against charges that the Court had been "packed" by Grant to overturn the legal tender decision. *A Statement of Facts Relating to the Order of the Supreme Court of the United States for a Re-Argument of the Legal-Tender Question in April 1870* (printed for private use), box 28, Bradley Papers. Bradley's son indignantly denied that his father had been nominated to "pack" the Court and pressured historians to alter the texts of their books in favor of his position. See Woodrow Wilson to Charles Bradley, December 20, 1900, box 18, Bradley Papers.

88. *Daily Arkansas Gazette*, February 24, 1870.

89. *Charleston (S.C.) Courier*, April 21, 1870.

90. *San Francisco Daily Evening Bulletin*, April 2, 1870.

91. *New York Tribune*, quoted in *San Francisco Daily Evening Bulletin*, April 11, 1870.

92. *Nation* 10 (March 24, 1870): 188.

93. Samuel Miller to William Pitt Ballinger, February 10, 1870, Miller Papers.

94. John L. Thomas, "Romantic Reform in America, 1815–1865," *American Quarterly* 17 (Winter 1965): 656–61; Grodzins, *American Heretic*, 62–76.

95. Joseph P. Bradley, autobiography, July 14, 1872, box 26, Bradley Papers; Cayton, *Emerson's Emergence*, 45–59.

96. Emerson, *Complete Works*; Emerson, *Prose Works*; Emerson, *Culture, Behavior, Beauty*; Emerson, *Essays*; Emerson, *Representative Men*. For an example of a column of his aphorisms, see *Hawaiian Gazette*, May 5, 1866. For Emerson in the American press, thousands of times, see *19th Century U.S. Newspapers*, Gale Digital Collections, Cengage Learning, http://www.gale.cengage.com.

97. Emerson, "Introductory Lecture," December 2, 1841, in *Collected Works*, 1:167–76; Shklar, "Emerson and the Inhibitions of Democracy"; Van Cromphout, *Emerson's Ethics*, 22–23, 34–35, 53, 101; [Ralph Waldo Emerson], "Illusions," *Atlantic Monthly* 1 (November 1857): 60; Eaton, "From Inwit to Conscience"; Langland, *Piers Plowman*, Passus 4, 166–78.

98. Bradley, autobiography; Parker, "Mr. Justice Bradley," 158 (first and second quotations), 176 (third quotation).

99. Bridgman, *Concord Lectures on Philosophy*; *Catalogue of the Library of the Late Joseph P. Bradley*.

100. Sedgwick, *Atlantic Monthly*, 1–6, 31–38; [Ralph Waldo Emerson], "Illusions," *Atlantic Monthly* 1 (November 1857): 58–62; [Ralph Waldo Emerson], "Solitude and Society, *Atlantic Monthly* 1 (December 1857): 225–29; [Ralph Waldo Emerson], "Books," *Atlantic Monthly* 1 (January 1958): 343–53; [Ralph Waldo Emerson], "The President's Proclamation," *Atlantic Monthly* 10 (November 1862): 638–42; Ralph Waldo Emerson, "Boston," *Atlantic Monthly* 37 (February 1876): 195–97.

101. "The Strong Government Idea," *Atlantic Monthly* 45 (February 1880): 273–77.

102. *Catalogue of the Library of the Late Joseph P. Bradley*. Bradley owned Allibone, *A Critical Dictionary of English Literature and British and American Authors*; see in that volume 1, 557–58, which included an entry for Emerson. R. D. Richardson, *Emerson*, 522–3; Teichgraeber, "Our National Glory," 499–500; Buell, *Emerson*, 319; Gura, *American Transcendentalism*, 240–42.

103. Buell, *Emerson*, 256–59; Congress, Senate, Senator Davis of Kentucky on Suffrage in the District of Columbia, 39th Cong., 1st sess., *Congressional Globe* (January 12, 1866): pt. 1:216; Joseph P. Bradley, "Before the Citizens of Newark," July 4, 1848, box 15, Bradley Papers.

104. Joseph P. Bradley to Charley Bradley, June 4, 1876, box 4, Bradley Papers; *Catalogue of the Library of the Late Joseph P. Bradley*.

105. Crane, *Race, Citizenship, and Law*, 87–95.

106. Adelman and Aron, "From Borderlands to Borders"; Brooks, *Captives and Cousins*, 2–79.

107. Finkelman, "Foreign Law and American Constitutional Interpretation," 45.

108. *Brownsville v. Cavazos, et al.*, 4 F. Cas. 460 (1876); Finkelman, "Foreign Law and American Constitutional Interpretation"; *Dred Scott*, 60 U.S. 393; Bradley to Charley, June 4, 1876.

109. Bradley, *Miscellaneous Writings*, 246–47.

110. Joseph P. Bradley to Charley Bradley, March 1, 1880, box 4, Bradley Papers. The passage Bradley quoted appears in numerous sources. See, for example, *The Works of Lactantius*, trans. William Fletcher (Edinburgh: T. & T. Clark, 1871), 370–71. G. W. Featherstonhaugh claimed to offer the first translation into English of *The Republic of Cicero, Translated from the Latin* (New York: G. & C. Carvill, 1829).

111. Joseph P. Bradley to daughter, Carry, January 15, 1864, box 3, Bradley Papers.

112. Joseph P. Bradley to daughter, April 30, 1867, box 3, Bradley Papers.

113. *Semmes v. United States*, 91 U.S. 21 (1875).

114. Ross, *Justice of Shattered Dreams*, 198.

115. *Live-Stock Dealers & Butchers' Ass'n. v. Crescent City Live-Stock Landing & Slaughter-House Co., et al.*, case 8408, 12 F. Cas. 649 (1870); Ross, *Justice of Shattered Dreams*, 198–200.

116. *Live-Stock Dealers & Butchers' Ass'n.*, 12 F. Cas. 649.

117. Ibid.

118. Richard Busteed testimony, June 23, 1871, Congress, House, Joint Select Committee to Inquire into the Condition of Affairs in the Late Insurrectionary States, *Testimony . . . Alabama*, 42d Cong., 2d sess., 1872, 1:320–30.

119. Charles Hays testimony, June 2, 1871, Congress, House, Joint Select Committee to Inquire into the Condition of Affairs in the Late Insurrectionary States, *Testimony . . . Alabama*, 42d Cong., 2d sess., 1872, 1:12–25.

120. Trelease, *White Terror*, 271–73; Hennessey, "Political Terrorism in the Black Belt," 35–48. The *New York Times* did not cover this story.

121. Amos Akerman to J. H. Caldwell, November 10, 1871, Amos Tappan Akerman Letter Books, microfilm M1379, Manuscripts Department, Alderman Library, University of Virginia, Charlottesville, hereafter cited as Amos Tappan Akerman Letter Books; McFeely, "Amos T. Akerman."

122. Amos Akerman to Benjamin Conley, December 28, 1871, Amos Tappan Akerman Letter Books; U. S. Grant to Senate, June 16, 1870, in Grant, *Papers*, 20:174; *New York Times*, June 17, July 10, October 26, 1870.

123. Samuel B. Brown, complaint, October 28, 1870, case no. 62, *United States v. John J. Jolly, et al.*, Criminal Case Files, U.S. Circuit Court, Southern District of Alabama, Mobile Term, Records of the United States District Courts, RG 21, National Archives Southeast Region, Atlanta (NASR); John G. Pierce testimony, June 21, 1871, Congress, House, Joint Select Committee to Inquire into the Condition of Affairs in the Late Insurrectionary States, *Testimony . . . Alabama*, 42d Cong., 2d sess., 1872, 1:317.

124. Warrant and summonses for witnesses, October 29, 1870, case no. 62, *United States v. John J. Jolly, et al.*, Criminal Case Files, U.S. Circuit Court, Southern District of Alabama, Mobile Term, Records of the United States District Courts, RG 21, NASR.

125. Trelease, *White Terror*, 271–73.

126. Robert G. Hamlett, James M. Brown, William Perkins, bonds, November 14, 1870, case no. 62, *United States v. John J. Jolly, et al.*, Criminal Case Files, U.S. Circuit Court, Southern District of Alabama, Mobile Term, Records of the United States District Courts, RG 21, NASR.

127. Indictment, December 26, 1870, *United States v. John J. Jolly, et al.*, case no. 62; indictment, December 26, 1870, *United States v. John Hall, Jr., and William Pettigrew*, case no. 76; indictment, December 26, 1870, *United States v. Beverly Pierce, Joseph Elliott, and William C. Hall*, case no. 83, all in Criminal Case Files, U.S. Circuit Court, Southern District of Alabama, Mobile Term, Records of the United States District Courts, RG 21, NASR.

128. *An Act to Enforce the Right of Citizens of the United States to Vote in the Several States of this Union, and for other Purposes, Statutes at Large*, vol. 16, 140, 141 (1870).

129. Joseph P. Bradley to William Woods, January 3, 1871, box 3, Bradley Papers.

130. Blaine, *Twenty Years of Congress*, 2:407–8.

131. "Tennessee Election," *Philadelphia North American and United States Gazette*, August 4, 1870; "The Election in Tennessee," *Boston Daily Advertiser*, August 6, 1870.

132. "The North Carolina Election—The Conservatives Victorious," *Portage, Wisconsin State Register*, August 13, 1870; "Surprise and Consternation on Account of the North Carolina Election," *Daily Cleveland Herald*, August 31, 1870.

133. "The Election in Kentucky," *Newark Advocate*, August 19, 1870. Calhoun, *Conceiving a New Republic*, 24–25; Blaine, *Twenty Years of Congress*, 2:466.

134. Bradley to Woods, January 3, 1871, box 3, Bradley Papers.

135. *An Act to Enforce the Right of Citizens of the United States to Vote in the Several States of this Union, and for other Purposes, Statutes at Large*, vol. 16, 140, 141 (1870).

136. Bradley to Woods, January 3, 1871.

137. Congressional hearings investigating the Ku Klux Klan took considerable and detailed testimony on the Eutaw riot, including testimony by Congressman Charles Hays, one of the Republicans at the Eutaw rally. Hays told Congress that he did not think it safe to testify in court about what had happened. Charles Hays testimony, June 2, 1871, Congress, House, Joint Select Committee to Inquire into the Condition of Affairs in the Late Insurrectionary States, *Testimony . . . Alabama*, 42d Cong., 2d sess., 1872, 1:12–25. Willard Warner testified that one Eutaw riot case went to trial but had to be postponed because Hays would not testify. Warner testimony, June 3, 1871, House, Joint Select Committee to Inquire into the Condition of Affairs in the Late Insurrectionary States, *Testimony . . . Alabama*, 42d Cong., 2d sess., 1872, 1:37.

138. Joseph P. Bradley to William Woods, March 12, 1871, box 18, Bradley Papers.

139. Ibid. Curly brackets indicate interlineations, text inserted by the writer as an afterthought.

140. Ibid. Legal scholars have disagreed over whether the Fourteenth Amendment incorporated the Bill of Rights. In a superb summary of this scholarship, Benedict shows that the scholarly consensus has now shifted in favor of recognizing that the Fourteenth Amendment did incorporate (*Preserving the Constitution*, 222–23n46). For the death of the Alabama solicitor in Greene County, see Willard testimony, Congress, House, Joint Select Committee to Inquire into the Condition of Affairs in the Late Insurrectionary States, *Testimony . . . Alabama*, 42d Cong., 2d sess., 1872, 1:39. Willard said, "Boyd was killed while the matter was pending, and that was the end of it."

141. 26 F. Cas. 79, 81 (1871).

142. Baggett, *Scalawags*, 51.

143. Rogers, *Scalawag in Georgia*, 111.

144. Henry Farrow to Attorney General George H. Williams, September 29, 1872, Letters Received by the Department of Justice from the State of Georgia, 1871–1884, microfilm, M996, reel 1, National Archives, College Park, Maryland.

145. "The Enforcement Act," *Georgia Weekly Telegraph and Georgia Journal & Messenger*, October 29, 1872.

146. "Fuss, Feathers, and Farrow," *Savannah Republican*, quoted in ""The Georgia Press," *Macon, Georgia Weekly Telegraph and Georgia Journal & Messenger*, May 13, 1873.

147. "The State of Georgia Sent to Jail without a Hearing," *Macon, Georgia Weekly Telegraph and Georgia Journal & Messenger*, November 5, 1872.

148. Motion to Quash & Objections to Grand Jury, May 10, 1873, *United States v. Appleton P. Collins*, drawer 66, Fifth Circuit Court of the United States for the Southern District of Georgia, Records of the District Courts of the United States, RG 21, NASR.

149. *United States v. Collins, Rich v. Campbell, United States v. Gardner*, Case no. 14,837, 25 F. Cas. 545 (1873).

150. Samuel Miller to William Pitt Ballinger, January 18, 1874, Miller Papers.

151. *Slaughterhouse Cases*, 83 U.S. 36 (1873); Aynes, "Freedom," 627–86; Ross, *Justice of Shattered Dreams*, 189–210; Labbe and Lurie, *Slaughterhouse Cases*.

152. *Slaughterhouse Cases*, 83 U.S. 36 (1873) at 81–82.

153. *Slaughterhouse Cases*, 83 U.S. 36.

154. Miller, *Lectures*, 411.

155. *Slaughterhouse Cases*, 83 U.S. 36 (1873) at 111–24.

156. Joseph P. Bradley to Frederick Frelinghuysen, July 19, 1874, box 18, Bradley Papers.

157. Ibid.

158. By distinguishing what he called "private" from "individual" rights, Bradley followed Tom Paine, who had recommended a similar duality of rights. Paine, *Rights of Man*, 78–79; Foner, *Tom Paine and Revolutionary America*, 80–93.

159. Bradley to Frelinghuysen, July 19, 1874.

160. James R. Beckwith to George H. Williams, April 18, 1873, Source Chronological File, Louisiana, 1871–1874, Letters received by the Department of Justice, microfilm publication M940, reel 1, frame 604, National Archives, College Park, Maryland.

161. James R. Beckwith to George H. Williams, June 25, 1874, Source Chronological File, Louisiana, 1871–1874, Letters received by the Department of Justice, microfilm publication M940, reel 1, frame 947, National Archives, College Park, Maryland.

162. James R. Beckwith to George H. Williams, June 11, 1874, Source Chronological File, Louisiana, 1871–1874, Letters received by the Department of Justice, microfilm publication M940, reel 1, frame 933, National Archives, College Park, Maryland.

163. Beckwith to Williams, June 25, 1874.

164. Ibid.

165. *United States v. Cruikshank,. et al.*, 25 F. Cas. 707 (1874).

166. *Cruikshank,. et al.*, 25 F. Cas. at 710.

167. Joseph P. Bradley to Frederick Frelinghuysen, July 19, 1874, box 18, Bradley Papers.

168. *Cruikshank,. et al.*, 25 F. Cas. 707; Brandwein, "Judicial Abandonment of Blacks?" 356. Brandwein resurrects an argument made by Michael Les Benedict, in "Preserving Federalism," 39–79.

169. "More Blood," *Chicago Daily Inter-Ocean*, September 11, 1874.

170. "The South," *Chicago Daily Inter-Ocean*, December 30, 1974.

171. "The Enforcement Act," *Macon, Georgia Weekly Telegraph and Messenger*, July 21, 1874.

172. Joseph P. Bradley, undated note, box 18, Bradley Papers.

173. Hoar, *Charge against President Grant*, 17.

FIVE.   The Jury Cases

1. *Giles v. Harris*, 189 U.S. 475 (1903) at 488.

2. Klarman, *From Jim Crow to Civil Rights*, 36; *Vicksburg Evening Post*, April 13, July 9, 1903; December 28, 1901.

3. *Vicksburg Evening Post*, August 4, 1883. Cashman himself had changed. Though he had once served in the Confederate army, in 1883 he called secession "a foolish and futile attempt to break up the Union and establish a separate Government, the corner-stone of which should be African slavery." *Vicksburg Evening Post*, November 21, 1883.

4. *Vicksburg Evening Post*, September 8, 1883.

5. Ibid.

6. Ibid., September 26, 1884.

7. Testimony of Augustus R. Wright, July 13, 1871, in Congress, Testimony Taken by the Joint Select Committee to Inquire into the Condition of Affairs in the Late Insurrectionary States, *Georgia*, 42nd Cong., 2nd sess., Rep. 41, pt. 6, p. 121; testimony of Joshua Morris, July 18, 1871, Congress, Testimony Taken by the Joint Select Committee to Inquire into the Condition of Affairs in the Late Insurrectionary States, *Mississippi*, Rep. 41, pt. 11, p. 322; Waldrep, *Roots of Disorder*, 130–69.

8. Waldrep, *Roots of Disorder*, 130–69.

9. Joseph P. Bradley to Nicolai Grevstad, not dated, box 3, Bradley Papers.

10. Amos Akerman to William E. Walker, September 8, 1871, Amos Tappan Akerman Letter Books.

11. *Worcester Transcript*, quoted in the *Lowell (Mass.) Daily Citizen*, April 27, 1860; Congress, Representative English of Indiana in The Political Crisis, 36th Cong., 1st sess., *Congressional Globe* (May 2, 1860): app., 284–85.

12. Delaware, Massachusetts, New Hampshire.

13. *Laws of the General Assembly of the State of Pennsylvania* (Harrisburg: Henry Welsh, 1834), 357 ("sober, intelligent, and judicious persons"); *Laws of the General Assembly of the State of Pennsylvania* (Harrisburg: Singerly and Myers, 1867), 62 (the new law).

14. R. S. Alexander, *North Carolina Faces the Freedmen*, 124–51. For the military orders, see *Washington Daily National Intelligencer*, June 5, 1867; for Gilliam's ruling, see

Raleigh Register, August 27, 1867; for Fowle's decision, see *Raleigh Register*, August 30, 1867; Hamilton, *Reconstruction in North Carolina*, 221–34. Hamilton was a student of William A. Dunning, and his work reflects all the biases of the Dunning school. It must be used with great caution.

15. *Journal of the Constitutional Convention of the State of North-Carolina*, 233, 235–38.

16. T. B. Alexander, *Political Reconstruction in Tennessee*, 79–198; Patton, *Unionism and Reconstruction in Tennessee*, 103–69. Both of these books reflect the biases of their times and should be used only with considerable caution.

17. In contrast to many other states, Louisiana has an excellent, up-to-date study of Reconstruction. See Tunnell, *Crucible of Reconstruction*, 153–56.

18. Kentucky Gen. Stat. (1873) c. 62, art. 3, sec. 2; West Virginia Acts, March 12, 1873, c. 47; Wagner's Missouri Stats., 1:797; Virginia Acts, February 3, 1871, c. 57; Tennessee Acts, January 31, 1868, c. 31; Louisiana Acts, September 29, 1868, no. 110; South Carolina Acts, March 23, 1869, no. 155; Simkins and Woody, *South Carolina during Reconstruction*, 120–22.

19. *Account of the Proceedings*, 36–39.

20. *New York Times*, January 21, 24, 1874; *Boston Daily Advertiser*, January 20, 22, 1874; *Galveston News*, January 22, 1874; *San Francisco Bulletin*, January 20, 1874.

21. *Macon, Georgia Weekly Telegraph*, January 27, 1874.

22. *Toledo Blade*, quoted in *Little Rock Daily Republican*, February 19, 1874; *New York Times*, January 22, 1874.

23. *Edwards v. Elliott*, 88 U.S. 532 (1874); Bogen, "Slaughter-House Five," 355–56.

24. Congress, House, Representative Conger of Michigan speaking "In relation to the Qualifications of Jurors in Courts of the United States," HR 3499, 43d Cong., 1st sess., *Congressional Record* (May 27, 1874): 2:4299; "Educated Jurors," *Galveston News*, June 17, 1874.

25. Congress, House, Representative Blount of Georgia, speaking on Civil Rights, 43d Cong., 2d sess., *Congressional Record* (February 4, 1875): 3:977–78. Historians have spent decades trying to explain why northern Republicans would push through such a comprehensive civil rights act when their own states discriminated and support for Reconstruction had faded. By February 1875, some proponents of civil rights had lost their jobs and had no obvious political reason for advocating the bill. See McPherson, "Abolitionists"; Jager, "Charles Sumner"; Spackman, "American Federalism."

26. *Edwards*, 88 U.S. 532. Historians have generally criticized Waite for his deference to the states. Stephenson, "Waite Court"; Robert Kaczorowski accuses Waite of leapfrogging back in time (*Politics of Judicial Interpretation*, 214); Lou Falkner Williams says that Waite sacrificed his good sense (*Great Ku Klux Klan Trials*, 138–40). Worse, for Waite's reputation, are the efforts to defend him by early historians of the Dunning school, who opposed Reconstruction. Dunning himself credited Waite with removing the chief supports for Reconstruction (*Reconstruction*, 263–64); Charles Warren congratulates Waite for demolishing Radical Reconstruction (*Supreme Court in United States History*, 3:324); Bruce Trimble credits Waite with overthrowing the congressional plan of reconstruction within seven years of the Fourteenth Amendment's ratification (*Chief Justice Waite*, 171–72). C. Peter Magrath, sees Waite as an instrument of Hayes's reconciliation plan (*Morrison R. Waite*, 153–59).

27. Congress, Senate, Senator Frelinghuysen of New Jersey speaking on Civil Rights, 43d Cong., 1st sess. *Congressional Record* (April 29, 1874): 3451–55; Joseph P. Bradley to Frederick Frelinghuysen, July 19, 1874, box 18, Bradley Papers.

28. Congress, Senate, Senator Thurman of Ohio speaking on Civil Rights, 43d Cong., 2d sess., *Congressional Record* (February 26, 1875): 3:1791.

29. Congress, Senate, Senator Boutwell of Massachusetts speaking on Civil Rights, 43d Cong., 2d sess., *Congressional Record* (February 26, 1875): 3:1792–93.

30. Congress, House, Representative Merrimon of North Carolina speaking on Civil Rights, 43d. Cong., 2d sess., *Congressional Record* (February 26, 1875): 3:1796.

31. Mayes, *Lucius Q. C. Lamar*, 195–228; Murphy, *L. Q. C. Lamar*, 51–131, 126 (quotation); Cate, *Lucius Q. C. Lamar*, 68–229.

32. Congress, House, Representative Hale of New York speaking on Civil Rights, 43d Cong., 2d sess., *Congressional Record* (February 4, 1875): 3:980.

33. Congress, House, Representative Lamar of Mississippi speaking on Civil Rights, 43d Cong., 2d sess., *Congressional Record* (February 4, 1875): 3:980.

34. Congress, House, Representative Roberts of New York, speaking on Civil Rights, 43d Cong., 2d sess., *Congressional Record* (February 4, 1875): 3:980.

35. *An Act to Protect All Citizens in Their Civil and Legal Rights*, 18, pt. 3, Stats. 336–37.

36. Foner, *Reconstruction*, 556; Gillette, *Retreat from Reconstruction*, 196–206.

37. Indictment, July 8, 1873, Record, *State of West Virginia v. Taylor Strauder*, folder 18, box 24, Ar1800 Supreme Court of Appeals, West Virginia State Archives, Charleston, West Virginia, archive hereafter cited as WVSA; Cresswell, "Case of Taylor Strauder."

38. Lonn, *Reconstruction in Louisiana after 1868*, 222; Ross, "Obstructing Reconstruction"; Haskins, *Pinckney Benton Stewart Pinchback*, 158–95; Tunnell, *Crucible of Reconstruction*, 153–72.

39. Brief for Plaintiff in Error, *John H. Kennard v. State of Louisiana, ex rel. Philip Hickey Morgan*, no. 272, Supreme Court of the United States, *U.S. Supreme Court Records and Briefs*.

40. *Kennard v. Louisiana ex rel. Morgan*, 92 U.S. 480 (1876).

41. Warmoth, *War, Politics, and Reconstruction*, 92.

42. *Walker v. Sauvinet*, 92 U.S. 90 (1876).

43. Magrath, *Morrison R. Waite*, 195.

44. Brief and Argument for Plaintiff in Error, *Hall v. DeCuir*, no. 294, *U.S. Supreme Court Records and Briefs*.

45. *Munn v. Illinois*, 94 U.S. 113 (1877); *Munn v. People*, 69 Ill. 80 (1873); *Mrs. Josephine DeCuir v. John G. Benson*, 27 La. Ann. 1 (1875); Lofgren, *Plessy Case*, 130; Palmore, "Not-So-Strange Career."

46. Palmore, "Not-So Strange Career," 1777–78.

47. *Munn*, 94 U.S. 113; *Hall v. DeCuir*, 95 U.S. 485 (1878); *Munn*, 69 Ill. 80; *Mrs. Josephine DeCuir v. John G. Benson*, 27 La. Ann. 1 (1875); W. C. Goudy, brief and argument, *Ira Y. Munn and George L. Scott v. People of Illinois*, October Term, 1874, *U.S. Supreme Court Records and Briefs*.

48. *Strauder v. West Virginia*, 100 U.S. 393 (1880), headnote written by Justice Strong.

49. *Acts of the Legislature of West Virginia for 1872–73*, c. 47, sec. 1, 102.

50. Motion, May 5, 1873, Record, *State of West Virginia v. Taylor Strauder*, folder 18, box 24, Ar1800 Supreme Court of Appeals, WVSA.

51. Fontaine, *Trial*; Swanberg, *Sickles the Incredible*; Ireland, "Libertine Must Die"; Ireland, "Insanity and the Unwritten Law"; Hartog, "Lawyering."

52. Notes, not dated, *State of West Virginia v. Taylor Strauder*, folder 18, box 24, Ar1800 Supreme Court of Appeals, WVSA.

53. *State v. Strauder*, 8 W. Va. 686 (1874).

54. Transcript of Record, *Taylor Strauder v. State of West Virginia*, filed May 3, 1879, no. 754, Supreme Court of the United States, *U.S. Supreme Court Records and Briefs.*

55. *State v. Strauder*, 11 W. Va. 745 (1877) at 803–4.

56. *Strauder*, 11 W. Va. at 817.

57. Campbell, *White and Black*, 291; Maddex, *Virginia Conservatives*, 194–200.

58. Melton, *Thirty-Nine Lashes—Well Laid On*, 191; Pincus, "Negroes on Juries in Post-Reconstruction Virginia"; Maddex, *Virginia Conservatives*, 23–28.

59. Petition of Prisoners for Removal, filed March 10, 1879, Transcript of Record, Ex Parte: In the Matter of the Commonwealth of Virginia, Petitioner, no. 3, Supreme Court of the United States, p. 7, *U.S. Supreme Court Records and Briefs.*

60. *An Act Further to Provide for the Collection of Duties on Imports, Statutes at Large of U.S.A.* 4, sec. 7, 634–35; *An Act to Provide Further Remedial Justice in the Courts of the United States, Statutes at Large of U.S.A.* 5, sec. 1, 539.

61. Congress, Senate, Senator Cowan speaking on Habeas Corpus, HR 238, 39th Cong., 1st sess., *Congressional Globe* (April 20, 1866): pt. 3:2056; Federman, *Body and the State*, 1–28; Duken, *Constitutional History of Habeas Corpus*, 181–211.

62. Congress, Senate, Senator Cowan speaking on Habeas Corpus, HR 238, 39th Cong., 1st sess., *Congressional Globe* (April 20, 1866): pt. 3:2056.

63. 14 Stats. 46–47; 14 Stats. 385.

64. Maddex, *Virginia Conservatives*, 14–15.

65. *Washington Daily National Intelligencer*, May 11, 1866; *Lynchburg Virginian*, October 14, 1870.

66. *Richmond Daily Dispatch*, October 25, 1878; Maddex, *Virginia Conservatives*, 189–91.

67. Naragon, "From Chattel to Citizen"; *Ex Parte Reynolds, et al.*, 20 F. Cas. 586 (1878).

68. *Richmond Daily Dispatch*, December 16, 1878.

69. Ibid., December 17, 1878.

70. Ibid., December 21, 1987.

71. Alexander Rives, Answer, Transcript of Record, Ex Parte: In the Matter of the Commonwealth of Virginia, Petitioner, no. 3, Supreme Court of the United States.

72. Brief for the Petitioner, Ex Parte, the Commonwealth of Virginia, upon Petition for a Mandamus, no. 3, Supreme Court of the United States.

73. *St. Louis Globe Democrat*, March 20, 1879.

74. Brief for Petitioners, Ex Parte, J. D. Coles and Ex Parte, the Commonwealth of Virginia, no. 3, Supreme Court of the United States, *U.S. Supreme Court Records and Briefs.*

75. *Washington Post*, April 15, 1879.

76. Ibid., May 19, 1879, October 15, 1879.

77. Kershen, "Jury Selection Act of 1879," 731–58, 743 (quotation).

78. For Devens, see Ropes, "Memoir," 1–25; for Devens's views of the Fourteenth Amendment and the Declaration, see his oration "The Battle of Bunker Hill," in Ropes, "Memoir," 120–22. *Washington Post*, October 18, 1879. For Hayes and Devens, see Calhoun, *Conceiving a New Republic*, 136–56; Wang, *Trial of Democracy*, 134–79.

79. *Boston Daily Advertiser*, September 29, 1879; *Milwaukee Daily Sentinel*, October 13, 16, 22, 1879; *San Francisco Daily Evening Bulletin*, October 16, 1879; *Washington Post*, October 18, 1879.

80. For the San Francisco city ordinance, see *Ho Ah Kow v. Matthew Nunan*, 12 F. Cas. 252 (1879); *Washington Post*, September 16, 1879.

81. For discussions of the jury cases, see Benedict, "Judicial Infamy," 53–82; Kens, *Justice Stephen Field*, 184–91; Klarman, *From Jim Crow to Civil Rights*, 39–43; Schmidt,

"Juries, Jurisdiction, and Race Discrimination"; Gillespie, "Constitution and the All-White Jury."

82. *Strauder*, 100 U.S. 303.

83. *Virginia v. Rives*, 100 U.S. 313 (1880) at 321 (quotation).

84. *Rives*, 100 U.S. at 321–22.

85. *Rives*, 100 U.S. at 322.

86. *Rives*, 100 U.S. at 322.

87. *Ex Parte Virginia*, 100 U.S. 339 (1880) at 348.

88. *Ex Parte Virginia*, 100 U.S. at 348.

89. *Boston Daily Advertiser*, March 10, 1880; *Vermont Watchman and State Journal*, March 10, 1880.

90. *New York Times*, March 8, 1880.

91. *Nation* 30 (March 25, 1880): 227–28.

92. *Washington Post*, March 2, 1880.

93. *San Francisco Daily Evening Bulletin*, March 2, 1880.

94. *St. Louis Globe-Democrat*, March 3, 1880.

95. *Milwaukee Daily Sentinel*, March 10, 1880.

96. *Rives*, 100 U.S. 313.

97. Transcript of Record, Ex-Parte: In the Matter of Albert Siebold et al., petitioners, no. 7, Supreme Court of the United States, *U.S. Supreme Court Records and Briefs*.

98. *Ex Parte Siebold*, 100 U.S. 371 (1880).

99. Frederick Frelinghuysen to Joseph P. Bradley, March 17, 1880, box 3, Bradley Papers.

100. Transcript of Record, *William Neal v. State of Delaware*, no. 865, Supreme Court of the United States, *U.S. Supreme Court Records and Briefs*.

101. The other judges were Leonard E. Wales, appointed in 1864 by William Cannon (Rep.); Edward Wooten, appointed in 1847 by William Tharp (Dem.); John W. Houston, appointed in 1855 by Peter F. Causey (American); Willard Saulsbury, chancellor, appointed in 1873 by James Ponder (Dem.). John Cochran (Dem.) appointed Comegys. Three judges made a quorum; Comegys, Wales, and Houston heard *Neal v. Delaware*. For Delaware's judicial system, see Delaware Constitution, 1831, Art. VI.

102. For Comegys's biography, see Comegys to Charles Lanman, May 15, 1858, Charles Lanman Collection, Special Collections, University of Delaware Library, Newark; for Comegys and the white man's party, see Joseph P. Comegys to Samuel Townsend, April 16, 1870, Townsend Family Papers, Special Collections, University of Delaware Library, Newark.

103. Transcript of Record, *William Neal v. State of Delaware*, no. 865, Supreme Court of the United States, *U.S. Supreme Court Records and Briefs*.

104. Przybyszewski, *Republic according to John Marshall Harlan*, 14–42; John Harlan to Melville Fuller, August 24, 1896, general correspondence, box 5, Papers of Melville Weston Fuller, Manuscript Division, Library of Congress, Washington, D.C.

105. Przybyszewski, *Republic according to John Marshall Harlan*, 43–72.

106. *Neal v. Delaware*, 103 U.S. 370 (1880).

107. *Neal*, 103 U.S. at 385–87.

108. *Neal*, 103 U.S. at 392.

109. *Neal*, 103 U.S. at 393–94.

110. *Neal*, 103 U.S. at 396.

111. *Neal*, 103 U.S. at 397.

112. *Neal*, 103 U.S. at 398–408.

113. *Neal*, 103 U.S. at 398.

114. *Bush v. The Commonwealth*, 78 Ky. 268 (1880).

115. Brief for the Defendant in Error, *John Bush v. Commonwealth of Kentucky*, no. 1130, October term, 1882, Supreme Court of the United States, p. 12, *U.S. Supreme Court Records and Briefs, 1832–1978.*

116. Ibid.

117. Ibid.

118. Brief for the Plaintiff in error, *John Bush v. Com'wealth of Kentucky*, October term, 1882, Supreme Court of the United States, page 22, *U.S. Supreme Court Records and Briefs.*

119. Best, *Principles of the Law of Evidence*, 3–5; Twining, *Rethinking Evidence.*

120. Whitman, *Origins of Reasonable Doubt*, 106, 181–93.

121. *Bush v. Kentucky*, 107 U.S. 110 (1883); *Commonwealth v. Johnson*, 78 Ky. 509 (1880).

122. Brief of Plaintiff in Error, *Joseph Hurtado v. People of the State of California*, Supreme Court of the United States, pp. 8–9, *U.S. Supreme Court Records and Briefs.*

123. Ibid., p. 28; *Murray's Lessees v. Hoboken Land and Improvement Co.*, 18 Howard 276–77 (1856); Streichler, *Justice Curtis*, 98–118.

124. Reply Brief of Plaintiff in Error, *Joseph Hurtado v. People of the State of California*, no. 1207, October term 1883, Supreme Court of the United States, pp. 2–3, *U.S. Supreme Court Records and Briefs.*

125. *Hurtado v. California*, 110 U.S. 516 (1884).

126. Melville W. Fuller, "Jefferson and Hamilton," *Dial* 4 (May 1883): 5.

127. Melville W. Fuller, "John C. Calhoun," *Dial* 3 (July 1882): 52. For a good overview of the Fuller era, see Przybyszewski, "Fuller Court."

128. *Topeka Daily Capital*, June 17, 1883, in folder 126, box 3; David Brewer, "Address to Yale Law School," June 23, 1891, folder 129; David Brewer, "Address to the New York State Bar Association," January 17, 1893, folder 132; "The Liberty of Each Individual," unidentified newspaper clipping in folder 133, all in Brewer Family Papers, Manuscript Collections, Yale University Library, New Haven, Connecticut, hereafter cited as Brewer Family Papers.

129. David J. Brewer, "The Jury," folder 148, box 3, Brewer Family Papers.

130. David J. Brewer, untitled speech, n.d., folder 197, box 5, Brewer Family Papers.

131. David J. Brewer, untitled speech, n.d., folder 198, box 5, Brewer Family Papers.

132. David J. Brewer, "Jubilee Address" to the American Missionary Association, October 21, 1896, folder 137, box 3, Brewer Family Papers.

133. "Public Opinion," *Yale Literary Magazine* 21 (July 1856): 23–24. Brewer cut the article out of the magazine and placed it in a file of his own writings.

134. When New York wanted to execute prisoners through the unprecedented means of shooting electricity through their bodies, Fuller approved, saying, "The Fourteenth Amendment did not radically change the whole theory of the relations of the state and Federal governments to each other," in re *Kemmler*, 136 U.S. 436 (1890). When Utah convicted Charles L. Maxwell with an eight-man jury instead of the traditional twelve, Fuller and his brethren had no more concern than the Waite Court had when California dispensed with the necessity of grand juries altogether. *Maxwell v. Dow*, 177 U.S. 442 (1900); Cortner, *Supreme Court*, 12–29. Fuller's Court, and Fuller personally, nonetheless confirmed that the Fourteenth Amendment did not allow the states to arbitrarily deny due process in the administration of criminal justice. In re *Coverse*, 137 U.S. 624

(1891); *Caldwell v. Texas*, 137 U.S. 692 (1891); *Leeper v. Texas*, 139 U.S. 462 (1891); *Hallinger v. Davis*, 146 U.S. 314 (1892); Ely, *Chief Justiceship of Melville W. Fuller*; King, *Melville Weston Fuller*.

135. Cornelius J. Jones, Brief of Petitioner in the Matter of *Ex Parte John Gibson*; Cornelius J. Jones telegram to Edward W. White, April 10, 1897, both in Supreme Court of the United States, Miscellany, box 16, Papers of Melville Weston Fuller, Manuscript Division, Library of Congress, Washington, D.C..

136. *Gibson v. Mississippi*, 162 U.S. 565 (1896). For the sometimes troubled history of Mississippi's judiciary and its relationship to the federal authority throughout the nineteenth century, see Lang, *Defender of the Faith*. For the problem more generally, see Huebner, *Southern Judicial Tradition*. For arguments that the federal government brought law and order to the South, see Miller, *Revenuers and Moonshiners*; Cresswell, *Mormons, Cowboys, Moonshiners, and Klansmen*, 1–78, 133–80.

137. *Smith v. Mississippi*, 162 U.S. 592 (1896); Brief of Plaintiff in Error, October Term 1895, *Charley Smith v. State of Mississippi*, Supreme Court of the United States, *U.S. Supreme Court Records and Briefs*.

138. *Williams v. Mississippi*, 170 U.S. 213 (1898).

139. 14 Stat. 885; Kutler, *Judicial Power and Reconstruction Politics*, 102–3; Joseph P. Bradley, habeas corpus notes, not dated, box 3, Bradley Papers; Cho, "Transformation of the American Legal Mind"; Wiecek, "Great Writ and Reconstruction."

140. In *re Wood, Petitioner*, 140 U.S. 278 (1891).

141. C. P. Barrett to John M. Harlan, August 15, 1896; John M. Harlan to Melville Fuller, August 17, 1896; John M. Harlan to C. P. Barrett, August 24, 1896, all in general correspondence, box 5, Papers of Melville Weston Fuller, Manuscript Division, Library of Congress, Washington, D.C.

142. *Galveston Daily News*, November 25, 26, 27, 1897; March 18, 19, 1898.

143. *Perry Cavitt v. State*, 15 Tex. Ct. App. 190 (1883) quotation at 197.

144. *Perry Cavitt*, 15 Tex. Ct. App. at 198.

145. Article 661 of the Code of Criminal Procedure.

146. Article 662 of the Code of Criminal Procedure.

147. *Gus Williams v. State*, 44 Tex. 34 (1875).

148. *Seth Carter v. State*, 39 Tex. Crim. 345 (1898) at 348; *Galveston Daily News*, March 19, 1898.

149. *Seth Carter*, 39 Tex. at 352.

150. C. L. Maxwell by J. W. N. Whitecotton, his attorney, Petition for Writ of Habeas Corpus, *Charles L. Maxwell v. George N. Dow*, no. 384, October Term 1899, Supreme Court of the United States, *U.S. Supreme Court Records and Briefs*.

151. *Maxwell v. Dow*, 176 U.S. 581 (1900).

152. Nancy Cohen, *The Reconstruction of American Liberalism, 1865–1914* (Chapel Hill: University of North Carolina Press, 2002); H. C. Richardson, *Death of Reconstruction*; Paul, *Conservative Crisis*, 20–21.

153. *Julliard v. Greenman*, 110 U.S. 421 (1884); *Fong Yue Ting v. United States*, 149 U.S. 698 (1893); *United States v. Kim Wong Ark*, 169 U.S. 649 (1898). For doubts about Gray's commitment to nationalism, see Davis and Davis, "Mr. Justice Horace Gray," 421–24, 468–71.

154. *Capital Traction Company v. Hof*, 174 U.S. 1 (1899) at 7–8.

155. *Carter v. Texas*, 177 U.S. 442 (1900) at 447; Davis and Davis, "Mr. Justice Horace Gray," 421–24, 468–71.

156. *Carter*, 177 U.S. at 443–49.

SIX.   Getting Blacks on Mississippi Juries

1. Oshinsky, *Worse Than Slavery*, 43–53; Dabney Marshall to Miss Alice Shannon, December 27, 1898, Crutcher-Shannon Family Papers, MDAH. By the time Marshall went to prison, Mississippi had outlawed convict leasing, but the practice nonetheless continued through Marshall's term.

2. Marshall to Shannon, December 27, 1898.

3. Dabney Marshall to Alice Shannon, May 7, 1896, Crutcher-Shannon Family Papers, MDAH.

4. Marshall, "Escape," 76. Interestingly, Marshall makes a point of describing his nameless protagonist-prisoner as married with children. Marshall himself never married.

5. Marshall to Shannon, May 7, 1896.

6. Dabney Marshall to Miss Alice Shannon, September 10, 1896, Crutcher-Shannon Papers, MDAH.

7. *Vicksburg Evening Post*, January 6, 1896; May 18, 1901; July 8, 1901. McLaurin had pardoned Fox and Coleman, his promise not to pardon his client apparently not extending to them. *Vicksburg Evening Post*, July 9, 1901. Sumners, *Governors of Mississippi*, 83–86.

8. *Vicksburg Evening Post*, July 31, August 2, 7, 1901.

9. *Greenville (Miss.) Daily Democrat*, February 5, 1904.

10. *Charleston (Miss.) Democratic Herald*, February 11, 1904; *Memphis Commercial Appeal*, February 4, 1904.

11. *Memphis Commercial Appeal*, February 4, 5, 1904.

12. Ibid., February 8, 1904. Luther Holbert married Annie Lee Ward on February 5, 1886. Scott County Marriages, Index to Marriage Records (Blacks), 1865–83. Annie Holbert was still alive in 1910. 1910 Population Census Schedule, Scott County, Mississippi. Luther Holbert's female companion was not his wife.

13. Holmes, *White Chief*, 58, 88, 132–33; *Greenwood (Miss.) Commonwealth*, February 13, 1904.

14. *Greenwood (Miss.) Commonwealth*, February 13, 1904.

15. Ibid.

16. *Vicksburg Evening Post*, February 13, 1904.

17. Holmes, *White Chief*, 34–39; McCormick, "Discovery That Business Corrupts Politics"; I. C. Mollison, "Negro Lawyers in Mississippi." Mollison's article is a virtual oral history with his father, Willis Mollison.

18. Gaines, *Uplifting the Race*, 6–9, 14.

19. Williamson, *Crucible of Race*, 140–79; Gaines, *Uplifting the Race*, 67–99; Muller, "Look Back without Anger," 325–38; Shklar, *Redeeming American Political Thought*, 104; Dunning, *Essays on the Civil War*; Dunning, *Reconstruction*; Abraham Lincoln, Gettysburg Address, in *Collected Works*, 7:18–19.

20. Du Bois, *Souls of Black Folk*, 2–3; Gaines, *Uplifting the Race*, 6–9, 14.

21. McCormick, *Party Period and Public Policy*, 263–88.

22. Miraldi, *Muckrakers*; Mattson, "History as Hope," 22 (quotation); Noll, *Scandal of the Evangelical Mind*, 163.

23. Edward, *Angels in the Machinery*, 111–66.

24. Chambers, *Tyranny of Change*, 279–80. Basing historical analysis on late twentieth-century conservative skepticism of government—a paradigm that has captured not only self-described "conservatives" but the Left as well—also runs the risk of becoming dated. There is at least some chance that predictions by journalists such as Paul Krugman and George Packer that America's "hard right turn" is being reversed might prove accurate.

"It's a Different Country," *New York Times*, June 9, 2008; George Packer, "The Fall of Conservatism," *New Yorker*, May 26, 2008.

25. *Vicksburg Evening Post*, September 8, 1904.

26. Ibid., May 30, June 4, 17, September 9, 1904.

27. T. Dabney Marshall, "Law", *Green Bag* 20 (1908): 6–7.

28. *Vicksburg Evening Post*, April 3, 1894.

29. Ibid., March 22, 1886.

30. Marshall was mentioned in the newspapers with black clients, so we know about them. Perhaps he had many white clients who did not make the papers. Or did white clients shy away from a lawyer so publicly identified with the defense of black defendants?

31. *Vicksburg Evening Post*, March 21, 1905.

32. Ibid., February 13, 1907.

33. Ibid., February 20, 1908.

34. Ibid., June 2, 1908.

35. Ibid., February 21, April 7, 1908.

36. White, *Metahistory*, 9.

37. Waldrep, *Vicksburg's Long Shadow*, 182.

38. *Vicksburg Evening Post*, February 13, November 7, 1907.

39. Ibid., February 21, 1908.

40. *Edward Ammons v. State of Mississippi*, 80 Miss. 592 (1902).

41. *Peter, a slave v. State*, 24 Miss. 512 (1844); *Van Buren, a slave v. State*, 24 Miss. 512 (1852); *Jordan, a slave v. State*, 32 Miss. 382 (1856). These are all discussed in Waldrep, *Roots of Disorder*, 46–48.

42. Testimony of Captain William Price, *Ed Ammons v. State*, case 10340, Mississippi Supreme Court, MDAH.

43. *Edward Ammons*, 80 Miss. 592; *Brown v. Mississippi*, 297 U.S. 278 (1936); *Lynumm v. Illinois*, 372 U.S. 528 (1963); *Escobedo v. Illinois*, 378 U.S. 438 (1964); *Miranda v. Arizona*, 384 U.S. 436 (1966).

44. I. C. Mollison, "Negro Lawyers in Mississippi."

45. Several witnesses described the shooting. Adeline Davis testimony, *Joe Hill v. State of Mississippi*, case 12017, box 14359, Supreme Court of Mississippi, MDAH.

46. Chief Justice Comegys, Opinions of Court of Oyer and Terminer, *State of Delaware v. William Neal*, May Term 1880.

47. *Neal v. Delaware*, 103 U.S. 370 (1881) at 397.

48. Wellman, *Art of Cross-Examination*, 151, 13, 25–26.

49. Harris, *Hints on Advocacy*, 36–40. Harris repeatedly warns of the dangers inherent in cross-examination.

50. Best, *Principles of the Law of Evidence*, 610–11.

51. *Williams v. Mississippi*, 170 U.S. 213 (1898).

52. Testimony Taken on Motion to Quash Indictment, *Joe Hill v. State of Mississippi*, case 12017, box 14359, Supreme Court of Mississippi, MDAH.

53. Ibid.

54. Ibid.

55. Ibid.

56. Ibid.

57. W. Mollison, *Leading Afro-Americans*.

58. H. H. Coleman and Dabney Marshall, Motion for a New Trial, December 16, 1905, *Joe Hill v. State of Mississippi*, case 12017, box 14359, Supreme Court of Mississippi, MDAH.

59. Sentence of the Court, December 21, 1905, *Joe Hill v. State of Mississippi*, case 12017, box 14359, Supreme Court of Mississippi, MDAH.

60. H. H. Coleman and Dabney Marshall, Abstract of Facts and Brief, March 22, 1906, *Joe Hill v. State of Mississippi*, case 12017, box 14359, Supreme Court of Mississippi, MDAH. The published synopsis of Marshall's brief does not include this quote. *Joseph Hill v. State of Mississippi*, 89 Miss. 23 (1906).

61. *Carter v. Texas*, 177 U.S. 442 (1900). Rosenberg, *Hollow Hope*, 17.

62. *David Posey v. State of Mississippi*, 86 Miss. 141 (1905); *Elias Cain v. State of Mississippi*, 86 Miss. 505 (1905).

63. Calhoon, *Negro Suffrage*, 7–11.

64. *Journal of the Proceedings of the Constitutional Convention of the State of Mississippi*, 9–11. The convention decided not to publish transcripts of speeches delivered after Calhoon's opening address. This saved money, but it also saved creating a record for federal judges to peruse when considering whether Mississippi's new constitution violated the Fourteenth and Fifteenth Amendments. Subsequently other states, including Alabama, felt more comfortable creating full transcripts of their disfranchising conventions.

65. Skates, *History of the Mississippi Supreme Court*, 64–65.

66. *Vicksburg Evening Post*, December 20, 1906.

67. *Joseph Hill*, 89 Miss. at 25–26.

68. *Joseph Hill*, 89 Miss. at 26.

69. *Joseph Hill*, 89 Miss. 23.

70. *Vicksburg Evening Post*, January 8, May 24, 1907; December 20, 1906.

71. *George Lewis v. State of Mississippi*, 91 Miss. 505 (1907).

72. *George Lewis*, 91 Miss. at 508.

73. *George Lewis*, 91 Miss. at 507.

74. "Masterful Plea Saves Three Slayers," *Chicago Defender*, February 26, 1921, p. 1.

75. *Chicago Defender*, June 14, 1924.

76. *Vicksburg Commercial Herald*, May 11, 1884.

77. Ibid., April 4, 1884.

78. *Vicksburg Evening Post*, February 19, 1884.

79. *Vicksburg Herald*, May 2, 1888.

80. *Vicksburg Commercial Herald*, May 13, 1884; January 22, 1887; *Vicksburg Evening Post*, May 13, 1884; December 17, 1883.

81. *Vicksburg Evening Post*, May 6, 1908; May 10, 1913; December 1, 1921; April 23, 1934.

Bibliography

PUBLISHED PRIMARY SOURCES

An Account of the Proceedings on the Trial of Susan B. Anthony on the Charge of Illegal Voting at the Presidential Election in November 1872. Rochester, N.Y.: Daily Democrat & Chronicle Book Print, 1874.

Adams, John. *The Adams Papers: Legal Papers of John Adams.* Edited by L. H. Butterfield. New York: Atheneum, 1968.

Adams, John Quincy. *Address of John Quincy Adams to His Constituents of the Twelfth Congressional District, at Braintree, September 17, 1842.* Boston, 1842.

Allibone, S. Austin. *A Critical Dictionary of English Literature and British and American Authors.* 3 vols. Philadelphia: Lippincott, 1859–71.

Alvord, James C. "Trial by Jury, in Questions of Personal Freedom." *American Jurist and Law Magazine* 17 (April 1837): 94–113.

Ames, Herman V., ed. *State Documents on Foreign Relations: The States and the United States.* Philadelphia: University of Pennsylvania, 1904.

Aughey, John H. *The Iron Furnace; or, Slavery and Secession.* Philadelphia: William S. and Alfred Martien, 1863.

Barton, William. "An American." *Observations on the Trial by Jury with Miscellaneous Remarks concerning Legislation and Jurisprudence.* Strasburg, Pa.: Brown & Bowman, 1803.

Beecher, Henry Ward. *Freedom and War: Discourses on Topics Suggested by the Times.* Boston: Ticknor & Fields, 1863.

Best, W. M. *The Principles of the Law of Evidence.* 8th ed. Boston: Boston Book Co., 1893.

"Biographical Sketch of James C. Alvord." *American Jurist and Law Magazine* 4 (January 1840): 373–81.

Birney, James G. *Letter on Colonization Addressed to the Rev. Thornton J. Mills.* New York: Office of the Antislavery Reporter, 1834.

Blaine, James G. *Twenty Years of Congress: From Lincoln to Garfield.* Norwich, Conn.: Henry Bill, 1886.

Boston Slave Riot, and Trial of Anthony Burns. Boston: Ferriage, 1854.

Boutwell, George S. *Speeches and Papers relating to the Rebellion and the Overthrow of Slavery.* Boston: Little Brown, 1867.

Bradley, Charles, ed., *Miscellaneous Writings of the Late Hon. Joseph P. Bradley.* Newark, N.J.: Hardham, 1902.

Brayley, Edward Wedlake, James Norris Brewer, and Joseph Nightingale. *A Topographical and Historical Description of London and Middlesex.* London: Sherwood, Neely & Jones, 1810.

Bridgman, Raymond L., ed. *Concord Lectures on Philosophy.* Cambridge, Mass.: Moses King, 1883.

Browne, J. Ross. *Report of the Debates in the Convention of California on the Formation of the State Constitution in September and October, 1849.* Washington, D.C.: John T. Towers, 1850.

Browning, Orville Hickman. *Diary of Orville Hickman Browning.* Edited by Theodore Calvin Pease and James G. Randall. Springfield: Illinois State Historical Library, 1925–33.

Caines, George. *A Summary of the Practice of the Supreme Court of the State of New-York.* New York: Isaac Riley, 1803.

Calhoon, S. S. *Negro Suffrage.* Jackson, Miss.: Commonwealth Steam Print, 1890.

Campbell, George. *White and Black: The Outcome of a Visit to the United States.* New York: R. Worthington, 1879.

[Candler, Isaac]. *A Summary View of America.* London: T. Cadell, 1824.

Carter, Nathaniel H., William L. Stone, and Marcus T. C. Gould. *Reports of the Proceedings and Debates of the Convention of 1821 Assembled for the Purpose of Amending the Constitution of the State of New-York.* Albany: E. & E. Hosford, 1821.

Chase, Salmon. *The Salmon P. Chase Papers.* Edited by John Niven. Kent, Ohio: Kent State University Press, 1997.

Chitty, Joseph. *A Practical Treatise on the Criminal Law, Comprising the Practice, Pleadings, and Evidence.* 3 vols. American ed., corrected and enlarged. Springfield, Mass.: G. and C. Merriam, 1836.

Cole, Arthur Charles, ed. *The Constitutional Debates of 1847.* Springfield: Illinois State Historical Library, 1919.

Cooley, Thomas M. *A Treatise on the Constitutional Limitations Which Rest upon the Legislative Power of the States of the American Union.* Boston: Little, Brown, 1868.

Cooper, James. *Speech of the Hon. James Cooper, in the Case of the United States v. Castner Hanway for Treason.* Philadelphia: King & Baird, 1852.

The Complete Juryman; Or, a Compendium of the Laws Relating to Jurors. London, 1752.

Devens, Charles. "The Battle of Bunker Hill." In *Charles Devens: Orations and Addresses on Various Occasions, Civil and Military,* edited by Arthur Lithgow Devens, 81–134. Boston: Little Brown, 1891.

Dorr, Thomas W. *An Address to the People of Rhode-Island from the Convention Assembled at Providence, on the 22d day of February and Again on the 12th Day of March, 1834.* Providence: Cranston & Hammond, 1834.

Dorsey, Clement, comp. *The General Public Statutory Law and Public Local Law of the State of Maryland.* 3 vols. Baltimore: John D. Toy, 1840.

Douglass, Frederick. *The Frederick Douglass Papers.* Series 1. Edited by John W. Blassingame. New Haven, Conn.: Yale University Press 1982.

Dubin, Michael J. *United States Congressional Elections, 1788–1997.* Jefferson, N.C.: McFarland, 1998.

Emerson, Ralph Waldo. *The Collected Works of Ralph Waldo Emerson.* Cambridge, Mass.: Harvard University Press, 1971.

———. *The Complete Works of Ralph Waldo Emerson.* Boston: Houghton Mifflin, 1911.

———. *The Complete Works of Ralph Waldo Emerson: Comprising His Essays, Poems, and Orations.* 2 vols. London: Bell & Daldy, 1866.

———. *Culture, Behavior, Beauty, Books, Art, Eloquence, Power, Wealth, Illusions*. Boston: Houghton, Mifflin, 1870.

———. *The Early Lectures of Ralph Waldo Emerson*. Cambridge, Mass.: Harvard University Press, 1964.

———. *Essays*. Boston: Houghton, Mifflin, 1876.

———. *Miscellanies: Embracing Nature, Addresses, and Lectures*. Boston: J. R. Osgood, 1876.

———. *The Prose Works of Ralph Waldo Emerson*. Boston: Fields, Osgood, 1869.

———. *Representative Men: Seven Lectures*. Boston: J. R. Osgood, 1876.

Farrand, Max, ed. *The Records of the Federal Convention of 1787*. New York: Yale University Press, 1937.

Finkelman, Paul, ed. *A Brief Narrative of the Case and Tryal of John Peter Zenger, Printer of the New York Weekly Journal*. St. James, N.Y.: Brandywine Press, 1997.

———, ed. *Fugitive Slaves and American Courts: The Pamphlet Literature*. New York: Garland, 1988.

Fisher, Sidney George. *A Philadelphia Perspective: The Diary of Sidney George Fisher Covering the Years 1834–1871*. Edited by Nicholas B. Wainwright. Philadelphia: Historical Society of Pennsylvania, 1967.

Fontaine, Felix G. *Trial of the Hon. Daniel E. Sickles for Shooting Philip Barton Key, Esq., U.S. District Attorney, of Washington, D.C. February 27th, 1859*. New York: R. M. De-Witt, 1859.

[Forten, James]. *Letters from a Man of Color*. Philadelphia, 1813.

Fowler, H. *Report of the Debates and Proceedings of the Convention for the Revision of the Constitution of the State of Indiana, 1850*. Indianapolis: A. H. Brown, 1850.

A Friend to the Constitution. N.p.: 1801?

Goodell, William. *Views of American Constitutional Law in Its Bearing upon American Slavery*. 2d ed. Utica, N.Y.: Lawson & Chaplin, 1845.

Graham, David. *An Essay on New Trials*. New York: Halsted & Voorhies, 1834.

Grant, Ulysses. *The Papers of Ulysses S. Grant*. Edited by John Y. Simon. Carbondale: Southern Illinois University Press, 1967–2009.

A Guide to English Juries: Setting Forth Their Antiquity, Power, and Duty. London, 1725.

Harris, Richard. *Hints on Advocacy in Civil and Criminal Courts*. 3d American ed. St. Louis: William H. Stevenson, 1884.

Hawles, John. *The Englishman's Right: A Dialogue between a Barrister at Law and Juryman*. 1680. Reprint, London, 1732.

Hoar, George F. *The Charge against President Grant and Attorney General Hoar of Packing the Supreme Court of the United States, to Secure the Reversal of the Legal Tender Decision, by the Appointment of Judges Bradley and Strong, Refuted*. Worcester, Mass.: Charles Hamilton, 1896.

Holzer, Harold, ed. *The Lincoln-Douglas Debates: The First Complete, Unexpurgated Text*. New York: HarperCollins, 1993.

The Honest Jury; or Caleb Triumphant: A New Ballad. London, 1729.

Journal of the Constitutional Convention of the State of North-Carolina at Its Session 1868. Raleigh: Joseph W. Holden, 1868.

Journal of the Proceedings of the Constitutional Convention of the State of Mississippi. Jackson: E. L. Martin, 1890.

Kendrick, Benjamin B. *The Journal of the Joint Committee of Fifteen on Reconstruction*. New York: Columbia University, 1914.

Langland, William. *William Langland's Piers Plowman, the C Version*. Translated by George Economou. Philadelphia: University of Pennsylvania Press, 1996.

Laws of the State of Maine. 2 vols. Brunswick: J. Griffin, 1821.

Laws of the State of New York Passed at the Sixty-third Session of the Legislature Begun and Held in the City of Albany. Albany: Thurlow Weed, 1840.

Lee, Richard Henry. *Observations Leading to a Fair Examination of the System of Government, 1787*. In *The Roots of the Bill of Rights*, edited by Bernard Schwartz, 1:466–73. New York: Chelsea House, 1980.

Lincoln, Abraham. *Collected Works of Abraham Lincoln*. Edited by Roy P. Basler. New Brunswick, N.J.: Rutgers University Press, 1953.

———. *The Papers of Abraham Lincoln: Legal Documents and Cases*. Edited by Daniel W. Stowell et al. 4 vols. Charlottesville: University of Virginia Press, 2008.

Madison, James. *Letters and Other Writings of James Madison, Fourth President of the United States*. New York: R. Worthington, 1884.

———. *The Papers of James Madison*. Edited by William T. Hutchinson and William M. E. Rachal. Chicago: University of Chicago Press, 1971.

Marshall, Thomas Dabney. "The Escape." In *New Stories from the Chap-Book: Being a Miscellany of Curious and Interesting Tales, Histories, &c; Newly Composed by Many Celebrated Writers and Very Delightful to Read*, 71–86. New York: Herbert S. Stone, 1898.

———. "God and the Working Man." *Quarterly Review of the M. E. Church, South* (October 1890): 133–44.

McCord, David J., ed. *The Statutes at Large of South Carolina*. Columbia: A. S. Johnston, 1840.

McPherson, Edward, comp. *The Political History of the United States of America during the Period of Reconstruction (from April 15, 1865, to July 15, 1870)*. Washington: Solomons & Chapman, 1875.

Melton, Herman. *Thirty-Nine Lashes—Well Laid On: Crime and Punishment in Southside Virginia, 1750–1950*. Privately printed, 2002.

Miller, Samuel Freeman. *Lectures on the Constitution of the United States*. New York: Banks & Brothers, 1891.

Mollison, Irvin C. "Negro Lawyers in Mississippi." *Journal of Negro History* 15 (January 1930): 38–71.

Mollison, Willis E. *The Leading Afro-Americans of Vicksburg, Miss., Their Enterprises, Churches, Schools, Lodges and Societies*. Vicksburg: Biographia, 1908.

Nicholas, Samuel Smith. "Report of the Joint Congressional Committee," June 14, 1866. In *Conservative Essays Legal and Political*, 4 vols., 3:21–34. Philadelphia: J. B. Lippincott, 1863–69.

Owen, Robert Dale. "Political Results from the Varioloid." *Atlantic Monthly* 35 (June 1875): 660–70.

———. *The Wrong of Slavery, the Right of Emancipation*. Philadelphia: J. B. Lippincott, 1864.

Paine, Thomas. *The Rights of Man*. In *Thomas Paine: Political Writings*, edited by Bruce Kuklick, 49–203. Cambridge: Cambridge University Press, 1989.

The People's Ancient and Just Liberties Asserted, in the Trial of William Penn & William Mead. Sheffield, England: Constitutional Society, 1794.

The Perpetual Laws of the Commonwealth of Massachusetts, from the Establishment of Its Constitution to the First Session of the General Court, AD 1788. Worcester: Isaiah Thomas, 1788.

Pickering, Charles. *The Races of Man; and Their Geographical Distribution*. London: H. G. Bohn, 1854.

Pole, J. R., ed. *The Federalist*. Indianapolis: Hackett, 2005.

Proceedings and Debates of the Virginia State Convention of 1829–30. Richmond, 1830.

Proceedings of the Maryland State Convention to Frame a New Constitution, Commenced at Annapolis, November 4, 1850. Annapolis: Riley & Davis, 1850.

Remarks of Henry B. Stanton, in the Representatives Hall on the 23d and 24th of February, 1837. Boston: Isaac Knapp, 1837.

Report of the Proceedings and Debates in the Convention to Revise the Constitution of the State of Michigan, 1850. Lansing: F. W. Ingals, 1850.

Report of the Trial of Thomas Wilson Dorr for Treason. Providence, R.I.: Tappen & Dennet, 1844.

Resolutions of the General Assembly of South Carolina in relation to the controversy between the States of New York and Virginia, on the subject of surrendering fugitives from justice, February 7, 1842. Printed in 27th Congress, 2d sess., 1842, S. Rep. 96, p. 2.

Revised Statutes of the State of Maine, Passed April 17, 1857. Bangor: Wheeler & Lynde, 1857.

The Revised Statutes of the State of New York. Albany: Packard & Van Benthuysen, 1829.

Richardson, James D. ed. *A Compilation of the Messages and Papers of the Presidents, 1789–1897*. Washington, D.C.: U.S. Government Printing Office, 1897.

Ropes, John Codman. "Memoir." In *Charles Devens: Orations and Addresses on Various Occasions, Civil and Military*, edited by Arthur Lithgow Devens, 1–26. Boston: Little Brown, 1891.

Scudder, Fayssoux. "History of Mississippi Flag." In *Minutes of the Twenty-eighth Annual Convention, United Daughters of the Confederacy, Mississippi Division*, 75–76. Vicksburg, 1924.

Smith, J. V. *Report of the Debates and Proceedings of the Convention for the Revision of the Constitution of the State of Ohio, 1850–51*. Columbus: S. Medary, 1851.

Spooner, Lysander. *An Essay on the Trial by Jury*. Boston: John P. Jewett, 1852.

Stanton, Henry B. "Ultraists—Conservatives—Reformers." In *Address by Henry B. Stanton and Poem by Alfred B. Street Pronounced before the Literary Societies*. Utica, N.Y.: Roberts & Sherman, 1850.

Starling, Samuel. *An Answer to the Seditious and Scandalous Pamphlet, Entitled the Tryal of W. Penn and W. Mead, at the Sessions Held at the Old Baily, London, the 1, 3, 4, 5, of Sept. 1670*. London: W. G., 1671.

Stewart, Alvan. *A Legal Argument before the Supreme Court of the State of New Jersey, at the May Term, 1845, at Trenton, for the Deliverance of 4,000 Persons from Bondage*. New York: Finch & Weed, 1845.

Storing, Herbert, ed. *The Complete Anti-Federalist*. Chicago: University of Chicago Press, 1981.

Tucker, Henry St. George. *Commentaries on the Laws of Virginia*. 2 vols. Winchester: Winchester Virginian, 1831.

———. *A Few Lectures on Natural Law*. Charlottesville, Va.: James Alexander, 1844.

U.S. Congress. House. *Pardons by the President, Message from the President of the United States in Answer to a Resolution of the House of 10th December Transmitting Names of Persons Pardons by the President Who Have Engaged in Rebellion*. 39th Cong., 2d sess., H. Doc. 31, serial 1289.

U.S. Supreme Court Records and Briefs, 1832–1978. Gale Digital Collections, Cengage Learning, http://www.gale.cengage.com.

Warmoth, Henry Clay. *War, Politics, and Reconstruction: Stormy Days in Louisiana.* New York: Macmillan, 1930.

Webster, Daniel. *The Papers of Daniel Webster.* Edited by Charles M. Wiltse and Michael J. Birkner. Hanover, N.H.: University Press of New England, 1986.

———. *The Writings and Speeches of Daniel Webster.* Boston: Little Brown, 1903.

Welch, Richard E., Jr. *George Frisbie Hoar and the Half-Breed Republicans.* Cambridge, Mass.: Harvard University Press, 1971.

Wellman, Francis L. *The Art of Cross-Examination.* 1903. Reprint, New York: Macmillan, 1913.

Whitfield, A. H., T. C. Catchings, and W. H. Hardy. *The Mississippi Code of 1906 of the Public Statute Laws of the State of Mississippi.* Nashville, Tenn.: Brandon Printing, 1906.

Wilson, James. "Of Juries." In *Collected Works of James Wilson,* edited by Kermit Hall and Mark David Hall, 2:954–1011. Indianapolis: Liberty Fund, 2007.

Yates, William. *Rights of Colored Men to Suffrage, Citizenship and Trial by Jury.* Philadelphia: Merrihew & Gunn, 1838.

SECONDARY SOURCES

Adelman, Jeremy, and Stephen Aron. "From Borderlands to Borders: Empires, Nation-States, and the Peoples in between North American History." *American Historical Review* 104 (June 1999): 814–41.

Alexander, Roberta Sue. *North Carolina Faces the Freedmen: Race Relations during Presidential Reconstruction, 1865–67.* Durham, N.C.: Duke University Press, 1985.

Alexander, Thomas B. *Political Reconstruction in Tennessee.* Nashville, Tenn.: Vanderbilt University Press, 1950.

Allen, Austin. *Origins of the Dred Scott Case: Jacksonian Jurisprudence and the Supreme Court, 1837–1857.* Athens: University of Georgia Press, 2006.

Alschuler, Albert W., and Andrew G. Deiss. "A Brief History of the Criminal Jury in the United States." *University of Chicago Law Review* (Summer 1994): 867–928.

Amar, Vikram David. "Jury Service as Political Participation akin to Voting." *Cornell Law Review* 80 (January 1995): 203–58.

Aynes, Richard L. "Freedom: Constitutional Law; Constricting the Law of Freedom; Justice Miller, the Fourteenth Amendment, and the Slaughterhouse Cases." *Chicago-Kent Law Review* 70 (1994): 627–86.

Baggett, James Alex. *The Scalawags: Southern Dissenters in the Civil War and Reconstruction.* Baton Rouge: Louisiana State University Press, 2003.

Bailey, T. J. *Prohibition in Mississippi, or, Anti-Liquor Legislation from Territorial Days with Its Results in the Counties.* Jackson, Miss.: Hederman Bros., 1917.

Bailyn, Bernard. *The Ideological Origins of the American Revolution.* Cambridge, Mass.: Harvard University Press, 1967.

Baker, J. H. *An Introduction to English Legal History.* 3d ed. London: Butterworths, 1990.

Barney, William L. *The Secessionist Impulse: Alabama and Mississippi in 1860.* Princeton, N.J.: Princeton University Press, 1974.

Barry, Peter. "The Charleston Riot and Its Aftermath: Civil, Military, and Presidential Responses." *Journal of Illinois History* 7 (2004): 82–106.

Beattie, J. M. "London Juries in the 1690s." In Cockburn and Green, *Twelve Good Men and True,* 214–53.

Benedict, Michael Les. *A Compromise of Principle: Congressional Republicans and Reconstruction, 1863–1869.* New York: Norton, 1974.

———. "James Ashley: Toledo Politics and the Thirteenth Amendment." *University of Toledo Law Review* 38 (2007): 814–37.

———. "'Judicial Infamy': The Black Testimony Cases." In *Virginia and the Constitution*, edited by A. E. Dick Howard and Melvin I. Urofsky, 60–61. Charlottesville: Virginia Commission on the Bicentennial of the United States Constitution, 1992.

———. "Preserving Federalism: Reconstruction and the Waite Court." *Supreme Court Review* (1978): 39–79.

———. *Preserving the Constitution: Essays on Politics and the Constitution in the Reconstruction Era*. New York: Fordham University Press, 2006.

Biographical and Historical Memoirs of Mississippi. 2 vols. Chicago: Goodspeed, 1891.

Blight, David. *Frederick Douglass' Civil War: Keeping Faith in Jubilee*. Baton Rouge: Louisiana State University Press, 1989.

———. *Race and Reunion: The Civil War in American Memory*. Cambridge, Mass.: Harvard University Press, 2001.

Blinka, Daniel. "'This Germ of Rottedness': Federal Trials in the New Republic, 1789–1807." *Creighton Law Review* 36 (February 2003): 135–89.

Blue, Frederick J. *Salmon P. Chase: A Life in Politics*. Kent, Ohio: Kent State University Press, 1987.

Bogen, David S. "The Individual Liberties within the Body of the Constitution: The Privileges and Immunities Clause of Article IV." *Case Western Reserve Law Review* 37 (1987): 794–861.

———. "Slaughter-House Five: Views of the Case." *Hastings Law Journal* 55 (December 2003): 333–98.

Bowling, Kenneth R. "'A Tub to the Whale': The Founding Fathers and Adoption of the Federal Bill of Rights." *Journal of the Early Republic* 8 (Fall 1988): 223–51.

Brandwein, Pamela. "A Judicial Abandonment of Blacks? Rethinking the 'State Action' Cases of the Waite Court." *Law and Society Review* 41 (June 2007): 343–86.

Breay, Claire. *Magna Carta: Manuscripts and Myths*. London: British Library, 2002.

Brooks, James F. *Captives and Cousins: Slavery, Kinship, and Community in the Southwest Borderlands*. Chapel Hill: University of North Carolina Press, 2002.

Brown, Samuel Gilman. *The Works of Rufus Choate with a Memoir of His Life*. 2 vols. Boston: Little Brown, 1862.

Buell, Lawrence. *Emerson*. Cambridge, Mass.: Harvard University Press, 2003.

Burin, Eric. *Slavery and the Peculiar Solution: A History of the American Colonization Society*. Gainesville: University of Florida Press, 2005.

Burton, Orville Vernon. *The Age of Lincoln*. New York: Hill & Wang, 2007.

Calhoun, Charles W. *Conceiving a New Republic: The Republican Party and the Southern Question, 1869–1900*. Lawrence: University Press of Kansas, 2006.

Camp, Bayliss J., and Orit Kent. "'What a Mighty Power We Can Be': Individual and Collective Identity in African American and White Fraternal Initiation Rituals." *Social Science History* 28 (Fall 2004): 439–83.

Castiglia, Christopher. "Abolition's Racial Interiors and the Making of White Civil Depth." *American Literary History* 14 (March 2002): 32–59.

Cate, Wirt Armistead. *Lucius Q. C. Lamar: Secession and Reunion*. 1935. Reprint, New York: Russell & Russell, 1969.

Cayton, Mary Kupiec. *Emerson's Emergence: Self and Society in the Transformation of New England, 1800–1845*. Chapel Hill: University of North Carolina Press, 1989.

Chambers, John Whiteclay, II. *The Tyranny of Change: America in the Progressive Era, 1890–1920*. 2d ed. New Brunswick, N.J.: Rutgers University Press, 2000.

Cho, Ji-Hyung. "The Transformation of the American Legal Mind: Habeas Corpus. Federalism, and the Constitution, 1787–1870." PhD diss., University of Illinois, 1995.

Clawson, Mary Ann. *Constructing Brotherhood: Class, Gender, and Fraternalism*. Princeton, N.J.: Princeton University Press, 1989.

Cockburn, J. S. "Twelve Silly Men? The Trial Jury at Assizes, 1560–1670." In Cockburn and Green, *Twelve Good Men and True*, 158–81.

Cockburn, J. S., and Thomas A. Green, eds. *Twelve Good Men and True: The Criminal Trial Jury in England, 1200–1800*. Princeton, N.J.: Princeton University Press, 1988.

Coleman, James H., Jr. "The Evolution of Race in the Jury Selection Process." *Rutgers Law Review* 48 (Summer 1996): 1105–37.

Constable, Marianne. *The Law of the Other: The Mixed Jury and Changing Conceptions of Citizenship, Law, and Knowledge*. Chicago: University of Chicago Press, 1994.

Cormack, Joseph M. "The Legal Tender Cases: A Drama of American Legal and Financial History." *Virginia Law Review* 16 (December 1929): 132–48.

Cortner, Robert C. *The Supreme Court and the Second Bill of Rights: The Fourteenth Amendment and the Nationalization of Civil Liberties*. Madison: University of Wisconsin Press, 1981.

Crane, Gregg D. *Race, Citizenship, and Law in American Literature*. Cambridge: Cambridge University Press, 2002.

Cresswell, Stephen. "The Case of Taylor Strauder." *West Virginia History* 44 (Spring 1983): 193–211.

———. *Mormons, Cowboys, Moonshiners, and Klansmen: Federal Law Enforcement in the South and West, 1870–1893*. Tuscaloosa: University of Alabama Press, 1991.

Crouch, Barry A. "Black Dreams and White Justice." In *The Dance of Freedom: Texas African Americans during Reconstruction*, edited by Larry Madaras, 54–68. Austin: University of Texas Press, 2007.

Davis, Curtis Carroll. "The Craftiest of Men: William P. Wood and the Establishment of the United States Secret Service." *Maryland Historical Magazine* 83 (Summer 1988): 111–26.

Davis, Elbridge B., and Harold A. Davis. "Mr. Justice Horace Gray: Some Aspects of His Judicial Career." *American Bar Association Journal* 41 (May 1955): 421–71.

Dennison, George M. *The Dorr War: Republicanism on Trial, 1831–1861*. Lexington: University Press of Kentucky, 1976.

Donahue, Charles, Jr. "Proof by Witnesses in the Church Courts of Medieval England: An Imperfect Reception of the Learned Law." In *On the Laws and Customs of England: Essays in Honor of Samuel E. Thorne*, edited by Morris S. Arnold, Thomas A. Green, Sally A. Scully, and Stephen D. White, 127–58. Chapel Hill: University of North Carolina Press, 1981.

Donald, David Herbert. *Charles Sumner and the Rights of Man*. New York: Knopf, 1970.

Du Bois, W. E. B. *The Souls of Black Folk*. 1903. Reprint, New York: Dover, 1994.

Duken, William F. *A Constitutional History of Habeas Corpus*. Westport, Conn.: Greenwood, 1980.

Dunning, William A. *Essays on the Civil War and Reconstruction*. New York: Macmillan, 1897.

———. *Reconstruction, Political and Economic, 1865–1877*. New York: Harper & Brothers, 1907.

Dworkin, Ronald. *Freedom's Law: The Moral Reading of the American Constitution*. Cambridge, Mass.: Harvard University Press, 1996.

Eaton, R. D. "From Inwit to Conscience in Late Middle English Literature." *Neuphilologische Mitteilungen* 105 (2004): 423–35.

Edward, Rebecca. *Angels in the Machinery: Gender in American Party Politics from the Civil War to the Progressive Era.* New York: Oxford University Press, 1997.

Eells, Robert J. *Forgotten Saint: The Life of Theodore Frelinghuysen, a Case Study of Christian Leadership.* New York: New York University Press, 1987.

———. "Theodore Frelinghuysen, Voluntarism and the Pursuit of the Public Good." *American Presbyterians* 69 (1991): 257–70.

Ellis, Richard E. *Aggressive Nationalism: McCulloch v. Maryland and the Foundations of Federal Authority in the Young Republic.* New York: Oxford University Press, 2007.

Elton, Geoffrey R. *Parliament of England, 1559-1581.* Cambridge: Cambridge University Press, 1989.

Ely, James W., Jr. *The Chief Justiceship of Melville W. Fuller, 1888-1910.* Columbia: University of South Carolina Press, 1995.

Ernst, Daniel. "Legal Positivism, Abolitionist Litigation, and the New Jersey Slave Case of 1845." *Law and History Review* 4 (1986): 337–65.

Fairman, Charles. "Does the Fourteenth Amendment Incorporate the Bill of Rights?" *Stanford Law Review* 2 (1949): 81–134.

———. "Does the Fourteenth Amendment Incorporate the Bill of Rights? The Original Understanding." *Stanford Law Review* 2 (1949): 5–173.

———. *Mr. Justice Miller and the Supreme Court, 1862–1890.* New York: Russell & Russell, 1939.

Federman, Cary. *The Body and the State: Habeas Corpus and American Jurisprudence.* Albany: State University of New York Press, 2006.

Fehrenbacher, Don E. *The Dred Scott Case: Its Significance in American Law and Politics.* New York: Oxford University Press, 1978.

———. *The Slaveholding Republic: An Account of the United States Government's Relation to Slavery.* New York: Oxford University Press, 2001.

Finkelman, Paul. "Foreign Law and American Constitutional Interpretation: A Long and Venerable Tradition." *New York University Annual Survey of American Law* 63 (2007): 29–61.

———. "James Madison and the Bill of Rights: A Reluctant Paternity." *Supreme Court Review* (1990): 301–47.

———. "The Kidnapping of John Davis and the Adoption of the Fugitive Slave Law of 1793." *Journal of Southern History* 56 (August 1990): 397–422.

———. "Legal Ethics and Fugitive Slaves: The Anthony Burns Case; Judge Loring and Abolitionist Attorneys." *Cardozo Law Review* 17 (May 1996): 1793–1858.

———. "Prigg v. Pennsylvania and Northern State Courts: Anti-Slavery Use of a Pro-Slavery Decision." *Civil War History* 25 (March 1979): 5–35.

———. *Slavery and the Founders: Race and Liberty in the Age of Jefferson.* New York: M. E. Sharpe, 2001.

———. "Story Telling on the Supreme Court: Prigg v. Pennsylvania and Justice Joseph Story's Judicial Nationalism." *Supreme Court Review* (1994): 256–66.

Foldy, Michael S. *The Trials of Oscar Wilde: Deviance, Morality and Late-Victorian Society.* New Haven, Conn.: Yale University Press, 1997.

Foner, Eric. *Reconstruction: America's Unfinished Revolution.* New York: Harper & Row, 1988.

———. *Tom Paine and Revolutionary America.* New York: Oxford University Press, 1976.

Forman, James. "Juries and Race in the Nineteenth Century." *Yale Law Review* 113 (January 2004): 895–937.

Fortescue, Sir John. *On the Laws and Governance of England*. Edited by Shelley Lockwood. Cambridge: Cambridge University Press, 1997.

Frankel, Oz. "The Predicament of Racial Knowledge: Government Studies of the Freedmen during the U.S. Civil War." *Social Research* 70 (Spring 2003): 45–81.

———. *States of Inquiry: Social Investigations and Print Culture in Nineteenth-Century Britain and the United States*. Baltimore: Johns Hopkins University Press, 2006.

Fredrickson, George M. *The Black Image in the White Mind: The Debate on Afro-American Character and Destiny, 1817–1914*. New York: Harper & Row, 1971.

———. *Racism: A Short History*. Princeton, N.J.: Princeton University Press, 2002.

Gaines, Kevin K. *Uplifting the Race: Black Leadership, Politics, and Culture in the Twentieth Century*. Chapel Hill: University of North Carolina Press, 1996.

Gillespie, John R. "The Constitution and the All-White Jury." *Kentucky Law Review* 39 (November 1950): 65–78.

Gillette, William. *Retreat from Reconstruction, 1869–1879*. Baton Rouge: Louisiana State University Press, 1979.

Graber, Mark. *Dred Scott and the Problem of Constitutional Evil*. Cambridge: Cambridge University Press, 2006.

Grant, Susan-Mary C. "Representative Mann: Horace Mann, the Republican Experiment and the South." *Journal of American Studies* 32 (1998): 105–23.

Greeley, Horace. *The American Conflict: A History of the Great Rebellion*. Hartford, Conn.: O. D. Case, 1866.

Green, Thomas Andrew. *Verdict according to Conscience: Perspectives on the English Criminal Trial Jury, 1200–1800*. Chicago: University of Chicago Press, 1985.

Grimsted, David. *American Mobbing, 1828–1861: Toward Civil War*. New York: Oxford University Press, 1998.

Grodzins, Dean. *American Heretic: Theodore Parker and Transcendentalism*. Chapel Hill: University of North Carolina Press, 2002.

Groot, Roger D. "The Early-Thirteenth-Century Jury." In Cockburn and Green, *Twelve Good Men and True*, 3–7.

———. "The Jury of Presentment before 1215." *American Journal of Legal History* 26 (January 1982): 1–24;

Guelzo, Allen C. *Lincoln's Emancipation Proclamation*. New York: Simon & Schuster, 2004.

Gura, Philip F. *American Transcendentalism: A History*. New York: Hill & Wang, 2007.

Hamilton, J. G. de Roulhac. *Reconstruction in North Carolina*. 1914. Reprint, Gloucester: Peter Smith, 1964.

Harris, William C. *The Day of the Carpetbagger: Republican Reconstruction in Mississippi*. Baton Rouge: Louisiana State University Press, 1979.

Harrison, Lowell, and James C. Klotter. *A New History of Kentucky*. Lexington: University Press of Kentucky, 1997.

Hart, Albert Bushnell. *Salmon Portland Chase*. 1899. Reprint, New York: Greenwood, 1969.

Hartog, Hendrik. "Lawyering, Husbands' Rights, and 'the Unwritten Law' in Nineteenth-Century America." *Journal of American History* 84 (June 1997): 67–96.

Haskins, James. *Pinckney Benton Stewart Pinchback*. New York: Macmillan, 1973.

Hennessey, Melinda Meek. "Political Terrorism in the Black Belt: The Eutaw Riot." *Alabama Review* 33 (1980): 35–48.

Herrup, Cynthia B. *The Common Peace: Participation and the Criminal Law in Seventeenth-Century England.* New York: Cambridge University Press, 1987.

Holmes, William F. *The White Chief: James Kimble Vardaman.* Baton Rouge: Louisiana State University Press, 1970.

Holzer, Harold, and Sara Vaughn Gabbard, eds. *Lincoln and Freedom: Slavery, Emancipation and the Thirteenth Amendment.* Carbondale: Southern Illinois University Press, 2007.

Horwitz, Robert F. *The Great Impeacher: A Political Biography of James M. Ashley.* New York: Brooklyn College Press, 1979.

Howe, Mark De Wolf, ed. *Touched with Fire: The Civil War Letters and Diary of Oliver Wendell Holmes, Jr.* Cambridge, Mass.: Harvard University Press, 1946.

Howsman, Gerald. *Thief-Taker General: The Rise and Fall of Jonathan Wild.* New York: St. Martins, 1970.

Huebner, Timothy S. *The Southern Judicial Tradition: State Judges and Sectional Distinctiveness, 1790–1890.* Athens: University of Georgia Press, 1999.

Hulsebosch, Daniel J. *Constituting Empire: New York and the Transformation of Constitutionalism in the Atlantic World, 1664–1830.* Chapel Hill: University of North Carolina Press, 2005.

Hyams, Paul R. *Rancor and Reconciliation in Medieval England.* Ithaca, N.Y.: Cornell University Press, 2003.

Hyman, Harold M., and Catherine M. Tarrant. "Aspects of American Trial Jury History." In *The Jury System in America: A Critical Overview,* edited by Rita James Simon, 23–44. Beverly Hills, Calif.: Sage, 1975.

Hyman, Harold M., and William Wiecek. *Equal Justice under Law: Constitutional Development, 1835–1875.* New York: Harper & Row, 1982.

Ireland, Robert M. "Insanity and the Unwritten Law." *American Journal of Legal History* 32 (1988): 157–72.

———. "The Libertine Must Die: Sexual Dishonor and the Unwritten Law in the Nineteenth-Century United States." *Journal of Social History* 23 (Fall 1989): 27–44.

Jager, Ronald B. "Charles Sumner, the Constitution, and the Civil Rights Act of 1875." *New England Quarterly* 42 (September 1969): 350–72.

Jeffreys-Jones, Rhodri. *The FBI: A History.* New Haven, Conn.: Yale University Press, 2007.

Johnson, David R. *Illegal Tender: Counterfeiting and the Secret Service in Nineteenth-Century America.* Washington, D.C.: Smithsonian Institution Press, 1995.

Kaczorowski, Robert. *The Politics of Judicial Interpretation: The Federal Courts, Department of Justice, and Civil Rights, 1866–1876.* New York: Oceana, 1985.

Kens, Paul. *Justice Stephen Field: Shaping Liberty from the Gold Rush to the Gilded Age.* Lawrence: University Press of Kansas, 1997.

Kerber, Linda K. *No Constitutional Right to Be Ladies: Women and the Obligations of Citizenship.* New York: Hill & Wang, 1998.

Kershen, Drew L. "The Jury Selection Act of 1879: Theory and Practice of Citizen Participation in the Judicial System." *University of Illinois Law Forum* (1980): 707–82.

Killenbeck, Mark R. *M'Culloch v. Maryland: Securing a Nation.* Lawrence: University Press of Kansas, 2006.

King, Willard L. *Melville Weston Fuller: Chief Justice of the United States, 1888–1910*. New York: Macmillan, 1950.

Klarman, Michael J. *From Jim Crow to Civil Rights: The Supreme Court and the Struggle for Racial Equality*. New York: Oxford University Press, 2004.

Kutler, Stanley I. *Judicial Power and Reconstruction Politics*. Chicago: University of Chicago Press, 1968.

Labbe, Ronald M., and Jonathan Lurie. *The Slaughterhouse Cases: Regulation, Reconstruction, and the Fourteenth Amendment*. Lawrence: University Press of Kansas, 2003.

Lane, Charles. *The Day Freedom Died: The Colfax Massacre, the Supreme Court, and the Betrayal of Reconstruction*. New York: Henry Holt, 2008.

Lang, Meredith. *Defender of the Faith: The High Court of Mississippi, 1817–1875*. Jackson: University Press of Mississippi, 1977.

Langbein, John H. "The Criminal Trial before the Lawyers." *University of Chicago Law Review* 45 (Winter 1978): 263–316.

Lawson, P. G. "Lawless Juries? The Composition and Behavior of Hertfordshire Juries, 1573–1624." In Cockburn and Green, *Twelve Good Men and True*, 117–57.

Levy, Leonard W. *The Palladium of Justice: Origins of Trial by Jury*. Chicago: Ivan R. Dee, 1999.

Lloyd, John P. "Revising the Republic: Popular Perceptions of Constitutional Change during the Civil War and Reconstruction." PhD diss., Claremont Graduate University, 2000.

Lofgren, Charles A. *The Plessy Case: A Legal-Historical Interpretation*. New York: Oxford University Press, 1987.

Lonn, Ella. *Reconstruction in Louisiana after 1868*. New York: G. P. Putnam's Sons, 1918.

Maddex, Jack P., Jr. *The Virginia Conservatives, 1867–1879: A Study in Reconstruction Politics*. Chapel Hill: University of North Carolina Press, 1970.

Magliocca, Gerald N. *Andrew Jackson and the Constitution: The Rise and Fall of Generational Regimes*. Lawrence: University Press of Kansas, 2007.

Magrath, C. Peter. *Morrison R. Waite: Triumph of Character*. New York: Macmillan, 1963.

Maltz, Earl. *Civil Rights, the Constitution, and Congress, 1863–1869*. Lawrence: University Press of Kansas, 1990.

——. "The Unlikely Hero of Dred Scott: Benjamin Robbins Curtis and the Constitutional Law of Slavery." *Cardozo Law Review* 17 (1996): 1995–2016.

Martel, James R. *Love Is a Sweet Chain: Desire, Autonomy, and Friendship in Liberal Political Theory*. New York: Routledge, 2001.

Martin, Waldo E., Jr. *The Mind of Frederick Douglass* Chapel Hill: University of North Carolina Press, 1984.

Mattson, Kevin. "History as Hope: The Legacy of the Progressive Era and the Future of Political Reform in America." In *Democracy's Moment: Reforming the American Political System for the Twenty-First Century*, eds., Ronald Hayduk and Kevin Mattson, 15–24. Lanham: Rowman & Littlefield, 2002.

Mayes, Edward. *Lucius Q. C. Lamar: His Life, Times, and Speeches, 1825–1893*. Nashville: Methodist Episcopal Church, South, 1896.

McCormick, Richard. "The Discovery That Business Corrupts Politics: A Reappraisal of the Origins of Progressivism." *American Historical Review* 86 (1981): 247–74.

——. *The Party Period and Public Policy: American Politics from the Age of Jackson to the Progressive Era*. New York: Oxford University Press, 1986.

McDermott, Stacy Pratt. "Gentlemen of the Jury: Juror Status and the Reputation of the Jury in the Antebellum Midwest." PhD diss., University of Illinois, Urbana, 2007.

McFeely, William S. "Amos T. Akerman: The Lawyer and Racial Justice." In *Region, Race and Reconstruction: Essays in Honor of C. Vann Woodward,* edited by J. Morgan Kousser and James M. McPherson, 395–415. New York: Oxford University Press, 1982.

———. *Grant: A Biography.* New York: W. W. Norton, 1981.

McPherson, James M. "Abolitionists and the Civil Rights Act of 1875." *Journal of American History* 52 (December 1965): 493–510.

Miller, Wilbur R. *Revenuers and Moonshiners: Enforcing Federal Liquor Law in the Mountain South, 1865–1900.* Chapel Hill: University of North Carolina Press, 1991.

Miraldi, Robert. *The Muckrakers: Evangelical Crusaders.* New York: Praeger, 2000.

Moglen, Eben. "Considering Zenger: Partisan Politics and the Legal Profession in Provincial New York." *Columbia Law Review* 94 (June 1994): 1495–1524.

Moneyhon, Carl H. *Republicanism in Reconstruction Texas.* Austin: University of Texas Press, 1980.

Morris, Thomas D. *Free Men All: The Personal Liberty Laws of the North, 1780–1861.* Baltimore: Johns Hopkins University Press, 1974.

Mulholland, Maureen. "The Jury in English Manorial Courts." In *The Dearest Birth Right of the People of England: The Jury in the History of the Common Law.* Edited by John W. Cairns and Grant McLeod, 63–73. Oxford: Hart, 2002.

Muller, Philip R. "Look Back without Anger: A Reappraisal of William A. Dunning." *Journal of American History* 61 (September 1974): 325–38.

Murphy, James B. *L. Q. C. Lamar: Pragmatic Patriot.* Baton Rouge: Louisiana State University Press, 1973.

Murrin, John M. "Magistrates, Sinners, and a Precarious Liberty: Trial by Jury in Seventeenth-Century New England." In *Saints and Revolutionaries: Essays on Early American History,* edited by David D. Hall, John M. Murrin, and Thad W. Tate, 152–206. New York: Norton, 1984.

Musson, Anthony. *Medieval Law in Context: The Growth of Legal Consciousness from Magna Charta to the Peasants' Revolt.* Manchester: Manchester University Press, 2001.

Naragon, Michael. "From Chattel to Citizen: The Transition from Slavery to Freedom in Richmond, Virginia." *Slavery and Abolition* 21 (2000): 93–116.

Neely, Mark E., Jr. *The Union Divided: Party Conflict in the Civil War North.* Cambridge, Mass.: Harvard University Press, 2002.

Newmyer, R. Kent. *John Marshall and the Heroic Age of the Supreme Court.* Baton Rouge: Louisiana State University Press, 2001.

Niven, John. *Salmon P. Chase: A Biography.* New York: Oxford University Press, 1995.

Noll, Mark A. *The Scandal of the Evangelical Mind.* Grand Rapids, Mich.: William B. Eerdmans, 1994.

O'Brien, Bruce R. *God's Peace and the King's Peace: The Laws of Edward the Confessor.* Philadelphia: University of Pennsylvania Press, 1999.

O'Connor, Michael P. "Time out of Mind: Our Collective Amnesia about the History of the Privileges or Immunities Clause." *Kentucky Law Journal* 93 (2004/2005): 659–735.

Oldham, James. *Trial by Jury: The Seventh Amendment and Anglo-American Special Juries.* New York: New York University Press, 2006.

Olson, Trisha. "The Natural Law Foundation of the Privileges or Immunities Clause of the Fourteenth Amendment." *Arkansas Law Review* 48 (1995): 347–437.

Oshinsky, David M. *Worse Than Slavery: Parchman Farm and the Ordeal of Jim Crow Justice*. New York: Free Press, 1996.

Palmer, Robert C. "Litigiousness in Early Modern England and Wales." University of Houston, O'Quinn Law Library, http://aalt.law.uh.edu/litigiousness/procedure/html.

Palmore, Joseph R. "The Not-So-Strange Career of Interstate Jim Crow: Race, Transportation, and the Dormant Commerce Clause." *Virginia Law Review* 83 (November 1997): 1773–1817.

Parker, Cortlandt. "Mr. Justice Bradley of the United States Supreme Court." *Proceedings of the New Jersey Historical Society*, 2d ser., 11 (1890–91): 145–77.

Parkinson, John Scott. "Bloody Spring: The Charleston Riot and Copperhead Violence during the American Civil War." PhD diss., University of Miami, 1998.

Patton, James Welch. *Unionism and Reconstruction in Tennessee, 1860–1869*. 1934. Reprint, Gloucester, Mass.: Peter Smith, 1966.

Paul, Arnold M. *Conservative Crisis and the Rule of Law: Attitudes of Bar and Bench, 1887–1895*. Ithaca, N.Y.: Cornell University Press, 1960.

Perry, Lewis. *Radical Abolitionism: Anarchy and the Government of God in Antislavery Thought*. Ithaca, N.Y.: Cornell University Press, 1973.

Pierce, Edward L. *Memoir and Letters of Charles Sumner*. Boston: Roberts, 1894.

Pincus, Samuel. "Negroes on Juries in Post-Reconstruction Virginia: The Rives Cases." MA thesis, University of Virginia, 1965.

Pinsker, Matthew. "Lincoln's Summer of Emancipation." In *Lincoln and Freedom: Slavery, Emancipation and the Thirteenth Amendment*, edited by Harold Holzer and Sara Vaughn Gabbard, 79–99. Carbondale: Southern Illinois University Press, 2007.

Pole, J. R. "Reflections on American Law and the American Revolution." *William and Mary Quarterly*, 3d ser., 50 (January 1993): 123–59.

Post, J. B. "Jury Lists and Juries in the Late Fourteenth Century." In Cockburn and Green, *Twelve Good Men and True*, 65–77.

Potter, David M. "Jefferson Davis and the Political Factors in Confederate Defeat." In *Why the North Won the Civil War*, edited by David H. Donald, 93–114. Baton Rouge: Louisiana State University Press, 1960.

Potter, David M., and Don E. Fehrenbacher. *The Impending Crisis, 1848–1861*. New York: Harper & Row, 1976.

Przybyszewski, Linda. "The Fuller Court, 1888–1910: Property and Liberty." In *The United States Supreme Court: The Pursuit of Justice*, edited by Christopher Tomlins, 147–67. Boston: Houghton Mifflin, 2005.

———. "Judicial Conservatism and Protestant Faith: The Case of Justice David J. Brewer." *Journal of American History* 91 (September 2004): 471–96.

———. *The Republic according to John Marshall Harlan*. Chapel Hill: University of North Carolina Press, 1999.

Remini, Robert. *Daniel Webster: The Man and His Time*. New York: W. W. Norton, 1997.

———. *The House: A History of the House of Representatives*. New York: HarperCollins, 2006.

Richardson, Heather Cox. *The Death of Reconstruction: Race, Labor, and Politics in the Post–Civil War North, 1865–1901*. Cambridge, Mass.: Harvard University Press, 2001.

Richardson, Robert D., Jr. *Emerson: The Mind on Fire*. Berkeley: University of California Press, 1995.

Richter, William L. *The Army in Texas during Reconstruction, 1865–1870*. College Station: Texas A&M University Press, 1987.

Ritter, Gretchen. "Jury Service and Women's Citizenship before and after the Nineteenth Amendment." *Law and History Review* 20 (Fall 2002): 479–516.

Roberts, Stephen K. "Juries and the Middling Sort: Recruitment and Performance at Devon Quarter Sessions, 1649–1670." In Cockburn and Green, *Twelve Good Men and True*, 182–213.

Rogers, William Warren, Jr. *A Scalawag in Georgia: Richard Whiteley and the Politics of Reconstruction.* Urbana: University of Illinois Press, 2007.

Roper, Donald M. "In Quest of Judicial Objectivity: The Marshall Court and the Legitimation of Slavery." *Stanford Law Review* 21 (1969): 532–39.

Rose, Anne C. *Transcendentalism as a Social Movement, 1830–1850.* New Haven, Conn.: Yale University Press, 1981.

Rosenberg, Gerald N. *The Hollow Hope: Can Courts Bring About Social Change?* Chicago: University of Chicago Press, 1991.

Ross, Michael A. *Justice of Shattered Dreams: Samuel Freeman Miller and the Supreme Court during the Civil War Era.* Baton Rouge: Louisiana State University Press, 2003.

———. "Obstructing Reconstruction: John Archibald Campbell and the Legal Campaign against Louisiana's Republican Government, 1868–1873." *Civil War History* 49 (2003): 235–53.

Rowland, Dunbar. *The Official and Statistical Register of the State of Mississippi, Centennial Edition.* Madison, Wis.: Democrat Printing, 1917.

Rubin, Richard. "The Ghosts of Emmett Till." *New York Times Magazine,* July 31, 2005.

Schmidt, Benno C., Jr. "Juries, Jurisdiction, and Race Discrimination: The Lost Promise of *Strauder v. West Virginia.*" *Texas Law Review* (1983): 1401–99.

Sedgwick, Ellery. *The Atlantic Monthly, 1857–1909: Yankee Humanism at High Tide and Ebb.* Amherst: University of Massachusetts, 1994.

Seipp, David J. "Jurors, Evidences and the Tempest of 1499." In *The Dearest Birth Right of the People of England: The Jury in the History of the Common Law,* edited by John W. Cairns and Grant McLeod, 75–92. Oxford: Hart, 2002.

Shklar, Judith N. "Emerson and the Inhibitions of Democracy." *Political Theory* 18 (November 1990): 601–14.

———. *Redeeming American Political Thought.* Edited by Stanley Hoffmann and Dennis F. Thompson. Chicago: University of Chicago Press, 1998.

Shoemaker, Robert. *The London Mob: Violence and Disorder in Eighteenth-Century England.* London: Hambledon & London, 2004.

Siddali, Silvana R. *From Property to Person: Slavery and the Confiscation Acts, 1861–1862.* Baton Rouge: Louisiana State University Press, 2005.

Silbey, Joel. *The American Political Nation, 1838–1893.* Stanford, Calif.: Stanford University Press, 1991.

Simkins, Francis Butler, and Woody, Robert Hilliard. *South Carolina during Reconstruction.* 1932. Reprint, Gloucester, Mass.: Peter Smith, 1966.

Simpson, Brooks. *The Reconstruction Presidents.* Lawrence: University Press of Kansas, 1998.

Skates, John Ray. *A History of the Mississippi Supreme Court, 1817–1948.* Jackson: Mississippi Bar Foundation, 1973.

Skocpol, Theda, and Jennifer Lynn Oser. "Organization Despite Adversity: The Origins and Development of African American Fraternal Organizations." *Social Science History* 38 (2004): 367–437.

Smith, Douglas G. "The Privileges and Immunities Clause of Article IV, Section 2: Pre-cursor of Section 1 of the Fourteenth Amendment." *San Diego Law Review* 34 (May/June 1997): 809–57.

Smith, J. Clay, Jr. *Emancipation: The Making of the Black Lawyer, 1844–1944*. Philadel-phia: University of Pennsylvania Press, 1993.

Smith, James Morton. *Freedom's Fetters: The Alien and Sedition Acts and American Civil Liberties*. Ithaca, N.Y.: Cornell University Press, 1956.

Sorin, Gerald. *The New York Abolitionists: A Case Study of Political Radicalism*. Westport, Conn.: Greenwood, 1971.

Spackman, S. G. F. "American Federalism and the Civil Rights Act of 1875." *American Studies* 10 (December 1976): 313–28.

Stanton, William. *The Leopard's Spots: Scientific Attitudes toward Race in America, 1815–1859*. Chicago: University of Chicago Press, 1960.

Stenton, Frank Merry. *William the Conqueror and the Rule of the Normans*. New York: G. P. Putnam's Sons, 1908.

Stephenson, Donald Grier, Jr. "The Waite Court at the Bar of History." *Denver University Law Review* 81 (2003): 449–95.

Stimson, Shannon C. *The American Revolution in the Law: Anglo-American Jurispru-dence before John Marshall*. Princeton, N.J.: Princeton University Press, 1990.

Streichler, Stuart. *Justice Curtis in the Civil War Era*. Charlottesville: University of Vir-ginia Press, 2005.

Sumners, Cecil L. *The Governors of Mississippi*. Gretna, La.: Pelican, 1998.

Sunstein, Cass R. *A Constitution of Many Minds: Why the Founding Document Doesn't Mean What It Meant Before*. Princeton, N.J.: Princeton University Press, 2009.

Surowiecki, James. *The Wisdom of Crowds*. New York: Doubleday, 2004.

Swanberg, W. A. *Sickles the Incredible*. New York: Scribner, 1956.

Taylor, William A. *Ohio in Congress from 1803–1900*. Columbus: Century, 1900.

Teichgraeber, Richard F., III. "'Our National Glory': Emerson in American Culture, 1865–1882." In *Transient and Permanent: The Transcendentalist Movement and Its Con-texts*, edited by Charles Capper and Conrad Edick Wright, 499–526. Boston: Massa-chusetts Historical Society, 1999.

Thompson, E. P. *The Making of the English Working Class*. New York: Vintage, 1966.

Trelease, Allen W. *White Terror: The Ku Klux Klan Conspiracy and Southern Reconstruc-tion*. Baton Rouge: Louisiana State University Press, 1971.

Trefousse, Hans. *Thaddeus Stevens: Nineteenth-Century Egalitarian*. Chapel Hill: Univer-sity of North Carolina Press, 1997.

Trimble, Bruce R. *Chief Justice Waite: Defender of the Public Interest*. Princeton, N.J.: Princeton University Press, 1938.

Tunnell, Ted. *Crucible of Reconstruction: War, Radicalism, and Race in Louisiana, 1862–1877*. Baton Rouge: Louisiana State University Press, 1984.

Twining, William L. *Rethinking Evidence: Exploratory Essays*. Evanston, Ill.: Northwest-ern University Press, 1994.

Van Cromphout, Gustaaf. *Emerson's Ethics*. Columbia: University of Missouri Press, 1999.

Vorenberg, Michael. *Final Freedom: The Civil War, the Abolition of Slavery, and the Thir-teenth Amendment*. Cambridge: Cambridge University Press, 2001.

Von Frank, Albert J. *The Trials of Anthony Burns: Freedom and Slavery in Emerson's Bos-ton*. Cambridge, Mass.: Harvard University Press, 1998.

Waldrep, Christopher. *Roots of Disorder: Race and Criminal Justice in the American South, 1817–80.* Urbana: University of Illinois Press, 1998.

———. *Vicksburg's Long Shadow: The Civil War Legacy of Race and Remembrance.* Lanham, Md.: Rowman & Littlefield, 2005.

Walsh, Kevin. "The Legal Tender Cases and the Post-Civil War Origins of Modern Constitutional Interpretation." PhD diss., Southern Illinois University, 1999.

Wang, Xi. *The Trial of Democracy: Black Suffrage and Northern Republicans, 1860–1910.* Athens: University of Georgia Press, 1997.

Warren, Charles. *The Supreme Court in United States History.* 3 vols. Boston: Little Brown, 1926.

Welch, Richard E. *George Frisbie Hoar and the Half-Breed Republicans.* Cambridge, Mass.: Harvard University Press, 1971.

White, Hayden. *Metahistory: The Historical Imagination in Nineteenth-Century Europe.* Baltimore: Johns Hopkins University Press, 1973.

Whitman, James Q. *The Origins of Reasonable Doubt: Theological Roots of the Criminal Trial.* New Haven, Conn.: Yale University Press, 2008.

Whittington, Keith E. *Constitutional Interpretation: Textual Meaning, Original Intent, and Judicial Review.* Lawrence: University Press of Kansas, 1999.

———. *Political Foundations of Judicial Supremacy: The Presidency, the Supreme Court, and Constitutional Leadership in U.S. History.* Princeton, N.J.: Princeton University Press, 2007.

Wiecek, William. "The Great Writ and Reconstruction: The Habeas Corpus Act of 1867." *Journal of Southern History* 36 (November 1970): 530–48.

———. "Popular Sovereignty in the Dorr War—Conservative Counterblast." *Rhode Island History* 32 (1973): 35–51.

Wildenthal, Bryan H. "Nationalizing the Bill of Rights: Revisiting the Original Understanding of the Fourteenth Amendment in 1866–67." *Ohio State Law Journal* 68 (2007): 1509–1626.

Wilentz, Sean. *The Rise of American Democracy: Jefferson to Lincoln.* New York: Norton, 2005.

Williams, Charles R. *The Life of Rutherford Birchard Hayes, Nineteenth President of the United States.* 2 vols. 1914. Reprint, New York: DaCapo, 1971.

Williams, Lou Falkner. *The Great Ku Klux Klan Trials, 1871–1872.* Athens: University of Georgia Press, 1996.

Williamson, Joel. *The Crucible of Race: Black-White Relations in the American South since Emancipation.* New York: Oxford University Press, 1984.

Winch, Julie. *A Gentleman of Color: The Life of James Forten.* New York: Oxford University Press, 2002.

———. "The Making and Meaning of James Forten's *Letters from a Man of Color.*" *William and Mary Quarterly,* 3d ser., 64 (January 2007): 129–38.

Wolf, Eva Sheppard. *Race and Liberty in the New Nation: Emancipation in Virginia from the Revolution to Nat Turner's Rebellion.* Baton Rouge: Louisiana State University Press, 2006.

Wood, Gordon. *The Creation of the American Republic, 1776–1787.* New York: Norton, 1969.

Wyatt-Brown, Bertram. *Southern Honor: Ethics and Behavior in the Old South.* New York: Oxford University Press, 1982.

Index

9 780820 330020